1 00 049316 3

£4. -

A fine will be charged if not returned by the date stamped above

UNIVERSITY LIBRARY

3 0 JUN 20

HALL 64

KU-546-360

Dominique Eudes

The Kapetanios

Partisans and Civil War in Greece, 1943-1949

Translated from the French by John Howe

Monthly Review Press
New York and London

. . . If our comrades ask you any questions about me,
Don't say I stopped a bullet, don't say I was unlucky,
Just tell them I've got married
In the sad lands overseas . . .
With a big flat stone for a mother-in-law,
New pebble brothers and the black earth for my bride.

Klephtic song

Copyright © 1972 by New Left Books
All Rights Reserved

First published as Les Kapetanios by Librarie
Arthème Fayard, Paris, France. Copyright © 1970
by Librarie Arthème Fayard.

Selections from Closing the Ring by Winston S. Churchill,
copyright © 1951 by Houghton Mifflin Company and from
Triumph and Tragedy by Winston S. Churchill,
copyright © 1953 by Houghton Mifflin Company
are reprinted by permission of the publisher.
Selections from Greek Entanglement by Edmund Myers
are reprinted by permission of Rupert Hart-Davis Ltd.
The map on page ii was drawn by Paul White.

First Printing

Library of Congress Cataloging in Publication Data
Eudes, Dominique.
    The kapetanios.
    Bibliography: p.
    1. World War, 1939-1945 — Underground movements —
Greece. 2. Greece, Modern — Politics and government —
1935 —   3. Communists, Greek. 4. Greece, Modern —
History — 1944-1949. I. Title.
D802.G8E913   940.53'495   72-92032   ISBN 0-85345-275-X

Monthly Review Press
116 West 14th Street, New York, N. Y. 10011
33/37 Moreland Street, London, E.C. 1

Manufactured in the United States of America

List of Abbreviations

This list contains only those abbreviations which occur throughout the book. All abbreviations are explained the first time they occur.

EAM National Liberation Front (*Ethnikon Apeleftherotikon Metopon*)

EDES Greek Democratic National League (*Ellinikos Dimokratikos Ethnikos Syndesmos*)

EKKA National and Social Liberation (*Ethniki kai Koinoniki Apeleftherosis*)

ELAN Greek National Liberation Navy (*Ellinikon Laikon Apeleftherotikon Navtikon*)

ELAS Greek National Liberation Army (*Ellinikos Laikos Apelftherotikos Stratos*)

EPON United Panhellenic Youth Organization (*Eniaia Panellinios Organosis Neolaias*)

KKE Communist Party of Greece (*Kommounistikon Komma Ellados*)

OPLA Organization for the Protection of Popular Struggle (*Omades Prostasias Laikou Agonos*)

PEEA Political Committee for National Liberation (*Politiki Epitropi Ethnikis Apeleftherosis*)

Foreword

Dominique Eudes's book is an important contribution to our understanding of contemporary history, and not only to that part of it which concerns Greece.

In the field of Greek history it is the only work of its kind. Eudes covers in continuous detail a period whose story has never been told before, even on the all-important factual level: those who wonder why will find part of the answer in the text. For the sake of readability the author has used a popular style. However, this does not mean that the book is merely an imaginative reconstruction; even its details are based on thorough and serious research, and the narrative takes us from the written documents to oral testimony, with everything doubly cross-checked. Here the author was greatly helped by his nationality since, for a number of reasons, many of the participants who agreed to speak to a Frenchman would not have done so as freely if their questioner had been a compatriot. Even so, the author is unable to give all his sources. This may be unfortunate in an historical work, but it is essential in this case to protect witnesses who confided in the author.

Narrative history is not criticized because it narrates a sequence of events; that, after all, is essential. What sometimes earns it a bad name is a tendency to jumble significant facts in a rambling tissue of dramas. Eudes has managed to avoid this pitfall. Not that one has to agree with all his interpretations and judgments; a number of points will probably give rise to arguments. Nevertheless, he has arranged his story in such a way as to emphasize the difference between the two strategies which have dominated the workers' movement in recent years. He has organized his narrative around this line of demarcation, following it from each side alternately.

Even if we might not agree that the differences pose themselves in terms of the alternatives the author suggests, they undeniably do represent two fundamental political and strategic positions. On the one hand, a position which advocates a concrete analysis of the real situation, leading to a prolonged 'people's war' and mass line with its own strategy; on the other, a position cut off from the masses, advocating a fixed strategy of urban insurrection or a classic war of position: on the one hand a line that favours the political over the military, on the other a line that favours the military over the political. On another level: on the one hand a line which, in a country like Greece with an overwhelming peasant majority, advocates encirclement of the towns by the countryside; on the other, a line which clings through thick and thin to the idea of towns as revolutionary storm-centres. Finally: on one side, a line which bases its assessment of the revolutionary possibilities of a worker-peasant alliance on a proper consideration of the 'people' or popular masses; on the other, a line which both underestimates the potential of people's alliances and fundamentally mistrusts the peasantry. To this second line Eudes attaches the name of Stalin and the leadership of the Greek Communist Party; the first he identifies with the kapetanios, a spontaneous Greek movement with strong tendencies in this direction.

As for the Greek Communist Party – apart from the fact that it followed the second line, which emerges strikingly from the text – the essential thing seems to be that within this line it always progressed, not exactly at random, but in a series of sudden swerves to left and right, as if the correct line would automatically emerge as a spontaneous end-product of all the zigzags. Nor was it simply a question of successive changes; there were often two simultaneous strategies, so that the party seems permanently to have been committed to what might be described as a 'leftist-rightist' line.

Clearly the problems raised in this book are still with us and go beyond the framework of Greece. The Greeks, after all, are the only people in Europe who have attempted to carry out a genuine socialist revolution in the period since the end of the Second World War.

The interest of this book for Greeks themselves is obvious. It is the first available text which, by covering the whole sequence of events and asking the relevant questions, enables us at last to open a debate which has been delayed far too long.

Nicos Poulantzas
Paris, 1970

Author's note

Of all those whose help and testimony have made it possible to sketch this history of the Greek tragedy, there are too many whom I am unable to thank by mentioning their names here, for obvious reasons. Most of them talked not about their own lives but about those of others. Their experiences are linked together to form the story of this book – which does not claim to exhaust the subject. It is just possible, despite the oblivion which enfolds most of the official records and the fearsome conspiracy of silence which stifles the country, that these few elements of the mosaic may help to bring a particular facet of the living Greece into the light. . . .

Let those I could name here forgive me, on behalf of all those I would compromise by doing so. Let the reader forgive me for not always citing my sources. I extend my warmest thanks to all the kapetanios, all the political cadres, all the former partisans in Athens, Paris, Bucharest, Prague and Belgrade, who gave me the inspiration to write their book.

1. Aris Velouchiotis
(*extreme right of group photo, and above*), chief kapetanios, administrative leader of ELAS
(*L'Humanité; author's collection*)

2. George Siantos,
leader of KKE from 1942 to 1945
(*L'Humanité*)

3. Napoleon Zervas,
head of EDES
(*Author's collection*)

4. Andreas Tzimas,
political leader of ELAS
(*Author's collection*)

5. Colonel (later General) Stefanos Sarafis,
military leader of ELAS
(*Author's collection*)

6 (*left*). Markos Vafiadis, kapetanios,
later Commander of the Democratic Army
(*L'Humanité*)

7 (*right*). Dimitros Partsalidis,
General-Secretary of EAM,
later Prime Minister
of the Provisional Democratic Government
(*Author's collection*)

8 (*left*). Nikos Zachariadis,
General-Secretary of KKE, its leader from 1945
(*Author's collection*)

9. George Papandreou, Prime Minister of Greece
by grace of the British, with General Scobie,
C-in-C British forces in Greece
(*Author's collection*)

10. Churchill and Archbishop Damaskinos in Athens, December 1944.
Behind them, Colonel Popov of the Soviet Mission
in Greece (*on the left*), Harold Macmillan and Anthony Eden
(UPI)

Part One

Popular Uprising

1942-1944

The poster featured three police mugshots; one taken full face, wide and stern, and two in profile which made the face look thinner, aquiline. It was an intense face, darkened by a thick beard, with the keen-eyed expression of a hunter; heavily underlined by a police serial number allotted during the witch-hunt of democrats that had been raging in Greece since 1936.

WANTED

Thanasis Klaras

alias Miserias

alias ARIS VELOUCHIOTIS

and so on, leading up to a reward of hundreds of thousands of drachmas. Paper drachmas devalued a thousandfold, the currency of a Greece bled white by two years of frenzied looting under the triple occupation of Germany, Italy and Bulgaria.

The black, official notice was surrounded by red and green graffiti. On every white wall in Athens, Piraeus and the suburbs, EAM, the National Liberation Front, was recording the daily progress of the Resistance and the Allies in the red paint favoured by its strong communist support; the Panhellenic Youth Organization EPON, whose inspiration was much the same, used green.

At the beginning of March 1943, which was unusually cold and grey, the freshest inscriptions celebrated the Russian victory at Stalingrad and the advances of the British in the Middle East. But the main body of this palimpsest concerned the activities of the partisans in the liberated mountain areas of Greece, where an old epic was being reborn: the story of the Klephts, of four centuries of resistance to Turkish occupation, of Greece's indomitable will to remain Greek. A spontaneous revolt against the invader had begun in the bare, dry mountain country where rebellion was an ancient tradition; the untamed inhabitants, the *andartes*, had risen under the leadership of their legendary battle-proved chieftains: the *kapetanios.* The moving spirit behind this living guerilla saga, the kapetanios whose name was being woven into the opening lines of old klephtic songs, was Aris Velouchiotis.

Three priests walked down a narrowing street in the outskirts of Athens. Their robes were splashed with reddish mud and grey circles of sweat stained their armpits. The middle priest was clearly recognizable, under his cassock, as Aris. Smaller than the other two – he was a little under five feet five tall – he dominated them with a solid but wiry bearing and an abrupt, imperious manner. As the suburbs closed in around him, an increasing number of tattered posters flashed his imprisoned image from the walls, but he did not seem to notice them. He was taking a real risk in coming to an Athens quartered day and night by German and Italian patrols.

Aris had been summoned to Athens by the Central Committee of the Greek Communist Party (KKE). Although he was the hero of popular songs, another image of him was gaining currency in bourgeois liberal circles: that of a bloodthirsty fanatic. He had agreed to come and explain himself, but had refused to shave the black beard which was part of his legend. Now the streets were awakening and he might be recognized by the first passer-by. Aris's only concession to secrecy had been wearing the priests' clothes; they may not have rendered the three men completely unrecognizable, but their folds concealed a most unholy arsenal.

As the three guerillas clumped past the first Italian command post, an observant eye would have noted that their bearing was more military than clerical. But the sleepy sentry knew his omens: three priests on waking is a bad-luck sign. Crossing his fingers, he allowed the evil to pass without asking questions. Shops and taverns were opening, famine in their windows. People were appearing in the streets, beginning the hopeless daily search for a cup of oil, a few chick-peas, half a bottle of wine, a quarter-pound of sugar, things which existed only in fantasy; in the evening they would return home with the usual disgusting loaf of straw bread wrapped in newspaper. Skinny but intractable people, grimly determined to submit neither to force nor to hunger.

It was getting too dangerous for Aris and his companions to carry on in the open and they hailed a taxi. Giving the driver a false destination, they suddenly ordered him to stop, leapt out and disappeared down a side street, leaving a heavy black satchel on the back seat. The three priests had vanished before the driver could call them back; their satchel contained equipment for an unexpected form of worship. It was filled to the brim with grenades.

News of Aris's arrival spread through the town; the telephone was humming with it. Early in the afternoon Andreas Tzimas, a member of the Political Bureau of the KKE and the Central Committee of EAM, met the three men in a safe house at the foot of the Acropolis, the white Acropolis stained by the swastika. It seemed that 'policy' required Aris to shave off his guerilla's beard on the spot. And that, in the interests of prudence, he must replace a gold tooth marked in his police dossier.

Behind this childish argument, limited for the time being to the superficialities of personal adornment, lay real issues of far-reaching importance. A conflict between two realities, two opposing images; two different but complementary conceptions of the struggle. Rock versus tar. In Athens, where resistance must remain underground, the covert methods elaborated by revolutionary theorists held sway in an atmosphere of secrecy, mistrust and extreme caution. In the freer air of Aris's country, the mountains of Roumeli, overt resistance could be adapted to the problems of each new day, maintained openly from the heart without any reference to dogma or to canonical models.

In challenging the people's confidence so openly, Aris had deliberately chosen the path of provocation. Now, fourteen months after the birth of ELAS (the Greek National Liberation Army), he was about to be judged by guardians of dogma who half suspected him of being a provocateur.

The Birth of ELAS

Ten months earlier, one morning in June 1942, fifteen men armed to the teeth had appeared in the village square of Domnista, a small place 300 kilometres north-west of Athens, in the Karpenisi region. At that time the Axis was maintaining the German Fifth Army, the Italian Eleventh Army and a couple of Bulgarian army corps, amounting in all to some 300,000 men, on Greek territory. The little detachment marched down the village street, bandoliers across their chests and damascened daggers stuck in their belts; they looked like guerillas, but the Greek flag and bugler at their head added a novel touch that was soon to become nationally familiar. The villagers gathered under the olive trees in the little square. Aris spoke:

'Patriots! I am Aris Velouchiotis, Colonel of Artillery. Starting today, I am raising the banner of revolt against the forces occupying our beloved country. The handful of men you see before you will soon become an army of thousands. We are just a nucleus.'

And so it turned out. The National Liberation Army ELAS, whose name sounds like the Greek word for Greece (Hellas) soon numbered tens of thousands of men.

Aris's real name was Thanasis Klaras. His *nom-de-guerre* derived from the mountains of Velouchi, where he was born, and from the god of war Aris or Ares. He was stretching the truth a little in describing himself as a colonel of artillery. His military service in 1925, during the military dictatorship of General Pangalos, had been spent mainly at Kalpaki in a disciplinary company whose function was not, strictly speaking, the training of officers. But the imposture was only an expedient, a mere formality; a member of the British Mission in Greece, Chris Woodhouse, who had no special love of Aris, endorsed both his name and his commandeered rank by describing him in his memoirs as 'the fighting genius of ELAS'. The career officers who came later on to swell the ranks of ELAS treated 'Colonel of Artillery' Velouchiotis as a general, without asking awkward questions about his former regiment.

Aris's fast-spreading fame and his decision to go ahead on the simple assumption that people would support him, marching his units through the villages in broad daylight in defiance of all the rules of safety, galvanized the Roumelian peasants. All over the mountainous heart of Greece partisans gathered to fight the occupying forces.

Under Aris and the guerilla chieftains 'The Mountain' became an independent reality. Cut off from Athens and the EAM Cental Committee by differences of temperament as well as the practical difficulties of communication, the movement developed like a wild growth, adapting itself to the exigencies of the terrain but frequently straying from revolutionary orthodoxy. It soon became an organization within the Organization, with its own leaders, its own legends and its own hymns:

> Like a solid wall, always unfinished,
> onto the field of battle rolls
> the People's Army formed and led by Aris

Aris's family belonged to the liberal bourgeoisie whose fortunes had fluctuated for decades with those of the Republican opposition. His father was a lawyer. As a boy Aris was inspired by the rugged landscape of his native Roumeli and attracted to the texture and depth of the peasant life; he did not identify with the Greek middle class, forever suspended in an uncomfortable limbo between the great mass of the people and the cosmopolitan circle centred on the Palace. He studied agronomy and came into contact as a student with the revolutionary elements grouping round the nascent KKE. During his military service he tasted official repression for the first time; in the military prison at Kalpaki the young Klaras established himself as a stubborn and insubordinate rebel.

In 1929, at the age of twenty-three, he became a leader of the Young Communists. The Party numbered about 3,000 members at that time. Militancy in Greece has always carried with it the certainty of imprisonment and political exile; Aris's generation and the one following were to see a good part of their youth and young manhood wasted in this way.

He spent forty-five days in gaol in 1929. The following year, badly hurt in a fight between demonstrators and police, Aris was thrown in prison again, this time for two months. That was only the beginning. A few months after his release he was rearrested and exiled to Gavdos, a swampy forgotten island to the South of Crete.

Eleven men were dropped on this remote outpost of Greece, among them Aris and one Andreas Tzimas. Tzimas was also a mountain man, a native of Macedonia. Thin-lipped and with a sharp profile, he combined great sensitivity with a formidable strength of character. He was more refined and cultivated than Aris and knew every stone of mainland Greece. The deep bonds of friendship that sprang up between the two men during their time on Gavdos would play an important part, later on, in the formation of a 'Mountain Clan' inside the KKE.

The eleven exiles were dumped on the mosquito-infested north coast of the island and left to rot. There was a risk of malaria, but moving to the other side of the island would involve them in an extra task: every time the weather allowed a boat to cross over from Crete, they would have to carry their supplies across the island on foot. From the moment Aris took command of the group, there was no question of succumbing to malaria, or to idleness for that matter. He decided to move the camp to the south coast and build a solid shelter. Within a few weeks 'Gavdos Palace' rose from the pebbles. Every evening, after running the building site at top pressure all day and organizing the transportation of victuals, he would suggest a spartan swim in the sea, whatever the weather or season. People seldom argued about Aris's suggestions. While he was there, exile on Gavdos weakened no one either in body or in will. Aris returned to Athens in 1932, but not for very long. He spent much of the next four years in the political prisons of Syngrou, Aegina and on Agios Evstratios.

George II, king of Greece by grace of the British, was a member of the Danish Glucksburg family and related to the Hohenzollerns. His regime served the interests of both Britain and Germany, and enjoyed their protection in return. On 4 August 1936, he crushed the liberal democracy which was making its tentative appearance in Greece by setting up the dictatorship of General Ioannis Metaxas. There followed an unprecedented witch-hunt of communists. In addition to the stimulus this gave to the general refinement of police interrogation techniques, the Minister of Security, Maniadakis, devised a major innovation to the machinery of repression. This was a form of inquisition: political prisoners could obtain their release by renouncing their faith and signing a public 'declaration of repentance'. Copies of the declaration were sent to the authorities in the 'penitent's' home village. By publishing the statements, both true and false, of these *dilosias* (renegades), Maniadakis was able to poison all the Party organizations to the core. He set up a parallel leadership in competition with the Central Committee. The communist newspaper *Rizopastis* began to appear simultaneously in two versions, both published in such secrecy that it was sometimes impossible to tell which one came from the Ministry of Security.

Aris was arrested at the end of 1936. In 1937, while being transferred from Aegina prison to Athens, he escaped. He was soon recaptured, given four years and sent back to Aegina. It was there that he suddenly signed the celebrated 'declaration of repentance' in July 1939, and became a *dilosias*.

Klaras was branded, a marked man. Before adopting the name Aris Velouchiotis, he was known for a while as Miserias. It was a basic rule that a communist should not submit to coercion, and the long list of martyrs to Maniadakis's torturers had made the ruling absolute. Aris's transgression introduced a taint into his legend, a blemish that damaged his powers of decision and that was to inhibit him for a long time to come from expressing open opposition to the Party line. There are plenty of rumours about the reasons that could have induced him to sign the declaration, including the story of a fiancée tortured before his eyes. But although these ceremonies were usually preceded by treatment which makes any assumptions about the victim's reactions entirely conjectural, it seems unlikely that a man of Aris's calibre would have given way. Other people whose histories do not place them on his exceptional level of toughness and bravery were able to endure in silence. Most of those who broke under this treatment and became *dilosias* withdrew from the struggle for good; Aris rushed back into the fray as soon as he was released.

It is well known that Nikos Zachariadis (General Secretary of the KKE Central Committee) ordered an imprisoned militant called Michaelidis to sign the declaration at about this time in order to get back in touch with the outside world. It seems possible that Aris was officially ordered to recant in the same way: as we shall see, his death in 1945, and Zachariadis's attitude towards him, leave this question open. It is quite likely, finally, that Aris would have decided on his own authority that he would be more useful in action than adding his name to Maniadakis's grisly list of martyrs.

What is quite certain is that this renunciation – or apparent renunciation – left its mark on Aris. Communists have a sense of sin. A transgression can be forgiven, but the sinner must rehabilitate himself through a kind of revolutionary self-abnegation. Aris was a stubborn, wounded rebel who would never be able to bring himself to jump to the whistle like a Party hack; some communists regarded him as a fanatical anarchist. But from now on he was vulnerable when the Party machine called him to order in the name of the orthodox line. He had signed.

While Metaxas maintained law and order in Greece, the shadow of a related phenomenon was spreading across Europe to the north and west. In Hitler's scheme of things the Mediterranean was reserved as a zone of influence for Italy. In the summer of 1940, however, he was anxious to avoid any move that might encourage the British to menace his Rumanian oilfields; Mussolini had in any case staked out a rough claim to the Eastern Mediterranean with the Ethiopian war and the invasion of Albania in 1939. But the Duce's appetite for military glory could not wait. On 28 October 1940, without warning Hitler, he sent an ultimatum to the Greek government demanding free passage for Italian troops across Greek territory. Despite extensive German commercial penetration into the Balkans, the Greek monarchy reneged on a choice which had kept it isolated from the nation since the First World War: it sorted out the tangle of foreign interests enmeshing Athens by aligning itself with England, the major guardian power in the kingdom.

Pulled in all directions by the bribery and threats of the two conflicting power blocs, this regime – the product of a century of Balkan intrigue and unashamedly fascist in inspiration – resolved its dilemma by entering the family of 'democracy', if British interests in that part of the world can be described in such ideological terms.

The Italian *chargé d'affaires*, Grazzi, arrived to deliver the Duce's ultimatum to Metaxas at three in the morning on the night of 28 October. Whether or not the dictator's historic *ochi* (no!) was as contemptuous as some versions would have us believe, the Greek people managed to back up their discredited and unpopular government with an overwhelming counter-offensive. The foreign invasion found itself facing not only an army, but what can only be called a popular uprising. Where there was a shortage of lorries, where the roads were useless or non-existent, village women and even young children carried arms and supplies on their backs across the mountains of Epirus. By the end of the year the Italians had been thrown back sixty kilometres from the frontier and the Greeks were occupying a third of Albania. A notice at Ventimiglia, on the Italian frontier near Nice, proclaimed in big black letters: 'If you want to visit Italy join the Greek army.'

The sixteen Greek divisions involved did not get as far as Italy, but they immobilized twenty-seven overequipped Italian divisions for six months. It is not impossible that the British intervened to prevent the army from pressing its advantage still further during the winter. The British Staff did not want to get too deeply involved in the Balkans: it would have over-extended their lines of communication, and they also had good reason to suppose that Germany was preparing to attack Russia and open the Eastern front further to the north. But Mussolini had botched his expedition. This had the effect of forcing Hitler to intervene; the disastrous results of the Duce's initiative had dealt a severe blow to the reputation of the Axis war machine, which was supposed to be invincible. Something had to be done about it. On 6 April 1941 troops of the Third Reich entered Yugoslavia en route for Greece. The operation lasted a good deal longer than expected and some elite German units were badly mauled in the course of it. The first parachute regiments – a new instrument of war from which Hitler expected great things – shattered against the defences of Crete. The first wave of paratroops was quite literally chopped up on the cobbles of the port of Chania. 'In Crete,' wrote Churchill, 'Goering only won a Pyrrhic victory, since the forces which he expended there could easily have given him Cyprus, Iraq, Syria and perhaps Persia.'

Finally, the Greek campaign delayed the German offensive against Russia for several weeks, so that it was overtaken by winter. When Crete fell, the king, the government and the British troops fighting in Greece all left the country. The Germans reached Athens on 27 April 1941 and set up their own collaborationist government.

The Albanian campaign and the resistance in Crete had shown with what determination Greece could face an invader. The Greeks had only been warming up: the shadow of the swastika floating over the Acropolis did not mean that all resistance had ceased to exist. While the underground was gathering its forces for the struggle in Athens and the big towns, bands of armed men were leaving their villages and taking to the hills. Partisans, or bandits. Klepht is another word for bandit in Greek; the old epic was coming back to life.

In October 1941 the Party newspaper *Rizospastis* was being printed on a small secret press in a cellar in Kaisariani, on the edge of Athens. Both the press and the type had been stolen by Aris, but he had not the slightest intention of sitting about looking at his loot.

Armed bands were operating freely around his native village in Roumeli; though they plundered the population from time to time in the traditional Klephtic manner, they were also beginning to make life uncomfortable for the occupying forces. A leader was needed to turn these bandits into national Resistance heroes.

Aris knew the country like the back of his hand and was champing at the bit in the confines of Athens. For some time now he had been asking to be sent to the mountains. He was harassing Tzimas, who belonged to the Political Bureau and who shared his interest in the development of a peasant guerilla force: 'What are you keeping me in Athens for? I don't think this work suits me. Send me to the mountains.'

The Central Committee was deeply suspicious of the emerging movement, rooted as it was in rural banditry flavoured with folklore. The insurrectional model current at the time leaned heavily on the urban proletariat, and its adherents tended to an atavistic Stalinist distrust of the peasantry. But the Greek peasants were already fighting. In the end Tzimas managed to overcome some of the Party leadership's reservations and get Aris sent away to the mountains; but the Party regarded the project as an experiment and retained the right to disown him. Ypsilantis, another future kapetanios with a name that became legendary in the war of independence, left to contact armed bands in Macedonia in the same atmosphere of caution and mistrust.

Aris reached the walled town of Lamia, commanding Roumeli from the entrance to the pass of Thermopylae, early in the winter of 1941-42. The local branch of EAM had already listed the names of between fifty and seventy volunteers who were willing to join the maquis or support the andartes and partisans in their activities. Accompanied by a certain Georgis Houliaris (codenamed Pericles), Aris left the town for the mountains proper where goats, bandits and rock reigned supreme.

After a preliminary tour of the region, the two men established themselves in the Sperchios valley, where they were joined almost immediately by three companions. Hidden in a mill outside the village, these five were supplied with arms by local EAM officials. An excursion to Mount Goulina after a few days increased the strength of the Roumeliot armed Resistance to twelve men. They were still much weaker in numbers than the local organization had led them to expect, but there were enough of them to make a start. Thanks largely to Aris's boldness and genius for guerilla work, this handful of men grew into the formidable Resistance army ELAS.

Some of the armed bands in Roumeli at this time were led by self-proclaimed 'kings of the mountains' who were clearly more interested in plunder than in national or ideological struggle. Many of these men later became Resistance heroes: Bellis, Tzavelas, Karalivanos. Those who found it impossible, or inconvenient, to give up their indiscriminate looting soon found Aris to be a ruthless administrator of the People's Justice.

From June 1942, when the andartes started marching through the villages behind the flag and bugle, they called the population together and set up the basis for self-administration in the villages. Where the existing officials were unsatisfactory, new councillors were elected by show of hands. Each councillor was entrusted with a particular job: Security, People's Justice, Supplies, Recruitment. Justice was carried out by popular assemblies; one punishment, much feared by the andartes and usually imposed for disciplinary offences, was the confiscation of personal weapons. An ancient Utopia was gradually taking shape; side by side with daily violence, the reality of a free Greece was drawing nearer. A Greece subject to raids by enemy units, but free from the stranglehold of total occupation and from the poisonous pettiness of military government.

Communications with Athens were slow and inadequate. In 1942 the Central Committee sought above all to avoid frightening the liberal bourgeoisie; alarming stories were circulating about the radical methods Aris was using to recruit mountain bandits to the national struggle and to administer his territory. Ignorance of the problems and attitudes of the peasant resistance was widespread and profound.

Early in the summer of 1942 a KKE member called Andreas Mount-richas made a tour of Voiotia to organize the political side of EAM in the region. He took a trunk full of aspirin and quinine with him to sell in the villages, dividing his time between political contacts and this more or less innocent charlatanism.

The bandits infesting the mountains were making the roads unsafe by this time. As he approached the small village of Kaparelli, near Thebes, Mountrichas passed a shepherd sitting beside the road. It was a hot day and the shepherd, who had lost an eye in the Albanian campaign, offered the passing pedlar the traditional glass of water. The two men fell into conversation and after a few minutes Mountrichas learned that bandits had pillaged a nearby monastery on the previous day. He said experimentally: 'Italians, Germans and now bandits; it's getting too much!'

'You're wrong,' replied the shepherd, 'these are Klephts. They're going to liberate the country.'

'How?'

'You'll see, the bandits are going to get together, they'll become a new Greek army. They're going to help the peasants to liberate the country.'

The majority of Mountrichas's contacts, as well as casual conversations of this sort, confirmed his feeling that if these primitive pockets of spontaneous resistance could be unified and organized, they might indeed become a liberation army. On his return to Athens he reported to the Central Committee:

'The bands in the mountains have no organization, no discipline and no ideology. There is a real danger that they will go over to the enemy or, failing that, simply remain a burden on the people in addition to that of the triple occupation. The only solution is to turn these bandits into partisans by giving them the blessing of the Resistance.'[1]

His first report got no response. He sent two more, with the same result on each occasion. In the end Mountrichas became impatient and began to think in terms of going ahead with the experiment without waiting for the Central Committee's approval. He mentioned it to other Party members: 'The Party has no experience of the andartes. It only understands urban struggle.'

Nobody seriously opposed his departure, but he was given no official mission. If he succeeded he would be justified; if he failed he would be disowned.

Six months after Aris's departure, with the Resistance well under way in Roumeli, the cadres in Athens were still as doubtful as ever. Mountrichas, who became the kapetanios Orestis, joined Nikiforos and Diamantis,

[1] Orestis (oral testimony; all such references are to direct or indirect oral testimony).

who were fighting near Aris in the south of Roumeli. He organized armed resistance in the immediate surroundings of Athens and throughout Attica and Voiotia. In a difficult region where the enemy could use the comprehensive road network to intervene rapidly at any time, Orestis finished up in control of the Parnis mountains and a territory that reached the very gates of Athens.

In March 1943 the misunderstanding was still there, and the guerilla had been summoned to Athens in the person of Aris to be examined by the representatives of dogma. But in the meantime a new element had appeared in the mountains, a handful of bearded, anachronistic replicas of Lawrence of Arabia. The first representatives of the British SOE (Special Operations Executive) did very little to keep conflicts within bounds.

Pulling Strings

The British Staff in Cairo had kept in touch with the Greek Resistance through the 'Prometheus' networks set up at the time of the Allied retreat in 1941. They decided to send a military mission into the field to co-ordinate acts of sabotage carried out by the andartes.

The first members of the British military mission to emerge from the SOE's Cairo offices parachuted into Greece on the night of 1 October 1942. Their orders were to collaborate with partisan groups to organize a major sabotage of the Athens–Salonika railway line, the umbilical cord of Rommel's forces in Libya. The detachment was commanded by Colonel Eddie Myers and Major Chris Woodhouse.

'With his maquisard's beard, high forehead and long ascetic face, Myers looked like a saint in a Byzantine icon.'[1] Apart from this facial qualification he had no special knowledge of Greece. His assistant Woodhouse, a giant of twenty-three, was brave and indefatigable and spoke modern Greek perfectly. They arrived with a great deal of demolition equipment and a rather unreal image of Greece. Following the somewhat hazy directions supplied by the Prometheus II network, Myers and his men landed in territory controlled by Aris; to be exact, after wandering about for a while they made contact with the kapetanios Karalivanos.

Karalivanos was hardly the sort of person His Majesty's officers were

[1] A. Kedros, *La Résistance Grecque, 1940–44*, Paris, 1966, p. 138.

expecting to meet in Byron's adopted country. His partisans wore Evzones' kilts and fezes, and were armed with pearl-inlaid muskets and damascened knives. The Britons could hardly believe their eyes, and were not entirely happy to find themselves under the protection of the andartes. They had been instructed to contact a different Resistance organization called EDES (Greek National Democratic Union), which was led by Colonel Napoleon Zervas.

The ambitious, portly Colonel Zervas wore a beard as thick as Aris's and had also become a respected guerilla leader, in Epirus on the West coast of mainland Greece, but the resemblance between the two men stopped there. Zervas was a long-time dabbler in military putsches who would adopt democratic or republican opinions whenever it was expedient to do so.

With some other Greek officers he had begun at the end of 1941 sending intelligence reports to Allied Middle East headquarters, channelling them through Athens. The network was discovered by the German services and deliberately corrupted before being allowed to disappear; as a result of this German infiltration, it seems that misleading information reached Cairo suggesting that the Germans were getting ready to invade Turkey. It is quite possible that this episode in the 'war of the networks' left Zervas under some sort of cloud that gave the British a hold over him. In any case, in the Spring of 1942 he was under suspicion resulting from the accusations of a certain Alexatos.

This Alexatos was a redoubtable figure, a smuggler and something of a pirate by his own account. He had frequented the backwaters of the Aegean Sea for years and established liaison with the Middle East on Zervas's behalf. One day he appeared suddenly to ask for the KKE's protection; he did not realize that his men had been subverted by the occupying services and suspected Zervas of having betrayed him.

'Old Man' Siantos, General Secretary of the KKE, was not very happy about him but gave him what he wanted: a house to hide in and body-guards to protect him against Zervas and the Gestapo.

Locked in a bedroom with an armoury of knives and pistols, Alexatos became an EAM wireless operator to pay for his keep. He established an effective liaison with the Middle East; his first messages were followed by an air-drop of arms in the Dilofon region in the southern Pindus.

Alexatos's possibly sordid motives for accusing Zervas of treachery will never be known; whatever they were, he was not the only person to nourish such suspicions. Zervas received an ultimatum from Cairo a few days later: 'If you are not guilty, go into the mountains. If you do not do this we will be obliged to accuse you publicly over Radio London.'

This warning from Cairo, and the incompetence of the Greek liberals, between them provided Zervas with a near-monopoly of the non-communist resistance inside the country.

In September 1941 the republican General Plastiras,[1] a leader of the Greek radical movement living in exile in France, had sent a representative to contact Greek liberal personalities with a view to organizing the resistance and ensuring the country's return to democracy after the war. His emissary, Komninos Pyromaglou, was young, brave and intelligent, a former Greek army officer who had finished his education in Paris where he had also gained some political experience.

Plastiras had instructed him to have nothing to do with political organizations and to deal only with 'secure friends'. Zervas was specifically excluded from this category and Pyromaglou was warned to approach him with the greatest caution. But Pyromaglou's contacts proved neither as receptive nor as unanimous as expected. Sofoulis, Kafandaris, Papandreou and the rest of the liberal establishment accused Plastiras of trying to split the forces of democracy, while the military expressed verbal enthusiasm but felt that the time had not yet come for direct action. In the end Pyromaglou could only find one attentive ear: that of Napoleon Zervas, the man he had been told to distrust. Zervas was under pressure from London to rehabilitate himself and was in any case eager to play a political role. In September 1942 he and Pyromaglou founded a new Resistance organization called the Greek National Democratic Union (EDES).

According to its own statutes, EDES was a republican movement with socialist ideals. Pyromaglou, who had in all probability drawn up the statutes himself, was to be the only member to feel himself bound by the spirit of the initial programme to the bitter end. Initially the relations between EDES and EAM were quite good. When Zervas and Pyromaglou left Athens on 23 July 1942 to form the first 'national bands' of partisans in Zervas's home district, Epirus, they asked for support from ARTA, the communist Resistance organization that preceded ELAS. But when Zervas started operating in the mountains of Epirus he found himself in competition with Aris's men, installed in the neighbouring region. Aris was fiercely imposing the Resistance's monopoly on the armed groups which

[1] Plastiras had headed several Republican plots, revolutions and coups d'etat in 1922–23 and in 1933.

had appeared spontaneously, but for very diverse reasons, in Roumeli. He had decided once and for all that these 'kings of the mountains' and their gangs must be integrated, dissolved or wiped out. He was half inclined to treat Zervas's units in the same way.

The Pindus, Aris's territory, is separated from Epirus, which Zervas intended to dominate, by the River Acheloös. Two rival organizations of armed partisans fighting in the same area and recruiting from the same villages must inevitably come into conflict sooner or later. A tacit agreement recognized the Acheloös as the demarcation line. Nevertheless, the rivalry intensified with the proliferation of the inevitable minor frictions. Zervas had been sent into the mountains by the British; since he was sure of their support, he was not much inclined to coddle his neighbours; Klephts and Armatoloi.

Open conflict betwen ELAS and EDES could only serve the detractors of ELAS, whose basic argument was that the communists wanted to monopolize the Resistance with a long-term view to pursuing the class struggle. In these difficult circumstances Aris's policy oscillated between making punitive expeditions against EDES units on his territory and suggesting to Zervas that they should join forces: dissolution or integration. The objectives listed in the statutes of the two organizations were palpably similar. Since it was necessary to allow for Zervas's ambition, Aris even went so far as to offer him the military command of ELAS. But the resistance's apple of discord was growing on the banks of the River Acheloös, and served the long-term interests of the British so well that it would have been unnatural if Myers had not cultivated it a little.

For the time being, however, the mission was under the orders of the SOE which had parachuted it into Greece, rather than the Foreign Office. SOE was a military agency and its objectives were primarily strategic; it suited the Cairo Staff that ELAS and EDES should collaborate on its sabotage programme for a while.

Only half reassured by his first contact with the partisans, Myers left to reconnoitre possible sabotage targets, leaving Woodhouse to get in touch with Zervas and Aris.

Zervas greeted Woodhouse like manna from heaven, throwing himself into his arms and calling him 'Evangelos' – the Herald Angel. He was not over-scrupulous about the nuances of national sovereignty, and such was his need of money and arms that Chris's arrival seemed to him a gift of providence. Aris was contacted indirectly through Karalivanos's men, and agreed to take part in the sabotage operation.

Woodhouse arrived back in ELAS territory in the middle of the night of 17–18 November. He shook Myers awake and told him that Zervas was on the way, followed at half a day's distance by Aris Velouchiotis with a hundred partisans.

Myers and Zervas met for the first time the following day. The jovial, demonstrative Napoleon of the Mountains captivated Myers from the outset; he was an impressive figure in his officer's leather, exactly what the head of the British Mission had been hoping to see.

Myers joined Aris and his men after a day's march towards the village of Mavrolithari. This time the welcome was a good deal less cordial. Aris did not display any transports of enthusiasm and the first contact between the British Mission and the chief kapetanios of ELAS was distinctly cool. None of their subsequent meetings would be much warmer.

During his reconnaissance trip Myers had chosen the viaduct over the river Gorgopotamos as the target. After a final visit, the plan of battle was drawn up. The kapetanios Nikiforos, who was present at the meeting, recalls that Aris dictated the battle plan from beginning to end, hardly consulting the English. The mission was carried out by 150 men from ELAS, sixty from EDES and the British contingent of twelve saboteurs. General Zervas was in command of the operation. The final approach to the objective was made on the afternoon of 25 November. Zero hour was fixed for 11 p.m.

A minute or two before eleven o'clock [Myers wrote[1]], Zervas, Aris, Chris [Woodhouse] and I advanced to within a few feet of the crest of the gently sloping ridge behind which the reserve was sheltering, and we peered over the edge. Through the light mist we could clearly see the viaduct ahead of us. It looked huge and gaunt. All was silent. For fourteen anxious minutes we waited thus, lying on our stomachs on the ground. Then at last, when we had begun to think that something had gone seriously wrong, that all the parties were late, or that in the darkness they had gone astray, pandemonium was let loose right in front of us round the north end of the viaduct.

Rifle and automatic fire seemed to come from every direction at once, a tremendous volume of it. I could distinguish four or five light machine-guns cracking away in a deafening manner. The attacking party at this end of the viaduct had only two such guns. We were up against something fairly strong. Bullets were flying high over our heads in considerable numbers. After about twenty minutes of this intense small-arms fire Zervas became worried and said to me, through Chris, that, at that rate of fire, we would soon run out of our ammunition. Shortly afterwards heavy firing broke out from the south end, and

[1] E. C. W. Myers, *Greek Entanglement*, London, 1955, p. 78 ff.

we distinctly heard captain Michalli's voice, loudly cheering his andartes on. Then the firing somewhat died down in front of us, and a few minutes later an excited andarte approached and told us that the group attacking the north end of the viaduct had been beaten back. They had tried to cut their way silently through the barbed wire round the Italian guard-post, and had succeeded in getting a few people through a narrow gap when they had been spotted by the enemy, who had trained some light automatics right on the gap. The andartes, inexperienced in a deliberate operation such as this, had not been able to face the intense fire, and they had all withdrawn to a position of cover.

From the cheering still occasionally audible above the noise of the firing at the far end of the viaduct, we gathered that all was going well there. The situation at our end demanded drastic action. We decided to put in the whole of our reserve to re-establish the situation. Zervas' second-in-command, Komninos Pyromaglou, was in charge of this party. Once a teacher of Greek in Paris, he was not only an able person but full of courage. He was therefore entrusted with supreme command of the fresh attack on the north end. Not long after he had gone forward with the reserve, brisk firing broke out again in front of us. But there were still too many light automatics to be heard for my liking. After another twenty minutes' continuous firing Zervas became even more anxious. He told me that he was almost convinced that we had been betrayed, that the Italians had been forewarned of our attack and had been reinforced. He said that he would fire the green Very light for the general withdrawal if the north end of the bridge was not captured in the next ten minutes, and he asked for the Very pistol. No one had it! Fortunately, though inadvertently, it had been taken forward by Komninos in his pocket. I sent Chris forward to get it, with instructions to keep it in his own hands and on no account to allow anybody to handle it except under my orders. Ten minutes later he returned with it, and with the news also that Komninos was in good heart and hoped, before long, to gain possession of his end of the bridge.

Nearly an hour after the battle had started exceptionally loud cheering went up from the south end of the viaduct. It was followed almost immediately by a white Very light. The far end was in our hands.

The steel piers, which the demolition party were going to destroy, were nearer that end than ours; so I decided to take the risk of ordering Tom Barnes and his party forward to their work. I ran down to a point where I could look straight across to the other side of the valley, where Tom and his men were lying up, waiting for my signal. I flashed my torch and shouted at the top of my voice: 'Go in, Tom! The south end of the bridge is in our hands. Go in! I will join you as soon as possible.'

'OK,' Tom shouted back.

I returned to wait with Zervas and Aris, and with Chris, who was essential to me as interpreter.

On the battle went in front of us. Zervas was convinced that we had almost run out of ammunition. I told him we could not consider a withdrawal now, because the demolition party already had their task partially completed.

After about another fifteen minutes, unable to wait inactive any longer, I told Chris that I would go forward and join Komninos, who spoke English moderately well, and that I would leave him as my sole representative with Zervas and Aris. I repeated to him my instructions that on no account was the withdrawal signal to be fired without my orders. With one andarte, who did not speak a word of English, as my personal bodyguard, I crept over the odd hundred yards between our rise in the ground and the place where I could see the flashes coming from the rifles of Komninos' men. I crawled up alongside the leader of one of his sections; but he spoke no English. I could not find Komninos. By gesticulation I urged the section leader to move his men forward; but he would not do so. The enemy fire was by now far from intense, and I realised that the resistance in front of us was crumbling. A few moments later, above the noise of battle, a shrill whistle was heard. It was Tom Barnes' signal for everyone to take cover, as he was about to light fuses. Our firing ceased as we put our heads down, and almost automatically the enemy firing also eased. Two minutes later there was a tremendous explosion, and I saw one of the seventy-foot steel spans lift into the air and – oh, what joy! – drop into the gorge below, in a rending crash of breaking and bending steel-work.

At last I succeeded in getting the andartes around me to charge, and in the darkness they overran the few Italians who had not by now escaped. Seconds later, from somewhere just behind me, a white Very signal was fired into the air. Simultaneously with the successful accomplishment of half our task the Italian garrison had been completely overcome.

Through the barbed wire and tall grass at the foot of the viaduct I made my way down to the river, intending to cross it in order to join Tom Barnes. But I found a raging torrent and, with no rope and unassisted except for the single bodyguard at my side, I realised, after one attempt, that I could never keep my feet in it. I shouted at the top of my voice to Tom, who could only have been about fifty yards away from me. But I failed to make myself heard. As quickly as I could, I retraced my steps to the end of the viaduct, where I got onto the top of it and walked along until I reached its jagged end. In front of me I clearly discerned two complete spans which had been dropped into the gorge below, as a result of the demolition of one of the steel piers. Forty feet above the river which, even where I then stood, roared loudly below me, I shouted again at the top of my voice, and at last got Denys Hamson to hear me. He told me that they needed another forty minutes to bring down the other steel pier and a further span, and to twist and cut the other two spans already lying partially on the ground.

At that moment there was a loud explosion from the north. Heavy firing broke out from that direction. Enemy reinforcements were approaching by rail from Lamia. I could but hope that Themie's party was doing its job properly. I shouted to Denys that they must be as quick as they could, as we had now insufficient ammunition to hold off any fresh enemy force for many minutes.

A few moments later I heard Chris' voice behind me, shouting from somewhere up the hill: 'Zervas says he can only give you another ten minutes, and then we must fire the withdrawal signal.'

'On no account will you allow it to be fired,' I shouted back, 'until you hear the next explosion from the bridge. This cannot be less than twenty minutes from now.'

'All right', Chris shouted, 'I'll do my best; but for heaven's sake don't make it more than twenty minutes.'

I went back to the overhanging edge of the viaduct and shouted across to Denys the gist of this conversation. I told him to be as quick as he possibly could.

Some fifteen minutes later Tom blew his whistle again. I heaved a sigh of relief. The enemy firing from the north was getting nearer, and I knew it was touch and go whether we could hold out any longer. I went back to the end of the viaduct and took cover. There was another tremendous explosion. I couldn't see exactly what happened. No further span fell down, as I expected; but I distinctly saw the two already fallen ones jump up into the air and subside again. A second later a green Very signal went up into the air.

The andartes did not leave a single man on the field; three were slightly wounded. Fresh snow was falling which obliterated their tracks. The war diary of the Wehrmacht High Command contains this entry dated 27 November 1942:

During the night of 25–26 November, a group of 200 men blew up the Gorgopotamos bridge, to the south of Lianokladi; the Salonika-Athens railway line was severed in the attack, in all probability for at least a week.[1]

The High Command was indulging in wishful thinking. The viaduct was not in fact finally repaired until the end of February 1943. Rommel's essential supply route was cut for three months. The day after the operation Myers distributed the customary praise and rewards, even going so far as to shake hands with the doughty Karalivanos.

In recognition of ELAS's 'valiant services' he gave its leader two hundred and fifty pounds in gold, which Aris accepted without demurring. But when Myers announced his intention of proposing him for a high military decoration, Aris stared at him coldly with one eye halfclosed and replied that he would think it more suitable to be given 'boots

---

[1] Andreas Hillgrüber, *Kreigstagebuch des Oberkommandos der Wehrmacht*, Vol. II, Frankfurt, 1963, p. 1030.

for his andartes'. Denys Hamson, who took part in the expedition, wrote in his memoirs:

They were in a shocking state of equipment. Their nondescript clothes were mostly in rags, and many were literally barefoot, which must have been considerable hardship in this weather. Our boots were soaked through by the snow and our feet were wet and cold, but at least we had boots. Their guns ranged mostly from sixty-year-old Graz, firing an antiquated but murderous lead bullet, through Martinis and Mausers of all types and vintages to the Greek Mannlicher. One or two even had our Lee-Enfields.

Zervas' men, the EDES team, were somewhat older men, at least not boys, and rather better – but not much better equipped. They were far more friendly, and their young officers seemed good.[1]

A few days later the BBC broadcast a poetic account of the Gorgopotamos sabotage, emphasizing the part played by EDES and praising General Napoleon Zervas to the skies. ELAS and its chief Aris Velouchiotis were not mentioned once. The English had made their choice.

In the country of Homer, legends can survive without the help of the BBC. Much of the credit due to Aris for his role in the Gorgopotamos affair was restored to him by the Athens newspapers, by songs and by word of mouth. He became the leading figure of the armed Resistance. By this time his popular image was incomplete without his escort: the *mavroskufides* or 'black bonnets'. Always close to their chief, riding the best horses the region could provide, thundering about like a herd of buffalo, bearded and wearing their black sheepskin caps, their qualities were such as to inspire either terror or epic lyricism, depending on the circumstances.

The sheepskin bonnets were trophies, originally the property of bands of Vlach collaborators living in the valleys of Thessaly and Epirus whom the Italians had armed in the hope that they would secede. Aris had wiped them out and adopted their headdress, turning a traitor's attribute into a symbol of national resistance.

The 'black bonnets' were the elite corps of the Resistance. There were about twenty-five of them and they had their own way of doing things; they shared out their chores among themselves and lived like monks in a convent of which Aris was the superior and Tzavelas the second-in-command. Alongside their reputation for bravery they developed a name for extreme violence, even cruelty.

[1] Denys Hamson, *We Fell Among Greeks*, London, 1946, p. 104.

The British were puzzled by these armed anchorites. The methods that Aris used to transform banditry into sacred patriotic struggle suited the peculiarities of the situation but were distinctly alien to the concepts handed down by British Hellenism. In his memoirs Myers recounted with wry admiration that he had seen Aris have a man executed for stealing a chicken in a village. On another occasion a *mavroskufis*, one of those closest to him, was accused of stealing a watch from a peasant woman. The andartes passed the usual sentence and Aris, pale as death, ordered the firing squad into position. He was about to kill a man he held in the highest esteem for a trivial offence. The rifles were aimed at the condemned man's chest. Bolts clicked. At the last possible moment the accuser came rushing out of her house, yelling, and waving the watch which had simply been mislaid. Aris, still impassive but soaked in perspiration, dismissed the firing squad and shut himself in his room for several hours.

Doors could be left open in mountains which had been plundered by bandits for centuries. Locks became a thing of the past. This monastic discipline extended into the sexual domain, especially when young women began joining the partisans in increasing numbers.

On yet another occasion in 1942 the Voulgareli andartes' court condemned a resistance fighter to death for attempting to rape a girl. Aris sternly lectured his men: 'You had better understand once and for all,' he said, 'that as long as you are here your rods are just for pissing.'

Rumours reached Athens more quickly than reports, and Aris's epic had its ambiguous side. On one hand, popular mythology was enlivened by the songs that were written to celebrate his exploits; on the other, his brutalities loomed large in bourgeois accounts and helped the Resistance to acquire a rather bloodthirsty image in liberal circles. The EAM Central Committee was becoming increasingly disturbed by the alarming rumours which were circulating, exploited and swollen by official propaganda. Reassuring the Athens politicians was not their only problem; they had to find arms and equipment for ELAS. To this end they were prepared to pay almost any price to get ELAS recognized in its own right by British Middle East HQ.

Under these circumstances nobody could bring himself to attribute the BBC's treatment of ELAS after Gorgopotamos to a deliberate manoeuvre by the British. The most widespread explanation of it, and also the most comfortable for the communist leadership, blamed Aris for his inept handling of the situation.

Aris was being attacked from all directions. Violently criticized by his own party for failing to appear in the BBC's roll of honour, he also became the target of a straight attempt at liquidation organized by his neighbour Napoleon Zervas. Following its original orders the British Mission had moved in with EDES. The English presence bestowed a semi-official status on Zervas's organization, and he felt secure enough to step up his provocations. The ELAS attitude hardened in response: escalation. Zervas had the wind in his sails, and a murky plot began to take shape in his Mavrolithari headquarters. This was no less than a scheme to kidnap Aris. An ELAS member called Kostorizos was given the task of arresting him and his staff, and handing them over to EDES with all arms and equipment. To ensure the loyalty of his new acolyte, Zervas had reinforced his arguments with a few golden sovereigns.

On the morning of 13 December Aris discovered that Kostorizos and his twenty-five men had deserted. His first thought was that Zervas had something to do with the incident and that the deserters had probably fled to his territory. The fact that Kostorizos's motives for crossing the river Acheloos had almost certainly been sordid made the problem especially serious for ELAS; Zervas's sovereigns were a good deal more important than the theft of a chicken, and Aris had not hesitated to make an example of that. He must strike now, and strike hard. An assembly of four hundred andartes passed judgement on the Kostorizos case, Aris intervening without making any notable pleas for clemency. It was decided that ELAS would enter Zervas's territory, seize the culprits and punish them in accordance with the rules of war.

The detachment sent to carry out the punitive expedition clashed with an Italian regiment on the way and left seventy Italian dead on the field, including the colonel in command of the unit. Aris crossed the river Acheloös and plunged into Zervas's territory without meeting any serious resistance from EDES.

Both Woodhouse and local EAM officials intervened to stave off disaster, and managed between them to arrange a meeting between Aris and Zervas. The two men walked to meet one another covered by two tense lines of andartes, standing with fingers trembling on the triggers of cocked guns and ready to start a massacre at the slightest false move.

Aris announced that he was willing to negotiate a merger between ELAS and EDES with Zervas as military commander. Aris would remain the kapetanios – that is, overall chief of partisans – and a political figure enjoying the trust of both groups would be brought in as political adviser to the unified movement. Zervas had the British on his side and knew that he could expect preferential treatment from Cairo. He wrecked the conference by saying that he could only envisage the unification of the two movements under his exclusive command.

There was no shortage of competitors for the rich rewards strewing the path of exclusive allegiance and collaboration with the British, and it was not long before Zervas found himself being overtaken by the machinations of his partners. A few days after his meeting with Aris he intercepted a secret note from the staff of the exiled king to two monarchist officers who were fighting with EDES. It instructed them to 'cultivate good relations with EDES and acceptable relations with ELAS, but to bring about discords and clashes between ELAS and EDES by all available means'.

Post-war British interests in Greece were closely tied to the fortunes of the Glucksburg dynasty, which was the best guarantee that the semi-colonial structures of the kingdom would be maintained. Despite a rather shopsoiled Republican label, Zervas for his part was really only interested in advancing his career. The mechanism was in place.

Officially, Myers had only volunteered to carry out the Gorgopotamos sabotage. At the beginning of 1943, however, he was given another job instead of being sent back to Egypt: to meet the leaders of the political parties and strengthen the armed Resistance. Churchill was at this time toying with the idea of making a landing in the Balkans, and had begun taking a closer interest in the political problem posed by Greece.

Woodhouse was sent to Athens about the first week in January; Myers himself stayed behind with Zervas. The SOE's giant travelled the last few kilometres crouched under the seats of a small bus and entered the capital without incident.

Woodhouse contacted the heads of the Liberal and Social Democratic parties, Sofoulis and Papandreou, and received quantities of verbal encouragement and one or two pieces of good advice. After a while he asked to be put in touch with the people running EAM.

The meeting took place in a house in Kolokynthou. EAM was represented by Siantos, Tzimas and another Central Committee member, a socialist lawyer called Tsirimokos. In his perfect modern Greek, Woodhouse got straight down to business. 'I have orders for you from my HQ in Cairo to increase your efforts in the area of armed resistance. We are collaborating closely with your king, whom we intend to restore to his throne.'

It would have been difficult to be more explicit about the general direction of British policy in Greece. Woodhouse wrote later in his memoirs: 'Taking into account the state of events in 1943, this was rather like asking the English ambassador in Moscow to remind Stalin every time he saw him of the British government's devotion to the cause of the Romanovs.'[1]

The military in Cairo and their intelligence service, the SOE, were looking for strategic support from the Greek Resistance, whatever its political colour. The Foreign Office on the other hand persisted in making an issue of the 'debt of recognition' owed to King George of Greece by Britain, enabling him to regard his kingdom as a guarded preserve.

General Wilson, Commander-in-Chief of Allied troops in the Eastern Mediterranean, could not conceal the serious difficulties that arose for him out of the diplomats' quarrels with the SOE over Greece:

... Our diplomats [he wrote later] were strongly averse to any encouragement being given to parties which might prejudice the return of the King and the existing Greek Government, while SOE wanted to build up resistance regardless of the politics of any of the bands they had contacted. From the war effort point of view the latter course was preferable and I personally did not like the idea of tying our liaison officers exclusively to one political party. (The right and right centre parties did not figure in the resistance movement, while Zervas was a Republican); I felt that the wisest course was to work with the left wing parties and endeavour to guide them rather than to resist them.[2]

Woodhouse's opening statement in the house in Kolokynthou expressed the ambiguity of his mission to the full. The EAM representatives replied that the question of the king's possible return could only be settled by a national referendum, which must be called to decide on the future of the Greek institutions as soon as the country was liberated. They knew that a plebiscite would be certain to reject the Glucksburg dynasty, whose rule had never extended far beyond the parties of reaction in any case. It is most unlikely that the British had any illusions on this matter, for they were already starting to set up a praetorian military force which could be used to uphold a concept of legality that would serve the Empire's best interests.

Meanwhile both parties, Woodhouse on the one hand and Siantos,

[1] C. M. Woodhouse, 'Zur Geschichte der Resistance in Griechenland', Vierteljahreshefte für Zeitgeschichte, April 1958, p. 141.
[2] Lord Wilson of Libya, Eight Years Overseas, London, 1948, p. 167.

Tsirimokos and Tzimas on the other, were trying to ally themselves with the devil. EAM's immediate concern was to get arms, and Middle East HQ was trying to promote intensified Resistance activity in Greece. Any solution to the political problem which might limit the SOE's basic options was shelved by tacit agreement; for one reason or another, nobody was ready to jump that hurdle just yet. It was not going to become an easier obstacle with the passage of time.

After listening to a report on EAM activities, Woodhouse made a number of comments based on his limited experience of ELAS; he was particularly vehement on the subject of Aris. He did not conceal the fact that he found the reputation and activities of this bearded guerilla and his entourage of fierce black horsemen more frightening than admirable. Despite the oddity of a situation in which an English officer was upholding the monarchy before a group of revolutionaries, his judgements on Aris made a considerable impression on his audience.

Although Siantos and most of the other KKE cadres subscribed to a value system radically opposed to that of the British, Aris's methods of warfare seemed equally unorthodox to both parties. The suspicion of both sides combined to swell Velouchiotis's dossier. At the end of the meeting the Englishman asked his hosts with some embarrassment if he could use their radio to get in touch with Cairo. Leading Woodhouse into the next room to compose his message, Tzimas asked: 'Why are you using our radio when you've got your own?'

'Ours has just fallen into the hands of the Germans.'

Leaving Woodhouse seated at a table, Tzimas rejoined the others: 'Woodhouse's Athens set-up has been burnt. We'd better keep him here and let him use our communications.'

Siantos was reluctant. He knew that it would be running an enormous risk to protect a British agent whose political aims in Greece were openly admitted. Tzimas persisted: 'Everyone in Athens knows this Englishman is in town. If he tries to get back to his friends, he may well be arrested. We'll be accused of not looking after him. This is our opportunity to show what we can do, and to establish a permanent connection with Cairo.'

Tsirimokos and Siantos exchanged glances. They agreed. In the next room, Woodhouse was still poring over his message.

'I suggest you stay here with us,' Tzimas told him. 'Your radio's been discovered already; you're in danger of being captured by the Germans.'

It was a reasonable suggestion. Churchill's emissary accepted the protection of EAM and the communists. At Tzimas's request he added a paragraph to his radio signal: 'EAM would like to send a mission to Cairo. Could you possibly work out a scheme for getting them there ?'

This was the first official contact between EAM and the British Government. Over the next few days Woodhouse's blond hair was dyed black under Tzimas's personal supervision. Then he was taken with three other men to the Aspropirgos suburb where Theos, EAM's best liaison agent, took charge of his return to Zervas. They left Athens without the slightest trouble. Woodhouse had just inaugurated the 'Mountain Boulevard' which he attributed in his memoirs to 'EAM's divine machinery'.

The Mountain on Trial

In Greece one is never very far from the mountains. The white and gold quarries of the Pendeli, the ash-grey slopes of Lycabettus, Hymettus and Parnis are visible from every corner of Athens, reminders even in the capital of the rugged and uncompromising nature of this country: the sea stretches away in front like a moat, the rampart of the mountains rises behind. A domain of sharp stones shimmering like blue metal under the dazzling Greek sky, the kingdom of klephts, of those who refuse to submit or compromise, bandits and heroes. Beyond Attica and Voiotia, among the dense mountain chains of the Pindus, there was Aris's domain.

Even in Athens itself an unprecedented urban resistance had taken shape. The necessary style of its existence, with coded messages exchanged and furtive contacts made in an atmosphere of dumb tension, contrasted sharply with Aris's cavalcades through the mountains at the head of his Black Bonnets. How could those engaged in the city assess the rumours that filtered in from Roumeli ?

'Old Man' Siantos, general secretary of the KKE, was behind the decision to summon Aris to Athens at the beginning of March 1943. Bringing Aris to the city through occupied territory, at a time when the conflict between ELAS and EDES was erupting in daily incidents on both sides of the Acheloös, meant depriving the Mountain of its chief during a particularly critical period.

Tzimas wanted to send him an emissary authorized to speak for the Central Committee, who would have been able to conduct an inquiry on the spot and assess Aris on some other basis than a few rumours and Woodhouse's hostile report. Siantos was stubborn. The smear campaign being waged against ELAS by the forces of the right was making more and more capital out of Aris's excesses. He thought it might be necessary to replace him. Aris must appear.

George Siantos was born in Karditsa in 1890. The tobacco trade provided the region's only industry, which was poorly paid and subject to fluctuations in the international market. He joined the Tobacco Workers' Union at the age of fifteen and took an active part in strikes, demonstrations and labour unrest. He joined the KKE in 1920 and lived through all the currents and internal movements that accompanied the birth of Stalinism. There was a conflict between the flexible 'opportunist' line, which Siantos supported, and the dogmatic line advocated by the new generation of Party cadres, which was characterized by unconditional alignment with Moscow. Most of these opponents of the tendency favoured by Siantos were men trained outside Greece in the Soviet Union's Communist University of the Peoples of the East (KUTV).

After various ups and downs the confrontation between the two tendencies ended in a compromise in 1934. The Party shelved its internal dissensions while promoting the claims of the Slavic minorities in Macedonia, which suited the purposes of the Comintern but clashed sharply with the still-new Greek national consciousness.

Siantos was elected secretary of the Piraeus organization and became an influential member of the Party. He was arrested in August 1936 during the first few days of Metaxas's dictatorship and exiled to the island of Anafi, from which he escaped the following year. He was recaptured in October 1939 and imprisoned on Corfu. He managed to escape once again while being taken to Athens for trial in 1941. The General Secretary of the KKE, Zachariadis, was sent to Dachau. The shattered Communist Party was just beginning to reorganize itself. Siantos was fifty-one years old and had never adopted too extreme a position in the Party's internal struggles. He was a level-headed man; the movement needed a democratic figure to unite the diverse currents of the resistance, rather than a doctrinaire. EAM was being formed at this time, and he was virtually the only person who could take over the leadership of the Communist Party without frightening away its allies from the democratic centre. Thin and dry, with hair black for his age but with a high bald forehead, wearing a small clipped moustache and round schoolmaster's spectacles, the 'Old Man' was elected First Secretary of the KKE Central Committee in

January 1942. His experience of all the varieties of police repression had left him with a deep horror of violence. Aris's excesses, both real and alleged, had touched him on a sensitive spot. He was determined to deal firmly with the matter.

Around Siantos the Central Committee was dominated by a nucleus of dogmatists, the Soviet-trained Comintern men sometimes called 'kutvists'. Every time Siantos's opinion was consulted as a matter of form on some doctrinal problem, the dialectical experts would say: 'George is a great militant, but he hasn't a clue about ideological problems.'

In trying to understand the 'Old Man's' decisions, then, it is necessary to take the presence of these *éminences grises* of the Revolution into account. The main watchdog of orthodoxy on the Central Committee was the 'kutvist' Yannis Ioannidis. He was the spiritual heir of Nicos Zachariadis, whose spectral presence still seemed to haunt every meeting.

Ioannidis was born in Volos. Volos was the third largest industrial town in Greece, situated midway between Athens and Salonika, and was the cradle of the KKE. Ioannidis was working as a barber there when he joined the Party in 1923. His health was delicate and in 1928 he was sent to the Soviet Union gravely ill with tuberculosis. While undergoing three years of medical treatment there he had enough free time to receive parallel intellectual treatment at the University of the Peoples of the East. Returning to Greece with his health restored and ideas cast in ferro-concrete, he was subjected to the tribulations reserved for left-wingers under the Metaxas regime.

In 1943 he was the second most influential man in the Central Committee; sheltering behind Siantos, he wielded a considerable ideological influence. He belonged to that special revolutionary caste within the Revolution, the upholders of the infallibility of the capital of orthodoxy: Moscow. A follower of Stalin's pure, hard line, he had to believe in the supremacy of proletarian struggle. Even in Greece, where the proletariat was small and undeveloped and the peasant masses were ready to take up arms, his training and belief led him to enshrine the October Revolution as a permanent model and proclaim the decisive role of the urban struggle.

When the Comintern was dissolved in May 1943 to give greater freedom of manoeuvre to fraternal parties, men like Ioannidis would become similar to orphans, searching endlessly for outside authority. He was the kind of communist other communists would always recognize if they passed him in the street. He was archetypally doctrinaire, committed to the very marrow of his bones, driven by the unswerving certainty of canonical faith. He was less shocked by Aris's intransigence than by his rustic and homeric appearance: a wild, bearded figure who owed something to Chapaiev and prefigured Castro. The enmity between the bearded and the smooth-shaven is more than a simple matter of adornment in the revolutionary history of our time.

In the person of Aris Velouchiotis, the peasant resistance, which had instinctively adopted the historic forms of the Greek national struggle, was now brought in for questioning by the Central Committee of the KKE. Aris had burnt his ecclesiastical robes, shaved off his beard and allowed his gold tooth to be replaced. He sat facing Siantos, Ioannidis and Tzimas. Siantos opened the proceedings:

'Comrade Klaras, as you know, even traitors should not be brutalized; they have to be convinced. Our weapon is conviction, not terror. We are being accused of neglecting the national struggle and of conducting a class struggle instead by exterminating feudal elements. Our only objective at the moment should be to struggle against the invader.'

Aris kept still, one eye half-closed, his hand resting on his crossed knees, the picture of submission. The Party in disciplinary guise reminded the king of the mountains of the *dilosi* in his past, the man who had denied his faith under Metaxas. He was disarmed. He knew that the future of ELAS was in the balance, that the Old Man was ready to relieve him of his command and impose another face on the Roumelian resistance.

He knew the penalties for the excesses he had been accused of committing, but he also knew the extent of his popularity. Certainly, there were people who disapproved of his methods; but if these methods 'terrorized' those whom they were designed to crush, they had also succeeded in rousing the great majority of peasants to revolt. Siantos continued: 'Zervas is fighting the occupying forces, but ELAS's attitude towards him has been such that people are now accusing us of wanting to monopolize the Resistance for purely political ends.'

Aris came suddenly to life, but managed to speak calmly: 'Zervas is a careerist. We're going to have either to destroy him or to integrate him by giving him military command of ELAS.'

For the moment, nobody was willing to confine himself to this choice. The official line demanded that the liberals should not be alarmed; revolutionaries are not always very skilled at that game. Ioannidis interrupted: 'An alliance has to be made with Zervas; the circumstances of the struggle make it essential. But there can be no question of putting

Zervas in charge of ELAS. The British must aid and recognize *our* organization.'

The position was simply untenable, but nobody in the Central Committee had the slightest experience of the mountains, where insults and Homeric provocations were daily events.

Aris read out his report on the activities of ELAS slowly and calmly. With an intentional lack of expression, he read all the figures, the list of victories, the list of self-administered villages controlled by the andartes, the report on his whole administration; when he came to deal with the problem of ELAS's future, he had trouble controlling his voice.

'The possibilities for developing the struggle are still considerable, and could well play a crucial role. In my opinion, from now on the Central Committee's proper place is in the mountains. . . .'

His last sentence dropped into an uneasy silence, as if he had just said something shockingly incongruous. There was a short pause; Ioannidis and Siantos remained expressionless. Then, with an emphasis which seemed all the more out of place for having been so long suppressed, Aris let himself go with Danton's formula: '*De l'audace et encore de l'audace.*'

It was the only piece of audacity that the kapetanios showed in the whole confrontation.

During this first trial of the Mountain the violent side of Aris's personality was not aroused by the indictment he had been expecting. No sentence was passed. The 'rebel' took all the criticisms that were levelled at him without a murmur. The terrible Aris, beardless and choking back his natural arrogance, had proved himself capable of reassuring behaviour. He would go back to the mountains, but accompanied by a political adviser.

'Comrade Tzimas has repeatedly urged us to support Aris; now he will return with him to make sure that the Party line is respected by the andartes of Roumeli.'

Tzimas had been struggling for some time to bring home the importance of the partisan struggle to the Political Bureau and the Central Committee. He had sent them report after report underlining the need to send at least one member of the Central Committee into the provinces. His departure with Aris enabled Siantos and Ioannidis to kill two birds with one stone: they were placing their own man close to Aris at the same time as cutting Tzimas off from direct contact with the Central Committee. They kept the orthodox nucleus of the Central Committee intact, more monolithic than ever and still almost unaware of the prodigious development which was already throwing the Party's base into confusion.

Urban Resistance

Athens was a powder-keg. The winter of 1941–42 had turned the city into an extermination camp where swollen-bellied children and fleshless old men and women died like flies in the streets. When one of them dropped, no one came to identify the body; the ration card of a dead relative might mean survival for the living. 300,000 people had starved to death in two months. Athens was bloodless, stretched to breaking point, sensitive and unpredictable as decaying gelignite. The slightest spark might touch off an explosion of popular fury that the occupying forces would not be able to contain. The cadres of EAM and the KKE had sound reasons for not underestimating the urban Resistance.

At the beginning of March 1943 every wall in the city carried one or two fresh slogans in the jumble of graffiti surrounding the advertisements for Aris's head: NO WORKERS FOR GERMANY. DOWN WITH GERMAN JAILS. Occupied Athens had started a fierce, open resistance against the Axis.

On 20 February the Greek radio had broadcast a laconic announcement from the official German agency:

In recognition of the bravery shown on the field of battle by the Greek people, Adolf Hitler, Chancellor of the Third Reich, wishes to associate them closely with the New Order whose historic path he has marked out, and asks that their help in achieving this end become more positive and energetic. . . .

It did not take the anonymous writers of red graffiti very long to respond to this message. The wall newspapers mounted an immediate campaign against the civil mobilization which was to associate the youth of Greece with the glories of the Third Reich.

On the evening of 22 February the mobilization order was handed to the staff of the official newspaper by Feldkommandant Speidel, whose career was far from being at an end:

In accordance with the powers vested in me by the Führer as Supreme Commander of German armed forces, I order:

Article I: Every male inhabitant of Greece aged between sixteen and forty-five must, if circumstances require it, carry out work allotted to him by the German and Italian services.

Specifically, he must present himself at his correct place of work, he must work proper hours and his output must match his physical capacities. Men will be required to work away from their homes if necessary; when this is the case they will live in labour camps.

Supreme Commander of German Armed Forces,
GENERAL SPEIDEL

The newspaper staff passed on the contents of this text, which was circulating among the underground organizations long before it was printed. A demonstration was arranged for the next day. The strategy had been established on 22 December of the previous year, when popular gatherings had thrown the German and Italian security services into confusion. Pedestrians would close ranks at a signal and become demonstrators; within a few seconds the flood of passers-by would crystallize into a riot. The first groups would form very quickly at predetermined rallying points and converge on their objective.

On 23 February the occupying forces were taken by surprise and had to confine their troops to barracks. The Ministers of the puppet government were forced to beat a prudent retreat, receiving German delegations and denying rumours despite all the incriminating evidence.

This was only a rehearsal. The next day, 24 February, Athens took to the streets again. This time the Germans and Italians were ready; patrols were tripled and machine-gun nests had been set up during the night on the roofs and in the windows of public buildings.

At about 9 a.m., under a fine freezing rain, the first processions arrived in Syntagma (Constitution) Square, the nerve-centre of Athens. The presence of the Parliament and Ministry of the Interior make it a political and administrative centre, the Tomb of the Unknown Soldier focuses patriotic emotion, and it has always been the stamping-ground of the foreign presence. The enormous Hotel Great Britain was now occupied by the Axis Staff. In palmier days it had been frequented by a varied international clientele which liked to glimpse the Acropolis in the background as it watched from the balconies the swarming of a population reduced to semi-colonial status; busy, cosmopolitan Hellenists whose love of the classics was not the only reason for their presence on the shores of the Aegean. Demonstrators flooded into the square. The armed cordon of German and Italian troops formed a prickly but flimsy barrier in front of the sea of humanity. Soon the big quadrangle was filled with a dense crowd which genuflected towards the Tomb of the Unknown Soldier and began to sing the national anthem:

> I know you
> By the bright flashing of the sword.
> I know you
> By your gaze, the way it falls on soil
> Enriched by the sacred bones of Greeks.
>
> And as in ancient times, inspired,
> We greet you, Liberty. . . .[1]

The rattle of German and Italian small arms interrupted the last line:

> Hail Liberty!
> Hail Liberty!

The occupying security forces had so far gone no further than firing in the air. . . . The demonstrators took heart and climbed the trees in the square to pick their fruit, small wild oranges as hard as pebbles. They started to bombard the sentries outside the former Royal Palace serving as government headquarters. The crowd gained entry to the building and wrecked everything in its path. The security force in the square was overwhelmed and withdrew. After a few minutes of disorder, reinforcements arrived. Feldpolizei Volkswagens and Carabinieri motorcycles charged into the crowd, and the people began to drain away down side streets.

Before the crowd had time to disperse a new order was passed through its ranks: 'Everyone to the Ministry of Labour.' The dense mass surged swiftly into University Street, passed in front of the over-ornate Ionic-style university buildings which look more like a theatre-set of a town hall than anything in ancient Greece, and swarmed up Patissia Street as far as the Archaeological Museum. This route had been planned ever since the demonstration on 22 December. By now the occupying forces had learnt their lesson and reinforced the security arrangements. The Labour Ministry was guarded by two companies of Carabinieri. The enfilades were all covered by automatic weapons and a detachment of light tanks was lurking nearby at the alert. Very few of the demonstrators were armed. Most of them were brandishing sticks, stones or the little oranges. The Carabinieri aimed their rifles at the advancing crowd and machine-guns commenced their irregular barking, scything down the front ranks like wheat. A few puny pistol shots answered as the machine-guns cut into

[1] Costa de Loverdo, *Les Maquis rouges dans les Balkans*, Paris, 1967, p. 147.

the mass of people; the demonstrators were going berserk, gripped by a blind, irresistible determination, exalted by the mad ancient war-cry of Greece: *Aera!*

Aera: wind, tempest, delirium.

Before this particular tempest even automatic weapons soon ran out of breath. Indifferent to danger, trampling its dead and wounded underfoot, the crowd silenced the machine-guns with its bare hands and penetrated the Ministry buildings. It began wrecking offices and burning files. Guns were still spitting in the streets. By the time Italian reinforcements arrived in sufficient strength to disperse the demonstration an hour later, the Ministry had been completely sacked and fires were spreading in the district. Most of the hundred or so dead and wounded were taken away by the demonstrators. The fight was not over yet.

The next day a strike was called in the Athens central telephone exchange in Stadium Street. Although the strike was called almost on the spur of the moment, anger was in the air and almost all the employees supported it. Threatened with total paralysis of the telephone system, the Gestapo tried to deal with the crisis in its usual way. Two hundred of the staff were rounded up at gunpoint before they had time to leave their offices, beaten up and locked in the cellars of the exchange with a heavy guard on the door. When the lorries arrived to take the prisoners to Gestapo headquarters at the end of the morning, the cellar doors were opened to disclose an empty space. All of the arrested men and women had managed to wriggle out through a ventilator which the Germans had failed to notice.

From this time onwards the soldiers of the Axis found it difficult to strut through the streets of Athens like conquerors; they generally appeared in groups, protected by frequent patrols as though in an unsafe zone. They gave up visiting certain areas of the suburbs altogether except to make lightning raids. In the provinces the troops stayed shut up in their barracks most of the time, besieged and sometimes totally stranded by the unanimous hostility of the population. Field-grey islands in the steadily rising flood of Free Greece.

Hardly a day passed in late February without the Italians and Germans receiving some proof of the extraordinary spirit of resistance which inspired the population. On 27 February a huge crowd attended the funeral of the poet Kostis Palamas, singing patriotic songs. The funeral orations were delivered in front of an immense audience and contained undisguised exhortations to national resistance. The Axis security force present at the ceremony panicked and charged the cortège, but they could not arrest those responsible for the inflammatory speeches because they were protected by the multitude; the crowd was unstable, ready to explode into violence at any moment. The agitation was unpremeditated. On 4 March EAM and the underground trade union organizations ordered a general strike of public service employees.

The collaborationist government was led by a certain Logothetopoulos. He had taken office on 30 April 1941 and was a wholehearted admirer of the new Spartan virtues from the North. Logothetopoulos could see that the civil servants' strike would tarnish his reputation, and was afraid that the military administration might make him their scapegoat.

After consulting the jackbooted Oracles who dictated his policies he decided to negotiate. The last explosion had resulted in deaths and widespread disorder; this time, he hoped to sap the Athenians' determination by throwing doubt on the agitators' assertions. Accordingly, on 4 March all the government-controlled papers carried an official announcement:

The President of the Council yesterday issued the following statements:

'Preachers of discord and professional agitators are once again spreading panic among the people by circulating stupid rumours about an alleged civil mobilization.

'These evil rumours are in no way commensurate with certain measures which the military authorities have been preparing for some time, in accordance with international law, to facilitate necessary public works. I advise the people to stay calm and to pay no attention to the stupid suggestions of communist propaganda.'

Despite its new legal packaging, this was obviously another attempt to protect the civil mobilization project. Nobody was taken in by it for a moment. The next day all the civil servants came out on strike.

The past fortnight's demonstrations had cost them dear, but the Athenians prepared to march on the machine-guns once again. Groups formed in every part of the town. The streams converged into a sea of humanity; German and Italian troops were widely dispersed in emergency patrols and the fighting started early in the morning. When the first procession came into sight of the Academy, machine-guns opened fire without warning. German soldiers dropped grenades from the roofs into the packed flesh of the crowd, wreaking terrible carnage. But the Athenian sea was flowing into the centre of the city from all directions: innumerable, anonymous, trampling the first cordons underfoot . . . 200,000 men, a quarter of the population of Athens, marching empty-handed through a hail of bullets.

The flood swept down on the Labour Ministry, which had now become a veritable fortress: ten times as many soldiers as there had been on the last occasion, with a German company supporting the Carabinieri. The first wave of demonstrators hesitated, eddied – a moment of uncertainty: the wave that piles itself up for a slow moment before breaking on the shore.... Aera! The Athenians charged, insane but irresistible, transported towards their objective with a battle-crazy momentum that could not be touched by mere blood, by a scattering of deaths. Grenades and machine-guns were useless. The demonstrators reached the defenders within seconds and the soldiers were overrun, trampled, snatched up and torn to pieces by the multitude. Flames rose once again from the Ministry buildings. The bloodshed continued in the district until every file and every office had been reduced to ashes.

A few days earlier, Hitler's voice had cracked with emotion as he delivered a funeral oration for the German heroes of Stalingrad. He knew that he was not going to be able to relax his grip on Greece enough to withdraw the reinforcements he needed so desperately for the Russian front. He gibbered: 'We must have done with these lice!'

Easier said than done. No one will ever know how many dead lay in the streets of Athens on 5 March. More than two hundred of the attacking side were seriously wounded, not counting those who were rescued by friends or taken in by nearby householders. More than sixty occupation troops were seriously wounded and nearly twenty killed. Most of the dead had succumbed to skull fractures ... or strangulation.

Archbishop Damaskinos, Primate of Athens, was a thickly-bearded, imposing figure, nearly six and a half feet tall. He owed his enthronement to the collaborationist government; Metaxas had distrusted his prestige and his ambition, and had kept him out of the highest ecclesiastical office as long as he was in power. The history of the Greek Orthodox Church is interwoven with the story of the klephts and with the Greek Resistance tradition. Damaskinos calculated that the moment had come to live up to this legend. He had an extremely domineering personality and both Altenburg, the German chargé d'affaires, and his Italian opposite number Chighi, had spent more than one uncomfortable quarter of an hour in his company. They had disagreeably vivid memories of one particular occasion when he had made occupation troops dig up the corpses of thirty-two hostages under a full moon, and delivered a sermon over the gaping graves. The heroism of the Greek people had fired the Archbishop with the ambition to present himself as a worthy successor to the Archbishops of Byzantium.

Although the Greek Church had not played a leading part in organizing the resistance in Athens or the street actions against civil mobilization, Damaskinos felt that he was authorized to speak for his flock. He had gone to see Altenburg on the day before 5 March.

'Your Excellency, I have come to give you clear warning of my decision to assume personal leadership of the campaign against "civil mobilization".'

Altenburg did not believe his ears.

'If I understand you correctly, I shall shortly be obliged to have the Archbishop Primate of Greece arrested as the leader of a so-called rebellion.'

Damaskinos had not come to listen to the diplomat's irony. He glared down at him from his full height.

'If the "civil mobilization" is not officially cancelled by 7 March, the church bells will ring the alarm as a sign of supreme emergency. Doubtless the Reich will make its own assessment of the consequences.'[1]

The 5 March demonstration had nothing to do with the Archbishop. Altenburg was perfectly well aware of the fact, but he was faced with the problem of finding someone to negotiate with. The *Oberkommando Süd-Griechenland*'s daily paper was quite clear about the origins of the movement, despite the telegraphic modesty of its descriptions of recent events:

4 March 1943: For the first time in Athens, major strikes occurred in the Greek press, the administration and the Bank of Athens. The strikes are communist-inspired and directed against civil mobilization.

5 March 1943: Various demonstrations took place in Athens during the morning. They were dispersed by the Feldpolizei and the Italians. The demonstrations were communist-inspired and directed against civil mobilization.

Hitler was desperate for more troops and favoured a peace overture. Altenburg tried to get the Archbishop's backing for it. What he proposed was a curtailment of the original measures: only 'specialist' workers would be subject to individual requisition orders, and he added the assurance that they would not be taken out of Greece under any circumstances. The panic was such that the government tried to buy the civil servants off with a fifteen-percent pay increase backdated to 1 January. But the strike continued and Logothetopoulos's concessions failed to stop the insurrection. Damaskinos made a great show of inflexibility with the cornered Altenburg.

[1] Conversation reported in Loverdo, op. cit., p. 144.

'Absolutely not, Your Excellency. We'll ring the alarm.'

Altenburg called Berlin: 'The Archbishop's going to ring the bells.'[1]

The chargé d'affaires was the only one to hear the brief reply. Defeated but showing his relief, he turned back to Damaskinos: 'Civil mobilization has been dropped.'

The Germans and Italians were in an intolerable situation. Mass resistance had got the better of their weapons; in a country under total occupation the defeat was bitter. Soothing announcements flowed from the collaborationist government and the Archbishop. The people of Athens had won. A scapegoat was required and Logothetopoulos was sacked. On 6 April he was replaced at the head of the government by Ioannis Rallis, whose German secret service file made interesting reading:

Former leader of the Populist Party (monarchist). Convinced anti-communist. Drunkard. Passes for a British agent.

The immediate future would show that he was the man for the job and that his British connections were no obstacle to his career.

We shall see presently that the British, in their dealings with the Greek army in the Middle East, never hesitated to make use of elements overtly favourable to the Axis. 'Anti-communism' was a qualification of the first importance to both sides. Rallis established a praetorian guard for the collaborationist government: the Security Battalions, whose future career would be as ambiguous as their founder's *curriculum vitae*.

Aris's Return

By 10 March 1943 the Athenian population's victory was being proclaimed in big red letters by every EAM wall newspaper. A few tattered notices were still offering a healthy reward for information leading to Aris's arrest; but armed intimidation had lost some of its power over the last week or so, and Axis patrols were becoming rarer in the poor parts of the city. It had been a costly victory, but the people were still in a state of exaltation, carried away by their success in disarranging the invulnerable image of a helmeted and jackbooted army.

Tzimas could not avoid the feeling that his separation from the rest of

[1] Conversation reported by Loverdo, op. cit., p. 145.

the Central Committee had a slight taste of exile about it. But he was going to the mountains to keep Aris in check and his introduction to the new environment could not wait.

By the time they reached the edge of Athens – still in the very jaws of the wolf – and started up the 'Mountain Boulevard', Aris was leading a procession that defied all reason. Aris marched in front, a submachine-gun slung across his chest. His beard had grown long enough to restore his legendary profile, and he was flanked by four men in bandoliers and black bonnets. When the houses began to thin out they flung off the robes which concealed their arsenal, feeling no doubt that they had finished with secrecy. The party included two officers: Zoulas and Fivos Grigoriadis, whose father General Grigoriadis headed the Left Liberal Party. They were wearing full dress uniform. Tzimas found this ostentatious escort a little unnerving; but Aris was coming back to life at his side, taking eager breaths of mountain air as if testing it for the scent of provocation. He was clearly anxious that nobody should mistake the purpose of his entourage. Twenty men supplied by the local organization marched behind him, followed by four horses laden with provisions and footwear.

Like all the suburbs of Athens, Peristeri bore some resemblance to a Wild West town, built too hastily along wide unpaved roads. A small crowd gathered to watch the detachment march past. Aris was immediately recognized and hailed as a liberator. The crowd began singing klephtic songs whose words had been rewritten to describe his own exploits.

If the Greeks had any special talent for secrecy, it would still be vastly outweighed by their sense of occasion. Aris's arrival in Athens had hardly been discreet, but his departure was positively rowdy. Instead of dispersing and urging the crowd to be quiet, the men of his escort marched a little straighter and emptied their magazines into the air. Aris was shaking the dust of the capital from his feet and meant to show whose word was law in the mountains.

The detachment stopped for the first night in a small village in Voiotia. The Italians had a garrison a few kilometres away and Aris's presence in the region was common knowledge, but he had nothing to worry about. In the unlikely event of the Italians' daring to move, he would be warned and would have ample time to vanish into the undergrowth. ELAS was like a fish in water.

Before eating, he sat in the village square and drank several glasses of ouzo to celebrate his return to life. Ouzo is a bitter, translucent Greek absinth which turns soft and milky when a drop of water is added to it. Aris was notoriously fond of it. Captain Fivos Grigoriadis sat beside him. He was surreptitiously changing the glasses round and emptying those intended for Aris. This touching attention was one of the first fruits of the plethora of surveillance instructions that the Athens leadership had lavished on Velouchiotis's new escort.

Aris noticed what the officer was doing and seized him by the wrist: 'The EAM line! We can't get away from the line.'

His laugh died away in his beard. He leaned towards Grigoriadis and stared into his face. The young socialist captain had distinguished himself fighting the Germans in 1941, on the Metaxas line at the Yugoslav frontier. Although he knew the story, Aris was scrutinizing his new recruit's boyish face with something like disapproval.

'You're going to let your beard grow?'

Grigoriadis, surprised, answered that he was not.

'Listen, when you've fought and proved yourself you can do what you like. In the meantime, you're going to let your beard grow.'

When the detachment marched off the next day Captain Grigoriadis was still wearing dress uniform, but his face was darkened by a day-old beard. He did not shave it for three months. Aris took his leave of the villagers. He and his men bade a respectful farewell to the priest who came to give them his blessing. Grigoriadis had to behave like the rest; the young anti-clerical socialist bent awkwardly over the priest's extended hand. It was the first time in his life that he had kissed a priest's ring.

While the Athenian population was paying in blood for its refusal to man the Reich's labour camps, the Mountain movement was developing apace. Early in the year an acting member of the Central Committee called Kostas Karageorgis had been sent into the Olympus region of Thessaly. Superficially, he was not at all like Aris. He was a doctor by training who, after studying medicine in France and Germany, had decided to devote his life to political struggle as a journalist and permanent Party cadre.

Karageorgis was elegant and cultivated. He lacked Aris's faith in direct action and had no special ambition to become a legendary chieftain. He had contacted the local organization on his arrival and set about extending guerilla activity to the eastern part of Thessaly which, though less wild and impregnable than Olympus, was potentially more valuable to the andartes by virtue of its wealth and large population. By February he was harassing the occupying forces with some success, and he made rapid progress in extending the movement across Thessaly. At the end of January, when Myers had installed himself on Zervas's territory in Epirus, a new member of the British Military Mission had appeared on Karageorgis's doorstep.

Colonel Hills had probably been dropped there as a result of the good relationship Woodhouse had established with the EAM Central Committee during his visit to Athens. In view of the confused situation in Cairo, where the SOE and the Foreign Office were pursuing different and sometimes contradictory goals, it is quite possible that Hills had been instructed to follow a slightly different policy from his nominal chief. It is known that Myers was furious that he had not even been warned of Hills's arrival; in principle, he was his commanding officer. Hills was as different from Myers as Karageorgis was from Aris. Leslie Rufus Sheppard, to give his real name, not only spoke perfect Greek but lacked any ingrained prejudice against 'Reds'.

His political open-mindedness, encouraged by Karageorgis's diplomacy, soon made him a warm ELAS supporter. The fact that he was sent to Greece without Myers's knowledge, and the fact that the British Mission in Greece was never unified, despite the repeated requests of Pyromaglou and others, bear eloquent witness to the diversity (not to say incompatibility) of the tasks SOE agents were expected to carry out.

During Aris's return trip to Athens his lieutenants, Tzavelas and Hasiotos, had not been idle in Roumeli. On 10 February a unit of 256 Italians stationed at Kalabaka, near the Meteora, set out on a punitive expedition. The Meteora are rocky pinnacles smoothed by erosion into tall thin columns, some of them three hundred feet high. Four of them are topped with large monastries, others contain the homes of religious hermits practising the asceticism of St Simon Stylites. Some of these holy men could only reach their retreats by means of a cord and pulley; neighbouring villagers would bring them food which was placed in baskets and hoisted up in the same way. The Italians would only venture into this lunar landscape in considerable force, making lightning raids and quickly returning to their barracks. On 10 February the village of Oxineia was the victim; its houses were looted and several women raped. Tzavelas and Hasiotos came running and prepared an ambush. The next day the Italians, heavy with feasting and weighed down by their booty, fell straight into the andartes' trap. The fighting lasted from three in the afternoon on 11 February until ten the next morning. Throughout the night long lines of people from neighbouring villages came through the snow and frost bringing food and support for the partisans.

At the end of the morning the Italians were utterly defeated. A hundred of them were dead; 146 were taken prisoner. In a country they were supposed to be occupying, the number of Italians ELAS had taken prisoner was beginning to pose a serious supply problem. The andartes also captured some more useful material: 4 mortars, 20 automatic weapons, about 250 rifles and more than 2,000 grenades. But the most important battle of the later winter took place near the village of Siatista in south-west Macedonia on 5 March, the day of the big demonstration in Athens.

The Greek Spring

Still veiled by the last shadows of night, the road below curved through a natural amphitheatre in the mountains before slipping into the Siatista pass. At each end of the long curve a stone bridge carried the road across a torrent swollen by the thaw. The short-lived Greek Spring was bursting from every fissure in the rock in an explosion of red, yellow and blue flowers. The south-facing slope had been laboriously terraced and planted with vines, by generation after generation, until the man-made steps of earth and stone blended perfectly with the steeper, bolder natural outlines of the surrounding hills.

Invisible from the road, a man was huddling behind every wall, trying to retain his bodily warmth under the sheepskin thrown over his shoulders. Dawn was breaking on 5 March 1943, between Grevena and Kozani, in the foothills of the Pindus range which stretches its five fingers over northern Greece.

A hundred men lay hidden among the vines, facing towards Kozani. Most of them were ELAS reservists, villagers who belonged to no specific guerilla unit. They had been there for two days, lying in wait for a large Italian convoy bound for Grevena. Nerves stretched to breaking-point by the long vigil, they were longing for the moment to spring their trap. They did not mean to let a single rifle escape them. Their advantage lay in surprise and their knowledge of the terrain; their actual armament was a mixture of Gras rifles from the last century, many of them inlaid with mother-of-pearl, carbines abandoned by the defeated army two years previously, and shotguns. They were short of ammunition, but axes and the damascened knives stuck through their belts would make good the shortage when it came to hand-to-hand fighting.

A faint rumbling of engines could just be heard from the direction of Kozani. It grew louder. Cleaned, oiled and loaded, the ancient ornamental rifles eagerly scanned the empty road for the first sign of movement. The first lorry shot suddenly into sight and roared at high speed round the sweeping curve through the defile, followed closely by a second, a third, others. By the time it reached the bridge at the end of the curve, nine lorries were in the partisans' field of fire.

The antique weapons crashed in unison, nailing the first and ninth lorries to the ground with a concentrated blast of assorted bullets and shot. The trap had closed, missing only the tenth lorry which managed to pull back from the edge of the grave by executing a dizzy, improbable U-turn and retreating at full throttle. For three hours the mortar-like detonations of the old Gras rifles answered the dry hammering of Italian Martinis and Berettas; then it was hand-to-hand, with knives restoring the technical balance. When the convoy became overdue at Grevena, an Italian company was loaded into three lorries and sent up the road to look for it.

The ELAS regulars were elsewhere, and most of the reservists were busy at Siatista. When news of the approaching Italian reinforcement spread through the villages, only reserve reservists were left to deal with the situation. Old men and very young boys who could only just be called adolescent hurried from their villages to prepare an ambush on the road. They were still arriving in droves when the firing started, and they pinned the reinforcements down all day several kilometres from Siatista, near the village of Agios Georgis.

At Siatista, the hand-to-hand attack ended the battle; menaced with cold steel, the Italians raised their hands. Ninety-three of them threw down their rifles. Seventeen men had been wounded in the battle, most of them Italians. Five of the nine lorries in partisan hands were still in running order. They loaded these with the contents of the damaged vehicles: a heavy machine-gun, a mortar, ten light machine-guns, flour, rice, sugar, boots and ammunition.

The rest of the Grevena garrison set out early in the afternoon to relieve Siatista and Agios Georgis. Six hundred men left the barracks, leaving behind the merest skeleton guard. The veterans of Agios Georgis clung tenaciously to their rocky strongholds, and the column could not get past them until nightfall.

On the morning of 6 March the Italians reached the defile where their supply convoy had been taken the day before. This time they were on their guard; at the first rifle shots, three mountain cannon started to pound the andartes' positions, and they were forced to withdraw. Men were still arriving from all the neighbouring villages. One of the groups, led by a certain Paleologos, schoolteacher of the little village of Polilakos, managed to outflank the enemy by swimming across the river Aliakmon. Pressed hard on all sides, the Italians found themselves at nightfall scattered among the vines near the village of Fardikambo, where they dug in for the night.

When the sun rose on 7 March, long lines of peasants could be seen winding over the mountains towards the spot. Some of the hills were black with people; they were flooding in from all directions, from their land and their villages, spontaneously, unanimously. Some were totally unarmed, without knives or even stones; they were there simply because they had not been able to resist joining the procession. As far as they were concerned it was a rural demonstration, and they emitted ferocious yells which sowed panic in the enemy's ranks.

Old Gras rifles banged away like mortars. Shouts rose from behind every rock. The Italians found it impossible to evaluate the forces ranged against them. By the end of the morning the sun was beating solidly down on the rocks, the blinding sun of the Greek spring. There was no water in the sector where the enemy had dug in. Italian aeroplanes appeared in the sky. The ruses of war are an institution in the land of Ulysses; throwing their 'doulamas' or sheepskin cloaks over handy rocks, the partisans took cover at a respectful distance. The aeroplanes used up their ammunition strafing these stone dummies.

Heavier aircraft lumbered overhead, the bright domes of parachutes flowering in their wake. The pilots miscalculated the drop and cheers and laughter arose from the villagers as most of the containers fell into their waiting hands. The gift of arms and ammunition was distributed on the spot.

The Italians held out all the afternoon, wasting their ammunition on an adversary they could not see but whose multiple voice ricocheted all around them in waves of bewildering echo. They were suffering cruelly from thirst. Paleologos began trying a formula appropriate to the occasion, repeating it several times at the top of his voice between the andartes' bursts of random yelling:

'*Fratelli, arrendete vi!*' ('Brothers, surrender!')

Through the general uproar, he could just hear a voice from the enemy position answering in Greek: '*Paradinomaste* ("We surrender"). Our commanding officer is going to show himself and walk forward to parley.'

The Italian major rose from behind a rock, flanked by the battalion doctor who acted as interpreter. He walked majestically forward in his glittering uniform and Paleologos stood up to receive him. The schoolteacher was twenty-nine years old. He had been a partisan for eight days. The doctor translated the major's opening remark: 'I am carrying grenades. What shall I do with them?'

'Throw them down. You can keep your pistol.'

Paleologos knew that he was dealing with a career officer, and sensed the existence of a mysterious warrior code of honour. He had a vague feeling that it would be courteous to allow the Battalion Commander to keep his pistol during a parley. The major murmured something in Italian.

'Who is your general?' asked the doctor.

Paleologos was still wondering what to say when a quick-witted villager brandishing a billhook answered: '*I'm* the general.'

The splendidly-uniformed Italian towered over the little teacher by a good head and shoulders. He repressed a strong urge to be sick. It had just dawned on him that he was surrendering a fully-equipped battalion to a largely-unarmed rabble of peasants. He tried a last face-saving manoeuvre.

'I give you my word as an officer that if you allow us to withdraw from our positions I will spare Siatista, which I have been ordered to destroy.'

The novelty of the situation had worn off and the teacher was not impressed. Escorted by six andartes, he crossed to the enemy lines and walked up and down them. He only knew one phrase of Italian: '*Fratelli, arrendete vi.*'

A familiar face detached itself from a group of soldiers. It belonged to an Italian called Alfredo whom he had met in his home village.

'I've heard your voice all day and I've been firing in the air.' He turned to his compatriots: 'He's a friend. I've known him for a long time. He's not cruel. He's a good teacher.'

Moved more by their thirst than by this example of shameless fraternization, the Duce's soldiers adapted their answer to what had become their main preoccupation: '*Aqua, aqua.*'

The moment had come. Alfredo interpreted for the teacher: 'Don't worry. You'll get plenty to drink when you get to Siatista. But you don't need your guns to look for water. Throw them down and we'll take you to Siatista.'

The partisans collected 12 machine-guns, 3 mountain cannon, 500 rifles, 3 lorries, 2,000 grenades and 40 mules laden with ammunition.

The major's impressive appearance seemed to count for less after his men had surrendered. Walking beside him, Paleologos began to regret letting him keep his pistol. He suddenly blocked his path.

'It occurs to me that you aren't going to need your gun or your papers any longer.'

A small automatic joined the rest of the loot. The major's mind had not yet accepted completely the fact that he had surrendered to a force of ragged villagers.

'You tricked me. I promised not to touch Siatista if you would let me go. If I'd known you wanted to take our arms, I'd never have come out to talk in the first place.'

The column reached Siatista after a night's march. The major asked to be allowed to telephone General Geloso, Commander of Italian forces in northern Greece. His report was laconic: 'I have been forced to surrender to partisan forces superior to our own.'

Paleologos was not satisfied, but they had already rung off at the other end of the line. He called the Italian HQ again and dictated another clause to his prisoner, who recited it to Geloso's aide-de-camp who took the call: 'If a single aeroplane, or any other kind of unit, goes anywhere near Siatista, the partisans will not be answerable for our safety.'

A few days later aircraft did fly over the village and, either out of spite or as a matter of form, dropped a solitary bomb which landed in a vine-yard a few hundred yards from the houses. A fortnight later, on 21 March, a new battalion left Larisa and set out for Grevena. It clashed with partisan forces on the way but managed to reach the town. The Italians had no intention, however, of continuing to occupy the region; they had come simply to rescue the stranded skeleton guard from Grevena barracks. When they left, Grevena remained empty of occupation troops for good.

On 25 March, the anniversary of the proclamation of independence and a Greek national holiday, an ELAS unit paraded through the streets of the first liberated town in Europe behind the Greek flag. Archbishop Gerasimos held a service in the cathedral, attended by all the EAM organizations. The prelate blessed all the andartes, even the most in-delibly Red amongst them.

Throughout the country, the Axis forces were confronted with enormous demonstrations. The Athenians, who could not be dissuaded from taking to the streets of their city by the mere presence of occupying troops, celebrated independence in their own fashion. Only twenty days after the fierce struggle over civil mobilization, more than a hundred dead and wounded reaffirmed the irrepressible insolence of the Greek people.

The battle of Fardikambo had far-reaching results in the Grevena district. The victory had been won not by an ELAS unit but by the whole population, armed and unarmed alike; rising against the enemy had given it an idea of its own strength, and at the same time had brought it firmly into the Resistance. The captured arms were distributed very quickly. Within a few weeks the effective strength of ELAS in eastern Macedonia had risen from 50 andartes to 2,000. Soon the whole northern region would be liberated, from Salonika to the Albanian frontier.

The succession of defeats suffered by the occupying forces did not make things any easier in the large towns, where acts of reprisal were beginning to mount up: arrests, executions, pillage, repression. . . .

From 15 March onwards Jewish Salonika was in the toils of the Rosenberg Commission. Members of the Jewish community were loaded into cattle wagons and sent in convoys of several thousand at a time to 'colonize the spaces of the East'. Dockets on some of the trucks gave their destination as Weimar; others were not marked with any known name. 55,000 Jews had made Salonika a Jewish city in the same tradition as Alexandria, Toledo and Livorno. 46,061 of them went off to the ovens. Before the war, 77,000 Jews had lived in Greece without experiencing or causing the slightest racial problem. 68,000 were arrested and 66,000 of these were murdered.

National Resistance Bands

In Epirus, Woodhouse was sparing no effort to keep Zervas on the path that had been mapped out for him by the Cairo diplomats. By this time the Napoleon of the Mountains had fought a victorious battle against two Italian Alpine Battalions and captured a considerable quantity of arms; but the regular supply shipments he was getting from the British were the main reason for his mounting arrogance. Incidents between EDES and ELAS were a feature of almost every supply-drop. Accounts were often settled in the most direct manner.

The increasing strength of ELAS on the other side of the river Acheloos convinced Zervas that it would be a good idea to pay some attention to Woodhouse's advice. A declaration in support of the king might not secure him a monopoly of official British recognition, but it would ensure a measurable increase in material aid from Cairo at ELAS's expense.

Woodhouse had discreetly suggested that it would be expedient for the military leader of the National Bands in Epirus to send the king a congratulatory telegram on his birthday. Zervas, a declared Republican, sent not one but two telegrams to London.

The second telegram was more important. It informed HMG that Zervas would not only be the first to welcome the king back if the Greek people expressed their free opinion in his favour, but even that if HMG wished the king to be restored 'for wider reasons and without the people's wishes', he would not oppose it. For that declaration there are only two names: one is unscrupulous opportunism, the other is unquestioning loyalty.[1]

EDES remained deeply Republican at grassroots level, and its leader's posturings committed nobody but himself. The organization's second-in-command, Pyromaglou, did not discover the manoeuvre until later; when he did, Zervas was forced to back-pedal for a while. For the time being the Napoleon of the Mountains had every reason to believe that the British would find the necessary means to create and develop resistance movements to compete with ELAS.

On 4 February Myers had received a visit from an officer who had a large personal following in the country. Colonel Sarafis was one of the most prestigious figures in the Greek army, a former assistant director of the Officers' School in Athens and in 1933 Military Attaché to the Greek embassy in Paris, where he had attended the École de Guerre some years before. He was a convinced Republican. He had supported Venizelos in 1916 in the Greek army's pro-Allied, anti-monarchist revolt. Exiled by the post-war royalist government, he was one of the main executants of Venizelos's Republican coup d'état in 1935. When the attempt failed he was demoted with ignominy in front of his troops. Metaxas exiled him to the island of Milos from 1937 to 1940. He had been imprisoned twice by the Italian authorities since the outbreak of war.

[1] C. M. Woodhouse, *Apple of Discord*, London, 1948, p. 74.

Though a democrat, Sarafis had succumbed to the arguments of certain individuals, notably one Tsigantes who was deeply involved in setting up rival organizations to EAM, and joined a group of officers whose intention was to fight in cooperation with Cairo Staff HQ on a more conventional military footing than the existing partisans. This movement was called AAA: Liberation Struggle Command.

Sarafis was not well informed on the situation in the mountains. From the reports given him by Tsigantes's people he had gained the impression that ELAS was a minority organization whose politics were too extreme to be compatible with national unity.

He had joined AAA in the hope of creating a true national army. The movement was led initially by a nucleus of long-serving men who were all Republicans with socialist leanings: Grigoriadis, Hajibeis, Vlachos and Bakirjis.

Sarafis had gone into the mountains early in the year. His second-in-command was an ex-member of EAM, Major Kostopoulos, who headed a band of about eighty andartes in the Trikkala region, on the same territory as Karageorgis, and who had set up his own underground organization under the influence of friends of Tsigantes who guaranteed him support from Cairo. When Tsigantes's untimely death at the hands of the German police in Athens broke Kostopoulos's connection with the Middle East, Sarafis travelled to Zervas's HQ to see if Myers could help.

The two men discussed the formation of apolitical 'National Bands'. The Greek was thinking of making the Resistance acceptable to all shades of democratic opinion by adopting a political line midway between EAM and EDES. But the idea of National Bands had a different meaning for the leader of the British Military Mission: it occurred to him that 'apoliticism' could be used to hamper the development of ELAS. Myers pounced on the idea eagerly and fired off a message to the SOE urging them to 'give the maximum support to all the completely non-political "National Bands" throughout Greece, wherever we could find or form them, and that when they were sufficiently strong we would invite ELAS to join this National Movement'.[1]

It was this glittering prospect that had led Zervas to abandon half-measures and, without telling the other cadres of EDES, send his telegrams of allegiance to the king as proof of his 'apoliticism'.

From the viewpoint of EAM-ELAS, it did not need a genius to understand Myers's apoliticism, nor to see that they were soon going to have to

[1] Myers, op. cit., p. 115.

drop everything else to smash these new organizations which were planning to monopolize British aid instead of relying on political and popular bases. They did not have to search very far for pretexts.

Another ex-EAM man had just joined Kostopoulos's group: the same Kostorizos who once tried to capture Aris on Zervas's behalf. As if by chance, Kostorizos always seemed to be present when EAM's monopolistic pretensions were being unmasked. Encouraged by their certainty of British support, he and Kostopoulos were associating with a group of royalist officers whose overtly anti-ELAS activities had made them a thorn in Karageorgis's side. Kostopoulos was an energetic officer. He interpreted the National Bands project very freely and, without telling Sarafis, decided to teach ELAS a lesson.

His chosen adversary was the ELAS kapetanios Koziakas, whose own courage and character were equal to the challenge. Turn and turn about, the two groups plundered one another's food-caches. On 25 February Koziakas arrested Lt-Colonel Antonopoulos, a friend of Kostopoulos's who was trying to set up a new band on his territory.

Sarafis, Kostopoulos and Kostorizos (who would have been better advised to stay out of sight) decided to intervene and went to the local ELAS headquarters at Vounesi. At Vounesi they met Nikitaras, Koziakas's second-in-command, and after a stormy but inconclusive discussion they decided to stay the night there and carry on in the morning.

In the middle of the night Nikitaras's men took a step which was effective, though in dubious taste. They surrounded the house in which their guests were asleep and arrested the lot. The men were released immediately, but the officers were placed under heavy guard and sent to ELAS headquarters at Kolokythia, in Roumeli. While Sarafis was travelling south in handcuffs, noticing, despite his awkward situation, how extensive the territories controlled by EAM-ELAS seemed to be, Aris was nearing Kolokythia from the other direction on his way back from Athens.

News of Sarafis's arrest reached Myers in the form of a dramatic oral report from Vlachos, a monarchist officer from Thessaly. On 21 February 1943 the head of the British Mission had received top-secret instructions from the SOE. It had been decided that the Allied landing would take place in Sicily, after a diversionary attack in the Dodecanese. The first phase, the diversionary attack, could well develop into an eventual invasion of the Greek mainland. The operation was planned for June, and the Mission was asked to step up the training and equipping of andartes with these ends in view:

1. *In event of invasion of the mainland of Greece :* to harass enemy lines of communication and generally to support invasion plans.

2. *If axis troops attempted a general withdrawal from Greece or became disaffected :* to attack, harass and pursue them.

3. *Should neither of the above occur :* to be ready at a later date, and at the right moment, to promote general organized and co-ordinated revolt.[1]

Despite all his efforts, in fact, Churchill had failed to get his allies to agree to his plan for a landing in Greece, which he felt had the double advantage of forcing Turkey to enter the alliance at the same time as offering an immediate solution to what he called in his memoirs 'the Greek torment'. The short-term objective was therefore purely military: to create a diversion by making the Germans believe that Churchill's rejected plan was really going to be carried out.

A grisly piece of theatre was used to mislead the Axis intelligence services. SOE arranged for a corpse, wearing British officer's uniform and carrying documents referring to an invasion of mainland Greece, to be dropped into the sea some fifteen hundred kilometres away, off the Spanish coast. The next day he was washed up on a beach near Alicante.

Myers was going to have to work fast if he wanted the National Bands to be operational in time to help him carry out his latest orders. Cairo approved his 'great projects' and asked him to support Colonel Psarros, military leader of yet another Resistance organization called EKKA (Movement for National and Social Liberation). Everybody knew that EKKA was a Republican movement, but their first priority was to surround ELAS with competitors. Time would do the rest.

Myers's immediate concern was with the arrest of Sarafis, which was in danger of throwing all his elaborate plans into confusion. He despatched a furious ultimatum to EAM: 'Unless Sarafis is released all supply-drops will cease forthwith.' At the same time, he made full use of Vlachos's information to step up his alarming dispatches to Cairo. The SOE was still getting regular reports from Hills on Karageorgis's territory, and the reports from the two agents differed in more than one nuance. Unable to disentangle the situation, HQ hedged by asking Myers not to sever all his connections with ELAS.

Swallowing the temptation to argue, he and Chris Woodhouse drafted the 'First Military Agreement between the Forces of the Greek Resistance and the Middle East'. Pocketing the draft, Myers crossed the river Acheloos and entered ELAS territory, where the population gave him a

[1] Myers, op. cit., p. 122.

delirious welcome. While travelling to Aris's HQ he had ample time to assess the progress which had been made by EAM-ELAS, as Sarafis had done a few days earlier. All shades and tendencies of the Resistance were converging on Kolokythia, some more willingly than others.

The secrets of the royal entourage were not always as well-guarded as they might have been. By a devious route, the news of Zervas's allegiance to the king was also on its way.

Aris, Sarafis, Samariniotis

Tzimas had been sent to supervise the Mountain's orthodoxy on behalf of the Central Committee; on his journey through ELAS-controlled territory, he had had plenty of time and opportunity to gauge the true extent of Aris's popularity. However severely he might be criticized in Athens, in the mountains the guerilla chieftain enjoyed a prestige which it would be difficult to exaggerate. Even so, the problems awaiting the two men when they reached Kolokythia showed that Tzimas's presence might have its uses.

As soon as he learned that the traitor Kostorizos was at his mercy, Aris forgot all the counsels of moderation which had been lavished on him so recently in Athens. He was hardly disposed to allow subtle distinctions between Kostorizos and Kostopoulos; the first real test of Tzimas's influence was preventing a massacre on the spot.

The career officers, Major Zoulas and Captain Grigoriadis, were sent to interview the prisoners. They were shut in a house in the village, where Kostopoulos had been trying to work out an escape plan from the moment they had arrived. Sarafis seemed thoughtful. The arrival of the two career officers, two familiar faces, calmed the atmosphere a little. Kostopoulos rushed up to Grigoriadis: 'What are you up to with these bandits? Come in with us.'

Grigoriadis smiled: 'They say you're with the king these days.'

Sarafis interrupted: 'How can you say such a thing when you know your father is with us? . . .'

Then, after a short pause: '. . . But I must say I've been able to get an idea of what you're doing here. It's true that Aris is well organized. There's no reason for not joining him.'

When Zoulas and Grigoriadis reported on their visit Sarafis was released, and the treatment of the other prisoners softened perceptibly.

In their first interview with Sarafis, Aris and Tzimas asked him to join their organization. Far from imagining at this stage that anyone was thinking of giving him military command of the whole movement, Sarafis accepted the simple participation they offered him without a moment's hesitation. Incredible though it may seem, this providential conversion resulted from Sarafis's discovery that the true state of affairs was completely at odds with the picture of ELAS still being peddled in Athens. These hostile prejudices were not restricted to liberal circles. Several days after Sarafis had joined ELAS, an emissary from the Central Committee arrived at Aris's HQ. He carried a message from Siantos ordering the immediate release of Sarafis.

The attitude of the Party cadres themselves shows how much more slowly reports were circulating than wild alarmist rumours, and gives some idea of the ignorance prevailing in Athens on the subject of the Mountain's activities. Sarafis still knew far less than Siantos about Aris's activities; why then was he not at least as suspicious as the First Secretary? The reasons for Sarafis's conversion can be found in his own experience of the Mountain. He describes them simply in his memoirs:

I found that [EAM-ELAS] was a nation-wide organization, loved by the people, and with tremendous strength and power, which, if the politicians and professional soldiers would only support it, might develop into a unique resistance movement and draw to itself everything in the country that was sound and honest, thus serving the allied cause more effectively and contributing to the securing of civil liberties, to the punishing of collaborators and those responsible for our disasters, and to a quiet transition for the country to a normal civilian life. I found that the Zervas-Psarros-Sarafis organization had been a mistake and not only did not contribute to the allied cause the help it should; but, on the contrary, weakened it and, through the personal aims and ambitions of the leaders that would be given stimulus and direction by various local and foreign interests, was preparing the way for a civil war.[1]

When Eddie Myers arrived at Kolokythia he knew nothing of Sarafis's conversion and was still simmering with rage. He met Tzimas for the first time; he did not know Tzimas's function there but immediately sensed that he was an important KKE cadre. He waxed very indignant on behalf of Middle East HQ. His superiors had been outraged by ELAS's action in disarming and arresting resistance fighters working directly under the

[1] Stefanos Sarafis, *Greek Resistance Army*, London, 1951, p. 183.

Allies. He threatened as usual to cut off ELAS's supplies. Aris, who was present at the meeting, walled himself up in his most contemptuous silence, and it was Tzimas who had to reply. ELAS had good reason to distrust Zervas, he said: he had gone underground on British gold and looked very like a future candidate for military dictator. It seemed that British policy was aiming at dividing the Resistance in order to support a discredited monarchy lacking any popular support.

More and more irritated, Myers called on Tzimas to release Sarafis at once if he wanted Middle East HQ to reconsider the situation and send further supplies to ELAS. Aris looked the Englishman in the eye and settled a little deeper into his armchair. Tzimas allowed the silence to gather for several seconds before dropping his bombshell: 'Sarafis is at liberty.'

Myers thought they were pulling his leg. He was so incredulous that he simply asked calmly whether he might visit the prisoner. Sarafis went to see Myers at his house the next morning. He confirmed that he had been released along with Kostopoulos and all the other prisoners, except for Kostorizos and three of his men who would have to stand trial in front of an andartes' assembly. The head of the British Mission heatedly urged Sarafis to go back to Thessaly and recommission the AAA National Bands there. He had more surprises to come.

Sarafis said composedly that he had had plenty of time to think over the problem of the National Bands, and had come to the conclusion that it would be a mistake to continue with the experiment. ELAS seemed to be both effective and wide-based enough to form a focus of national unity. He had decided to join it.

Myers had been counting on Sarafis to spearhead a spectacular development of the 'apolitical' opposition to ELAS within the Resistance movement. He was paralysed with astonishment by what he called 'a most shocking volte-face'. But he had been given very specific instructions by his military superiors. Cairo's tortuous policy required him to water his wine for the time being and negotiate an agreement between the various Resistance organizations. The next day Eddie Myers asked to meet ELAS General Staff 'on behalf of his government'. His authority until now had always been Middle East HQ.

The building occupied by Aris and his 'Black Bonnets' was hardly the ideal setting for such an official meeting. ELAS 'General Staff' decided to see Myers in his own house. Three men arrived at the appointed hour: Aris, Tzimas and Sarafis. The astounded Englishman wanted to know why Sarafis was present. Tzimas, who liked to drop surprises one by one with calculated slowness, took a technician's pleasure in his latest effect: 'ELAS is considering placing Colonel Sarafis in command of all its military forces.'

Myers's face crumpled. The three men gave him time to master his feelings and waited calmly for the statement from His Majesty's Government. Aris sank deep into an armchair, crossed his legs and took out his tobacco, watching with an impassive eye as the crucified Englishman struggled to regain his composure. Myers took refuge in a formal stiffness, making himself as British as possible behind his Byzantine saint's beard. The interpreter translated: 'I have to pass on to you a note from His Britannic Majesty's Government. Please rise so that I can read it out.'

Tzimas and Sarafis stood up. Aris stretched out his legs, jammed himself in his chair and carried on filling his pipe. Myers stopped. He did not dare look at Aris and turned helplessly to Tzimas, who knew that it would be useless to take sides with him against Aris.

Each phrase was translated before the next was read out:

Should ELAS persist in its policy of disbanding other resistance groups, His Majesty's Government reserves the right to take all necessary steps to ensure the return and maintenance in power of the legal order in Greece.

Delivered in the presence of Sarafis, there was something laughable about this ultimatum, but Myers continued with it. It demanded a formal undertaking that ELAS would give up all forms of partisan strife and recognize the authority of Middle East HQ. Aris savoured the situation in silence while Tzimas answered.

'We helped Psarros and Kostopoulos when they were starting their group and we were prepared to collaborate fraternally with them. But instead of fighting the enemy they have been attacking us. Furthermore, Britain has always given them preferential treatment over us, and has not kept its promises to supply ELAS with arms and ammunition. This is our preliminary response; only the Central Committee of EAM has the authority to give a definitive answer to your proposals.'

A rambling discussion followed in which the three ELAS men freely expressed their anger over the support the British were lending the monarchy – a monarchy which the greater part of the Greek population would reject out of hand. The spectacular dream of setting up National Bands was coming down in flames. To carry out his orders Myers was forced into a *de facto* recognition of ELAS's authority. He dictated a cable to the SOE; embittered by the collapse of his 'great project', he included a number of home truths which would later be held against him. He even went so far as to declare that the British must make an announcement as soon as possible promising that free constitutional elections would be held under Allied control immediately after the liberation, and making it clear that Great Britain did not intend to impose the king's return on Greece.

He added that unless a declaration of this sort was made EAM would continue to suspect Allied motives and he, Myers, would have little or no opportunity to influence the organization. . . .

Quite apart from the defeat of his 'great apolitical project', Myers had discovered the reality of the Mountain some days earlier. The experience of travelling for several days through territory controlled and administered entirely by ELAS had altered his opinions noticeably. Excursions to the mountains seemed to have a considerable educational potential. Tzimas redoubled his efforts to get more members of the EAM Central Committee to make the trip.

Kostopoulos refused to follow Sarafis's lead and join ELAS. AAA was finished and he went off to join Zervas. His release earned ELAS a little extra prestige and did something to counteract an enormous whisper campaign now raging in Athens to the effect that Sarafis's conversion had been wrung from him by force.

Kostorizos did not get off so lightly. Despite the nature of his job, Tzimas understood that in this case it would be quite useless to tell Aris that traitors should not be punished but 'convinced'. Kostorizos was tried by andartes' assembly and executed. The British Government's solemn warning had turned out a damp squib. Two days later Myers came up with a plan for unifying the command of the Resistance.

The purpose of any such agreement would be to neutralize the internal dissensions which were still weakening the Resistance so that the large-scale operations planned for the near future could be coordinated under English authority. Under Myers's plan, these operations could not be organized in detail until the agreement had been signed.

'ELAS is ready to take part in any operation,' replied Tzimas, 'on condition that it is supplied with the necessary arms. This is our position whether any agreement is signed or not, and whether or not any other organization is taking part in the operation.'

Tzimas had to destroy the Englishman's new device by separating the two issues, by refusing to allow the carrying out of these operations to depend on Myers's conditions. To the extent that they set out to subject the Greek Resistance forces to the direct orders of the British Mission, the terms of this agreement were in fact unacceptable to ELAS. Right to the end, the andartes refused to sign a document which would deliver them tied hand and foot to the whims of the British officers in the field: Hills in Thessaly, and for some time now Arthur in Roumeli. ELAS would play its part in any common effort, but would not subject itself to outside orders. On the question of internal dissensions, Tzimas added: 'It's possible to avoid them with a little goodwill. But reconciliation on every level can only be achieved by the andartes themselves.'

Negotiations dragged on for three months. ELAS was accused freely of playing a reluctant and ambiguous role in some of the operations ordered by Cairo. The most widespread allegation was that its leaders believed that the Allies were about to land on the mainland and were conserving their forces so as to be able to unleash a civil war and seize power. In reality, however, the pressure to subject the Resistance forces to the direct orders of their own agents could only indicate the clearest political aims on the part of the British themselves.

ELAS countered with proposals for setting up a common andartes' General Staff to coordinate operations and arbitrate any conflicts which might arise. During these discussions a number of old quarrels returned to the surface; Aris, to give one example, was still more than bitter about the BBC's silence on the part he had played in the Gorgopotamos sabotage. It had been no accident, and omissions of this sort had subsequently become the rule. Among other things, ELAS insisted that any agreement should contain a clause requiring the BBC to broadcast information on ELAS activities. Myers answered this with an ingenuousness which set the tone of the discussions: 'The BBC is a private concern. The Government cannot interfere with its activities.'

Throughout these negotiations Myers was in direct and permanent contact with the Cairo Staff. The Mountain, on the other hand, could only contact Athens through the interminable medium of couriers whose journeys to and fro lasted about twenty days each.

During the first week in April, in the thick of the negotiations over the military agreement and when ELAS HQ was still at Kolokythia, a messenger from Siantos arrived to see Tzimas.

'You must release Sarafis immediately.'

Tzimas was a little taken aback.

'Go and see for yourself, then tell them in Athens that Sarafis *is* free.'

The poison campaign was still going on. Siantos himself was convinced that Sarafis's conversion was a myth, that he had been forced to change sides by violence.

Ever since the KKE Second Congress in December 1942, Tzimas had been fighting in Athens to persuade at least some of the Central Committee to move to the mountains. He had backed two reports on the development of local power, written by Tasos Lefterias and Ilias Madiakis, which emphasized the immense latent possibilities of the partisan struggle. He had not succeeded in changing anyone's mind. The canonical revolutionary model was based on the idea of a proletarian insurrection concentrated on the nerve-centres of the capital. He knew that his mission to Roumeli ostensibly to supervise a turbulent hero also served the purpose of removing him from Athens, where his support for the peasant guerilla struggle was found a little too enterprising.

But now Tzimas possessed new ammunition to support his personal statements. He decided to go to Athens in company with Sarafis, whose conversion could not be exploited politically until he had explained it personally to the leaders of AAA. Siantos's courier had been given letters from Sarafis for the Central Committee, but only his physical presence would convince the politicians that the letters were genuine, that they had not been written under duress.

During the journey Sarafis was able to reinforce his new convictions, and Tzimas to see how much progress had been made in the Karpenisi, Gravia and Lamia regions in the few short weeks since his journey in the other direction on the way to the mountains. The decision to make Sarafis military commander of all ELAS forces had not yet been ratified by the Central Committee, and Samariniotis expected enough good to come of his return to the capital to justify the time wasted in travelling.

He had another good reason for hastening his steps. His departure for the mountains on 10 March had interrupted his honeymoon.

After the initial meetings between Ioannidis, Siantos and Tzimas, Sarafis was present at all the discussions that took place in Athens. A Plenary meeting of the Central Committees of EAM and ELAS was called for 2 May. Tzimas's first proposition was adopted: the High Command of ELAS was officially constituted with Sarafis, Aris Velouchiotis and Andreas Tzimas (Samariniotis) at its head. From that day onward, ELAS General Staff was a triumvirate, soon to be echoed on a lower level at the head of every unit. A chief of partisans responsible for contacts with the population, administration and recruitment: Aris. A military chief: Sarafis. A political chief: Tzimas, inscribed in the brand-new ELAS legend under the name of his native mountain: Samariniotis.

Tzimas's second proposal was concerned with the need to bring the movement's governing bodies physically closer to the mountains, and came up against the usual fierce opposition.

Over the next few days Sarafis went to see all the AAA leaders; he was keen to give them the reasons for his choice before the decision was made public. Tzimas went with him to see General Grigoriadis and gave him news of his son, who was fighting with ELAS in the Giona region.

Sarafis still had to visit as many liberal political personalities as possible in order to cut short the rumours which were still circulating. One night a car called for Tzimas and took him to a friendly house where Sarafis was waiting for him with an eminent liberal figure: George Papandreou. In the course of the conversation Papandreou began to bewail his inactivity: 'I've wasted the best years of my life. I've written a book on democracy and socialism, but I'm not satisfied; I want to create something . . . closer to reality.'

'But, Mr President,' replied Tzimas, 'you've just been listening to Colonel Sarafis: there's the Mountain. That's where reality is at the moment.'

Papandreou was still very impressed by the account Sarafis had just given him, and said as he showed them out to the car: 'Go on, I'll follow you.'

But his spirits fell after his guests had gone. When he finally moved it was to Cairo rather than the mountains; and when he returned to Athens after the liberation, he was accompanied by British troops.

In the end it became more or less established in Athens that Sarafis had not been martyred but had, in fact, become the fanatics' new military leader. The political impact was considerable, and large numbers of officers who had been hesitant about joining the underground began flowing into ELAS, where their numbers soon rose as high as seven hundred.

Sarafis and Tzimas set out to return to the mountains. In Tzimas's pocket was the much-amended but still not ratified text of the proposed military treaty with the British, now further decorated with a preliminary amendment: 'This agreement has been drawn up between Middle East Staff and ELAS in its function as the competent Allied body in this theatre of operations'.

The original draft had envisaged a simple takeover; placing the

Resistance organizations on the same footing as the British forces had not been considered.

Myers had been hoping that Tzimas would come back with some constructive proposals, even if a signed agreement was too much to hope for. He made no effort to be gracious about his disappointment. ELAS refused to budge on the issue of its own sovereignty.

The length of the talks had at least made Eddie Myers stay at ELAS headquarters, where his presence indicated an implicit, if not official, recognition of ELAS authority. Zervas, who knew only too well what benefits he might yet extract from the Mission Chief's presence at his own HQ. began dropping very broad hints to Cairo that Myers was flirting with the communists.

EAM's political need for clear and official recognition by the British Government was now felt to be a matter of some urgency by the Central Committee in Athens. Though pressed from all sides, Tzimas was trying to wait for the right moment to negotiate the treaty from a position of strength. At the end of May ELAS moved its headquarters to the small village of Agia Triada, on Mount Velouchi. Myers burst out, exasperated: 'You're stubbornly holding to negative positions.'

'We're a very touchy people,' Tzimas replied.

'You're refusing to sign because you can't bear to let Cairo clip off a little bit of your authority. I warn you, if this goes on Cairo won't just carry on growling; it's going to bite.'

The orders Tzimas was getting from Athens all this time did not make his position any easier. In substance, all they did was repeat that he should sign the agreement at any cost, since it was politically essential that the movement be recognized by the British who were themselves perfectly well aware of the strength of their position and never gave an inch. They were alone in possessing the power to confer a kind of legality on the activities of EAM-ELAS. This political strength was to prove very helpful to them after the Liberation; by the time EAM realized that a break with the British was unavoidable, it was too late to break their hold on the country.

Sarafis played a leading role in the negotiations. The man Myers had been counting on to help him out-manoeuvre ELAS was now facing him at the conference table at the elbow of his *bête noire* Aris Velouchiotis.

As long as it was allowed to exist, the triumvirate controlling the combined forces of ELAS was never split by a single internal conflict. Aris respected Sarafis's undeniable military prestige, and Sarafis trusted him just as much in guerilla matters; the two men were solidly supported by Samariniotis, who had always been the Mountain's political brain.

Sarafis's qualities of effort and organization quickly bore fruit. He moved ELAS Staff Headquarters to Pertouli, where he set up an officers' school. A new telephone and telegraph network was being extended to all parts of the country. Popular administration and people's justice gave a real autonomy to the Free Greece of the mountain areas. In Spring 1943 the active strength of ELAS was an estimated 5,000 men; five months later it was nearer 40,000. Zervas was not at all unwilling to see this rapidly-growing force fall under British control. Incidents continued to mount up, especially between the bands controlled by the EDES bully-boy Houtas and the ELAS bands led by Aris's first companions – veterans whose tempers had not been much sweetened by the multiple demands of policy. Tzimas was still trying to realize his vision of an overall andartes HQ. Myers thought that he might recover a portion of his lost authority by presiding over a meeting between Zervas and the ELAS leadership. The meeting was arranged for 5 June 1943.

Since not even his most fervent admirers could see Aris in a diplomatic role, Tzimas and Sarafis set off without him for the little village of Laskovo, near the Korakas bridge across the Acheloös. They were escorted by a detachment of young EPON andartes.

Zervas was there several hours before them and welcomed them with a Homeric insult. As the ELAS delegation entered Laskovo, the silhouettes of the men Zervas had placed on the surrounding hills appeared on the skyline.

EDES was represented by Zervas and Pyromaglou. They were accompanied by Chris Woodhouse, which meant that with Myers present British interests were also represented by two men. Zervas did not waste time trying to show goodwill; he at once aligned himself with the British, announcing that he was ready to subject his units to their direct authority. He knew full well that as long as he remained a British lap-dog he would get the lion's share of whatever was going, or at least as much as ELAS. Tzimas's counter-proposal was based on a more realistic assessment of the forces involved.

There was general agreement on the relative strengths of the three main Resistance organizations: ELAS, 12,500; EDES, 1,300; EKKA, 300. Tzimas proposed a unified HQ comprising three ELAS members, one from the British Mission, one from EDES and one from EKKA. There was nothing unreasonable in this arrangement, which would not even give ELAS the automatic majority justified by its numbers. But Zervas's appetites seemed to know no bounds, and one by one he rejected all the proposals that were put to him. The talks made no progress for two days and finally, despite all Myers's efforts, ground to a halt. This collapse did not prevent Zervas from holding a public meeting in the village and declaring: 'EAM and EDES are in perfect harmony. The Resistance has now been unified nationally.'

After he had left, ELAS held its own meeting to explain how Zervas had ruined the negotiations. It was not the first time that a pact had failed to ripen on the unhealthy banks of the Acheloos.

The first negative result of the breakdown was Myers's departure for Zervas's HQ at Tzoumerka. Eddie sent Tzimas a note before leaving: he was summoning delegates from ELAS, EDES and EKKA (Psarros's group) to his house at Tzoumerka so that he could redistribute responsibilities in the operational framework required by Middle East HQ.

Athens was still breathing down Tzimas's neck. The Central Committee was now asking for a document guaranteeing that operations were being carried out in strict accordance with the directives of Allied HQ. Since the campaign against Sarafis's arrest had turned into a joke, ELAS's detractors had changed their tune: the allegation these days was that ELAS's ill-considered actions against the occupation forces were to blame for the terrible reprisals sweeping the country. The number of hostages and martyred villages was reaching dramatic proportions. Reports from Section 1(c) of the Abwehr, which specialized in anti-guerilla warfare, show how nervous the occupying forces were becoming:

The activities of andartes, who at first limited themselves to propaganda efforts among the population, have gradually assumed a more combative form. Elements favourably disposed to the Axis are being persecuted and assassinated. There are daily reports of large-scale acts of sabotage and killings of Italian soldiers. Since November 1942 more and more andarte groups have been entering German-occupied regions and attacking police posts to capture arms and ammunition. Thirty of these attacks have occurred since December in the military district of Salonika alone. Elsewhere, too, killings and acts of sabotage are daily events. This activity reached a peak when more than five hundred Italians were forced to surrender to the andartes with their artillery at Fardikambo.

The first direct attack by these bands, and also the first sabotage of our lines of communication, was the sabotage of the Gorgopotamos bridge on 25 November 1942. During the month of March the main Salonika-Lamia artery was severed six times. These facts show indisputably that andarte activity is endangering our supply position.

After the collapse of the Laskovo negotiations, Tzimas left for the north of Greece to inspect units in Macedonia and Thessaly. ELAS forces were being organized into divisions. . . . The first Macedonian Division, surrounded by a considerable array of Axis forces, had managed to pierce the enemy lines and regroup intact near Pertouli, where ELAS High Command decided to install its new HQ.

Sarafis stayed at HQ while Tzimas made his way to Tsotili, where his presence was required for the commissioning of a new ELAS division. An emissary from the Yugoslav Resistance joined him there, carrying a favourable reply from Tito to a request for a meeting which Tzimas had sent him some time in 1942. A meeting was set up between Tzimas and Vukmanović, a representative from Tito. Its location was Grammos; five years later, at the end of the civil war, Grammos would be one of the last strongholds of the Democratic Army.

The Phantom Balkan HQ

The Grammos mountains are in the north-western corner of the country, near the meeting-place of three frontiers: Greek, Yugoslav and Albanian. Just as he was getting ready to join his Yugoslav contact there, Tzimas received a message from Athens. He was being summoned to Karpenisi to meet an envoy from the Central Committee on the same day as his Grammos rendezvous.

Karpenisi is in the Pindus range to the east of Lamia, more than 300 kilometres south of Grammos. If he wanted to show up for both meetings, Tzimas would have to make a return journey of 300 kilometres through occupied country. He had no choice: travelling by car, on foot and even on a bicycle, he managed to reach Karpenisi the same day. This exploit showed him yet again that the occupying forces had lost all control over the country except for the main roads, where they were moving about in force, and a few hundred yards on either side of them. This network was completely inadequate to contain the Free Greece of the mountains, which was slipping through the meshes from Macedonia to Attica and spreading across the country.

When he reached Karpenisi Tzimas was given new orders from Athens by the Central Committee's emissary Vlachopoulos. Unfortunately these instructions were already obsolete by the time he received them, something which had been happening since the beginning of the negotiations with Myers. Tzimas had had to give way on certain points to permit the coordination of some of the operations ordered by Cairo, but the document unifying the Resistance had still not been ratified. Vlachopoulos emphasized once again that Athens was anxious to reach a final agreement, whatever the price.

Tzimas, his back to the wall, decided to stall for a few more days, and set off for Grammos where Yugoslav and Albanian emissaries were expecting him. At this stage he had no idea how much the Yugoslavs were going to help him. He was accompanied by the Commander of ELAS Ninth Division, General Vasilis Tzotzos. Tzotzos was a retired career officer who until about a year earlier had been living quietly in his native village, maintaining sympathetic but distant relations with ELAS. Then, one fine morning, the village was attacked by Italians. The local andartes met them outside the village and repelled the first attack, but began to give ground. It was at this point that Tzotzos appeared in full uniform, joined the andartes, took command of the operation and beat the attackers off, this time more thoroughly. When he returned to his house he only stayed long enough to throw some clothes into a suitcase before taking to the mountains for good.

Tito's representative at Grammos was the head of the Yugoslav Macedonian resistance: Vukmanović, code-name Tempo. Myers felt uneasy about his appearance on the scene and sent a British officer to see him. Tempo gave him a stinging welcome: 'I have nothing whatsoever to do with the British. In my country they're parachuting arms to Mihailović who is fighting for the Germans.'

The talks quickly revealed the major tactical and political divergences between Greeks and Yugoslavs. Tzimas, who was undoubtedly closer to the Yugoslav attitude than any other EAM cadre, had the job of formally defending the Central Committee's line which had been laid down a world away in Athens. At this time EAM was hampered both by its desperate eagerness to be recognized legally by the British and by a dogmatic view of political struggle which prevented it from grasping the full importance of the peasant guerilla movement.

The KKE was finding enormous numbers of new recruits among the ranks of EAM. It numbered about 350,000 at the end of the war, compared with the 5,000 recorded in the Metaxas era. In the course of the struggle for national liberation an underground minority was developing into a mass movement by leaps and bounds, but without its controlling group undergoing the slightest mutation. Not a single man who joined the Party from the Resistance was admitted to the top echelons of the Party leadership.

The Yugoslav Party, on the other hand, had grown directly out of the Resistance, though admittedly in a climate less directly disturbed by the tangle of British intrigue and manoeuvre. It was totally committed to armed struggle, it tailored its structures to the needs of that struggle and it kept up to date with its own base.

Tzimas was a member of the K K E Political Bureau and the E A M Central Committee, and was probably the most accessible political mind in the whole Resistance to the ideas Tempo represented, the most convinced of the need to involve the Party apparatus in the events that were taking shape in the mountains. But the official line he had to support, fundamentally orthodox to the point of abstraction, was aimed at securing Anglo-Saxon recognition on the strategic level.

Tempo wanted to set up a Balkan Resistance H Q. A coordinated action by partisans from both countries should make it possible to liberate the town of Kastoria, in Greek Macedonia, and instal in it the components of a unified command. Tzimas was not authorized to decide on such a proposal by himself, but he signed a provisional agreement. The agreement was later rejected by the Central Committee on the ground that it would not be advisable to reconstitute any form of international association so soon after the dissolution of the Comintern. But at Tsotili, where the talks went on for several days in E L A S Ninth Division's H Q, the prospect of setting up a Balkan H Q was very much in the air, bringing Myers out in a cold sweat.

Tempo's main task in Greece was collecting information. He had been very impressed by his earlier travels across E L A S-controlled territory. When Tzimas suggested taking him into Thessaly so that he could study the liberated mountain areas in depth, he accepted at once. During the trip, Tempo could see for himself that communications were functioning in almost complete safety, and he was also struck by the eagerness of the population and the confidence that reigned in the villages. He felt that he had escaped for a time from the realms of secrecy and was witnessing a unanimous uprising which seemed to have considerable power.

Tzimas was more worried than ever by the pressure to reach an agreement with the British, but the day before he left Tsotili he had a pleasant surprise in the form of a personal visit from Myers. If not exactly warm, the Englishman was a good deal more forthcoming than he had been at their last meeting. The head of the British Mission began by passing on a pat on the back from his superiors: 'Middle East HQ are very pleased with the way you have carried out your tasks. They played a very positive part in making the Italian landing a success.'

It was a great day. Tzimas had hardly recovered from his surprise when Eddie announced that his superiors were going to sign an agreement accepting all ELAS's conditions: 'Members of the British Mission will be attached to EAM as liaison officers only, without any authority over Resistance units.'

Tempo's presence must have played a determining role in this decision. There was no shortage of reasons which seemed to promise the Balkan HQ a brilliant future; in the end they escaped nobody except the Party leadership. The reports Myers had been receiving from the British liaison officer at Tsotili certainly painted a gloomy picture of the future of British influence over the Greek Resistance.

Tzimas had done far better than expected; he had been instructed to sign the agreement at any price, but had managed to get all his conditions accepted. Tempo, watching from the sidelines, was still trying to work out EAM's reasons for wanting to sign such a treaty with the British: 'Look, after the way they've behaved with you how can you dare to sign anything with the British?'

But he continued his journey to Thessaly. Myers had to collect signatures from Aris and Sarafis, and asked if he could travel with them. Tempo spent a great deal of time conversing with Tzimas. He was trying to convince him that the British wanted to introduce more agents into the Resistance mainly in order to limit the expansion of ELAS; that, apart from the specific operations ordered by Cairo, they had every reason for discouraging ELAS from waging an all-out struggle against the Germans, since this struggle could only strengthen the Resistance in military terms and confirm it in its political stance.

'You should put everything you've got into the fight against the Germans, and accept anyone willing to take part in it. In the countryside, people who cannot bear arms should be in permanent contact with mobile administrative centres. In Yugoslavia we show up at British supply-drops on Mihailović's territory – he's fighting for the Germans. We know the Soviet Union can't help us; all we can do is fight, take arms from the enemy and manage for ourselves. Political problems will come later. The main thing at the moment is to develop the liberation forces, since they alone can shape the future.'

Every day of the journey further reinforced Tempo's impressions: he was discovering a whole country turning unanimously to the Resistance. He did not know that the man he was trying to enlighten had himself never stopped putting virtually identical proposals to the Central Committee in Athens.

When the group arrived at ELAS's Thessaly HQ in Kastania Tempo met another believer for the first time: Aris. But the Greek Resistance had already been seduced into some very tortuous byways and had not finished helping its enemies. The Kastania andartes held a big conference in honour of their guests. Tempo and Eddie were both invited to speak. Before the meeting began Tzimas took Tempo aside and asked him what themes he was going to bring into his address.

'I'm going to speak about our liberation struggle.'

Tzimas hesitated.

'Er . . . it would be better not to mention Russia or the Communist Party. We're not supposed to use KKE propaganda material here.'

Tempo was irritated by the attitude of the ELAS cadres to the British and had no intention of putting himself out to please Myers.

'In that case I won't speak at all. Where I come from it's the Party that supports armed struggle. The other democratic parties haven't stood up to the occupying forces at all.'

Tzimas shrugged. Tempo was going to voice convictions that he secretly shared; after all, he was not going to say it himself. Tempo mounted the rostrum and went straight to the heart of his subject without any preliminaries: 'We have a lot of enemies in Yugoslavia: the Germans, the Italians, the Bulgarians, the Rumanians, the Hungarians, the Quislings, the Chetniks and the British who are arming the collaborators. Nobody gives us any help. Tito told us: "If you need arms, take them from the enemy." Now we have artillery, machine-guns, tanks. All we ask of Great Britain is that she refrain from helping the Germans indirectly. We don't need anything else from her.'

An ovation drowned his last words. When the cheering had died down a white-faced Myers got up to speak in his turn.

'I don't know what's going on in Yugoslavia, but I do know that the British Government has always helped and will always help the Greek partisans. As for Yugoslavia, I don't think it possible that my Government could be following a completely different policy. . . .'

Tempo had been away from Tito's HQ for six months. During that time a British mission, which included Churchill's son Randolph among its members, had been sent to join the Yugoslav communists. The British were still supplying Mihailović with arms, but were destined to stop doing so when military requirements became more pressing than those of the diplomats. But Yugoslavia was lost to Great Britain for ever, outside its zone of influence. In the Southern Balkans only Greece remained to the British, and they would be that much more ruthless in their determination to maintain their traditional role there, using any and every means.

After Eddie had finished it was Aris's turn to speak. He had made no attempt to hide his pleasure during Tempo's speech, and could not resist an ad-lib at the end of his own: '. . . The British ought to realize that Greeks won't sell themselves for planeloads of pants. What we want is arms.'

Tzimas the politician had been sent into the mountains with specific orders to restrain people's passions. He stood up and entered a moderate defence of the Central Committee's line. When he separated from Tempo a few days later, he asked for a month to get a reply from the Central Committee on the subject of the Balkan Headquarters.

Tempo returned to Greece at the beginning of September. He did not see Tzimas at Trikkala although he had been defending the project warmly in the meantime – too warmly, perhaps. This is probably why Tempo had only Siantos and Ioannidis to deal with. Facing the high priests of Athens, he began to get an idea of the real distance between the official lines of the two Balkan resistance movements.

Siantos emphasized the need to build up a very wide-based political support in order to exercise enough pressure to secure the portfolios of the Interior and the Armed Forces by legal means. Ioannidis held donnishly to the canonical model: 'Whoever holds the four main towns will have the power in Greece.'

Partly to respect this dogma and partly to keep the British happy, the heroic battle being waged by the big-city reserves was kept apart from the guerilla struggle. When the day came for the urban forces to enter the armed struggle, they would be overwhelmed by the impossible task of leading the decisive assault without any backing from Mountain units.

On 11 July Allied troops landed in Sicily. The Greek Resistance had done its job well. The disorder caused by andartes activities in the weeks preceding the landing is reflected in these reports from the Wehrmacht High Command newspaper:

2 June 1943. An Italian leave-train burnt on the main Larisa-Athens line, after an explosion in the tunnel between Angi and Nezeros (25 km. north-west of Larisa). 80 wounded. The track will probably be closed for twenty-four hours. In Karditsa and Nestorion, bands are appealing for military clothing. A communist band at Aigion (100 well-armed men) has blown up the Diakopton-Kalavryta railway bridge. The presence of a new band in the Kalavryta region is confirmed. An attack on the Kalavryta-Pyrgos road bridge repelled . . .

3 June. The Vigose bridge to the west of Konitsa (40 km. north of Yannina) has been blown up. Supplementary report on the Nezeros railway incident: 92 Italians and 60 Greek prisoners killed, many missing . . .

100 communists shot in reprisal at Larisa concentration camp . . .

A band dressed in Greek military uniform is reported in the Soupraea region (40 km. north-east of Lamia) . . .

4 June. A 200-strong band south of Florina. 1,000 communists said to be in the Metsovo region (28 km. north-west of Yannina) . . .

Several strike attempts in Athens by civil servants and workers . . .

5 June. The communists have set up their own concentration camp south-east of Grevaina (115 km. north-west of Larisa) . . .

Metsovo-Yannina road cut in several places . . .

Incident to the south of Lamia between Italians and a communist band claimed to be 4-5,000 strong. Italian losses: 150 men. Enemy losses claimed to be considerable . . .

Another attempted strike suppressed in Athens . . .

12 June. Fierce fighting is going on in the Klisoura gorge between the Eberlein combat group and 4-500 bandits. 3 Germans killed, 15 wounded, 9 missing. Enemy losses unknown . . .

13 June. The bands are still holding the heights they originally occupied in the Klisoura gorge. The Eberlein combat group is strengthening its defensive positions . . .

21 June. During the night of 20-21 June, the Salonika-Athens railway line was cut in six places by explosions in the Katerini-Asopos region. Two spans of the Asopos bridge have been destroyed. It is presumed that this sabotage was carried out by Greek workers who have recently been reinforcing the bridge under the supervision of German engineers. The workers have been arrested. There were no passages of arms with the detachment guarding the bridge. It is not known how long repairs to the track will take . . .

22 June. Organized intensification of sabotage activity. Attack on the railway bridge north-east of Katerini. A column of 64 lorries and 118 men attacked by bands on the road to the south-east of Servia, in the Italian zone. Some vehicles burnt . . .

... During the night of the 22 June, all telephone communications between Yannina, Athens and Preveza, and with Albania, interrupted by sabotage ...

... Eleven incursions by enemy aircraft ...

23 June. ... Organized sabotage activity continuing. Telephone communication in the Kozani region, and the bridges between Larisa and Trikkala, have been sabotaged ...

Aerial photographs confirm the destruction of the motorized column southeast of Servia. Extensive damage all over the gorge ...

24 June. Planned sabotage continuing. Seres aerodrome bombed ... road bridge destroyed to the south of Petrana (south-west of Kozani). Telephone lines sabotaged and roads barricaded with barbed wire ...

More news of the attack on the motorized column: 5 fugitives, one wounded and 10 killed can be accounted for, the rest are missing. 36 lorries, 42 cars and 4 radio cars destroyed ...

Eleven enemy flights dropping supplies to the bands ...

29 June. The Lamia-Salonika railway line blown up in eight places ...Telephone sabotage south-west of Ptolemais. The inhabitants have been ordered to look out for further attempts. After an attack on a German NCO at Naousa, 25 Greek communist suspects have been shot in reprisal. ...[1]

The SOE's diversionary manoeuvre bore fruit. The secret report Ic:AO284-43, issued on 3 July and signed by Brigadier-General Foertz, concludes:

The recent spectacular growth in maquisard activity – manifestly carried out under Allied orders – endangers supplies to our troops in the South of Greece and the movement and transportation of our forces in general. Recent Allied bombing of our aerodromes in Greece, and the facts listed below, perhaps constitute the preliminaries for a landing in the Balkans.

Continuous supply flights to the andartes in western Greece; the information gathered by enemy agents, both on the logistical needs of the maquisards and on meteorological conditions around Corfu ...

Favourable conditions for a landing by air and sea ...

Finally, the frequency with which British submarines approach the islands of Cefalonia and Ithaca and even the port of Astateis (70 miles south of Arta). ...[2]

Myers's military treaty allowing for all ELAS's conditions had been signed by Tzimas, Aris and Sarafis at Kastania on 6 July, while Tempo exhorted ELAS to fight on alone. A few days later Eddie handed Tzimas a congratulatory telegram from General Wilson to the andartes.

[1] A. Kedros, *La Résistance grecque, 1940-44*, Paris, 1966, p. 280 ff.
[2] A. Hillgrüber, *Kriegstagebuch des Oberkommandos der Wehrmacht*, Frankfurt, 1963, vol. II, p. 826.

I would like to pass on to all ranks of the Greek partisans' army my thanks and my sincere congratulations for their recent great successes all over Greece. Operations minutely prepared by us, and carried out by you with great precision, have contributed to the success of the Allied armies in Sicily. The Axis was misled into expecting an offensive in the Balkans. Reinforcements in men and aircraft which had been intended for Italy were deployed in the Balkans. The Axis was distracted by events in Greece and a major convoy was able to cross the Mediterranean without hindrance. I am aware that the andartes' operations were dangerous and that the civilian population has suffered greatly. I beg you to assure the partisans, as well as the civil population, of my esteem for their devotion to the Allied cause. The war is now progressing towards its end. It will end with the unconditional surrender of the Axis. For the future, I ask the same trust and the same devotion of the military leaders of the Allied armies in the Mediterranean, of which the Greek andartes are a part. Long live the andartes!

18 July.
Wilson

This telegram brought to its close a military chapter in the relationship between the British and the Greek Resistance.

Churchill had not managed to hustle his Allies into the Greek landing which would have enabled him to enter Athens as a liberator and throw the whole weight of the Middle East army into the scale of the country's future. The Russians and Americans had insisted on making Sicily and Italy the first objectives of their offensive in the south of Europe.

The 'Greek torment', to use the British Premier's own phrase, was now entering its political phase. Myers not only gave ELAS General Wilson's congratulations; he was also the bearer of another message. This was a reply to the proposal made to Woodhouse by Tzimas, Siantos and Ioannidis during their first meeting in Athens. An EAM delegation was expected in Cairo. The delegates must be ready to fly to the Middle East on 10 August.

The Seraglio

A majority of the leading Greek politicians, setting aside for the moment the open collaborators, felt at this time that it was less useful to attach themselves to the Resistance than to go to Cairo where their civic virtues would be appreciated. In clearing a path for themselves through that

Levantine maze of palace intrigue, a warlike stance was judged super-
fluous or even condemned as bad form. Churchill wrote in his memoirs:

The decisions of the Conferences in Cairo and Teheran indirectly affected the
position in Greece. There would never be a major Allied landing there, nor was
it likely that any considerable British forces would follow a German retreat. The
arrangements to prevent anarchy had therefore to be considered.[1]

The paternal attention of Great Britain was still fixed on Greece as firmly
as ever, although it was now on the edge of the main theatre of operations.
As proof of Churchill's particular concern for the Empire's game reserves,
a close friend of Eden's called Wallace was sent into Greece early in
August to sample the terrain before the Resistance representatives arrived
in Cairo.

Myers's reports had reflected all the inconsistencies and contradictions
of the diverse objectives he had been given. Better to start again with a
clean sheet. In this context, Wilson's congratulatory telegram can be seen
as a preliminary to liquidating the shadowy liaison between ELAS and
British Middle East HQ.

The Resistance delegates were on their way to Cairo to meet the
members of a government-in-exile which represented almost nothing
between the Peloponnese and Macedonia, but which basked in the favour
of the Foreign Office on the banks of the Nile.

Since April 1941 the Greek Government in Cairo had been led by
Emmanuel Tsouderos, an economist and former director of the Bank of
Greece whose relations with the English had always been of the best. A
'liberal' label retained from his earlier association with the Venizelists had
helped to get him 'exiled' by the 4 August regime for voicing his opposition to the 'illiberal' methods of Metaxas.

When the king offered him the job of prime minister, he was still under
surveillance by the dictator's police. Times seemed to have changed. The
British needed a flexible and obedient figure to place beside the monarch,
but one who had had nothing whatever to do with the Metaxas regime.
Tsouderos was just the man. As time passed the number of willing
candidates grew to an impressive size. The best qualification was an
energetic denunciation of the communist menace, and Metaxists and
Liberals were even joined by some former Socialists who had decided to
wave the right flag. The whole camp competed in emitting cries of alarm

[1] Winston S. Churchill, *The Second World War*, vol. V, London, 1952, p. 476.

the better to please a British establishment committed to preserving, if not exactly the principles, at least the frontiers of Western influence.

George Papandreou, who was still in Athens, entered the lists at the end of 1942. He presented himself to Churchill simply as the man who 'could save Greece from the communist menace'. He would bide his time for two years and then, partly against his own inclinations, liquidate the nascent Greek democracy with the help of Scobie's tanks.

In 1941 the refurbishing of the Metaxist machine in Cairo was only skin-deep. Behind the 'liberal' Tsouderos the key posts in the cabinet were all manned by veterans of 4 August: Maniadakis, promoter of the inquisition technique that produced the 'declarations of repentance', Sakellariou, Dimitratos, Nikolaidis and others.

In a circular of 17 May 1941, Tsouderos had announced his intention of holding aloof from party squabbles: 'Follow a policy in keeping with my recommendations and cooperate with one another, forgetting the divergences of the past.'

The 'divergences of the past' were, however, of some importance between monarchists and republicans. At about the same time IDEA, a Metaxist organization well known to the British services, circularized its members with detailed instructions on placing themselves at the disposal of the Axis forces in the event of Alexandria falling to Rommel.

The British were, of course, perfectly well aware of all this. From their point of view it was better to deal with an organization prepared to sell itself to the strongest – that is, to the British after the victory – than to find themselves confronting the national Resistance and its aspirations to independence.

Tsouderos's role was to reassure the Greek nation that the democratic future of the country was guaranteed by the collection of right-wing officers and cadres grouped around the political clique in Cairo, under the authority of the same king who had called Metaxas to power in 1936. 'The final aim of the struggle we are carrying on overseas, in the camp of our great Allies,' he proclaimed, 'is the triumph of Liberty and Democracy.'

Alongside the royal clique of officers and politicians, however, the embryo of a new Greek army was forming in Egypt. Its strength had risen to more than 20,000 men, many of whom had crossed the Aegean by risky unofficial routes to come and fight with the Allies. In the minds of the great majority of these men the liberation struggle was closely associated with the liquidation of the monarchy, of fascism and of the influence of the great foreign powers in Greece. They constituted a highly politicized army fighting in cooperation with the Resistance inside the country, and they had no intention of becoming the praetorian guard of a puppet government tied to the old regime.

Even Tsouderos thought that the Metaxist officers running the army could have been more enthusiastic about fighting the Germans, and that they could have made a better job of concealing their affection for fascist ideology: '. . . either they say that they would rather see the army disbanded than functioning under the orders of democrats, or they moan that they have had enough fighting, that there is no need to go on fighting in the desert.'[1]

The old democrats hung on, turning a blind eye to all this, in the hope of being present for the great distribution of jobs and portfolios which must come sooner or later. Tsouderos managed to eliminate or displace certain Metaxist elements who proved themselves too enterprising or exhibitionist: 'Admiral Sakellariou resigned from the Vice-Presidency in March 1942. During his period of office in the Government he ran the secret intelligence services in a completely personal and absolute manner.' He had even been in contact with the Axis services, using as intermediaries certain members of the royal family who, with princely unconcern, had kept up their connections with every branch of their truly international cousinage. To quote Tsouderos again:

He (Sakellariou) had made contact on his own initiative with reactionary and undesirable persons in Greece, with whom he was in correspondence. He had given orders to the agency responsible for getting people out of Greece that only convinced royalists should be helped to escape to Egypt. When we were informed of this order, we countermanded it with the king's approval. He also tried to bring the three service ministries under his personal authority; when the attempt failed, he became angry and joined the opposition.[2]

Sakellariou in opposition retained all his contacts and influences in the army and the government. His 'removal' from the centre of things had the platonic significance of a gesture. Deprived of the job of vice-premier, he was given command of the fleet. By this time, however, the democratic forces in the army had become sufficiently organized to give Sakellariou good cause to worry about the ideology of his men.

[1] E. Tsouderos, *Greek Conflicts in the Middle East*, Athens, 1945, pp. 8–9 (in Greek).
[2] Tsouderos, op. cit., p. 32.

The First Mutiny

The Military Anti-Fascist Organization (ASO) had been founded in October 1941 by Yannis Sallas, whose name was to become a legend before he was finally murdered by government agents. The movement's main objectives were:
- development of the army and intensive preparation for fighting on any front;
- liberation of occupied Greece in cooperation with the Resistance;
- struggle against fascist elements attempting to instal a Metaxist type government in Greece against the popular will.

There was no regular liaison between ASO in Cairo and EAM in Athens. Sallas himself only learnt of the existence of the Greek movement when a naval officer from Athens came to see him and extracted a copy of EAM's statutes from the lining of his jacket. ASO's organization was triangular, each cell consisting of an officer or NCO and two ordinary troopers. This system was absolutely watertight, and every attempt at decapitating the movement resulted in the prompt emergence of a new leadership from its untouched base.

To fill the vice-presidency left vacant by Sakellariou the British found another traditional liberal politician, Kanellopoulos, and imported him from Athens at great expense. Swept suddenly away on Cairo's magic carpet, Kanellopoulos became a vocal supporter of the most democratic opinions. He was given the portfolio of National Defence as well as the vice-presidency, and declared himself determined to expel all fascist elements from the army and the government.

By June 1942 the worried Metaxist officers were ready to act, and the first wave of resignations was handed to the Staff: 'They have no confidence in their Commanding Officer, Lt-Colonel Daskarelis.' The movement grew, the list of resignations lengthened and it became clear that an attempt was being made to force the removal of all democrat officers from the army. ASO's rapid intervention to expose the manoeuvre set the plot back for a time. To show how the minds of these Metaxist cadres worked, one of these officers commented as he looked at the graves of some Greek soldiers just after the battle of El Alamein: 'They wanted to fight. Well, now they can eat sand.'

There was still a war on in the Middle East and Foreign Office manoeuvres were still counterbalanced to some extent by military imperatives. No action was taken against these extreme right-wing officers for resigning in time of war. They were simply asked to remain at their posts, and the democratic officers were not disturbed.

Another provocation in the same vein, involving the denunciation of democrat officers, reached such a point a few months later that the Greek brigades had to be withdrawn from active service. General Tsakalotas wrote later: 'Owing to the rapid advance of the Eighth Army and the serious mutiny which had broken out in the 2nd Battalion, the Brigade was not used in the English operations to destroy the Mareth Line. . . .'[1]

The political end had been achieved. Despite its need for fighting troops, the British High Command was allowing an unusable army to exist on the edge of a battlefield. That was only a start. The old liberal Kanellopoulos quickly proved to be more allergic to Red than to the *fasces*. After all his ringing declarations, he not only failed to purge the army of fascist elements but was soon leaning on the 4 August group of officers for support, sending to Greece for a reliable man called General Zygouris.

The arrival in the Middle East of General Zygouris and other high-ranking officers [wrote Tsouderos] provided the Minister of the Armed Forces, who was also vice-premier, with an opportunity to reorganize the two brigades into one division under the command of the newly-arrived General and also to replace certain battalion commanders who enjoyed the sympathy and respect of the soldiers in the 2nd Brigade. Those ordered to replace them were reputed by the soldiers and a section of the officer corps to be fascists, and certain of them had already made their fascist tendencies public.[2]

ASO continued to expose Kanellopoulos's manoeuvres. He had slandered EAM in passing and was now trying to bring the Middle East Army to heel.

Official thinking over the last few decades of Greek history has held that movements of opinion in the army are 'plots' which will disintegrate if struck on the head. Applying this remedy to ASO, the government decided to remove Colonel Hajistavris and two other battalion commanders of the Second Brigade who were thought intemperately 'leftist'. The brigade commander, General Bourdaras, was afraid that ASO would take action and temporized. He gave the three left-wing battalion commanders ten days' leave to go to Cairo and explain themselves.

On 23 February 1943, the day before they were due to leave for Cairo, a notorious fascist called Athanasiou appeared at Fifth Battalion HQ and

[1] Tsouderos, op. cit., pp. 28–9.   [2] *Akropolis*, Athens, 5 April 1960.

announced that he had come to take over from Hajistavris. The soldiers of the battalion took matters into their own hands and removed Athanasiou by force. General Bourdaras could see that the army's whole future was at risk, and agreed to go to Cairo to protest personally against the dismissal of the 'leftists'.

There was an immediate riposte. Once again, 'nationalist' officers began resigning en masse, following a preconceived plan which should not have been carried out until the king's arrival on 15 March. The Hajistavris affair gave them a reason to advance the original project by two weeks.

Twelve officers resigned from the Fifth Battalion, followed by officers from other units. Bourdaras found himself under pressure from political sources and from British agents to speed up the removal of the three battalion commanders. The Right had the wind in its sails, and some of the resigning officers went so far as to threaten those of republican opinions. ASO decided to mount a counter-offensive. Within minutes the officers who had resigned were placed under arrest and escorted to Second Brigade HQ. ASO officers filled the vacant posts. The resignation campaign spread to the Metaxist cadres in the First Brigade, stationed two hundred kilometres away near Tripoli. The Artillery Regiment, only eight kilometres away, threatened to turn its guns on the Second Brigade. Bourdaras was losing control of the situation and began to give way. Two ASO delegates, a soldier and a sub-lieutenant from the Fifth Battalion, brought him a message urging him to stand firm: 'General, you have the respect and confidence of the army. Today, you must show yourself worthy of your rank by dedicating yourself to the service of the Greek people. Do not forget that our struggling compatriots regard us as deserters. We must proceed to actions which will prove our involvement in our brothers' struggle for freedom; nothing else can justify our flight from Greece. . . . Instead of resigning, remain at your post and punish the fascists; rest assured that the country will recognize you for it and that your name will be venerated. If you resign you will be seen as a coward and a deserter. . . . We would inform you that we are with you, as long as you are with Greece. The partial mobilization that took place over Colonel Hajistavris will become general if the fascists dare to try replacing you. . . .'

When Bourdaras finished reading the letter tears were streaming down his face.

'A traitor! I've always fought for my country and they call me a traitor. . . . You have to understand that I'm acting to preserve the unity of the army. I can't stall any longer; I'm obliged to ask the three battalion commanders to go immediately.'

Bourdaras could not hold out any longer against the pressures brought to bear on him by the government. In the end, ASO had to accept the sacking of the three officers on condition that they would be sent not to Cairo but to Beirut, where they could seek Kanellopoulos's personal explanation. ASO also demanded that the officers who had resigned be arrested and expelled from the Brigade. In Beirut they found Kanellopoulos unwilling even to consider going back on his decision. On the contrary, he was preparing another assault on the 'leftists' and had arrest warrants in his pocket for another twenty-eight democratic officers.

While the three battalion commanders were on their way to Beirut, Kanellopoulos's right-hand man, General Zygouris, was travelling in the opposite direction to join the Second Brigade. He told Bourdaras to regard the three officers' transfer as permanent, and ordered the artillery to cover the 'mutinous' units; but the situation was entirely under ASO control, and the order was not obeyed. Zygouris then turned to the British and asked them to intervene with tanks.

This was at the beginning of March 1943 and the military still had the last word in British decisions in the Middle East. They replied evasively that they had no spare tanks in the area. Zygouris tried to get them to cut off the First Battalion's food supplies, but Allied HQ refused to starve troops to serve a political manoeuvre. After all, the same troops had behaved admirably at El Alamein, and their chief demand was to be allowed to fight shoulder to shoulder with the Allies.

Zygouris had run out of ideas. Kanellopoulos turned to Katsotas, head of the First Brigade, and asked him to march on the mutineers in the Second Brigade. An open armed conflict could only lead to the dissolution of the Greek forces in the Middle East, leaving nothing but a praetorian nucleus of overtly fascist elements – a weak popular base for a government that does not represent much in the first place. Katsotas listed his conditions. The bargaining began.

Meanwhile, the three battalion commanders had returned to Cairo where they were immediately arrested and shut in a hotel. After a good deal of argument, Zygouris finally persuaded the British to supply him with the authorization and the means to move the Second Brigade. He hoped to disband the 'leftist' battalions by dispersing their units. The order was due to be carried out on 3 March 1943.

On the appointed morning ASO mobilized all its members. The time for compromise was long past, and if necessary Bourdaras himself would be arrested by his own men. Towards 10 a.m. a British transport unit appeared at the camp entrance. The lorries Zygouris had borrowed to move the Brigade were halted by the sentries. The muzzles of Greek artillery swung round to cover them. Behind the guns, the Brigade's three battalions were drawn up in straight ranks. With bayonets fixed, battle-standards unfurled and their officers leading them, they marched on Brigade Headquarters.

All the soldiers were on parade, with the exception of the officers who had resigned. They had lost the first round. Keeping their formation, the three battalions halted two hundred yards from the HQ buildings. Three British liaison officers emerged and approached the troops. They asked for a list of ASO claims for transmission to the General Commanding the Ninth Allied Army, to which the Greek forces officially belonged.

While this brief negotiation was going on in front of the HQ building Bourdaras left through a side door, jumped in his car and set out for Beirut, where he had to meet Kanellopoulos. The three battalions marched back to barracks in the same order and carried on with their duties. The arrested rightist officers were handed over to British liaison officers.

That afternoon, a delgation consisting of a soldier and a reserve sub-lieutenant handed the British a memorandum addressed to the Greek government and Allied Command. ASO's demands were:
– the immediate removal of Kanellopoulos and reshuffling of the government, which must be composed of democratic figures trusted by the army and the Greek people;
– the reinstatement of the Second Brigade battalion commanders;
– the purging of all fascist elements from the armed forces, and effective leadership of the Brigade with a view to future participation in Allied operations;
– court martial for all officers who had resigned;
– dismissal of General Zygouris and General Bourdaras, who were held responsible for the events.

The British officer to whom they gave this memorandum informed the delegates that Ninth Army Command had already taken one decision: the Brigade was to be placed under the temporary command of a British officer who would be relieving Bourdaras. This provoked a violent reaction from the ASO delegates. Only the Greek government had the right to appoint a new brigadier, British or otherwise. Rather than see themselves under the authority of a foreigner, ASO proposed that the Brigade be taken over by Lt-Colonel Manidakis, Bourdaras's second-in-command, who had never hidden his reactionary leanings.

'We know Manidakis's ideological position and his attitude to ourselves. We hope that the soldier in Manidakis will recognize the responsibilities incumbent on every Greek at this time, when the very existence of our Brigade and all the Greek forces in the Middle East is in the balance; that he will see it as the duty of every Greek officer worthy of the name to fight for the liberation of his country instead of dabbling in political intrigues ... and that he will accept provisional command of the Brigade. Should Manidakis refuse, we will offer the command to a subordinate officer, but we will never agree to be placed under the command of a Briton even if we have to use our weapons to prevent it.'

The delegation went straight to Lt-Colonel Manidakis's quarters. Either through patriotism or through personal ambition he accepted the command.

Virtually the same situation was enacted in the First Brigade. A majority of the officers put their names on the resignation list. ASO countered by sending a delegation consisting of a Sub-Lieutenant and two soldiers to see Katsotas, the Brigade General.

'All the men declare their solidarity with the Second Brigade, and urge you to take measures against the reactionary movement, relying on the support of ASO and the democratic elements among your troops.'

Katsotas had already been in touch with Kanellopoulos, and his only reply was to imprison the three delegates and give orders for the arrest of ASO members. Just as there had been in the Second Brigade, there was a general rebellion. All the Metaxist officers were arrested immediately and confined to their tents under guard. Several officers tried to turn the artillery on the men but were quickly neutralized. The imprisoned delegation was released. To change when one's duty changes is constancy, not frivolity. Katsotas about-turned and agreed to cooperate with ASO; it was the only way for him to stay in command of the Brigade.

On his way back to Cairo, Kanellopoulos called at the military hospital at Hentaras, in Palestine. The troops had his measure from the moment he arrived. He was leaning on the door of his car and trying to calm their minds with soothing words when his speech was interrupted by a well-aimed bucket of curds which soaked him from head to foot. His driver slammed the car into gear and took off at full speed: his quick reflexes probably saved the ex-Vice-Premier, now sprawled dripping across the back seat, from a vicious lynching.

The Middle East Army, which the Greek politicians in Cairo had intended to use as a basis for their political authority, had demonstrated that it would not be turned into a world apart, a microcosm indifferent to the aspirations of the majority of the Greek nation. Everywhere – inside the country itself and in the Middle East – the majority was mobilized for the same struggle, supporting the same claims and demanding a return to democracy. The Cairo government would never be accepted as representative by any popular movement. It had lost the nation's army. Henceforth its main objective would be to keep its hands free to exercise in total isolation the share of power granted to it by its powerful protectors, even if it had to throw away its own army to do so.

In March 1943, however, the first concern of the British services in Cairo was the struggle against the Axis. General Holmes, commander of the Ninth Army (to which the Greek forces belonged), observed simply that some men who wished to fight had risen against a clique of officers who had abandoned their posts and who were in any case more interested in their putschist schemes than in the wider objectives of the war. He found the ASO claims 'honourable' and accepted the terms of the Second Brigade's memorandum before passing it on to the government and Middle East Staff. The officers who had resigned were sent to Merzeghioum camp in Syria. The three battalion commanders were restored to their units in the Second Brigade. ASO was in control.

On 14 March 1943 the king and Tsouderos arrived from London.

'Under pressure from this revolution,' wrote Tsouderos, 'the government was reshuffled. Vice-President Kanellopoulos and the ministers Sekeris, Kavadias and Nikoloudis resigned. On 24 March M. G. Rousos entered the government as Vice-President and Messrs Karapanayotis, Sofoulis, Voulgaris and, later, S. Venizelos (son of E. Venizelos) entered the ministries. The brigades were temporarily run by British brigadiers who were replaced after a month (in fact they stayed three months) by Generals Papas and Geghetis.'

It was only another face-lift, but the 'leftist' mutineers had nothing to lose by waiting.

The Spring of 1943 brought changes to the military situation on all fronts. After crushing the German forces trapped at Stalingrad, the Red Army passed to the offensive and drove towards the Balkans. Rommel got stuck in the desert and never reached Alexandria. Like ELAS, the Greek Middle East army was beginning to get in Churchill's way with its fantasies of national independence. Under these conditions, the ASO memorandum accepted by Ninth Army Command had no more significance than a pious wish, and was soon followed by reprisals.

The leftist-infected Second Brigade was broken up in a series of moves which scattered its units separately all over the deserts of the Middle East. The Fifth Battalion was hurried to the outskirts of Damascus, and the rest of the troops were soon drying out more than five hundred kilometres away, in the Racca desert on the Euphrates. There, in the ferocious heat and sandstorms of April, May and June, the troops were subjected to a programme of special training. One of their disciplinary marches lasted ninety days. The First Brigade suffered a similar fate in the Aleppo region; the time had passed when the Cairo officers could consider a mutiny 'honourable'. The Foreign Office was trying to revive the opportunity it had missed in February, but the men marched until they dropped without responding to the provocation.

Every time a unit was moved, cadres suspected of belonging to ASO were shuffled around in an attempt to break up the organization. The Metaxist officers removed in March were beginning to reappear in their former units. The new government of liberal personalities did not mean to become dependent on any possible form of mass support only to find itself later being railroaded into some sort of relationship with the organizers of the Greek Resistance. For the time being ASO adopted a policy of holding out, hoping to ensure the continued existence of a national army despite the provocations designed to push it towards dissolution.

With the Allied landing in Sicily, and the disappearance of any immediate prospect of a military intervention in Athens, Churchill began to give priority to the problem of harnessing the Resistance politically. The message summoning delegations from EAM, EDES and EKKA to Cairo on 10 August was given to Tzimas at the beginning of July. The king had recently received a manifesto from some 'liberal' personalities in Athens requesting him not to return to Greece until a plebiscite called him back. At about this time, under some pressure from the British, he broadcast a reply to this letter.

George II promised the Greek people that free elections would be held immediately after the liberation, that the Government-in-Exile would resign and an enlarged cabinet would be established. The king and his ministers were in their element in Cairo. They were about to show what they meant by an 'enlarged cabinet' by pulling the Resistance delegates into the British hornets' nest.

At this point in the development of British policy in Greece, when the military had just left the field clear for the Foreign Office diplomats, Churchill was inclined to attribute the complex political problems looming on the horizon to the Greek national temperament.

The Greeks rival the Jews in being the most politically-minded race in the world. No matter how forlorn their circumstances or how grave the peril to their country, they are always divided into many parties, with many leaders who fight among themselves with desperate vigour. It has been well said that wherever there are three Jews it will be found that there are two Prime Ministers and one leader of the Opposition. The same is true of this other famous ancient race, whose stormy and endless struggle for life stretches back to the fountain springs of human thought. No two races have set such a mark upon the world. Both have shown a capacity for survival, in spite of unending perils and sufferings from external oppressors, matched only by their own ceaseless feuds, quarrels, and convulsions. The passage of several thousand years sees no change in their characteristics and no diminution of their trials or their vitality. They have survived in spite of all that the world could do against them, and all they could do against themselves, and each of them from angles so different have left us the inheritance of their genius and wisdom. No two cities have counted more with mankind than Athens and Jerusalem. Their messages in religion, philosophy and art have been the main guiding lights of modern faith and culture. Centuries of foreign rule and indescribable, endless oppression leave them still living, active forces in the modern world, quarrelling among themselves with insatiable vivacity. Personally I have always been on the side of both, and believed in their invincible power to survive internal strife and the world tides threatening their extinction.[1]

This creaking homage opens the chapter of Churchill's memoirs which he called 'The Greek Torment'.

Hornets' Nest

5 August 1943: a British aircraft circling over Neraida in a sky rippling with heat, trying to locate the landing strip that would be required at the

---

[1] Churchill, op. cit., vol. V, pp. 470–1.

end of the week. On the ground, nothing but rock and the grey-green waves of olive groves. The scorched landscape seemed to be disintegrating in the heat of the sun. Every pebble was sharply outlined in white light, but the pilot could see no sign of a landing strip. For several long minutes the noise of the engine drowned the chirping of cicadas, then died away as the plane flew off to the south. That night a message arrived from Cairo: 'The airstrip should be almost finished, but work does not seem to have started. Explain.'

The explanation came by return. Myers and the party of andartes placed at his disposal had done an admirable job. Not only was the airstrip finished, but the camouflage arrangements had proved their effectiveness. During the day whole trees were placed on the strip to blend in with the surrounding groves.

Myers's technical prowess would have been somewhat tarnished in the eyes of his superiors if they had seen what was going on a few hundred yards from the camouflaged airstrip, in the village of Neraida. In the last few days before the delegates were due to leave for Cairo, an improvised Resistance Congress was springing up there.

Siantos, Karageorgis and Aris were the first to join Tzimas. They were soon followed by three members of the EAM Central Committee: Tsirimokos, a socialist lawyer, and Rousos and Despotopoulos, both members of the KKE Central Committee. Kartalis was also there on behalf of EKKA, and EDES was represented by Pyromaglou.

Myers was worried by the number of EAM people in the village. Doubtless as a result of new orders from Cairo, he suddenly announced that he was only going to take one delegate from each organization. Addressing Tzimas, he said: 'I've been thinking of taking you, Kartalis and Pyromaglou.'

'We're sending four delegates,' Siantos answered. 'Tsirimokos, Rousos, Despotopoulos and Tzimas. Either they all go, or we send nobody.'

Tzimas added: 'You told me you were inviting the delegation we've been trying to send to Cairo since the beginning of the year. And another thing: why did you tell me "*they* should be there on 10 August" if you only intended to take me? I was with you already.'

Wallace was just as uneasy as Myers. Siantos was anxious not to carry on the argument in the presence of Kartalis and Pyromaglou, for fear that the controversy would cause a breach in the Resistance. Myers was as embarrassed as he was, and awkwardly tried to compromise. He had run out of arguments. He became flustered and ended by claiming that the aircraft would only be big enough to take five passengers: himself, Wallace, Kartalis, Pyromaglou and Tzimas. Everyone knew that the airstrip had been designed to take a Dakota. Myers and Wallace hung on desperately, but lost ground. After months of good and loyal service, Myers was never sent back to Greece. Wallace did return and was eventually killed there.

The British had made their arrangements in Cairo on the assumption that there would be three Resistance representatives. Three more boarded the aircraft, three EAM delegates determined to obtain total recognition for their movement, not only militarily but on the political level as well. Myers and Wallace had botched the curtain-up on the Egyptian scene.

The Dakota landed at Cairo in the late morning on 10 August. Myers was the first to jump to the ground; after him, the deluge. The officer waiting to welcome the delegation was bewildered at first, but after a brief explanation he took his six guests in hand and ushered them into the waiting staff cars. Not a single Greek official had come to greet the Resistance envoys at the airport. They were surrounded by the mechanical activity of a military area in wartime. Tsouderos's government was functioning openly in Cairo but the Resistance men felt curiously trapped there; now they were shut into military vehicles and speeding towards an unknown destination.

Although they were on territory which had never been occupied by the Nazis, they experienced a strong sensation of being pushed about, manipulated. This impression was not diminished by the security arrangements at Wilson's headquarters. The place was a veritable fortress. As they advanced into it, a tight military security network closed in smoothly behind them. Somewhere in the middle of this web, the officer who had met them at the airport stopped the cars and announced that he would show them to their quarters. As they climbed out of the cars, Kartalis broke the heavy silence.

'We refuse to stay here. We want to stay in a hotel in the centre of the town. We have to see people and we need to move about in complete freedom.'

The officer registered this request and disappeared with an abrupt salute. The delegates were taken into the centre of Cairo the same evening and a building occupied by British officers was placed at their disposal. The next day they made their first contact with the Cairo government.

Tsouderos received the delegation with every outward sign of the most profound esteem: 'Welcome! It's through you that we're still surviving.'

This was true enough; 'through you' can be stretched to mean 'in spite of you' as well as 'thanks to you'.

The whole cabinet had come together for the occasion. Venizelos raised the bidding: 'We were in a state of complete decay. You are saving us.'

Tsouderos and his cabinet politely admired the Resistance and its exploits in the hope that this would make it easier to absorb the delegation. The delegates had not been counting on being crunched up and digested. They began to get some idea of why they had been summoned. Tsouderos took Pyromaglou's arm and led him to one side, asking slyly:

'Tell me, what's behind this story of Zervas's telegram to the king?'

Pyromaglou's thunderstruck reaction lacked the air of complicity that was probably expected of him. He knew nothing about the affair.

The first official contact with the British was a luncheon given by Sir Reginald Leeper, British ambassador to the court of the king of Greece, where the Resistance was entertained in the lavish style customary at this kind of ceremony. The party ended with a surprise. King George II made a personal appearance along with the fruit salad. He was dressed in shorts and tennis shoes. His subjects were less astonished by his costume than by his opening words: 'I've heard of your ways and I wanted to see you.'

George II spoke a rather idiosyncratic Greek and it was explained later that he had meant to refer to the exploits of Leeper's guests rather than their 'ways'. The ice was not exactly broken by this opening, but the monarch seemed interested in what was going on in his kingdom. For an hour and a half he asked searching questions on administrative problems and the quality of the partisans' diet, then abruptly consulted his watch and stood up to leave. The delegates requested a private audience, which was granted for two days later.

On 18 August the Mountain delegates presented themselves at the king's private residence, where His Majesty received them in full uniform. The three organizations had agreed on what they wanted to ask, and the EAM spokesman Tsirimokos spoke for all of them.

'. . . Your Majesty should stay abroad until the plebiscite. Then, if the people want you back and vote accordingly, nobody will be able to prevent you from returning. You should agree to wait for the election result, for the sake of Greek unity.'

The king did not betray the slightest emotion. He accepted the memorandum from Tsirimokos but answered none of the questions that were put to him. In a tone that managed to be both patronizing and astonished, he congratulated Tsirimokos on the 'way' (someone had thought it worth-while to explain the meaning of the word) in which he had explained the problem. The audience ended. The king cabled Churchill the same evening:

King of Greece (Cairo) to Prime Minister and President Roosevelt.

On July 4 I declared to my people that after their liberation they will be invited to determine by means of free election the form of their government.

I am now suddenly faced with the most curious situation, of the unexpected arrival of certain individuals from Greece who are supposed to represent various guerrilla bands; in addition, a representative of certain old political parties, who wish to press me to declare that I should only return after a plebiscite which would decide the form of the future regime. . . . In these circumstances I would much appreciate your advice as to the policy which would at this time best serve the cause of Greece and the United Nations.

My present personal inclination is to continue the policy agreed between us before I left England. I feel very strongly that I should return to Greece with my troops, even if I left my country after a short period to work for its national interests among our Allies, should subsequent developments make it politic for me to do so.[1]

The spirit of the Greek nation, and its brave revolt against the Axis, were thus dismissed as trivial claims made by shadowy individuals. The sovereign was envisaging a triumphal return to his kingdom backed by his faithful troops. To find a viable praetorian guard, the king was going to have to dissolve the two brigades of the Greek Middle East army ten months later and rely on the support of two battalions which escaped the purge of monarchist elements. In the final analysis these two battalions would constitute practically the sole popular base of his regime; just enough to provide the British with a pretext for intervening. Churchill replied the same day.

Prime Minister to Foreign Secretary.

If substantial British forces take part in the liberation of Greece the King should go back with the Anglo-Greek army. This is much the more probable alternative. If however the Greeks are strong enough to drive out the Germans themselves we shall have a good deal less to say in the matter. It follows that the King should demand equal Royalist representation with the Republicans now proposed [*sic*]. In any case he would make a great mistake to agree in any way

[1] Churchill, op. cit., vol. V, pp. 473-4.

to remain outside Greece while the fighting for the liberation is going on and while conditions preclude the holding of a peaceful plebiscite.[1]

It seems that 'we' (the British and the monarchy) were on one side and the Greeks on the other. Churchill had no illusions about the popularity of the Glucksburg dynasty, but he did not allow any thoughts about the legitimacy of a 'sponsored monarchy' to blind him to its practical advantages.

An even more rousing example of British realism is provided by a telegram sent to Churchill by General Smuts a few days later:

There appears to be strong suspicion that British Intelligence agents who brought Greek Patriots and other party representatives to Cairo are anti-Royalist, and that the Patriot representatives even have communist leanings. . .

This suspicion, which was unproven to say the very least, was to cost Myers and Wallace more than a reprimand. No doubt they would have been thought more impartial if they had subscribed to the view of Greek reality that emerges from the rest of Smuts's message:

. . . A plebiscite or General Election on the regime immediately on the Allied occupation of Greece should be ruled out as likely to lead to civil strife, if not to civil war, in the existing bitterness of feeling. . . .

. . . King George and the Royal Family might well return to Greece to lend their moral support and authority to the Allied administration.

I very much fear that, in the inflamed conditions of public feeling, not only in Greece but also in other Balkan countries, chaos may ensue after the Allied occupation unless a strong hand is kept on the local situation. With politics let loose among those peoples we may have a wave of disorder and wholesale Communism set going all over those parts of Europe. . . .

. . . The Greek situation brings matters to a head, and you may now consider it proper to raise this matter with the President, as a very important question of future policy is involved. The Bolshevization of a broken and ruined Europe remains a definite possibility, to be guarded against by supply of food and work and interim Allied control.[2]

Confronted with attitudes of this sort, the delegates began to wonder why they had been invited to Cairo at all. Perhaps the initiative had come from the Staff, which was still clamouring for supplies to be sent to the guerillas in the Balkans; if so, the Foreign Office was not going to be too pleased about it. The time for supporting partisans was over; the task now was to restore order in their countries.

[1] Churchill, op. cit., vol. V, p. 474.   [2] Churchill, op. cit., vol. V, pp. 474–5.

In a round of talks with Roosevelt in Quebec, Churchill was still pressing for the Allied landing on the Greek mainland, or at least in the Dodecanese, which he hoped would influence events in his favour. Despite all their efforts on the terrain, Myers and Woodhouse had failed to produce representatives of any 'popular movement' that would fit in with British policy.

Much had been expected, no doubt, of Zervas's rallying to the monarchy, but the Mountain Napoleon's manoeuvre had been neutralized by his own passion for intrigue. Since Zervas had not thought fit to inform his own people of his action, his political representative Pyromaglou was more genuinely astonished than anyone else when the news broke. Pyromaglou was determined to maintain the republican platform of the initial EDES programme, and dashed British hopes by forming a common front with the EKKA delegate Kartalis and EAM.

Kartalis and Pyromaglou were able to take a step which EAM had been considering for some time, but which would not have had the same chance of success from the hand of Tzimas, Rousos or Tsirimokos. They proposed the formation of a Government of National Union. With enormous zeal and energy they succeeded in convincing almost all the Cairo ministers who professed republican opinions.

On 19 August eight of these ministers sent the Prime Minister a memo formally announcing that they were 'against the king returning to Greece until such time as the people had chosen the new regime's constitutional form'. Only Tsouderos still hesitated. Faced with this development the king, who had a highly personal idea of 'National Union', withdrew to the Lebanon with a diplomatic illness.

The delegation had far better relations with the British military than the Foreign Office would have wished. A few days after their frigid audience with the king, the Mountain delegates were received by senior British officers responsible for logistics. Lord Glenconner and Colonel Templing were particularly friendly, and Tsirimokos's rendering of the andartes' epic was received with unrestrained enthusiasm. The next day General Wilson gave a private reception for them. The guests included a number of British politicians, and Tzimas took the opportunity to speak about ELAS.

'We would like to express our appreciation for the help you have given us so far. Our forces are capable of considerable further development; if you keep up your assistance, we will soon be 200,000. . . .'

There were various reactions in the audience. Wilson showed neither surprise nor disapproval, while the civilians awaited the rest of the speech with feverish interest.

'. . . We will then be strong enough to liberate ourselves. You will have no need to come to Greece, and will be able to bring all your forces to bear on other fronts to speed up the victory.'

The stenographer who had been recording the speech put down her pencil and stared at Tzimas as if he were a Martian. The faces around her registered not only astonishment but open hostility; it seemed that these pretensions to independence were found shocking and totally unacceptable.

Pyromaglou and Kartalis supported the EAM delegates. They echoed Tzimas's request for further aid and added that the conflicts between the different resistance organizations were a thing of the past.

Of the people present only Wilson's immediate entourage seemed to find the partisans' views reasonable, if not exactly desirable from the British point of view. But nobody made any promises.

While the National Government scheme was running its course, Tsouderos tried to defuse the bomb by inviting Pyromaglou and Kartalis to stay in Cairo and join the existing cabinet. Both men refused categorically. At about the same time, the EAM delegation managed to organize a secret meeting with Sallas and about ten officers belonging to ASO.

The British had told the king to return to Greece with 'his' army. The two Middle East brigades had decided that they were not going to be used as the spearhead of the old regime. But British agents were stepping up their provocations, looking for a pretext to disband the scattered army and replace it with a few battalions of extras. This was the first time that Sallas and ASO had been in contact with the EAM leadership. Everyone agreed that the situation called for extreme caution and vigilance.

'The only policy worth pursuing,' Tzimas said, 'is one that will ensure the army's return to Greece. Anything else will just be extremism.'

When they separated Tsirimokos urged: 'Even if they hold a knife to your throat, don't give way.'

Everyone was in agreement on this point, but within a few months the pressure of events would be overturning all these fine stoical resolutions and making 'extremism' inevitable.

The British were getting worried about the delegation's comings and goings about Cairo and the success of its first political contacts. In the late afternoon of 22 August, British liaison agents combed the still-sweltering town looking for the delegates and winkling them out one by one. They were invited – perhaps summoned would be a better word – to see Casey, His Gracious Majesty's Minister in the Middle East, the same evening.

In the Minister's office the delegation found itself facing a semi-circle of impassive soldiers and civilians, including Myers and Wallace. The Minister broke the silence with a short, dry announcement: 'Your presence here has confronted us with problems which we have not found easy to solve. It is not desirable for you to stay here much longer.'

Just like that. Myers, who already knew that he would not be returning to Greece, was suddenly trembling like a leaf. He left the British semi-circle and instinctively crossed the room to stand beside the delegates. The Minister had no more to say and the meeting was over almost before it had started. The delegates were escorted back to their house by Colonel Templing and Francis Noel-Baker. They were given just enough time to pack their clothes before being hustled to the airport where an aircraft was awaiting them on the runway, its engines already warming up. At the very last minute, Tsirimokos asked to make a final telephone call. He managed to get through to Tsouderos and deliver an indignant tirade.

'. . . What's the Mountain going to think if we're simply slung out of Cairo?'

Tsouderos had himself been overtaken by events. He thought for a moment and then agreed to invite the Mountain representatives, who had been the guests of the British until then, to stay on in the name of the Greek government.

Colonel Templing, who had been so warm during the Logistics Staff reception, was tapping his foot with impatience as he waited for the delegation to board the aircraft. Tsirimokos simply handed him the receiver without a word. Tsouderos told him to bring his guests back to Cairo; white-faced, Templing complied. Two months later he committed suicide in his office. It is not completely far-fetched to suggest that this failure could have contributed to the pressures making his life intolerable.

For the rest of the delegation's time in Cairo the British were leaning heavily on Tsouderos, trying to stifle at birth any idea of forming a Government of National Union in Cairo. The delegation received news from home when Exindaris, an envoy from Athens, came to see Tzimas and found him with Kartalis and Pyromaglou.

'Why bother? We're trying to set up a Government of National Union in Athens with the men inside the country. You're wasting your time here.'

Tzimas reacted violently. He knew that the British would question the legitimacy of any government formed without the participation of the Cairo group, and that the announcement of any such government would give them their excuse to intervene. With this reaction, he showed his hand to Kartalis and Pyromaglou, who realized abruptly that they had been playing the EAM-ELAS game ever since they had arrived in Cairo.

Before returning to Greece, Tzimas was invited to tea by Colonel Stevenson. He had made the Englishman's acquaintance in the mountains and had used his influence to persuade ELAN (the naval branch of ELAS) to transport him to Cairo. Pyromaglou and Kartalis were also present round the teacups. Stevenson told them that he would soon be leaving for Greece and that a new British group was to be parachuted into the Peloponnese. He was in radio contact with Woodhouse, and recounted the latest rumours on Aris's excesses. Pressed by his host, Tzimas agreed to send Aris a message repeating his eternal appeals for moderation.

The tension between the different Resistance organizations was considerably increased after the Italian surrender on 8 September. The British wanted to share out the booty in accordance with their own preferences, but Aris simply helped himself on the spot. Whatever truth there might be in the accusations against him, mention of Aris's name seemed to bring a breath of fresh mountain air to leaven the crushing torpor of Cairo.

The delegation boarded their plane back to Greece on 13 September, two weeks after being shown the door by the British. Myers did not accompany them. Woodhouse, who had stayed behind to keep an eye on Zervas, would be running the British Military Mission from now on. Churchill had instructed him not to extend guerilla activities any further, but simply to 'restrain all the partisans' political claims, both present and future'.

A new passenger disembarked at Neraida airstrip: Colonel Bakirjis, a Greek officer who was accompanying Kartalis back to Psarros's organization.

Italian Booty

New orders from Wilson now rained down on the British Mission in Greece. First and foremost, Woodhouse was instructed to use all the means at his disposal to stop any Italian arms from falling into ELAS hands.

On its return from Cairo the delegation found things a little changed at Neraida. A steadily increasing stream of Italian prisoners·was flowing into the ELAS prison camp which had been established a few kilometres away.

The Italian armistice, signed on 9 September 1943, had liberated officially whole regions in the interior of the country which as often as not had only been administered by the Italians in theory, since their forces could seldom leave the towns. In the period immediately following the armistice, the British were not alone in having a lot to do.

All the German forces in Greece were thrown into the effort to outrun the partisans in the race for Italian arms. In German service circles the Italian leadership had long been suspected not only of negligence but of actual treason. Wehrmacht reports referred to General Geloso, who commanded all Italian troops in Greece, as a 'dead man'. The Italian capitulation had been considered imminent for several months, and the Germans were not entirely unprepared for it. It had given rise to the 'Axis plan', under which German troops marched into Italy, occupied Milan, Turin, Bologna and Rome, and launched an organized repression of all manifestations of anti-fascist sentiment. In Greece, the object of the Axis plan was to replace the Italian Eleventh Army and make sure that it was relieved before being taken apart by the partisans.

The Italian units on Crete were disarmed without a shot being fired. On Rhodes, the support of a British destroyer and a small Allied commando succeeded in getting a modest resistance under way, but on 12 September the 40,000 Italians on the island surrendered to a force of 5,000 much more combative Germans. On Corfu, and especially on Cefalonia, the Italians defended themselves more energetically; strong measures were necessary and here, on 23 September, the German Commandant Hirschfeld opened the season with a resounding declaration to his troops: 'Hunters! The next twenty-four hours are yours.'

Four thousand Italian soldiers were shot.

A rumour spread that the Germans had been tipping whole truckloads of prisoners into the Corinth canal, where the railway bridge crosses the narrow vertical incision between the Peloponnese and mainland Greece at a height of nearly a thousand feet.

Throughout Thessaly, Roumeli and Macedonia ELAS was everywhere, secure in its control over the pockets left vacant by the armistice. Caught between two fires, hounded from pillar to post by the Germans on one side and the andartes on the other, the Italians were surrendering to the first comer. Despite the bitter aftermath of the recent fighting and reprisals, the many deserters often received a generous welcome from the populace. They would arrive in the villages bearing weighty gifts: their weapons, which whether given or sold or captured flowed to the andartes like the stock of some fantastic jumble sale for redistribution. Whole units surrendered directly to ELAS. Woodhouse had been instructed to prevent this happening at all costs, but found himself completely overtaken by events.

The people of Volos, the 'reddest' town in Greece, heard the news of the Italian surrender on the radio on the night of 8–9 September. There was an immediate, open, door-to-door mobilization of EAM. At daybreak a delegation of notables besieged the Italian commandant's office. They called on the commandant to pass over to the Allied side with all his troops, to release everyone who had been imprisoned for belonging to the Resistance, and to prepare to fight the Germans beside the andartes. While these matters were being discussed the garrison troops spread through the town and began fraternizing with the population, without waiting for a decision from headquarters.

For reasons connected with honour the Italian commandant was reluctant to surrender to civilians, and he expressed a wish to talk to a senior officer. There was no senior officer in the local ELAS, but there lived somewhere in the neighbourhood an old retired general whose advanced age had prevented him from joining the Mountain. He was mobilized immediately and proudly presented himself to the Italian commandant as regional head of the andartes.

The soldiers became impatient waiting for all these subtleties to sort themselves out and began leaving town for the wilds of Peliou, laden down with rifles and machine-guns. At the same time, civilians were emptying the dumps and magazines of Volos and sending the booty into the mountains on long caravans of overloaded mules.

The headquarters of the Pinerolo Division were in the town of Trikkala. General Infante and his staff could feel the partisans closing in and did not know which way to jump. They decided that it would be prudent to risk some overture to the andartes.

'We are ready to negotiate our entry into Allied ranks with representatives of the Mountain accompanied by their British advisers.'

Although it called for involvement by the British Mission, this proposal did not suit Woodhouse at all. General Infante was in ELAS-controlled territory and the orders from Cairo were quite clear: nothing for ELAS. But there was nothing he could do and the negotiations went ahead. General Infante took his whole staff to meet the Mountain's representatives in the village of Sotiria.

The Resistance was represented by Aris, who had no intention of leaving this windfall to the British, by the heads of ELAS First Division, and by Lt-Colonel Hills (suspected by Woodhouse of pro-communist leanings). The talks took place in a holiday atmosphere. Infante's small escort was fêted by the villagers, while news of the negotiations spread through Trikkala. The population was seized with impatience; despite the fact that the Italians still occupied all the strategic points, truckloads of ELAS men began arriving in the town and marching through the streets behind their flags. Yesterday's enemies mingled with the crowds, lining the pavements and joining in the cheering.

The Germans, meanwhile, were hurrying towards Trikkala at a forced march: several armoured units supported by an SS regiment. Though halted several times by the constant ELAS harassment, the Germans managed to recapture the towns of Kalabaka and Karditsa. Their advance was finally brought to a halt on the road between Kalabaka and Trikkala.

General Infante had to decide very quickly which side he was on, unless he wanted to get chewed up between the twin jaws of ELAS and the Germans. The treaty was signed on 13 September. Sarafis and Raftopoulos ratified it for ELAS. Chris Woodhouse, who had arrived while the talks were in progress, nervously initialled the document on behalf of the British Mission, and had this clause added to it: 'The Italians will be employed in separate units for an initial period, but the Division will be reconstituted in the near future and given the job of controlling part of Thessaly.'

Could Woodhouse really have believed that a Division whose only interest was to get out of the line of fire would be able to fulfil such a mission even for one day? For the moment, the main problem was to reinforce the barrier which was holding up the German column at Porta.

Porta is a narrow pass dominating access to the wilds of Thessaly. The Germans were facing two vast perpendicular slabs of grey stone swarming with andartes. For a time, the partisans had considerable difficulty holding their positions under a hellish bombardment, but the tide of battle was turned by the arrival of some 105mm guns surrendered to ELAS units (not altogether willingly) by the Aosta Italian cavalry regiment. The ss regiment gave ground under the sudden artillery fire, and presently withdrew for good.

The loan of units from the Pinerolo Division was by no means the decisive factor in this battle. The soldiers who had been allowed to retain their arms under the agreement had no experience of maquis fighting and, as a logical extension of their change of allegiance, were more interested in their own safety than in anything else. Carrying this logic even further, a large number of them simply nominated themselves prisoners of war, handed their arms over to ELAS and allowed themselves to be sent off to the camp at Neraida. Woodhouse was furious.

On 13 September 1943, the Dakota bringing the rejected Cairo mission back to Greece jolted to a stop at the end of the sun-baked Neraida airstrip. The six Resistance delegates had managed to form a united Mountain front to deal with the manoeuvres of Tsouderos and the British; now they returned home to find the guerilla forces in tatters and the Resistance divided. National unity had come to nothing between the Mountain and the Middle East politicians; now the unity of the Mountain itself was being threatened to an unprecedented degree by the scramble for Italian booty and the prospect of Allied intervention on Greek soil.

Pyromaglou went to see Aris as soon as the aircraft landed. The ELAS chieftain had helped himself to most of the Italian arms and was clashing with EDES detachments almost daily; tension had reached breaking point. Aris was not gentle with rivals in the field as a rule, and he could strike ruthlessly when pressed, but he had always understood the consequences of a split in the Mountain forces. He confided his anxieties about the worsening situation to the political representative of his main rival: 'We have to avoid fighting among ourselves at all costs. But Zervas is looking for trouble; he's playing his own game and won't align himself against the king. The Resistance can only unite on a republican basis.'

Pyromaglou had learned a good deal in Cairo, and he was determined to do everything in his power to prevent EDES from becoming a tool of British policy.

'I'll make it my business to get him to think again.'

The partisans still regarded Aris as undisputed leader of the Mountain. If he managed to reach an agreement with Zervas, the whole organization would go along with it – or so he hoped.

'Tell Zervas I'm ready to meet him in a small village. We'll talk in public. If he comes out against the monarchy, we'll have our agreement.'

Pyromaglou promised an answer within a week and left Neraida to join Zervas.

Churchill now had his pretext for forcing the Allies' hand over the Corfu landing: the Italians and Germans on the island were at each other's throats, and only a prompt intervention could save the Italians from a massacre.

Woodhouse was ordered to support this operation by attacking the German garrison at Larisa and destroying the town's airstrip. Because Woodhouse wanted to demonstrate as soon as possible that the Pinerolo Division was now under the sole authority of the British Mission, he asked General Infante to supply the troops.

Despite the Italian's severe doubts about his men's fighting spirit, the commando was formed and marched on Larisa airstrip. The operation was a total fiasco. The unit disintegrated during the first skirmish, abandoning all the demolition equipment entrusted to it by the British.

For reasons which were worked out by Churchill and Stalin at Teheran, and which went far beyond the Greek theatre of operations, the Corfu landing would never take place.

Woodhouse became very uneasy about the Pinerolo Division's lack of combativity; the Division was in an advanced state of decay and clearly more inclined to hand over its weapons to ELAS than to distinguish itself in battle. He tried to get the unit transferred to Epirus. If it disintegrated there its armament would go to Zervas, who would not fail to use it to extend his hegemony over ELAS's neighbouring territories.

It was at about this moment in time that the ELAS Central Committee began to adopt a hard line. Two courses remained open after the setback of the Cairo meetings. One was to unify the Mountain and continue the work begun in the Middle East by facing the political manoeuvres of the British with a common Resistance front. The meeting Pyromaglou was trying to arrange between Zervas and Aris could well lead in this direction. The other possibility was to assume that the liberation was imminent, meet the intransigence of Zervas and the British with an equally grim stubbornness, and open the power struggle by monopolizing the Resistance. It was this second course that began to prevail in the Central Committee from October onward.

On 15 October, following directives from Athens, ELAS High Command decided that Aris's proposed meeting with Zervas was no longer necessary and that ELAS would seize the Pinerolo Division's armament.

ELAS grouped the whole of its First Division round Porta, where the difficult battle with the Germans had taken place a few weeks earlier, and mobilized all the region's reserves. A grey mist obscured the mountainside and its vineyards. Sounds were deadened by the rain which had been falling since the previous day. By the time the Italians realized that they were being surrounded the trap had closed on them. They were ordered to lay down their arms. The troops did not plead to be allowed to keep their weapons; they had been hoping secretly that this would happen, and their relieved behaviour showed it. The operation lasted about two hours. A few isolated companies, and the Aosta Cavalry Regiment, resisted as a matter of principle for part of the morning. ELAS had captured modern arms and equipment which confirmed it in its broad superiority, but it had declared war on the British Mission and Zervas.

The British were not slow to react. They stopped all further assistance to ELAS and ceased in practice to maintain the Italian prisoners. A few months later, this horde would be forced to leave the Neraida camp to escape the Germans' major winter offensive. In the mountains, despite all the efforts of ELAS and the population, the Italians would find themselves in a dramatic and far from pleasant situation.

ELAS Taken in Hand

The hardening of the EAM-ELAS line brought the Central Committee's centre of gravity a little closer to the Mountain. Six months after Tzimas's last, vain effort to persuade them to do it, Siantos and Ioannidis decided to leave Athens.

If the Central Committee had moved in April, the KKE might have gained a new face to harmonize with the guerilla and the liberation struggle; the arrival in the maquis of the Old Man and his *éminence grise* at the beginning of the autumn was not destined to have quite the same effect. The decisive political battle was now imminent, but the Central Committee was not turning to the Mountain for strength; on the contrary, it had come to take the guerilla in hand and restore it to orthodoxy. Getting Aris and the other kapetanios to march in step was going to be part of the programme.

One of the last English supply drops to ELAS took place near Mavro-lithari in the Roumeli mountains, in Aris's district. Several kapetanios were present. The normal system was for them to share out the equipment on their own authority. Nikiforos, Diamantis, Orestis and Bellis were prominent partisan leaders and their authority counted for something all over the country. The containers were opened eagerly. One of them contained brand new battledress uniforms. There was an immediate, unanimous decision to give these uniforms to Aris's men, the Resistance's elite unit and most prestigious force. The Black Bonnets wore their new gear the same evening.

The influence of the kapetanios could no longer be allowed to eclipse that of the Central Committee. The task of restoring the proper scale of values fell to Maniatis, political commissar of Roumeli. The next day he sent a certain Lefterias to see the kapetanios. Lefterias had instructions to recover the uniforms and send them to the Roumelian Committee, whose sole right it was to decide what would be done with them. On the surface this was a trivial matter concerning nothing more important than a few smart uniforms; but Aris was forced to strip his men after they had worn the uniforms in public. The affront was not only to Aris and his men, but to the whole of ELAS, whose loyalty to its own was legendary.

Aris never argued about orders. He obeyed without turning a hair and his men changed back into their discarded rags. But the kapetanios could feel that there was more to the affair than a simple story of warrior finery, and their mood became resentful. When the uniforms had been handed over, Aris left for the village, accompanied by Tzavelas. Straw chairs, of the type which seems to spring up everywhere in Greece, under trees, on the quayside, in the streets, were arranged in front of the open-fronted building in the square which served as shop, post office and cafe. Aris had not unclenched his teeth all the way. He chose a table, wedged himself into one of the chairs and turned a frozen profile to Tzavelas.

The smooth, dry ouzo did nothing to soften or animate his expression. He drank ten glasses in a row. The flask was empty. Tzavelas stared at the horizon; the alcohol was doing its work and he felt an irresistible impulse to cry. He stole a glance at Aris; he had not stirred or spoken, but his cheeks and beard were wet with tears. Something intolerable was happening. Tzavelas got up and went to fetch Orestis.

Orestis had never had a flexible attitude towards political commissars: putting it simply, he contested their authority over his troops. His personality would later be the subject of much argument. What is certain, though, is that if at this time Orestis was a bad communist, he was an equally good kapetanios; there is nothing incompatible in that. The sight of Aris's face still bearing traces of tears brought on an outburst of his notoriously un-militant temperament.

'Aris. We'll all go and countermand the order. You won't give up a single button.'

Aris said nothing. Faced with the choice between the arrogantly-administered discipline of bureaucrats and a new act of indiscipline, he had already chosen to receive the spanking in silence. Orestis went on: 'You know Ioannidis? What faith do you have in his thought, his feelings?'

'None.'

'You know Siantos. Do you trust him?'

'Leave me alone.'

'Listen,' Orestis said, 'Kutvist domination of the Party is ancient history. That was before ELAS. It's the Old Testament. Now we kapetanios are taking over.'

Aris stared at him. 'You're crazy.'

'Not at all. Here's what we're going to do; if you agree the others will follow. We send for the heads of the Central Committee. If they come, we close in and get them to agree to everything in writing. We must have kapetanios in the Central Committee, that'll be the first point. Later on we'll arrange things so that the Central Committee can't take any tactical decisions without consulting ELAS.'

The example of Yugoslavia shows that there was nothing delirious about these proposals. In Greece, however, ELAS was doomed to remain a gigantic excrescence of the Communist Party, whose leaders refused to see it as the base for a new doctrine tailored to the local historical conditions. It is conceivable that at this time, the end of 1943, Aris, backed by men of Karageorgis's calibre, might have been able to command enough power and popular support to bring about the mutation, but he was inhibited by a terrible complication: he had signed a Metaxas confession. He had disobeyed orders once and did not want to repeat the experience. Now he obeyed and went on obeying, against the whole direction of his struggle.

'The Party will never go along with it.'

'Who needs the Party's blessing?' Orestis was virtually proposing a coup d'état. 'They're bound to turn up and then we can do what we like with them.'

Some expression returned to Aris's voice: 'What am I to do now that you've told me all this? Kill you? We've sworn on the cross that we're brothers. Report you to the Party? I can't do that either.'

'Listen,' Orestis replied, 'you know what I'll do if you carry on like that? I'm going to go round telling everyone that it's you who suggested everything I've just said – I know you agree with it in your heart. They'll believe me because I never signed, and they'll tell me to kill you. I'll refuse and the others will follow.'

Aris stood up suddenly, overturning his chair.

'Don't talk about my confession.'

'It's time you got over that business. Nobody gives a damn for your confession round here. Nobody even knows the person who signed; he was called Thanasis Klaras. Here they only know Aris. It was the same with Karaiskakis, he gave way under Ali Pasha and became an Independence hero anyway.'

'Shut up or I'll kill you.'

Orestis left. He knew that Aris would not do anything to free ELAS from the millstone of the Central Committee. He still wanted to accomplish a last rebellious act, and went to see Lefterias.

'Why were Aris's men stripped of their uniforms?'

'It was a Party decision,' murmured the commissar.

'And we don't belong to the Party? The uniforms are to be given back to Aris. Go and tell your boss Maniatis it's what the kapetanios have decided.'

Aris got the uniforms back. It was the nearest the kapetanios ever came to a coup d'état.

Escalation

The wave of operations undertaken by the Germans after the fall of Italy soon extended to every part of Greece, and the reprisals began. One or more villages were martyred every day. There were hundreds of Oradours in Greece. In Epirus and the western part of Roumeli matters were complicated still further for ELAS by the conflict with EDES, but the extra burden was unavoidable because both sides had decided to act. Zervas, supported by the British, was trying to hinder the development of ELAS; the EAM Central Committee had to reestablish its power base after the insult it had suffered in Cairo. There was no shortage of pretexts.

On 4 October, a delegation led by the mayor of Yannina under the auspices of Archbishop Spiridon appeared at Zervas's headquarters. The Germans had proposed a meeting to arrange an armistice and an exchange of prisoners; what they really wanted was to rescue Goering's nephew whom they believed to be held captive by EDES (in fact he had been killed in battle some days earlier). A British officer was present at all the discussions and sent to Cairo for a directive. The answer was quite clear: No contact with the Germans but stop the sabotage if you want and if you think that it will bring the reprisals to an end.

After leaving Zervas the delegation met the leaders of ELAS Fifth Division at Agnanda on the Yannina road. The Eighth Division sent the following report to Aris's HQ after the meeting:

The Yannina delegation assures us that EDES has agreed to cease fire until the 14th of this month or until further orders from unified HQ. We are provisionally accepting this armistice in the same spirit.

[Recent] acts of violence and destruction were described to us in the most sombre terms. There are more than 80,000 people without shelter in the region.

Herr Vickel, sector representative of the Red Cross, who arrived twenty-four hours after the others, believes that it will be impossible to keep the population alive without massive contributions from his organization, as the occupying forces have burnt the crops . . . Vickel is afraid that the Germans will refuse the necessary authorizations unless some concessions are made. . . .

EDES will be prepared to make the following conditions:

1. Preliminary release of hostages.
2. Stopping all executions of civilians.
3. Recognition of EDES and ELAS troops as regular soldiers.

We urge you to send us your orders before the 14th, on which date a meeting is expected with a German representative.

P. NASIS[1]

In asserting that Zervas and the British Mission had agreed to this meeting, the Yannina delegation was abusing ELAS's trust. Taking the message at its word, ELAS headquarters forbade all further contact and accused Zervas of treason. At about the same time the guerilla-priest Papakoumbouras, an intimate friend of Aris, fell into the hands of Zervas's lieutenant Houtas.

Papakoumbouras ('the blunderbuss priest') was an imposing, hirsute figure. His chest bore a confusion of bandoliers and crucifixes. He travelled the mountains on horseback, a rifle on his shoulder and a cutlass

---

[1] Quoted by Loverdo, op. cit., p. 226.

in his belt, preaching God and the Revolution. Another priest, Paparis-
tides from the village of Stroumi, an equally close friend of Aris's, enjoyed
immense authority over the partisans. The men feared and respected
these priests as much for their prowess as guerilla leaders as for their
spiritual qualities.

ELAS men behaved like missionaries in the villages that they passed through. On
Saints' days they would march to church in formation, and those with good
voices such as the kapetanios Orion sang hymns and praised God. Anyone who
did not sing loudly enough would be called to order with a frown, which would
soon set him shouting to make the ikons tremble. Out of church, the andartes
bought their food without haggling, so that the villagers began to wonder whether
these communists were really as bad as their reputation suggested.[1]

The image of communism in the mountains was composed of various
elements: the peasant guerilla, self-administration in the villages, people's
justice, decentralization, the national resistance tradition, bearded klephts
and, occasionally, priests. The unorthodox nature of this image by comparison with the Stalinist ideal does not make it any less profoundly
revolutionary. Its driving force was derived from a peasant reality which
had remained largely untouched by industrial upheavals, and which
recoiled spontaneously from the centralism and quasi-industrial organization of the orthodox Revolution. The meeting of communism and the
Greek Resistance was the local synthesis of a revolution in progress.
Certain members of the Central Committee could only see it as a misunderstanding; although the relationship had been useful over part of the
course, these individuals were prepared to renounce it at the decisive
moment to preserve an abstraction.

No such doubt clouded the minds of Zervas's men. As far as they were
concerned 'the blunderbuss priest' was a Red through and through.
Following a minor skirmish in the Metsovo region, where Papakoumbouras was trying to organize a meeting between Houtas and Aris, the
priest became suspect of the very murkiest kind of treachery and was shot
by Houtas's men 'while trying to escape'. The ELAS kapetanios Orfeas
was captured in the same incident. It signalled the end of the closed season
and the start of the hunt.

ELAS–HQ
Operational order to 8th Division:
We have just learned from Metsovo that one of our sections has been attacked
by EDES.

[1] Loverdo, op. cit., p. 227.

Confront this hostile action without mercy. The 9th and 10th Dviisions are
to send their spare units to the appropriate sector so that the area can be cleared
once and for all. Coordinate your activity with theirs. Orfeas's fate remains
unknown to us.

9 October 1943, 21.35 hrs.

ARIS–SAMARINIOTIS[1]

Myers's unified headquarters was a very long way from realization and
the united front formed in Cairo had run its course. The order really
originated from higher up. It was an expression of the Central Committee's new hard line. On his arrival at Karpenisi, Siantos had sent a
dispatch to Tzimas (Samariniotis):

'LET ARIS LOOSE ON ZERVAS.'

Pyromaglou's proposal of a meeting between Zervas and Aris would
receive no reply. Everything was ready to supply the British a year later
with the best possible excuse for armed intervention: a civil war. Despite
various setbacks the British Mission had done its job well.

ELAS Eighth Division cleared the Metsovo region as ordered. The
Thirteenth Division disbanded the EDES units in Roumeli and Valtos and
crossed the river Acheloös. The Germans were carrying out an offensive
in the region at the same time. In the last week in October an EDES detachment commanded by Pyromaglou was engaged by ELAS. The skirmish
had been going on for several hours when Pyromaglou learned that the
Germans had arrived in the neighbourhood. Using a village telephone, he
tried to contact Aris, who was directing the ELAS operations against him.
He could not get through to the kapetanios but spoke to one of his men,
Koziakas: 'The Germans are here. Let's join forces.'

Koziakas did not want to understand anything.

'The Germans are our enemies, but you're our enemies too and you're
worse than they are.'

Months later, Pyromaglou met Aris in Plaka.

'Why,' he asked, 'did you not answer my letter at the end of September
giving Zervas's reply on the meeting we were trying to organize?'

Aris spoke bitterly: 'Because by then I had no power left. My decision
would not have conformed to the Central Committee's wishes.'

'And why wouldn't you speak to me when I tried to telephone you in
October?'

'Because you were right. I couldn't bring myself to admit that you
were right.'

[1] Quoted in Loverdo, op. cit., p. 228.

A major hurdle had been cleared. Pyromaglou was no more master of EDES than Aris was in a position to sway the Central Committee. He had organized an EDES congress for 15 October 1943 which was supposed to 'denounce Churchill's and Roosevelt's interference in Greek internal affairs', but it had never taken place. Zervas was by now openly the instrument of King George II and of the British.

Takeover

Inside EDES, the influence of Pyromaglou and the republican faction was being diluted by the arrival in Epirus of a trickle of hopeful monarchists and former collaborators hedging their bets. The anti-communist struggle waged by Zervas's troops was not far from being the mountain version of the activities of Prime Minister Rallis's security battalions in Athens. Although the security battalions had been under the supreme command of an SS general called Stroop since 13 October, Rallis let it be known in certain quarters that he was acting in cooperation with Cairo.

The EAM Central Committee wanted an explanation. 'Mr Rallis has mentioned in private a letter allegedly sent him by a British personality, which urges him to crush the EAM organization because it is communist and therefore pro-Russian. He also maintains that the British secret agents in Greece have been ordered to fight EAM and help the monarchist organizations, and that secret instructions from George of Glucksburg and the British Government oblige them to hunt down Greek partisans.'

Rallis, whose German secret service dossier described him as a 'British agent', had given the Germans every satisfaction after the March riots. Various Greek notables who were close to the Germans were not likely to hesitate to do the dirty work of the British in the struggle against ELAS.

The British themselves were playing an increasingly ambiguous game. The Military Mission had seconded Captain Don Stott, a New Zealander, to Psarros's organization, where he had played a heroic part in several sabotage operations. In December 1943 Stott was ordered to Athens on a secret mission. ELAS escorted him to the kapetanios Orestis, who controlled the Attica region.

Stott had arrived at the penultimate stage of his journey and was about to enter the capital. When he came to take his leave of Orestis he was wearing British uniform. Orestis, who was responsible for his safety, could not get over it.

'Why are you wearing that uniform? Even the stones are going to recognize you.'

'If I'm arrested, I intend to be treated as a prisoner of war.'

It might have been thought better to avoid being arrested, but this did not seem to be Stott's major concern. Orestis provided an escort led by a certain Marougas. It had entered the Filadelfia suburb when a German patrol came into sight round the corner. The partisans dived into the nearest ditch, leaving Stott standing calmly in the middle of the road.

'No worries. Stay out of sight and leave it to me,' he muttered to the lurking andartes, and strode off towards the Germans. After a short conversation with them, he was driven away in a car.

The New Zealander was bound for a mysterious rendezvous in the Swedish embassy, followed a few days later by another meeting in Klisthenous Street at the house of the mayor of Athens, Angelos Georgatos. Another British officer was present at both meetings, together with representatives of the security battalions, the Special Branch of Bourandas's police, General Grivas's organization and the secessionist Athenian wing of EDES which was collaborating openly but had never been disowned by Zervas. The Germans themselves were represented by a uniformed Gestapo officer. Neubacher, Hitler's special envoy to the Balkans, gives no names but mentions in his memoirs the proposals made by 'certain British officers present in Athens at the beginning of the winter of 1943':

This war should end in a common struggle by the Allies and the German forces against Bolshevism. This is not yet the official opinion of His Majesty's Government or of Middle East HQ in Cairo, but it is the view held by a number of important officers at Middle East HQ. These officers see clearly that communist infiltration is already a serious threat to the whole Mediterranean region, and they think that their point of view could soon become the official British attitude. It is regrettable that the communist partisans in Greece should still be receiving British support in the form of arms and money [in fact, ELAS had received no British aid since the end of October]; it may be possible to correct this state of things by sending arms to anti-communist groups by submarine. The Germans should give it some thought too! Are the Germans ready to hold official talks on this matter?[1]

The Germans were not sure how far the opinion of a few British officers could influence Middle East HQ, and made no specific response. Never-

---

[1] Hermann Neubacher, *Sonderauftrag Südost*, Göttingen, 1956, p. 204.

theless they provided their British contacts with a safe-conduct which enabled them to reach the small Lavrion camp without mishap; from there they embarked on a fishing boat for Cairo.

Meanwhile Orestis's man Marougas, who had been involved in the start of this outrageous manoeuvre as the leader of Stott's escort into Athens, had made his report. It was passed on to Sarafis, who dispatched a note to Cairo in his turn.

As a result of ELAS's denunciation, Don Stott was actually tried in front of a military tribunal, but according to Panayotis Rongakos, who was present at the trial, Stott was not only acquitted but warmly congratulated by his superiors. He was later to receive a decoration for his handling of a mission regarded as 'thankless'.

On 27 November 1943 Churchill, Stalin and Roosevelt converged on Teheran from different directions. The next day the Big Three began tidying up the map of the world with blue crayon. The fate of Poland was sealed on paper then and there. In that room every word was worth an army, and the future would show that the principal actors were not indulging themselves in idle speculation.

Churchill made one final attempt to persuade his Allies into landing in Greece. 'We ourselves,' he wrote in his Memoirs, 'had no ambitions in the Balkans. All we wanted was to nail thirty enemy divisions to the ground.' His persistence failed to convince his colleagues. The British effort was to be concentrated on the cross-channel Operation Overlord, which would be supported when the time came by another landing in the South of France.

So British troops were not going to admire the Acropolis that winter (1943–44). The decision prompted Arnold Toynbee to note realistically that 'unity between the left and right wings of the resistance no longer constitutes a moral and military imperative'. This opinion was shared by the Central Committees of EAM and the KKE, though for diametrically opposite reasons.

The military situation was, however, extremely serious at this time. The Germans had rushed into the enormous vacuum left by the Italian collapse and were pressing home their major offensive against the Resistance on all fronts. Despite enormous losses everywhere, the Mountain continued to fight steel with stone and men of stone. They remained impregnable. On the plains of the Peloponnese, where towns and villages were vulnerable to lightning raids and reprisals, the situation was more dramatic.

The village of Katafigi in the southern Peloponnese opened the season. The inhabitants were shut into the settlement's seventy houses. The flames of incendiary grenades licked at the walls. Human torches running from the furnace were picked off efficiently by lines of hunters. The whole population was burnt alive in the tangle of red-hot beams. The next day at Monodendri, near Sparta, 118 died in the name of the Reich's ghoulish concept of order. Fifty were shot at Andritsa, near Argos. On 8 December a big punitive expedition set out from Patras. Its objectives were Kalavryta, Chazeika and Roghous. The fifty-seven men of the village of Roghous were shut in the church. The priest Papachristos knew what was coming.

'My sons, we have arrived at the moment of truth. Kneel down.'

After praying, he stood up and turned to the German officer: 'You supporters of the New Order are worse than the Huns. Barbarians, dirty scum.'[1]

He was the first to die, bowled over by machine-gun bullets in the light of the doorway. Fifty-six others followed. In the other villages the men refused to enter the churches. Forty-five were shot like hares in the streets of Kerpini.

Kalavryta was the expedition's main target. The Reds had been running the town and Colonel Läger, who was in command of the massacre, was gifted like Nero with an aesthetic sense. On the evening of 13 December all the men over fourteen years of age were herded into the square and taken to a slope overlooking the town. Colonel Läger enjoyed his gothic spectacle from the vantage point of a nearby balcony. The town blazed at his feet. Covered by machine-guns, the inhabitants watched their houses burning for hour after hour. The town hall clock struck twelve as the building collapsed. There was a stir round the machine-guns; the Kalavrytans recognized that the execution was about to start. One of the men spat at Läger as he lurched past half-demented.

'Fire! Fire at will!'

A report from the Greek gendarmerie in Patras to the Security Department in Athens, dated 15 December 1943, includes the following:

... I have the honour to inform you that according to reliable sources the German forces operating in the Kalavryta region have taken the following measures:

1. Burnt the town of Kalavryta and massacred 550 to 650 persons including State civil servants, intellectuals and priests;

[1] Quoted in Loverdo, op. cit., p. 240.

2. Burnt the village of Skepasto after an intensive artillery bombardment. The number of victims of the bombardment and of executions is unknown;

3. Burnt the monasteries of Agia Laura and the Great Grotto and executed their monks;

4. Burnt the village of Kerpini and executed 69 persons;

5. Burnt the village of Roghous and executed 46 persons;

6. Burnt the villages of Kato Zachlorou and executed 20 to 30 persons;

7. Burnt 4 or 5 houses at Kato Vlassia and executed 5 persons.

The operations are continuing.

Commandant of Gendarmerie,
IOANNIS DARCALOS[1]

This reprisal operation alone claimed 1,101 victims. Elsewhere, in Epirus, in Roumeli, in Macedonia, in Thessaly, it was the same bloody story. The military results of the great German offensive were derisory, but the price paid by the population was truly frightful.

'During the next month of November and into December,' wrote John Mulgan, 'it seemed to me that villages were burning all over Greece . . .

. . . The real heroes of the Greek war of resistance were the common people of the hills. It was on them, with their bitter, uncomplaining endurance, that the German terror broke. They produced no traitors. We moved freely among them and were guided by them into German-held villages by night without fear. They never surrendered or compromised, and as a result the Germans kept five divisions guarding Greece all through the war.'[2]

Sometimes, as they had done in Kournovo seven months earlier, the condemned men would ignore the rifles aimed at them, join hands in a circle and tread out the dance of the klephtic women, singing the indestructible insolence of Greece in the face of the ultimate vain attempt to subjugate them by force.

> Fish do not live on land
> Nor flowers in the sand
> And Greeks can never live
> Without their freedom.

On his arrival in the mountains the Old Man – Siantos – automatically assumed the authority which had formerly devolved on Tzimas, and with it he took over the political management of ELAS.

Siantos joined Tzimas at ELAS headquarters in Kerasovo. He was

---

[1] Loverdo, op. cit., p. 247.

[2] John Mulgan, *Report on Experience*, London, 1947, pp. 97, 99–100.

accompanied by Hajimichalis, a member of the Political Bureau, who two years earlier had been reproaching Tzimas for 'over-estimating' the importance of the guerillas. The two Athenians were fascinated by what they had seen in the mountains, but at the same time they were made uneasy by it. The later arrival of Ioannidis did nothing to lessen this anxiety.

The very different approaches of Tzimas and Siantos meant that they were in conflict from the very first meeting. The Old Man announced his intention of stiffening political control over the guerilla, and murmured something about sending Aris away. Tzimas was horrified.

'Aris is a national figure,' he answered. 'Sack him and you damage the very soul of ELAS.'

Siantos let himself be convinced for the time being; Aris and the Black Bonnets stayed at headquarters. But it was obvious that it was only a matter of time before they would be sent away on duty. The established image of partisan struggle was being obliterated, and not so slowly either, by the KUTV graduates' takeover.

Tzimas himself was sent to Athens on an errand. On the way he stopped in the devastated town of Pertouli, whose houses had been burnt by the Germans. During a meeting the local cadres proposed that Italian prisoners should be employed in reconstruction work. Tzimas thought this an excellent idea. All the men present still regarded him as the political boss of ELAS, and he believed that he still possessed the authority to send a personal request to the kapetanios Pelopidas for fifteen prisoners to be used on building work. He continued his journey and had reached Karpenisi when Siantos's messenger caught up with him. The Old Man wanted him back in Kerasovo, but not because he needed his help. Siantos complained about the project of using Italian prisoners on village reconstruction.

'We have other things to worry about. We have 10,000 men to feed in the middle of the Pindus. This business about the Italians can wait.'

Over this matter of detail Tzimas was being given clearly to understand that he was no longer entitled to use his personal initiative. In the end, he did not go to Athens to plead the cause of the peasant guerilla; Siantos had found him another assignment.

The general hardening of the political situation had made Tempo's idea of creating a Balkan headquarters, which the EAM Central Committee had rejected in the spring, appear in a new and more attractive light. Tzimas was detailed to re-establish contact with Tito.

Thus on 11 December 1943 the legendary triumvirate of Aris, Sarafis and Samariniotis lost one of its members. Tzimas, whose role in the KKE's new armed base, ELAS, should have assured him of a seat in the Central Committee, gave up his place to the granite heavyweights from Athens. His mission was important, certainly, but it was taking him far from the principal centre of decisions, not for the first time.

A meeting was arranged with Tempo for 25 December in the town of Karajova in Macedonia. Balgaranov, an envoy from the Bulgarian leader Dimitrov, was supposed to be coming to the conference. After stalling for the whole of January, he failed to turn up at all.

Tito's position had been strengthened by the Teheran agreements. The British had failed to obtain their landing in the Balkans and were obliged to give up supporting Tito's only competitor Mihailović who was collaborating openly with the Germans. But the creation of a Balkan HQ might give Tito a leading role in south-eastern Europe, a possibility which was not to Stalin's taste. Dimitrov had undoubtedly been asked to keep out of the Karajova conference. This was the beginning of a long story which would not reach its climax until 1948.

After kicking his heels for a month Tzimas returned to ELAS HQ at Kerasovo for a few weeks. The atmosphere there was beginning to change noticeably. Political cadres were everywhere, setting the tone and counterbalancing the prestige of the kapetanios. At the end of the year it was being firmly suggested to new recruits that the wearing of beards was incompatible with the rules of socialist hygiene. And behind the military decor, beneath the popular imagery, a whole tradition of the Greek resistance was being brought remorselessly into question.

Pendulum

The British desire to lend Zervas their exclusive support was offset and sometimes counterbalanced by the imperatives of Allied military strategy, and this conflict was reflected in policies that varied with the circumstances. It now became important to keep all the German units stationed in Greece fully occupied, partly to lighten the burden on the Italian front and partly to prepare for the landing in the South of France.

Zervas had 5,000 men at his disposal, while active ELAS forces were estimated at 45,000 partisans; thus any serious military effort in Greece must rely heavily upon the Red maquis. Although Resistance unity 'no longer constituted a moral and military imperative', the embryonic civil war looked only too likely to result in the straightforward elimination of Zervas and his cohorts.

The British services, whose excessive support for Mihailović in Yugoslavia had in the end obliged them to renounce him, hoped to find a compromise solution in Greece. The General Staff was preparing Operation Noah's Ark, and wished to arrange a diversion at the time of the landing in the South of France. The military were pressing for a reconciliation for the last time.

American officers had been joining the former British Military Mission since the end of September, and it had grown into the Allied Military Mission. So complex were the problems facing the Mission and so urgent the need for a solution that the Gorgopotamos veteran Tom Barnes was rushed to Cairo with instructions to bring back an armistice proposal which would stand some chance of reunifying the tattered Resistance. At about the same time Eden paid Tsouderos a personal visit in Cairo seeking an interim solution. Since the king was not going to be able to return to Greece without raising enormous difficulties, Eden suggested the installation of a regent and proposed the Archbishop Primate of Greece, Damaskinos, for the job.

The one figure presented to us as above party rancour [Churchill wrote] was Damaskinos, Archbishop of Athens. While in Cairo Mr Eden had impressed on the King the advantages of a temporary Regency. . . . The King would not agree to a Regency and returned to London.[1]

There is something surprising in the king's very decisive response to this British proposal, but George II was not, in fact, acting without any protection: this time he had turned to Roosevelt, who had advised him to refuse any compromise. Leeper, British ambassador to the Cairo Government, cabled Churchill:

I feel I must express myself with some bluntness. The King of Greece is playing with fire. He is endangering not only the interests of the monarchy but those of his country by not realizing in time the rapid trend of events. . . .[2]

In fact, *everyone* was playing with fire, or rather waiting for someone else to start the conflagration so that there would be an excuse to interfere.

[1] Churchill, op. cit., vol. V, p. 476.   [2] Churchill, op. cit., vol. V, p. 477.

Roosevelt's clumsy advice to the king was probably intended to hamper Churchill's manoeuvres to plant his flag in Athens by any means. The Damaskinos regency would not be able to achieve unity in a newly-liberated Greece, but it would have enough paper authority to justify British intervention. It would be held in reserve, a booby-trapped Christmas gift, until the bloodstained beginning of the following year.

Meanwhile, appeals for unity were flooding in from all sides: from Eden, from Cordell Hull, from the Soviet Union and from the BBC, which even went so far as to hint that the security battalions might be on the wrong side. Seen from close quarters, the common front being displayed by the Allies was less than reassuring from the ELAS point of view; a Soviet ambassador, Novikov, arrived to present his credentials to the king of Greece at the end of December.

Tom Barnes had not been idle in Cairo and returned with a scheme designed to put an end to internal struggles. This was based on a proposal to divide Greece into zones of influence, with thirty per cent going to EDES and seventy per cent to ELAS. Although this division was disproportionately favourable to EDES, Zervas was not satisfied with it and even threatened to disband EDES if his pro-British virtues were not better rewarded. Nevertheless an armistice was signed between ELAS and EDES on 4 February, and a conference was planned to take place within a few weeks.

ELAS's relations with EKKA, on the other hand, had improved greatly since the delegation's return from Cairo. Kartalis and Bakirjis had not hesitated to protest over Papakoumbouras's murder, even sending a symbolic unit of Psarros's 5/42nd Regiment against EDES.

Colonel Bakirjis had assumed military leadership of EKKA as soon as he arrived from Cairo, while Kartalis had retained political control. Although Bakirjis was nicknamed the 'Red Colonel' by right-wing circles, the British regarded him as a reliable man. Like Sarafis months earlier he was discovering the reality of the Greek mountains, and gradually building up a mental picture of ELAS for which he had not been prepared at all. At this time he certainly enjoyed the simultaneous trust of ELAS, which knew all about his connections with the British services, and Cairo HQ, which was no less aware of his republican leanings.

Sweet-Escott, one of the heads of SOE, had always regarded him as a leftist and convinced anti-monarchist. But support for the opinions of Bakirjis and Kartalis was by no means unanimous among Psarros's men, any more than Pyromaglou's convictions found universal favour with the members of EDES. A conspiracy led by a certain Dedoussis contrived various incidents between EKKA and ELAS which ended in an embryonic but potentially explosive split within EKKA. On 28 February 1944 68 officers of the 5/42nd Regiment sent a memo to the Cairo government swearing allegiance to the king and renouncing EKKA's political line.

A week earlier, on the 21st, delegates of the three organizations met in the small hamlet of Plaka, beside the river Araxos in Epirus. A preliminary conference had taken place in Myrofyllo on 12 February. A blood-debt of some magnitude had accumulated over the last few months, and the time when Aris had been willing to offer Zervas military command of the unified Resistance was past. ELAS now intended to impose a Commander-in-Chief from its own ranks, which did not suit Zervas at all. Only the continued division of the Resistance could maintain him in his privileged position *vis-à-vis* the British.

Nothing had emerged from the first meeting at Myrofyllo, and the same delegates came to Plaka: Sarafis, P. Rousos and Babis Klaras (Aris's brother) for ELAS; Pyromaglou, Nikolopoulos and Vergotis for EDES; Kartalis, Psarros and S. Doukas for EKKA. Doukas was one of the signatories of the memorandum swearing allegiance to the king.

In a small riverside hamlet still in the iron grip of winter, the players sat down for the last hand in the unity game. The stakes were very high. Behind the immediate issue of establishing agreement between the different guerilla movements, the faint outlines of a Mountain-inspired Government of National Union could be discerned in the background.

Kartalis and Pyromaglou, Cairo still fresh in their memories, were well aware of the odds. But ELAS's numerical strength gave it an arrogance that could easily infect its allies. Zervas had personal ambitions, the EKKA dissidents had no wish to achieve unity, and the EAM man Rousos was intractable from the first. The immediate past had left a heavy burden of rancour, and it would not take much to make any one of them dig his heels in and refuse to move from his point of departure.

A tortuous dialogue began on the terms and conditions of the reorganization. ELAS wanted to achieve close integration on all levels, Kartalis was thinking in regimental terms, and EDES based its haggling on whole areas of Epirus and central Greece. The weaker parties sought to avoid the dissolution of their units in the new army: EKKA was trying to preserve its regiment, while Zervas wanted to hang on to his territories. ELAS, on the other hand, had nothing to fear and could perfectly well afford to recognize the differing needs and anxieties of the groupings involved. But suspicion had become the rule, and the delegation hardened its position; the KKE had formulated its new hard line at the 10th Plenum in December, and Rousos would not give an inch.

Rousos was an Athenian, a doctrinaire. He was leader of the Mountain delegation. Tzimas had been sent to see Tito, and Sarafis had no freedom of manoeuvre whatsoever. The conference ground to a halt. In an atmosphere which had already become stifling, it moved on to another crucial item on the agenda: the nomination of a supreme commander. Everyone agreed on the name of an undisputed democratic personality, General Othonaios. But his nomination was a red herring; Othonaios was an old man, and the conference finally decided that he would not be up to the responsibility. The dialogue seemed fated to meander endlessly through the conditional when Woodhouse jerked it back to reality by proposing Bakirjis for the job. ELAS and EKKA were quick to agree; this time the opposition came from Pyromaglou. He was suspicious of the strange concurrence of ELAS and English support for Bakirjis. He favoured a form of collective leadership in which each organization would be represented in proportion with its numerical strength.

Every other subject was swamped by the general ill-will, especially the projected creation of a common political Commission. Some delegates seemed to have come to the conference only to prove how pointless it was, while others, like Rousos, wanted to impose arrogant conditions on it. Pyromaglou, who despite his opposition to Bakirjis regarded the Plaka conference as the last chance of saving the National Union, later discovered a document which helps to explain the rigid positions adopted by certain EDES delegates. This was a confidential telegram which Tom Barnes received from SOE during the conference:

178/9 RT 1 DD Cairo to Tom Barnes Personal:
1. We think ELAS will want an andartes army run from ELAS HQ. It will also try to obtain at all costs a coalition Government formed on Greek territory. See NP 111, 114, 115. Chris thinks, and we agree with him, that this would involve the integration of Zervas and Psarros into ELAS, and a reorganization of an andartes' unified HQ.
2. As we have already told Chris, this must not be allowed to happen. The treaty must be based on the division of the country into territories in accordance with the needs of Operation Noah's Ark. . . .
3. We are most anxious that you accompany Zervas's representatives to the conference and that you meet Chris there. We would like you to arrange things directly with him. It would be better not to show this telegram to Zervas before

the conference so that the business does not appear to have been settled in advance. Use it to help him formulate his demands, in such a way that he understands the need to hold certain cards for the negotiations. You must employ the utmost discretion in discussing these matters before the end of the conference.[1]

The British only wanted two things from the conference: to ensure Zervas's survival by prolonging the armistice, and to arrange for the tasks connected with Operation Noah's Ark to be carried out properly. Any other agreement that emerged from the conference would probably be against their interests. Woodhouse's covert manipulations, added to the opposition of the EKKA monarchists, the doctrinaire intransigence of the ELAS delegation and the smouldering memories of the recent fighting, torpedoed the Resistance's last opportunity of forming a National Union. No question this time of the Cairo clique trying to integrate itself into free Greece; what was happening was that the men of the Resistance were on the way to getting entangled once again in the Middle East spider's web.

The conference finally gave birth to a shapeless document which renewed the armistice agreement, condemned the collaborationist Athens government and made some provision for the coordination of Operation Noah's Ark. It was signed by the delegates of the three organizations. Woodhouse initialled it in a dual capacity, representing both the Allied Military Mission and the Greek Government in Cairo; this had at least the merit of clarifying the alignment of forces.

Aris took no part in the conference but paid a visit to Plaka before the end of the talks. He was photographed in a smiling group with Chris and Zervas. It's a picture and nothing more.

The KKE's tightrope-walking had placed the chief kapetanios in an impossible position once again. Superficially the Party's choice was a simple one: it could either wage an open class struggle or, subjugating political issues to the needs of the national liberation struggle in accordance with the statutes of EAM, seek working arrangements with all the resistance organizations.

Aris had left more than feathers on the stones of Epirus during his running battle with Zervas's men. For many partisans, the point of no return had been reached in the last months of 1943. But the attitude of the KKE Central Committee had set in an abstract position. Its hard new line was political rather than military. Doctrinaire models tend to lack flexi-

---

[1] Komninos Pyromaglou, *The Trojan Horse*, Athens, 1958, p. 216 (in Greek).

bility, and virtually all the Party cadres deemed it unnecessary to understand the Greek popular movement, which had been labelled 'petit-bourgeois'. Communist propaganda was out of favour, but its absence did not diminish the prevailing rigid distrust of everything not identifiable as an orthodox revolutionary force. The urban 'revolutionary elite' continued to be kept carefully apart from the Mountain.

Aris saw the Mountain as the wellspring and driving force of the Greek revolution; it was clear to him that political victory could only come from victory on the field, and that any ally against foreign interference was an ally of the Revolution. Ioannidis had now arrived in the mountains, and he was not there to broaden his education. He had come to put things in order and spread the true Word. The orthodox line had emerged from the Central Committee's 10th Plenum at the beginning of January:

... The merciless suppression of all agents of the enemy and of the Athens puppet government, and the isolation of those persons who are undermining National Unity, are the essential preconditions for the realization of our Party's political objectives.

Nobody was likely to disagree with this analysis. The trouble was that the interest which the political cadres were now showing in the Mountain was very far removed from the vision Tzimas had tried to conjure up for them a year earlier. For them ELAS was no more than a means to an end, an accidental phenomenon suitable for use as a lever to influence purely political events.

Two opposing tendencies were beginning to emerge on the level of the Party leadership. One side, led by Siantos, favoured a broadening of the EAM base to include the widest possible spectrum of opinion in accordance with the original statutes; the other, behind Ioannidis, was suspicious of 'provisional allies' of the Revolution and wanted to see a greater intransigence in negotiating agreements with them.

There was a third tendency: that of the combatants, of Aris himself. This was closer to the Yugoslav model, and held that the only way to ensure a definitive victory was to concentrate all available effort on the guerilla; that the 'politics' could wait until after the victory and would in any case be dictated by it in an organic way. But there were no Mountain men – not a single kapetanios – in key positions in the Party. ELAS remained a mere excrescence of the orthodox core. The proletarian panacea was being held in reserve for the final assault. It is certainly true that ELAS owed its development to the KKE, but there was a sort of imposture in the exercise of rigid authority by an ageing crew which refused to learn anything from the results of its own actions.

After the failure of the Plaka conference the EAM Central Committee gave up trying to establish a common platform with the other organizations. Backed by the power of ELAS and in a sense appropriating the success of the armed struggle, EAM set up its own provisional government on 18 April. It was called PEEA, the Political Committee for National Liberation. The committee provided an official framework for the administrative work being accomplished in the mountains, and was open to members from every part of the left. Its first version was led by Bakirjis in person. The colonel had now become a general and was on the point of following Sarafis's footsteps. EKKA was decomposing rapidly, and he was collaborating with ELAS while preparing to join it officially.

The Provisional Government reflected the composition of EAM, which was far from being exclusively communist. Influential members of the organization at this time included 6 bishops and a large number of priests, 30 university professors, 16 generals, 34 colonels and 1,500 other officers of the former Greek army. No mere kapetanios would ever be given a top executive job. After numerous sterile contacts with the traditional political organizations, PEEA announced its distribution of responsibilities on 11 March 1944.

Alexander Svolos, a democratic jurist and a professor at Athens University, took the Presidency. Bakirjis became Vice-President with responsibility for the Supply secretariat. Ilias Tsirimokos received the secretariat of Justice, George Siantos the Interior, Emmanuel Mandakas War, and two other Athens University professors, Angelos Angelopoulos and Petros Kokkalis, were made responsible for Finance and Hygiene respectively. Nikolos Askoutsis was Communications Secretary, Kostas Gavrilidis Secretary for Agriculture, and Stamatis Hajibeis, a socialist, Secretary for the National Economy. The first task of these men was the rationalization of the diverse 'Codes of Self-Administration and Popular Justice' which had sprung up in the Mountain since 1942.

Nothing had been done on the level of basic revolutionary reforms, such as the confiscation and redistribution of large estates, since Aris's visit to Athens a year earlier. He had been told on that occasion that he must not allow the battle for liberation to take on the appearance of a class struggle, and his bearded guerillas had stopped leaning on feudal elements. In any case landowners had for some time been displaced at the apex of the Greek governing class by the commercial and financial oligarchies.

Woodhouse himself describes the administrative achievements of EAM-ELAS in his memoirs:

Having acquired control of almost the whole country, except the principal communications used by the Germans, they had given it things it had never known before. Communications in the mountains, by wireless, courier, and telephone, have never been so good before or since; even motor roads were mended and used by EAM-ELAS. Their communications, including wireless, extended as far as Crete and Samos, where guerillas were already in the field. The benefits of civilization and culture trickled into the mountains for the first time. Schools, local government, law-courts and public utilities, which the war had ended, worked again. Theatres, factories, parliamentary assemblies began for the first time. . . . Followed at a distance by the minor organizations, EAM-ELAS set the pace in the creation of something that Governments of Greece had neglected: an organized state in the Greek mountains.[1]

EAM could do much better than that. At the beginning of April the movement organized an election, not just in the mountains but in the occupied towns as well. Militants carried it out by going from door to door. The operation had its risky side; if, as sometimes happened in Athens, the door was opened by a German officer, the mobile polling station would withdraw with an alacrity somewhat out of keeping with the dignity of its calling.

Despite these problems, however, EAM managed to collect the votes of more than a million Greeks, electing a hundred deputies to the 'National Resistance Council'. The Council met for the first time in the village of Koryschades in free Greece; sitting from 14 to 27 May, it adopted PEEA's decisions and confirmed it in its functions.

The news of PEEA's creation set a cat among Cairo's diplomatic pigeons. The British wanted any 'National Union' to be cooked up in the seraglio by the Tsouderos gang, and it was going to take one or two carefully organized provocations to enable them to contest the legitimacy of the rebel government.

The Second Mutiny

Before leaving Cairo Tsirimokos had left the leaders of ASO with the laconic order: 'Even if they hold a knife to your throat, don't give way.'

[1] Woodhouse, op. cit., pp. 146–7.

In the end it was the base that 'gave way'; times had changed since the previous year, when the British command had regarded ASO's demands to be allowed to go to war as 'honourable'. The Red Army's advance as far as Rumania, the growth of ELAS's power in the mountains, and the setting up of PEEA, unleashed a new wave of horseplay and reprisals. The pressure had been too great for all the counsels of prudence.

By 31 March 1944, the commanding officers of ASO-dominated units could no longer contain the movement. They presented Tsouderos with a petition signed by thousands of soldiers, sailors and officers, demanding his resignation and the formation of a Government of National Union. ASO delegates attempted to deposit a copy of the petition at the Soviet embassy; ambassador Novikov refused to see them.

Venizelos, who had been Navy Minister since the events of March 1943, now decided that the time was ripe for a personal intervention. He addressed the Greek population in a radio broadcast on 1 April, declaring himself in favour of unification. Tsouderos submitted his resignation to the king, at the same time recommending his Navy Minister as a suitable successor. Contacts were made with the British Labour Party. Francis Noel-Baker encouraged the movement. Meanwhile the British military authorities in Cairo started to act: a motorized column surrounded and disarmed the Fourth Regiment, stationed at Kassassin, and the same thing happened to the Artillery Regiment at Heliopolis. 280 militants were arrested and hurried under British guards to the camp beside the Pyramids.

Meetings and protest demonstrations came thick and fast in Cairo and Alexandria. On 4 April the Egyptian police went into action with British troops, arresting fifty union leaders and dockers. Next day, the unit attached to Greek HQ in the centre of Cairo was disarmed and the 'mutineers' sent to a prison camp. Feeling that things were going their way at last, the Metaxist officers tried to take the situation in hand, but ASO was ready for them. The republican soldiers and officers of the First Brigade, which was stationed just outside Alexandria, arrested their enemies and took over command. The movement spread to the Navy. The Metaxist officers on the destroyer *Pindos* were shut in the holds or thrown overboard. This rousing example was followed by the old cruiser *Averof* and three other vessels. The five ships elected a mixed committee of officers and sailors to take command decisions. A number of officers who supported the movement, but who were on shore leave when the action took place, rejoined their ships by launch under cover of night.

The horse-trading began the next day. A British delegation arrived to parley with the First Brigade insurgents. It undertook to send Greek troops to the front if the arrested officers were released. The officers were quickly freed, but HQ did not keep its promise and went on trying to disarm the Brigade. The knife was unmistakably at ASO's throat. Counsels of prudence somehow no longer seemed to apply to the situation.

We are keeping our arms: they are destined to liberate our country. We have consecrated them in blood in Albania, Macedonia, Crete and at El Alamein, and we will not give them up. Let the order be annulled and send us to the Italian front without delay.[1]

On the 6 April Churchill cabled Tsouderos:

I was much shocked to hear of your resignation, which seems to leave Greece forlorn at a moment of peril for her national life. The King, whom I have just seen, tells me that he has not accepted your resignation. He is coming out to Alexandria next week. Surely you can await his arrival.[2]

Another telegram in the same vein, announcing the refusal of Tsouderos's resignation and signed by Agnidis, Greek ambassador to London, escaped from the veils of diplomatic secrecy and on 7 April was circulating in the political circles of Cairo and Alexandria.

This was the ultimate provocation. Faced with the hardening of the British position, a large number of officers did a smart about-turn and withdrew from the movement. Leeper, the British ambassador in Cairo, simply did not see that the British were behind the provocation. He tried to delay the king's visit to Cairo, telegraphing the Foreign Office on the 7th:

What is happening here among the Greeks is nothing less than a revolution. . . .

. . . The King of Greece's return here at present would certainly provoke fresh trouble. Tsouderos and all his colleagues are strongly of this opinion. He would find himself isolated and unable to do anything, and would be a grave embarrassment to us. . . .

. . . In the circumstances in which we are living here at the moment the advice of people on the spot should, I submit, be accepted. My views are shared by everybody here.[3]

In fact, the Foreign Office was seizing the opportunity to disband the Greek Middle East Army. Its intention was to assemble a monarchist

[1] Loverdo, op. cit., p. 276.
[2] Churchill, op. cit., vol. V, p. 478.   [3] Churchill, op. cit., vol. V, p. 479.

militia from any reliable elements that could be salvaged. The king must enter Athens supported by 'his troops'; their numbers would be sufficiently reduced to justify the landing of a British unit or two. Churchill replied to Leeper the same day:

I have discussed the situation with the King. He is resolved to return to Cairo, leaving by air Sunday evening, and notwithstanding your telegram (which I have shown the King) I consider he is right to do so.

... You should inform M. Tsouderos that I count on him to remain at his post until the present crisis has found a lawful solution. ...

This is an occasion for you to show those qualities of imperturbability and command which are associated with the British Diplomatic Service.[1]

No Greek politician alive would be able to exercise much control over the immediate future. Churchill had taken over personally during Eden's absence. It would of course be left to the king to determine the 'lawful solution'. He was in no danger of being bewildered by subtleties on the English side.

The First Brigade was surrounded on 11 and 12 April. General Paget's orders were coming direct from Churchill. The Brigade's 4,500 men were completely cut off and their food and water supplies stopped. Churchill cabled on the 14th:

Surely you should let lack of supplies work its part both in the camp and in the harbour before resorting to firing[2]. ...

The mutinous ships were blockaded in the Bay of Alexandria. There were many arrests of civilians. The chief editor of the newspaper *Elin* was exiled to Abyssinia.

The Naval School was blockaded and deprived of water, and the situation there quickly became intolerable. Shock groups composed of women, and often supported by the Arab population, managed to approach the barricades from time to time and throw food over the barbed wire. But the heat and dust dried everything out and the men were in dire need of water.

There was a villa bordering the school's parade ground inhabited by a young Swiss schoolteacher. Giorgis Diamandaris, a leader of the Naval Revolutionary Committee, decided that he would seduce her. The enterprise was worse than hazardous; Diamandaris had no particular reputation as a seducer. He was so ugly that he had been nicknamed 'the

---

[1] Churchill, op. cit., vol. V, p. 479.
[2] Churchill, op. cit., vol. V, p. 482.

Widow'. Spurred on by the thought of his thirsty comrades, however, he invited the teacher out to dinner and took her dancing.

One way or another – either transfigured by his mission, bringing an unsuspected charm into operation or employing a particularly closely-reasoned dialectic – he managed to conquer the mutineers' fair neighbour. A hole was dug under the dividing wall, and the officer cadets were supplied with water through a garden hose for twenty days. The British were extremely puzzled by their endurance. In Alexandria harbour, small Egyptian fishing boats would change course abruptly to pass close to the isolated ships and pass supplies up to their crews.

The First Brigade was shrivelling rapidly in the heat of the desert. The Struggle Committee organized almost daily swoops on the area, and a few truckloads of supplies managed to penetrate the British blockade. The water problem was solved in the end by puncturing the 8th Army's main supply conduit, which passed nearby, and constructing a new branch. It would have been difficult after that to cut off their supply without inconveniencing the entire Eighth Army.

The king had arrived in Cairo on 13 April. Tsouderos offered his resignation again, and this time it was accepted. Venizelos was made Prime Minister without a cabinet. Like Tsouderos, he decided to call representatives of all the organizations in occupied Greece, including EAM, to the Middle East. Leeper proposed a new compromise solution. Churchill's reply was categorical:

Do not be influenced by possible anti-British sentiment among the local Greeks. It would be a great mistake to end this grave business up in a pleasant kiss all round. . . . We have got to get these men into our hands disarmed, without conditions, and I trust without bloodshed.[1]

The *Hephaestus*, one of the five mutinous ships of the Greek Navy, tugged gently at her moorings in Alexandria harbour. She was not a large vessel, but the thirty-nine torpedoes stacked in her holds were enough to blow up the entire Allied fleet anchored nearby. This fact worried the *Averof* committee, and they issued a statement designed to diminish the obvious danger: 'While we are well aware of the negative attitude being taken to our demands, we wish to make it clear that we do not intend to use our armament under any circumstances.'

The blockaded Greek units both in the camp and in the harbour were all holding out against privation and provocation. It was beginning to look

[1] Churchill, op. cit., vol. V, p. 483.

as if the authorities would have to compromise. The *Averof* was moored within a few cable's lengths of the *Hephaestus*; any serious attempt at armed resistance would not only be suicidal for the *Averof* but risk causing incalculable damage to the Allied fleet, a possibility which effectively disarmed the *Averof* committee. But Churchill was determined to drain the abscess. On 17 April he cabled the Naval C-in-C:

You should leave the senior member of the *Averof* in no doubt that his guarantee that the use of firearms will be avoided will not be reciprocated by us. We shall fire on mutineers whenever it is necessary. No officers or sailors of the Greek Navy have the slightest right to meddle in the formation of the new Government. Their duty is to obey the orders that they receive from the Greek Government recognized by the Great Allies.[1]

General Paget, whose troops were busy with the First Brigade, was also given very detailed instructions:

If you find it necessary to open fire on the mutineers' camp you should consider whether you might not start with a few ranging shots directed on their batteries which are aiming at you. If they make no reply, after an appropriate interval let them have a stiffer dose, and at the same time tell them the weight of fire which you are ready to direct on them if they persist. We are prepared to use the utmost force, but let us avoid slaughter if possible. It is proposed that the onus should lie to the account of the British rather than of the slender, tottering Greek Government.[2]

The final warning came on 23 April. Churchill told Venizelos that unless he brought the revolt under control British forces would open fire. That evening Admiral Voulgaris, Commander of the Greek Fleet, recruited a commando of two hundred reliable men. After issuing them with stokers' overalls and ordering them to smear their faces with grease, he embarked them in launches which sidled up to a British vessel.

Posing as a night shift of fitters, a group climbed openly on board the British ship while the rest flattened themselves in the bottom of the launch. The warm darkness covering the port was suddenly ripped apart by searchlight beams. Seconds later, Voulgaris's men opened fire on the mutinous ships with the British vessel's anti-aircraft guns. The rest of the commando boarded and occupied the two smallest units, the *Apostolis* and the *Saclitonis*, under cover of this fire.

The Struggle Committee had forbidden bloodshed, but twelve men were dead and thirty wounded. The searchlight beams illuminated the

[1] Churchill, op. cit., vol. V, p. 485.   [2] Churchill, op. cit., vol. V, p. 485.

sides of the *Hephaestus*, concealing her deadly load of torpedoes, lying immediately behind the *Averof*. If the cruiser fired back she might end up sinking everything in the harbour. The Struggle Committee handed over command of the Fleet to Voulgaris, and the Greek Navy uprising ended in the silent flashing of morse signals in the darkness.

When the First Brigade learned what had happened in the Alexandria roadstead, it decided to follow suit and lay down its arms. Within a few hours the troops were on their way to a concentration camp in the Libyan desert. Churchill had kept Roosevelt informed throughout the crisis, and Roosevelt had given him *carte blanche* to run things in his own way. The Soviets limited themselves to criticism:

We had also kept the Russians informed of these events, both by messages to Molotov and through the Soviet embassy in Cairo. The Soviet Government confined itself to criticism of our actions, and when on May 5 a formal request to Russia for cooperation in Greek affairs was made in Moscow the reply was that it would be improper to join in any public pronouncements on political matters in Greece.[1]

The censored British press maintained a total silence on these events from beginning to end.

The Greek Middle East Army was no more. Despite all EAM's warnings – even Chris Woodhouse admitted that EAM had had nothing to do with starting the mutiny – the anti-fascist organizations had been forced to revolt in the end. The British had got what they wanted; after the purge the king of Greece would have 'his army'. Most of the disarmed troops went to rot in British prison camps in Libya and later in the Sudan and Ethiopia. The first small groups began to trickle back into Greece at about the end of 1945.

A lucky handful managed to escape during their transfer to Abyssinia. They were crammed into the holds of an old French cargo ship, the *Trident*, which had never been converted for carrying troops. Conditions on board were appalling. The French crew began fraternizing with the Greeks and mutinied; although most of the ports were under British control, they managed to negotiate a safe landing after a protracted cruise.

Even before the mutiny the British had not found Venizelos's attitudes entirely to their taste. The imminent arrival of delegates from the organizations in Greece made a reshuffle a matter of some urgency, and Churchill at last believed that he had found the ideal candidate: George

[1] Churchill, op. cit., vol. V, p. 487.

Papandreou had landed at Cairo airport on 15 April, two days after the king and the day after Venizelos's investiture.

With the end of the mutiny [wrote Churchill] the question of the formation of a Greek Government became acute. It was not felt that Venizelos was suitable to this task, and the leader of the Greek Social Democratic Party, Papandreou, who had been specially brought out of Greece, took office on April 26.[1]

Three months spent in Averof jail at the beginning of 1942 gave Papandreou the aura of a resistant in the eyes of his Cairo colleagues. There was a short outline of his career and prospects in the files of the Athens Gestapo:

George Papandreou, 50, lawyer practising in the Peloponnese, deputy for the last fifteen years, twice Minister of State Education, democrat, opposed to the communists and the monarchy. . . . Should be regarded as the Statesman of the future.[2]

Papandreou always wore clothes that flapped around him as if they had been made for someone much fatter. He was tall and thin, with a nose like an eagle's beak and deep-set eyes under a high, bald forehead. A year earlier, when Tzimas and Sarafis had been trying to persuade him to join the Mountain, his parting words had been: 'Go on, I'll follow you.' By July of the same year, however, he had decided that it would be more expedient to send a statement to Middle East HQ – one which the British would be unlikely to misunderstand.

For the first time in History there is an absolute identification of Greek and British interests. . . .

. . . Today, a new antagonism is taking shape. Two world-wide ideologies are being born: Pan-Slavic Communism and Anglo-Saxon Liberalism. . . .

. . . In the next phase of World History every nation, even our present enemies after Italian Fascism and Hitlerian Pan-Germanism have been suppressed, will be natural allies of Anglo-Saxon Liberalism in its struggle against Pan-Slavic Communism. . . .

. . . Greece and Turkey are destined to be allies of the British, as they are the natural opponents of Pan-Slavic expansion in the Balkans and the natural sentinels of the gateway to the Mediterranean.[3]

He ended the manifesto with a suggestion that nationalist resistance groups be set up in Greece to counterbalance the power of EAM-ELAS. Republican or not, this Greek sounded like an oracle to the British.

---

[1] Churchill, op. cit., vol. V, p. 487.   [2] Quoted in Loverdo, op. cit., pp. 284-5.
[3] George Papandreou, *The Third War*, Athens, 1948, p. 16 (in Greek).

CATASTROPHE!

ELAS still held the real power in the Greek mountains. From the British point of view it was high time to drive the partisan movement into the last ditch and get the civil war rolling in earnest. EKKA would serve as the detonator; Psarros could not control the activities of the Dedoussis monarchist gang, and would soon lose his grip on the whole situation.

Bakirjis, Vice-President of PEEA, had always defended EKKA, but the organization's monarchist officers were determined to put an end to the idyll. It did not take much to poison relations between rival groups operating on neighbouring territories. Clashes were frequent and the Allied Mission was doing nothing to calm things down.

The situation was deteriorating rapidly. PEEA sent Psarros a threatening note ordering him to arrest the rebel officers and combine his forces with ELAS; at the same time Dedoussis, who had in all probability already secured his rear, proclaimed his intention to 'deliver his territory from the communists'.

While Psarros hesitated to disown his officer, Dedoussis was conspiring with a suspect figure called Kapetsonis to cause further mischief. He launched his men at the ELAS troops commanded by Nikiforos, arrested a hundred or so EAM cadres and undertook to clear the whole region. An ELAS leader called Varsos was killed in an engagement. Nikiforos counterattacked, the conflict spread, ELAS placed a price on Dedoussis's head. Psarros left Plaka to look for a compromise solution, while Dedoussis's hooliganism reached new heights.

Meanwhile, ELAS had sent Aris off to the Peloponnese to put things in order after the German winter offensive. While Aris's talents as a guerilla leader certainly suited him to this difficult task, it is also true that his removal from HQ following Tzimas's departure to Yugoslavia sealed the fate of ELAS's legendary triumvirate. His route to the Peloponnese took him through the Thebes region in southern Roumeli just as the battle with Dedoussis's forces was reaching its climax there. Aris was exasperated by the Central Committee's attitude. He was aware of the fate that History usually reserves for guerillas: 'If we win we'll be canonized. If we leave it be they'll call us murderers.'

He deployed two battalions of ELAS Fifth Brigade, a few units from the 36th Brigade and his own Black Bonnets. By 12 April, Easter Sunday, Psarros was completely surrounded. In response to ELAS's ultimatum he freed the hostages, returned the supplies captured by his men and arrested Kapetsonis, but he refused to hand Dedoussis over either through loyalty or because he was not in full control of the situation. ELAS replied that if Dedoussis was not tried before an andartes' assembly the 5/42nd Regiment would be disbanded by force. Psarros now made the ultimate concession: he agreed to integrate his beloved Regiment into ELAS, but added that he was still in no position to arrest his officer. It is not known whether this offer was passed on to Staff HQ and probably never will be. The next day, since Dedoussis had not been handed over, ELAS attacked.

Within a few hours the 5/42nd Regiment was just a memory. Dedoussis, Kapetsonis and most of the monarchist officers managed to break through the encirclement and were rescued by the Security Battalions operating in the Amfissa district. Psarros courageously refused to accompany them. He was alone when he surrendered, in the evening, to the kapetanios Nikiforos.

Nikiforos knew that feelings were running very high, and feared for Psarros's safety on the way to Aris. He entrusted him to a hand-picked escort and urged the leader to exercise the very greatest caution: 'Keep him out of sight and whisper in Colonel Rigos's ear that you've got Psarros and need his protection for him.'

Destiny now added its own absurd and dramatic flourish to the whole sinister episode. On the way to Aris's temporary HQ the escort met a small ELAS unit led by a certain Zoulas, who was still in a state of tension from the previous day's fighting. Zoulas recognized Psarros and, blinded with fury, covered him with insults. Psarros reacted angrily to an accusation of treachery that was flung at him. One of Zoulas's men fired a burst from his submachine-gun. Psarros fell, riddled with bullets.

At ELAS HQ, Siantos heard the news from Tsirimokos. The Old Man was paralyzed with horror.

'It's a catastrophe! A catastrophe!'

Kangaroo Court in the Lebanon

The conference which was now set up in Beirut had all the characteristics of a carefully-laid ambush. This was dimly apparent even to the British Labourites, and the *Observer* wrote, on 30 April 1944:

The suspicion is now being widely expressed that, notwithstanding his words a fortnight ago, the Greek King never really intended to bring the guerrillas into his Government; but rather to make it impossible for them to join it. . . .

In fact, since PEEA had been created and the kapetanios brought into line, it was no longer strictly accurate to talk about 'the guerillas' in this context. The left-wing delegation comprised seven members: Rousos for the KKE, Svolos, Angelopoulos and Askoutsis for PEEA, Porfyrogenis and Stratis for EAM, and Sarafis as military adviser. Whatever the political virtues of this group, with the exception of Sarafis it represented everything but the Mountain. The EAM septet seemed to sense the hungry wolf waiting for them, and were still hesitating at the very last minute.

Over the wireless [wrote Sarafis] we had heard that Papandreou had replaced Venizelos. We considered whether we ought to continue our journey or return to Viniani [PEEA headquarters], and we decided that if the planes came that day we would go, but that otherwise we would return and the journey would have to be cancelled.[1]

This was Russian roulette, no less. The players were out of luck, and the aircraft landed at the appointed hour.

The delegates had hardly set foot on Egyptian soil when Sarafis was summoned to British HQ in Cairo. Someone had remembered that he had once belonged to AAA and had had some contact with Papandreou; he was probably regarded as the most malleable of the delegates.

General Ballion, the Chief of Staff, was waiting for him with a number of other officers, including an American colonel called West. Sarafis was received with every sign of respect. He launched into an account of the National Liberation Army's needs in the context of Operation Noah's Ark and the general harassment of the occupation forces. They heard him out politely and then gave him to understand, with no less courtesy, that he was on the wrong tack altogether.

It seemed that Ballion and his colleages were thinking along totally different lines. Far from wanting to improve ELAS's effectiveness, their main concern was to dissolve it along with all the other guerilla organizations, the more easily to integrate them into the future regular army. Sarafis began to realize how very deluded the delegation had been in expecting any cooperation from the Allies. He warned his hosts that they were nourishing illusions themselves if they expected to dissolve ELAS round a conference table. But the British really seemed to expect a lot

[1] Sarafis, op. cit., p. 185.

from him. They wanted ELAS's 24th Regiment to evacuate the Preveza region and give it back to EDES. Sarafis's only reply was to telegraph the terms of the Allied request to the Cretan General Mandakas, his stand-in at the head of the Liberation Army.

Papandreou was sounding out the opposition before the Conference. When Sarafis came to see him he made it clear that he felt very little sympathy for ELAS, ending on a note of delicate inquiry: '. . . What's your attitude?'

Sarafis was not for sale. He answered stolidly: 'All the delegates who flew over with me are interested only in forming a Government of National Union.'

Pyromaglou had arrived with two other EDES delegates. He too passed through Cairo, where his two colleagues called on Leeper. The ambassador did not waste any time on details; he had called them in to give them an order.

'You must reach an understanding with Papandreou.'

Pyromaglou did not visit Leeper but went directly to see Papandreou.

'ELAS and EAM are totally dominated by the Communist Party,' declared the Prime Minister.

Pyromaglou disagreed: 'They're resistants first and foremost.'

Papandreou was not to be put off.

'They're communists. We've got to stop them from taking power at all costs.'

'Plenty of ELAS officers are not communists,' replied Pyromaglou, 'and I believe the important thing at the moment is to avoid forcing them into an extreme position.'

This was not Papandreou's view. On the contrary, he was determined to impose unacceptable conditions on ELAS. On another occasion Pyromaglou met a British diplomat who said: 'I find it quite impossible to understand why EAM should have refused to sign a treaty with the other underground organizations and then agreed to come to the Lebanon, straight into the gaping jaws of a hungry wolf.'

The delegates gathered in the sugary humidity of Beirut. While waiting for the talks to begin they were confined to their hotel 'for security reasons' and denied all access to the press. Leeper, who was to be seen everywhere behind the scenes at the conference, had installed himself nearby. The Conference opened on 17 May at Dur el Sauer, a hill resort outside Beirut.

The seven men representing EAM, ELAS, PEEA and KKE sat down at the conference table with the three EDES delegates led by Pyromaglou, Kartalis representing EKKA, and two unexpected new recruits to the 'Resistance': generals Ventiris and Stathatos, who claimed to be representing 'national organizations' with a membership of 150,000 men. These individuals had acquired glowing references in the struggle against EAM and ELAS, thanks to the generous indulgence of the occupying forces. The twelve delegates representing the 'Resistance' were ranged beside twelve representatives of pre-war political formations who represented nobody but themselves. It was an ambush.

Because the KKE had not yet given up its absurd attempts to be reassuring, nobody had dared to tell Svolos (leader of the PEEA delegation) about Psarros's death. Just before the conference opened Papandreou cornered him in a corridor and ground out through clenched teeth: 'How's Psarros?'

Slightly taken aback, Svolos answered in all innocence: 'Perfectly well, the last I heard.'

Papandreou waved a telegram in his face. It announced the EKKA chief's murder. That was the opening broadside. For the next three days, eighteen delegates hurled salvo after salvo at the seven men who represented the overwhelming majority of the struggling Greek people.

After the Army mutiny, the indignation aroused by the Psarros affair was Papandreou's best weapon. He opened for the prosecution: 'The present situation in our country resembles a hell on earth. People are being massacred on all sides, by the Germans, the Security Battalions, and the guerillas!'

It was an insult, but the protests of the Mountain delegates served only to trap them in the defensive. Around them, the musty relics of pre-Metaxas High Society stirred, nodded, murmured their sententious indignation. Papandreou warmed to his theme:

'. . . EAM is not fighting for liberation only; it is trying to pave the way for its own political dominance. To this end it has attempted to monopolize the national struggle; it will not allow anyone to join the underground to fight the invader; it prevents Greeks from doing their patriotic duty by threatening them with death. It has tried to terrorize and exterminate its opponents. It has deliberately confused itself with the State in order to be able to denounce its adversaries as enemies of Greece.'

The obvious retort would have been that the traditional parties had taken no part in the armed struggle and that ELAS's near-monopoly of the

Resistance had been an established fact almost from the word go. But the clashes and bloody operations against much smaller rival organizations had been carefully orchestrated and exhaustively recorded from the first. The present indictment had been prepared with cunning and forethought. The accused were placed in such a weak position that Woodhouse would be able to write later:

Agreement on a coalition was achieved by battering the delegates of PEEA, EAM' and the KKE into a mental daze in which they were hardly responsible for their actions.[1]

From the moment Papandreou started talking, the accused, who were the only people at the table to represent a popular movement of any size, had heard themselves abused and treated like criminals. Now all restraint was thrown to the winds and the accusations became libellous: 'The terrorist activities of the National Liberation Front (EAM) have created a psychological climate which has allowed the Germans to succeed in doing something they could not manage in the first two years of the occupation: setting up, in this third year of our nation's bondage, the Security Battalions that make civil war inevitable.'

Accusing the Resistance of terrorism had a familiar ring about it. Obviously, the Security Battalions had not been formed to fight Generals Ventiris and Stathatos, who were sitting demurely at the table: the British services, moreover, had some little knowledge of the development of these Battalions. The real authors of the civil war were sitting on the Bench on either side of Procurator Papandreou.

Finally and above all, the price paid by EAM-ELAS in the liberation struggle rendered the accusation completely despicable. It was as if 'de Gaulle had announced from London that the Fascist collaborator Doriot's militia originated in the "psychological climate" generated by the underground's "terrorist activities" against the French people'.[2]

Papandreou had not finished yet: 'I believe it is the duty of every man to protect his own rights and responsibilities, to pay his dues to History, to the people, and to the Law if there is any question of crimes in common law.' Common law criminals! Papandreou was outlining the future, and his prophecies were not over.

If then EAM . . . proposes to take over by force after the war, under the pretext of setting up a People's Republic and against the will of the majority of the Greek

[1] Woodhouse, op. cit., p. 191.
[2] Kedros, *La Résistance grecque*, Paris, 1966, p. 419.

people, then naturally an agreement is impossible. In that case it will be our clear duty to rouse the Nation and appeal to our Great Allies, their governments and public opinion for assistance in our struggle on both fronts: against the invader, and against the internal enemy.[1]

The scarecrow had been labelled. It was to serve the protégés of 'Anglo-Saxon Liberalism' both as doctrine and as programme. The army of the Great Allies would intervene, but only when the occupying forces had left the country; in the final analysis the victorious people would find that it had been designated the country's 'internal enemy'.

Instead of walking out of the conference or adopting the firm tone justified by the power of the movement it represented, the accused delegation stayed on the defensive and pleaded extenuating circumstances.

Its only instruction had been to bring back the signed agreement at any price and it had almost no margin for manoeuvre. Svolos, placed arbitrarily at the head of the PEEA delegation, had been suddenly accused of murdering Psarros at a time when he did not even know that he was dead. Rousos too was out of his depth, his long experience of militancy quite useless in dealing with skilled politicians. He adopted a mask that did not really suit him, and in his endeavours to sound reassuring only managed to seem pompous and insipid. He answered the accusation that PEEA had 'fomented' the Middle East mutiny with a clumsy, rambling disavowal:

'The Resistance and the bloody struggle being waged by the Greek people have a moral significance which lifts them far above the follies of certain irresponsible persons, acts which, though motivated partly by the desire to achieve National Unity, have had deplorable and disastrous results which must be condemned by all.'

Papandreou was seeking a rupture so that PEEA could be declared illegal and expelled. In its tense determination not to respond to provocation the delegation allowed itself to be manoeuvred into a corner. Sarafis apart, the Mountain had no genuine representatives at the conference; Rousos, for reasons diametrically opposed to Papandreou's, was far from having unlimited faith in Aris Velouchiotis and his heretical legend.

Papandreou's victims were not strong men fully aware of the force behind them; they were either liberals genuinely hurt and bewildered by the accusations levelled at them, or doctrinaires trying to look pleasant who were helpless in the face of a phenomenon foreign to their experience and training.

[1] Papandreou, op. cit., pp. 32–3.

The first resolution on the proposed treaty was aimed at the repression of the Middle East armed forces. The second point, which promised the most far-reaching consequences, was concerned with the reorganization of the National Army, in other words the dissolution of ELAS.

Such a document would be virtually a capitulation; the delegates of the Left could either submit, or break off the negotiations. In the end, very reluctantly and with some trepidation, they signed the record of their defeat, stipulating as a last resort that the decision would be subject to the final approval of PEEA.

1. The Armed Forces in the Middle East will be reconstituted under the flag of the 'Greek motherland';

2. *The Greek andartes' corps will be unified under the orders and discipline of a coalition government, in preparation for the mobilization of all the country's fighting forces against the occupant in due course;*

3. Suppression of terrorism in rural areas of Greece. Guarantees of personal safety and freedom of political opinion in areas evacuated by the occupant;

4. Provision of food and medical supplies in all areas of Greece;

5. After Liberation, law and order to be restored in collaboration with Allied forces to ensure that the Greek people can make their sovereign decision on the type and composition of their government without being subject to moral or material pressures;

6. Punishment of traitors and exploiters with severe sentences to those found to have profited from the public misery;

7. Immediate measures to supply the people's needs;

8. Full and complete satisfaction of Greek national claims.[1]

Few of the winners at Dur el Sauer would have much more opportunity in the future than they had had in the past to exercise their patriotism in the liberation struggle, but at least one of the seeds they had sown, the 'restoration of law and order in collaboration with Allied forces', promised a heavy crop.

On 25 May Papandreou took the oath of office in the king's presence and set up a twenty-minister cabinet. The delegates from EAM-ELAS, PEEA and KKE had arrived in the Lebanon intending to demand half the portfolios in the key ministries; when it came to the point Papandreou granted them a quarter of the posts, five portfolios of secondary importance. The delegation returned to Cairo. On the 27th it received a telegram from Greece. The underground disowned its representatives and demanded the reason for their capitulation.

---

[1] Quoted in Loverdo, op. cit., p. 300.

It was almost a repudiation [Sarafis wrote]. Svolos was hurt that, although he was President, they had answered him thus, and he wanted to resign. It was decided that I should leave at once for the mountains to inform the Political Committee [PEEA] about the proceedings of the conference and our decisions.[1]

Sarafis flew back to Greece on 29 May. He narrowly escaped death in a landing accident at the clandestine airstrip, and received a welcome which was not designed to put him back in command of his feelings. It was like landing on another planet.

The delegation to the Lebanon had allowed itself to be overwhelmed by politicians who were more given by nature to indignation than to resistance; in the mountains, however, EAM-ELAS shared its authority with nobody. Siantos and Ioannidis hit the ceiling. Sarafis found himself in the dock for the second time; feelings quickly reached such a height that Sarafis threatened to resign in his turn. Siantos and Ioannidis refused: 'Responsibility lay with the political delegates.'[2] Sarafis would keep his post as Commander-in-Chief of ELAS.

The other delegates stayed in Cairo waiting for instructions from PEEA. In fact, final ratification of the agreement took another three months, which did not prevent Papandreou from moving on to the active phase of his programme and purging the Middle East Army. The reliable elements were regrouped under the orders of General Ventiris.

Since the beginning of May there had been a new development of the 'Teheran tendency', the new idea of carving the atlas up into zones of influence dominated by Great-Power 'overseers'. After a long series of negotiations in London between Eden and Gusev, Soviet ambassador to Britain, a new Anglo-Soviet understanding on the Balkans was beginning to emerge. This promised the Russians dominant control over Rumania and Bulgaria on the understanding that the British would keep a free hand in the conduct of their affairs in Greece.

Cordell Hull, American Secretary of State for Foreign Affairs, was consulted as a matter of form and protested vigorously. But Stalin was ready to sign the agreement and Churchill appealed to Roosevelt personally, citing the sacrifices Great Britain had already made in Greece. 'There is no question, of course,' repeated the endless telegrams, 'of securing "zones of influence" for the future, but simply the problem of keeping things under control while hostilities last.'

On 12 June Roosevelt finally agreed to what was already a *fait accompli*.

[1] Sarafis, op. cit., p. 209.   [2] Sarafis, op. cit., p. 211.

Papandreou was kept informed throughout these dealings, which hardly disposed him to nurture EAM-ELAS.

Meanwhile, the Left delegates who had stayed in Cairo were trying to find new contacts. Rousos, the Greek Communist Party's official representative, managed to obtain an audience with the Soviet ambassador to Egypt. Not only was he not promised the slightest support, but he was strongly advised not to oppose the wishes of the British 'for the duration of this difficult war, whose outcome is still uncertain'.

A few days later Porfyrogenis, the other Communist delegate, reached the Greek mountains with a new report. When he left the house in which he had reported to the Party cadres, he was not the only person to be upset. Siantos and Ioannidis seemed to have sunk into a state of abysmal, perplexed indecision. PEEA was still refusing to ratify the Lebanon charter, but it had stopped publicly repudiating it and seemed to be waiting for something to happen.

The Andartes

Early summer was scorching the Peloponnese. Aris was as restless as a caged lion. Harassed by the Germans, Patras's collaborationist militia and the Security Battalions, conscious of the enormous task facing him in the region, he could not avoid the feeling that he had been sent off the field; that he was being excluded from the really important action. The peasants of Argolis and the mountain-dwellers of Mani had risen and were springing ambushes everywhere, withdrawing to the safety of their fortified farms.

Aris's intransigence and cruelty became virtually the sole theme of the Allied Military Mission's reports. ELAS had been condemned to dissolution by the Cairo oracles, and as it implanted itself more firmly than ever in the region the Mission's attacks began to adopt an almost fanatical tone. The Peloponnese adopted a song born two years before in the mountains of Roumeli:

> Aris, what mountain ridge are you treading
> Now? In what town is your swift step heard?
> On what hill, what high pass do you pause for breath?
> I'm treading a free Greece,
> Running with the people.

My chest fills, freely,
With the sweet breath of life.

And my shadow is the banner of the East and the West;
When they see it, men become brave,
Girls lovelier, and slaves
Find strength to smash their chains.

The Black Bonnets swooped down on the Patras hinterland, the stronghold of the Security Battalions. Within a few weeks Aris had cleared the hills and established ELAS control there. The region was crawling with members of the Allied Military Mission: Andrews, Reed, James, Campbell, Braun, Stevens. They were extremely anxious to form anti-ELAS organizations, and supported a certain Captain Karaknalios and the bands led by Papagandas and Kokkonios, which later joined the German-armed militia.

Michos, the head of ELAS in the Peloponnese, was a moderate, a former air force squadron commander who had fought beside the British. He had gradually discovered, however, that his former comrades-in-arms were behaving 'as if Greece had always been destined to become a British colony', and now fought ferociously at Aris's side.

The Peloponnese people's army had to confront the Germans, the collaborators and the ill-will of the British all at the same time. Aris was beginning to realize that he would soon have to fight PEEA's political line as well. When the report on the Lebanon negotiations reached his HQ, Hermes, who had always fought alongside Aris, saw his chief succumbing to despair for the first time.

'If you spit in the air it lands in your face. If you spit on the ground it gets caught in your beard. . . .'

And later, anger: '. . . It's a betrayal; of me, of all of us. We'll find the culprits later, it's right that we should know. . . . Listen, Hermes. It's obvious. We'll soon be finished with the Germans, but that won't be the end of it for us. Now we're going to have to fight the English. They're going to do everything in their power to occupy us in their own way.'

Somewhere along the line EAM's policy had split in two and lost all its strength. An armed people was being submitted to decisions over which it had no control whatsoever, sliding willy-nilly into a new tragedy from which politics could offer no escape.

The partisans in Aris's country, the upper slopes of the Pindus in the heart of mainland Greece, were by now taking all their orders from political officials. The *éminences grises* of the Revolution had experienced some little difficulty in persuading them that the Central Committee's policies were leading them to victory, but the ·most turbulent kapetanios had been removed at the same time as Aris and the opposition were virtually throttled into silence. Further north, the Macedonian andartes were terribly shocked by the wheeling and dealing in the Middle East. The Lebanon negotiations showed them just how little the politicians valued their struggle and their success in the field.

The regional cadres of EAM and ELAS met in the village of Daskio, at the foot of Mount Pieiria: Partsalidis, Lassanis who headed the resistance on Olympus, Vermiotis, Colonel Kikitsas, Troyanos, Smolikas, and the Macedonian kapetanios Markos Vafiadis.

Markos Vafiadis used his own christian name as a *nom-de-guerre* and was always known simply as Markos. In two years' time his name would feature in popular songs alongside Aris's. He was of medium height, blond and blue-eyed, with an aquiline nose and a bandit's moustache. His eyes narrowed to slits when he smiled, deepening the crow's-foot wrinkles that spread from their outer corners. When someone was speaking to him Markos listened with a quiet, concentrated attention that had something almost tender about it, and answered with great economy of words. He was a withdrawn man, rather shy, the image of a paternal and benevolent popular leader with a touch of the 'father of his regiment' to reassure the timid. An occasional metallic flash in his glance emphasized the craggy outlines of his face, the strong chin and prominent cheekbones.

Markos was thirty-eight years old in 1944. He was born in 1906 in the village of Tosia in Asia Minor. His father died in poverty in 1917, his mother in 1920. The failure of the 'Great Idea', which had infected Greece with a short-lived enthusiasm to reconquer the frontiers of the Byzantine empire, was followed by an exchange of ethnic minorities; by 1922 the Greeks of Asia Minor were returning to their country. Markos arrived in Constantinople in 1923, and managed to reach Salonika, which was overflowing with hundreds of thousands of refugees of Greek descent who had been scattered about the Balkans and Asia Minor for generations. Like all poor northern Greeks he was destined for the tobacco factories. He joined the Party in 1928 and became a leader of the Young Communists; after that it was the usual, almost mechanical alternation between militant activity and jail.

His first prison sentence lasted from 1932 to 1934. He was arrested again in July 1936 and in September escaped from the island of Agios

Evstratios; recaptured in Piraeus in 1938, he was sent to mildew at Aegina, Acronauplion and finally on the isle of Gavdos, where Aris had built the pebble 'palace' a few years before to protect the prisoners from malaria. He escaped from Gavdos in 1941, during the military collapse. He joined the Mountain and became kapetanios of the ELAS 10th Division in Macedonia.

The Macedonian resistance did not develop in the Homeric climate which had been bestowed on the movement elsewhere by the rugged Roumeli landscape and by Aris's personality. Markos's temperament had never risen against the Athens leadership's ukases, and his emergent legend was not yet in any danger of infringing the Central Committee's prerogatives. But it was June 1944 and the Lebanon deal had just been made public. Faced suddenly with the slandering of their epic in the interests of political bargaining of which they were the helpless object, the combatant people and their leaders reacted against what they could only experience as an imposture.

'This agreement amounts to a betrayal pure and simple. Those responsible for it should be disowned.'

All the Macedonian cadres agreed. A resolution along these lines was immediately telegraphed to PEEA headquarters. The Old Man was still busy there calming people down. Whether or not he had some consistent basic reasons for wishing to do so, these remained secret; the only argument he could develop openly and which also had some foundation was that pressure was being brought to bear on PEEA by liberal elements whose cooperation would be withdrawn if the negotiations were broken off.

Throughout this political withdrawal by PEEA, ELAS maintained its military progress. Statisticians give the name 'sufferance' to this dissonance between two curves.

Just as the dissolution of ELAS was becoming an important Allied priority, the battle against the occupying forces suddenly intensified. On 16 June the German garrison trapped in Levadia made a break for freedom and left the town. The andartes intercepted it near St Luke's monastery in Fokis, killing fifty men and destroying four lorries. The remains of this German column joined up with reinforcements and descended on the village of Distomo.

Torches and grenades. All the houses were burned one by one. Then rapes and machine-gun fire. The 228 inhabitants were terribly slashed and mutilated. 104 of the victims were male and 124 female; 20 were under five years old, 45 between five and twenty, 111 between twenty and sixty and 49 over sixty.

Almost all the young women were found cut open from the genitals to the breasts, others with their breasts cut off, and children were found disembowelled and with their entrails wound round their necks. The priest had been beheaded.[1]

Two days later, andartes trapped a large armoured detachment in the Pyrgos defile, on the road out of Lamia. The Germans lost forty men. At exactly midday on 26 June, a German column started up the forest trail leading to the Chrysovitsi sawmill in Arcadia. The first shot made the tense vertical sunshine of midday vibrate like a drum.

The battle lasted seventeen minutes: 75 Germans killed, including the senior officers. Spoils: two machine-guns with thousands of rounds of ammunition, grenades, all the Nazis' rifles. The comrades removed the tyres for resoling *tsarouchias* (improvised shoes), then doused the eleven or more vehicles with petrol and set them on fire.

The Germans never came to the sawmill again. They had to go further afield for their timber, as far as Tripolis. Our wood was the best for barrack building; it had a good pine smell.[2]

Parnassus stands in the south of Roumeli overlooking the treasures of Delphi and the whole northern coast of the Gulf of Corinth. Apollo's mountain had been the domain of andartes for two years now. The Germans attacked in force in the first week of July, deploying 2,000 men supported by tanks and armoured cars from the Amfissa garrison. The andartes managed to repel the enemy column and then hamper its retreat. Amfissa was left practically empty. The five battalions of ELAS 7th Brigade swooped on the town and destroyed the Wehrmacht transmitter, fifty vehicles and all the fuel dumps. The Germans had lost 150 men, but they had summoned reinforcements from every town in the region.

The Amfilochia garrison did not even have time to leave the town. On the night of the 12th-13th ELAS Seventh Brigade stormed the town and destroyed all the equipment it could not take away. This time the Germans lost 490 men. The partisans pulled out with three cars, several transmitters, and 70 mules and 38 horses laden with arms and equipment.

The idea of totally dismantling ELAS in the field was a utopian fantasy, which did not deter British agents from trying to work out the details. The Fardikambo schoolmaster Paleologos was now in command of a

---

[1] Kedros, op. cit., p. 446. [2] Loverdo, op. cit., p. 312.

battalion of the Macedonian Tenth Division. He was stationed near Grevena with his 800 partisans. The British officers in the region wanted to secure exclusive control of the airstrip. Why not disband the greater part of the ELAS battalion and recruit a few mercenaries at the same time? A British officer came to see Paleologos.

'Keep three hundred men and send the others away. We'll pay you personally a pound a day for each man; plus food and clothing for all of you.'

Paleologos couldn't get over it.

'What am I supposed to say to the andartes I send home?'

'Tell them you don't need them any more,' replied the Englishman blandly.

'And if the Germans come back and start burning villages again?'

The officer was talking business and found the question out of place. 'That's no concern of yours.'

Paleologos blew up completely: 'What the hell d'you think we're fighting for then? I talk to you about our houses, our relations, and you want me to send more than half my men home and sit here with the others doing nothing for a pound a day! Forget it, we're not mercenaries.'

The British officer blushed scarlet. Perhaps it hadn't been such a good idea after all.

The gold and supplies which had been reaching Zervas in such abundance found better employment.

Gradually [wrote Sarafis] Zervas' troops resumed their small-scale attacks on ELAS in the Arta district, and eventually, on June 19th, strong EDES forces attacked the 24th Regiment both in its coastal sector . . . and in its inland territory. The regiment counter-attacked and put them to flight. . . . The Political Committee addressed itself to the Prime Minister Papandreou and requested that Zervas . . . be instructed to stop these attacks. . . . Zervas asserted that he had been attacked on the previous day. . . .[1]

At the end of June Middle East HQ ordered Zervas to occupy the coastal zone between Preveza and Igoumenitsa, opposite Corfu. The sector had always been regarded as ELAS territory, and the 'Reds' reacted with a vehemence which would shortly add a stanza or two to the moaning Egyptian dirge for the victims of Bolshevik totalitarianism.

[1] Sarafis, op. cit., p. 214.

The Soviet Mission

Tzimas arrived at Tito's HQ on the Adriatic island of Vis at the end of June 1944, after an eventful journey. He wrote to the Soviet Government the moment he arrived, asking for arms and munitions to use against the Germans and for diplomatic support against the British. He did not find the quantities of good advice which he received in reply either useful or encouraging. The renewed prospect of a Balkan HQ was worrying to the British, and might prove capable of extracting a few concessions from them. Tzimas sent PEEA dispatch after dispatch urging it to reject the Lebanon agreement.

At about the same time the British were opening their diplomatic offensive against Tito. Wilson invited him to sit at a conference table side by side with Prime Minister-in-Exile Subotić; Churchill was setting up a Yugoslav version of the Lebanon coup. But Tito refused to have anything to do with the minister, insisting that the right to settle the country's political future belonged exclusively to the partisans.

PEEA was caught between two fires. Most of the Resistance cadres were violently opposed to ratifying the agreement, but the campaign of discredit against Bolshevik totalitarianism had built up to a very loud crescendo. Svolos and other lukewarm elements in the Provisional Government wanted to sign.

On 7 July Papandreou received two telegrams from the Mountain. The first, signed by Porfyrogenis and Sarafis, protested against the campaign of repression that was raging in the Middle East Army. The second, signed by Bakirjis, Siantos and Hajibeis on behalf of PEEA, demanded the constitution of a new 15-member Ministerial Council to replace the 20-man cabinet proposed in the Lebanon charter. PEEA wanted seven of the fifteen portfolios including the Ministry of the Interior.

Once again, in view of the extremely strong position of EAM-ELAS, there was nothing exorbitant about these demands. But reality was measured against a different standard in Cairo; certain services rendered to the Great Allies could easily outweigh a struggling people with all its sacrifices and all its victories. The opportunity was exactly what Papandreou had been waiting for. He declared the PEEA demands extravagant and broke off the talks.

We showed the Mountain Committee that we knew it had finally abandoned its subterfuges and pretexts and revealed its true intentions. From now on we would be able to make ourselves clear. We knew what they were demanding of us; we adopted a responsible position with regard to their claims: we refused.[1]

The only way to have done with ELAS was to provoke a civil war; then the Allies would be able to intervene. On 13 July Papandreou received the EDES delegate Pyromaglou at home.

'I would like to ask you one question, Mr Pyromaglou, and I beg you to answer sincerely and without beating about the bush: Are you in a position to disband ELAS?'

'I'll answer you in a moment, Mr President, but first of all I'd just like to mention that nothing has been done about our agreement on the subject of increasing our forces to 25,000 men. . . . Why not study the proposal we made at the Lebanon Conference to set up a National Army with a balance of forces that would make this civil war, which the Greek people hardly needs, unlikely to happen? And why is EDES expected to take the responsibility for the civil war, rather than the Government which can well afford to gamble with its prestige among the people? What are the officers doing training here? Why isn't the National Army being set up on the spot?'

'If that's the way you feel, I shall disband ELAS with the help of the British.'

'Before or after the Liberation, Mr President?'

'After the Liberation.'

'But by then, Mr President, the question will no longer be the exclusive concern of Middle East HQ; it will have become Allied business. You may find international complications arising.'

'No, no. *Believe me.*'[2]

Papandreou was not bluffing, as events quickly proved. Svolos and the PEEA delegation left Egypt to return to Greece on the day this conversation took place.

Tzimas was at Tito's headquarters on the island of Vis, maintaining a steady stream of messages urging the PEEA leadership to stand firm. At the end of July he had weighty news for them: the Soviet Mission in Yugoslavia was about to send a team of Russian 'observers' to Greece. Pressure to resist the British political offensive was now to be combined with the arrival of Soviet officers in the mountains! It looked a strong formula, but was to prove far less explosive than poor Tzimas imagined.

[1] Kedros, *La Résistance grecque*, Paris, 1966, p. 424.
[2] Pyromaglou, *The National Resistance*, Athens, 1947, p. 122 (in Greek).

On 28 July, a Soviet transport aircraft of Italian origin landed on the Neraida airstrip built by Eddie Myers a year earlier. Eight Soviet officers stepped down onto the soil of Free Greece: Colonel Popov, the Mission's leader, followed by Lt-Colonels Chernichev and Trojan, Commanders Ivanov and Aramanov, and three engineers. Their luggage consisted of several transmitters. Tzimas had met Popov at Tito's HQ before he left for Greece, and had immediately asked for arms. The Russian had replied imperturbably: 'I am being sent to Greece as an observer by Yugoslav HQ.'

Three days after the observers arrived at Neraida *The Times* carried the headline: 'Red Army Mission in Greece – Contacts with Partisans'.

Their arrival [wrote Sarafis] surprised the English, who had not been warned about it. Lieutenant Cook, who was stationed at the airstrip, was clearly very shocked. We had arranged quarters on the assumption that the Mission would live with the Anglo-Americans, but Colonel Popov wanted separate quarters, and we billeted him and his people in the hamlet of Petrillon, about three-quarters of an hour from HQ.

Popov then demanded detailed reports on the organization, its fighting strength and staff methods; he was interested in the intelligence service and in ELAS's military workings in general. He would make no promises about getting us supplies from the Red Army, having no instructions on the subject; he transmitted a list of our needs to Moscow, saying that it was a matter for Moscow to decide.

Colonel Hammond of the British Mission invited Popov and President Svolos to tea, which was how the Soviet and Allied Missions made their first contact.[1]

It was an extremely courteous meeting. The Soviets announced that they would soon be leaving for Albania and the British, who had heard of the Stalin-Churchill agreements through other channels, recovered some of their customary phlegm.

The PEEA leadership was still waiting for some gesture from its guests. If they could not supply arms, what diplomatic support would the Soviets be able to give the andartes? The question glanced off Popov's imperturbable mask without eliciting any answer whatsoever. In the mountains, later on at the window of the Hotel Great-Britain in Athens, wherever he showed himself in public, thousands of people would try to read some message of encouragement or menace into this mask. It always remained expressionless.

Siantos had a long private meeting with him, but what was said at it

[1] Sarafis, op. cit.; translation from Greek edition. Cf. English edition, pp. 224-6.

remained shrouded in the same mystery that surrounded what had passed at the Cairo meeting between Rousos and the Soviet ambassador, and for much the same reasons. Somehow or other it became clear that Russia was not going to intervene on behalf of a Greece earmarked for British influence, but the question of how, and from whom, the knowledge arrived remains unanswered to this day.

No doubt Popov's mask simply expressed the stance of a Pontius Pilate: There is nothing we can do for you; sort it out for yourselves. It is most unlikely that the head of the Soviet Mission would personally have wished EAM-ELAS to capitulate to the Anglo-Saxon Allies. Popov had never been an expansive man, and his responsibilities at this time would not have been especially conducive to good cheer. Siantos, for his part, was in no position to make Popov's message public in the form in which he had received it. There was nothing for it but to rely on discipline and blind faith in the infallibility of the party line. Everyone was waiting for a sign.

Popov's assistant Chernichev went to see Bakirjis in the evening, ostensibly to discuss certain military problems. Suddenly, Chernichev seemed to be giving the eagerly awaited signal.

'I have heard,' he said, 'that you are refusing to ratify the Lebanon agreements. It's illogical.'

Bakirjis leaned towards him.

'You ought to be saying that to Siantos, not to me.'

'General,' Chernichev answered, 'I don't represent any party. My business is making war. You too are a soldier. But if you're interested you can mention this to your Party.'

'Well, I'll pass it on.'

'I have no advice for you really. I'm simply telling you that the British are due to land at Piraeus "tomorrow", and that it would be absurd on your part not to welcome them as heroes.'

Bakirjis rushed to Siantos's quarters and repeated every word of Chernichev's remarks. Doubtless the Old Man had already heard some very similar whisper, for he had called a meeting of the Political Bureau for the same evening.

Within the Political Bureau the hard-line revolutionary tendency was represented by Ioannidis. He had espoused a line which closely resembled Aris's in most ways, but as a Party man rather than a Resistance fighter. The only difference, and it was a considerable one, was that Ioannidis had no thought of relying on the peasant guerilla movement for support, since his confidence in it was very limited.

'We're running a tremendous risk with all these men who have sprung up from the popular movement. . . .' He had said it a hundred times.

His idea was to use orthodox forces for the struggle – the proletarian revolutionary elite, most of which had been kept in the towns: an abstraction. Despite the fighting strength of the urban movement, he was violently opposed to ratifying the Lebanon agreement. Siantos opened the meeting brutally: 'We should reopen the negotiations and ratify the agreements.'

Ioannidis stood up: 'Not only should we not ratify them, but we should also get ready to fight the British.'

A violent quarrel ensued. The gentle Siantos, who had always preferred persuasion to terror, ended it with a completely uncharacteristic gesture, staring Ioannidis in the eye while fingering his pistol. The Line was the Line, and there was nothing more to be said.

PEEA sent a telegram to the Cairo government on 29 July. Compared to the demands made on 7 July it was a complete surrender: in it, the Mountain government agreed to participate in the framework laid down in the Lebanon. It insisted on one condition as a matter of form: Churchill's gift of providence Papandreou, of whom Tsirimokos had remarked: 'He's crusading for Greek Unity but the cross in his hand is a swastika', must be replaced.

Churchill was getting impatient. He wanted ELAS without conditions and bound hand and foot.

On July 7 the King of Greece had telegraphed from Cairo that after two months of 'cunning and futile arguments' the EAM extremists had repudiated the Lebanon agreement which their leaders had signed in May. . . .

. . . Surely we should tell M. Papandreou that he should continue as Prime Minister and brave them all. The behaviour of EAM is absolutely intolerable. Obviously they are seeking nothing but the Communization of Greece during the confusion of the war, without allowing the people to decide in any manner understood by democracy.

We cannot take a man up as we have done Papandreou and let him be thrown to the wolves at the first snarlings of the miserable Greek (Communist) banditti. . . .

Should matters go downhill and EAM become master we should have to reconsider keeping any of our mission there and put the Greek people bluntly up against Bolshevism. The case seems to me to have reached the following point: either we support Papandreou, if necessary with force as we have agreed, or we disinterest ourselves utterly in Greece.[1]

[1] Churchill, op. cit., vol. VI, London, 1954, pp. 96–7.

The second alternative was included only for the sake of style. Churchill was definitely 'interested' in Greece and had already obtained Stalin's partial agreement to his hunting rights.

The 'banditti' had just received good advice from the Soviets and were beginning an unexpected political retreat, but Churchill chose that very moment to pretend that he had been forced to escalate the conflict. What he wanted, what he had been after all along, was the go-ahead for an armed intervention in Athens. He was going to have to outflank PEEA's concessions. He cabled Roosevelt about his plans and got an answer the same day:

I have no objection to your making preparations to have in readiness a sufficient British force to preserve order in Greece when the German forces evacuate that country. There is also no objection to the use by General Wilson of American transport aeroplanes. . . .[1]

It was now a matter of urgency to cash the American credit chit, to finalize the military preparations before PEEA's surrender made the pretext null and void.

Prime Minister to Chief of Imperial General Staff
It may be that within a month or so we shall have to put 10,000 or 12,000 men into Athens, with a few tanks, guns and armoured cars. . . .

I repeat that there is no question of trying to dominate Greece or going outside the immediate curtilage of Athens, but this is the centre of government, and, with the approaches to it, must be made secure. . . . The utmost secrecy must enwrap this project.

You should note that time is more important than numbers, and that 5,000 men in five days is better than 7,000 men in seven days. The force is not of course expected to be mobile. Pray speak to me at the first opportunity . . . .

. . . As soon as the landing-ground has been secured by the 1,500 British parachutists the Greek Government would follow almost immediately, and within a very few hours should be functioning in Athens, where the people would probably receive the British parachutists with rapture. The arrival of the parachutists in the neighbourhood of Athens could be effected with complete surprise, and might well be effected before EAM had taken any steps to seize the capital. . . .[2]

On 10 August PEEA received a reply from four members of Papandreou's government, Venizelos, Mylonas, Sakalis and Rendis. It was astonishingly revealing on the subject of their enterprise's sovereignty: 'The British government has indicated privately that it will not

[1] Churchill, op. cit., vol. VI, p. 100.   [2] Churchill, op. cit., vol. VI, pp. 97–8.

countenance a change of President on the eve of Liberation.' Helpless and out of touch, PEEA agreed.

On 15 August, the day of the Allied landing in Provence, Council Vice-President Venizelos received a telegram from Greece. It was an unconditional capitulation, signed by Svolos for PEEA, Partsalidis for EAM and Siantos for the KKE. The Mountain agreed to be reduced to the status of political poor relation in the Government of National Union, turn a blind eye to the repression still raging in the Middle East Army, and stand by in a state of impotence while Churchill imposed a fraud on the country by remote control.

For the guerillas, the kapetanios, the National Liberation Army, the insult was intolerable. Only Party discipline remained to keep these men in check, men like Aris who had waged a bitter struggle and were determined to reap its rewards. In the name of this discipline, and of the infallibility of the Party leadership, an armed people was letting its victory be snatched from its grasp. Tzimas had just sent a characteristically outspoken telegram to PEEA from Tito's HQ when he received one from Siantos: 'We are sending our ministers to the Cairo government.'

The next day Tzimas learned that even Tito had been forced to give some ground. He had ended by accepting the British invitation on the condition that he would meet Churchill as the sole representative of his country. When he arrived, however, he found that he had to wait for the Foreign Office's candidate, Subotić, before the talks could start.

Churchill obtained the right on paper to control most of Yugoslavia's roads, and the military forces of the Resistance became theoretically subject to Allied orders except for courts martial.

With Mihailović virtually out of the way, Tito was in a better position than the Greeks, but the cards were substantially the same. The game was to be played against the same adversary. The outcome would depend on the forces chosen for the actual play.

The Last Battles

On 3 August 1944 Turkey severed diplomatic relations with the Third Reich. On the 15th, Allied troops landed in Provence. On the 20th, Generals Malinovsky and Tolbukhin launched their offensive on the

Prut and the Siret in Moldavia. On the 23rd, Michael of Rumania dismissed the dictator Antonescu, took over Radio Bucharest with the Royal Guard and announced that Rumania would no longer fight on the German side. The next day the German lines, weakened by the defection of Rumanian troops, were smashed by the Red Army.

In Greece, isolated on the promontory of Europe, the Germans had to secure their lines of retreat before they could withdraw. One of the most important barriers to their progress was Aris's former stronghold of Karpenisi, the fortress of Central Greece, about ten kilometres from Kerasovo where PEEA had been sitting until a few days before. From this bastion, clinging to the rock at a height of 3,000 feet, the andartes could dominate the main Athens-Salonika artery to the east, the Amfilochia-Arta coast road along the Adriatic to the west, and most important of all the only viable route between Epirus and Thessaly.

The Germans swarmed up to the attack from all directions at once: two columns from Agrinion to the south-west, a third from Amfissa to the south-east, the fourth advancing westwards from Lamia. The first column climbed painfully up a winding and vulnerable mountain road, harassed from the heights by ELAS Thirteenth Division. Every turn in the road signalled a minor massacre, and the Germans were finally brought to a halt at the village of Platanos, which they looted and burnt to ashes before retreating.

The second detachment from Agrinion set off in a northerly direction. It was supported by a sizeable armoured unit and several mountain batteries, and flattened three villages in its path. The Germans entered Viniani and were advancing on Kerasovo when they ran into the ELAS HQ guard detachment, which had not quite finished evacuating the village. The andartes clung to every boulder, counterattacked and pushed the assailants back.

The German column from Amfissa got as far as the foothills of Mount Giona; there, the ELAS Fifth Brigade quickly blocked its ascent and then smashed it to fragments. A column of reinforcements arrived and also flung itself at the partisans' wall of fire, losing half its men in the process. The Germans combined the survivors of the first two attacks and tried again but were driven back a third time. The andartes' ammunition was beginning to run low.

Emptying their garrisons completely, the Germans threw 3,000 fresh men into the battle and managed to progress a few kilometres to Lidoriki. The village was empty and, once again, they vented their rage on stones by pillaging and burning all the houses. They had left more than 1,000 dead on the slopes of Mt Ghiona since the beginning of the offensive, and their overflowing field hospitals could no longer cope with the wounded. The column from Lamia was detailed to strike the decisive blow. The partisans' ammunition problem was now very acute. The Germans plunged into the Sperchios valley and burned a dozen villages. ELAS mobilized everything it had left in the region: a battalion from Thessaly, the last Headquarters Battalion and the ELAS Officers' School.

The Germans were nailed to the spot once again, and called in every available force from a radius of 200 kilometres: the 41st Division set out from Lamia, the Third SS Regiment left Amfissa, and the last two regiments from Agrinion came hotfoot to the rescue, some 20,000 men in all. The reinforcements joined together and organized their attack, but when they launched it in the crushing sunshine the Mountain made no reply. Behind the rocks silhouetted like cardboard imitations in the white light, and andartes had silently vanished.

They were regrouped on Mount Delidymi, a few kilometres to the north, where they could still keep an eye on the main communications routes of Epirus and Thessaly. They had fired their last cartridges, but reserve supplies were already on the way from the Pindus and Macedonia. They had lost 300 fighting men. The Germans left 2,500 on the field. The Axis forces had received the order to retreat on the 26th.

ELAS struck incessantly for the next month, each battle leaving it in a stronger position than before. The members of the Allied Military Mission were worked almost to death. The Germans were burning everything behind them, and in order to limit the destruction the partisans were ordered to avoid useless confrontations. This order was certainly amply justified by the German massacres of the civilian population, but the Anglo-Americans saw it primarily as a means of limiting the partisans' share of the final victory.

Most of the studies of this period carried out by kremlinologists assert with relish that ELAS activity during the last few months before the Liberation was limited to preparations for the seizure of power carried out at the expense of the struggle against the occupant. In reality, if the Anglo-Saxons had any worries about the results of Operation Noah's Ark, they were because the operation exceeded all expectations.

All the large bridges and more than half of the small ones (less than 25-foot span) were demolished. The road from Athens to Salonika was cut in 31 different places and the parallel railway line had been blown up 19 times. 56 per cent of the road network and all the major railway tracks were unusable. 98 per cent of the rolling stock was destroyed: there were only 11 locomotives left in the whole of Greece. The telephone and telegraph systems could be regarded as totally sabotaged. Between 30 August and the end of September not an hour passed without a resounding explosion taking place somewhere in Greece (720 hours). Wehrmacht archives record 113 major sabotages in railway stations alone.[1]

After the Lebanon agreement had been signed, Aris was confined, smouldering, to the Peloponnese for a few days more. Thundering about on horseback at the head of the Black Bonnets, his word was still law in the region. Every military victory on the field was a political victory for the future – always providing that the armed struggle would be carried through to its logical conclusion. Anything smelling faintly of policeman, Security Battalions or traitor was hunted down without mercy. People's tribunals were established and passed brutal sentences. According to the German report Br. *b* No. 18262/44 for 9 July 1944, Aris proclaimed a Soviet in the village of Boumba, on the road between Kalavryta and Patras, in the presence of twenty deputies. The greater part of the kapetanios' activities fell outside the authority of the HQ from which he had been sent away; he was doing things in his own way. He pursued the Security Battalions with an unbridled violence which swept aside all the Allied Mission's efforts to calm things down.

On 8 September, Aris threw himself on Kalamata, the real stronghold of the militia. He took the town after a hard battle, but most of the defenders managed to escape and take refuge in Meligala.

ELAS Ninth Regiment attacked Meligala on 13 September. The town was defended by 1,500 militiamen equipped with artillery and heavy weapons, and the battle lasted forty-eight hours. As soon as Aris got inside the town a tribunal was immediately set up, and any militiamen captured were subjected to the most expeditious form of justice. The same thing happened at Pyrgos, then at Gargalianoi. In the ranks of the Security Battalions there was total panic, a rout. Militiamen surrendered to local organizations in their thousands rather than risk being tried by Aris's tribunals, and they were sent off to Spetsai prison camp.

The Allied Mission was completely swamped, unable to do a thing. The British services' *bête noire* had earned himself another black mark.

The Germans were retreating northwards throughout the rest of Greece, leaving a terrible wake of ashes and suffering behind them. On

[1] Loverdo, op. cit., p. 335.

2 September a Wehrmacht battalion was fired on as it entered the village of Chortiati, and managed to capture the village before the population could escape into the hills. 160 men, women and children fell into German hands; they were driven with blows from rifle-butts to the ovens belonging to the town's two bakers, Gouramanis and Daboudis, and there, without distinction by age or sex, baked alive one by one. There followed for good measure what must have seemed a rather anti-climactic house-burning.

The cruelty escalated to the very end. The peasants were fighting their last battles, and their fury spoke from every crag and every ravine, turning the German withdrawal into a rout. The rage was mounting in the towns as well. Raids and executions followed one another in rapid succession. A last wave of reprisals rolled across Athens.

Athens

It had been a long time since the conquerors had dared to venture openly into the side streets even in the centre of Athens. Certain peripheral areas could only be approached after the most elaborate preparations, and never by a small body of men: the eastern suburb Kaisariani, clinging to the slopes of Mount Hymettus (source of the sweetest honey of antiquity); to the west, Kokkinia, the Red quarter, below the Sacred Way of Eleusis.

By the end of August 1944 a kilo of bread cost 122 million drachmas; starvation rations cost a suitcase full of banknotes. The disastrous economic situation sharpened resistance to the occupant's every gesture, to every moment of his continued presence.

On 15 August, the day of the Allied landing in Provence, the Germans undertook to clear the 'Red-infested' outskirts of the capital and subjugate the population. During the night the SS sealed off the three districts of Katsipodi, Dourgouti and Faro. They searched every house and assembled all the men between sixteen and sixty in the street, holding the crowd in check with armoured cars and automatic weapons. A number of wanted persons were immediately set on one side, and then collaborators walked about picking people out at random; 3,500 hostages were taken in this one raid and hurriedly taken to concentration camps in Germany or to the Haidari camp. In the Faro quarter, eighty hostages were executed as an example to the thousands watching in the roadway.... Not far away, forty men were publicly shredded by machine-gun fire against the walls of the Kaisaria factory.

On the night of the 16th–17th 2,000 SS sealed off Kokkinia, a quarter which held particularly warm memories for them. The inhabitants were woken up by the clinking of tank tracks as armoured units established themselves at every crossroads. Presently boots began thudding against doors: '*Raus! Schnell!*'

Heavy boots clattered on staircases. Doors were kicked open. By dawn the quarter was practically empty and 30,000 people were massed in Osia Xeni Square. With the first glimmering of the new day there appeared a number of nightmarish figures, hooded men protected by squads of SS. They walked up and down the lines of people pointing first at one face, then at another.

One of these informers did his work with his face uncovered. He was called Bardanis. He stopped in front of a certain Apostolis who was known to everyone as an ELAS kapetanios. Bardanis sprang to attention, saluted and cried: 'At your service, Captain!'

A bayonet carved a deep furrow across Apostolis's face, taking out his left eye. The hooded men kept moving, fingering people as they went. One hundred hostages were executed on the spot, 8,000 others driven with kicks and rifle-butts towards the station, destined for Haidari camp.

On 24 August the Athenian population went on strike in protest against the massacre. There was no demonstration; the order was that people should shut themselves in their houses. At midday, instead of a wild mob, the occupying forces faced a formidable wall of silence. The town reflected the hot summer sun in an unbearable white glare, silent, the capital of the Void. Deaf stones, dumb defiance, the closed mask of a city petrified in marble hate.

Oppressed by this pall of silence, the Germans launched another offensive on the 27th and 28th. This time, the suburbs were on their guard: Kalithea, Kypseli, Tourkouvounia, Koukaki had all mobilized. Barricades turned each district into a fortress able to repel raids. Under such conditions the cadres of KOA (Athens Communist Organization) had the greatest difficulty in explaining to their rank and file members why EAM had walked into the Lebanon ambush.

Throughout the second half of August militants were going from house to house organizing another secret election, but this time they were less defensive about it. The list of Cairo ministers was even presented to officers of the fascist militia and senior police officers. It was a real provocation; armed men covered the electioneering militants from the street while they went through the buildings knocking on doors. Nobody dared any longer give public expression to pro-German opinions.

After curfew every night, wall-painting teams would swarm out of their backyards and start looking for clean wall surfaces on which to record the news and slogans of the day in red paint. By the end of the summer of 1944 the whole of Athens was daubed to the height of a man, and the teams had to use ladders to extend the fresco. The enterprise was becoming more and more difficult, but graffiti had become an institution. A friendly rivalry sprang up between the different quarters, each one claiming to have the 'best-looking wall' in town. In the event of pursuit, standing orders were to ring at the nearest door. The houses would always open and swallow the fleeing partisans.

It was with the same sort of insolence that militants went from house to house submitting the list of Cairo ministers to clandestine suffrage. In working-class districts the reaction was nearly always the same: 'Who is this Papandreou? We've had enough of bourgeois politicians.'

Two hundred yards from the Acropolis, in the same district as the Agora and the Theseion, were quartered the pro-Nazi nationalist commandos of General Grivas's X Organization. X was armed by the Germans, used police cars for its propaganda operations and loosed its packs against the Reds every night.

Since the beginning of the summer EAM had established special squads of three or four armed men to carry out counter-terrorism and various delicate missions. Their operations were coordinated by OPLA (Organization for the Protection of Popular Struggle), whose headquarters were hidden away in the labyrinth of Peristeri. OPLA network chiefs were designated by a letter: Alpha, Stamatiades; Beta, Mavros; Gamma, Pechtasidis; Delta, Kalodikis; Epsilon, Vasilopoulos. Its intelligence branch was fully up to date on the activities of certain British agents who were working with the German services, especially with a German organization called the Fourth Reich.

The Fourth Reich, which was more or less closely linked with the July movement and the Stauffenberg attempt (on Hitler's life), was preparing for a possible restructuring of alliances in which a purged German army would join the Anglo-Saxons in a struggle against Soviet expansionism. OPLA had infiltrated its Athens network and intercepted several British documents offering specific guarantees to the Security Battalions, which were still recruiting despite the imminence of the Nazi collapse. The Party's intelligence services had thus acquired the conviction that some kind of confrontation with the British was inevitable.

KOA, the Athens Communist Organization which directed all the activities of these militants and shock groups, was led by men who for the most part followed the revolutionary hard line represented by Ioannidis in the Central Committee. Major Makridis, the movement's strategist, and the elephantine, dogmatic Bartzotas, had finally reached conclusions not far removed from those of Aris himself; except that in their eyes the final struggle must be led by the revolutionary elite following the canonical model of the October Revolution. Aris and the kapetanios – the Mountain, bearded guerillas, 'roundheads' – were suspected of all the libertarian sins. Orthodoxy remained deeply suspicious of the country's largest progressive force.

For the time being the official line was to follow the legal path opened by the entry of EAM and KKE ministers into the Papandreou government. The capital's cadres were well-disciplined; they enlarged on all kinds of soothing ideas, they reassured and subtly threatened by reminding people of the Party's infallibility. But they did not allow all this to deter them from making secret preparations on the side, just in case there should be a struggle for power in the capital.

'The KOA leadership,' Bartzotas wrote in 1952, 'decided to prepare for armed insurrection in the course of two meetings held at the beginning of September.'[1]

Makridis was asked to work out a detailed military plan. It was never put into operation and the records eventually disappeared, along with many other documents, in the oubliettes of successive official inquiries.

Instead of taking stock of the forces at their disposal, Siantos and the EAM leaders continued to scrutinize Popov's monolithic mask for signs when they moved to ELAS's new headquarters. In case of disaster there would always be Athens, reassuringly proletarian, comfortingly orthodox. The Mountain, the armed masses, would always seem to these men to be an unreliable, uncontrollable card to play in a political game which now consisted of conquering a knotty and tortuous legality.

[1] V. Bartzotas, *The Policy of KKE Cadres during the last ten years*, 1950 (in Greek), p. 48.

The Great Surveyors

On 2 September 1944 the EAM ministers left for Cairo to join the government: two Communists, Zevgos and Porfyrogenis, and two Socialists, Svolos and Tsirimokos. Churchill had decided to withdraw the government from the disturbing Cairo atmosphere as soon as possible since the great majority of the Greek colony there had become converted to EAM views and seemed only too likely to complicate his enterprise. On the 7th, therefore, all the members of the government including Papandreou were invited to sample Italian air in the village of Cava dei Tirreni, near Caserta.

Tzimas was travelling through Italy at about this time on a fact-finding mission, and heard by chance that the ministers had arrived in Cava dei Tirreni. He decided at once that he would go there himself. His driver, a nursemaid supplied by Allied HQ, refused to take him there, but he managed to get a lift in a lorry as far as Naples and managed to reach the strange, quarantined government.

The ministers were installed in a hotel where they were simply killing time, completely out of touch with the outside world. Tzimas brought them the news of the liberation of Amfilochia, Agrinion and Preveza. The Greek government seemed to be in hiding; the ministers listened in confusion to this man who was getting regular information via Yugoslavia while they had not even the use of a radio transmitter. Tzimas's first concern was to set up contacts which would supply them with information bulletins in the days to come. Papandreou was not there. He lived in another hotel in the town, where he was probably better informed; at least he had a radio from that day on.

After dinner Porfyrogenis tried to send for the Prime Minister. The unexpected visitor's arrival did not seem to overwhelm Papandreou with pleasure; he pleaded fatigue and said that he would see him the next day. He must have been intrigued, because he turned up very early the next morning, before breakfast, escorted by fifteen men.

Tzimas pulled a few notes out of his briefcase and ran through the most recent ELAS successes. Papandreou grew paler at the name of each liberated town and blanched at the lists of equipment recovered from the enemy. He asked no questions at all but wanly registered the successes of a movement he was committed to dissolving at all costs. At the end of Tzimas' account he made no direct comment but asked for news of Yugo-slavia.

'Who is Tito?'

'He's the leading figure in Yugoslavia,' replied Tzimas. '15,000 right-wing *Ustashis* have just surrendered to him; Yugoslavia is lost to the West.'

The Prime Minister's face was beginning to twitch. He controlled himself with an effort: 'Has Tito said anything to you about his territorial claims?'

Tzimas had personally concluded a military agreement with Tempo which included a clause that 'Yugoslav troops in Greece must respect KKE policy towards the Slavic minority in Macedonia'. It is highly un-likely that this clause had been to Tito's taste, but Tzimas had not been asked about that.

'Tito has never mentioned any territorial claim to me.'

Papandreou did not seem convinced. The interview ended. The quarantined government was waiting in the wings. It needed a sign from Churchill, the real Master of Ceremonies, before it could appear on stage.

Needless to say Churchill had been keeping an eye on things through-out. He had found the ELAS successes against the Germans far from reassuring, and while his resident minister in the Mediterranean, Macmillan, was preparing new political master-strokes with Leeper and Papandreou, he concentrated on the military arrangements.

The projected British landing in Greece had now reached an advanced stage of planning and was named Operation Manna. As its name suggests, the plan was aimed at conjuring up a magical form of intimidation.

As from midnight September 13–14, the troops for 'Manna' were placed at forty-eight hours' notice.[1]

Despite the agreements recently outlined with Stalin, an intervention of this kind was contrary to the Teheran conventions which specified that 'the Allies will not use their armed forces on foreign territory . . . other than for the purpose of liberating occupied zones'.

Operation Manna needed a political dressing. Macmillan decided to go native. With Papandreou's help he adapted Ulysses's ancient stratagem to modern conditions; he would introduce a British Horse into the city of Athens. On 15 September Sarafis, for ELAS, and Zervas, for EDES, received a summons from General Wilson.

[1] Churchill, op. cit., vol. VI, p. 248.

The PEEA leaders were uneasy, but they had already sent their ministers to join the government. The process was in motion and they did not even have the time to change horses in mid-stream.

On the morning of 19 September Sarafis was at Neraida airstrip, preparing to board the aircraft that had come to take him to Caserta. The engines were already running when a dispatch rider arrived brandishing a telegram: Prime Minister Papandreou had just appointed the British General Scobie 'Chief of Allied Forces in Greece'.

The business had been accomplished in two stages. First of all, General Wilson had appointed his Chief of Staff, Lt-General Scobie, Commander of British Forces for the Greek landing. Since there was no question of landing at Athens before the Germans had left, Scobie's duties would be limited in practice to the conduct of Operation Manna. This would amount to nothing less than an intervention in the internal affairs of another country. But the document which served the Papandreou government in place of a Constitution entitled the Prime Minister to appoint a Commander-in-Chief. The appropriate passage was very laconic and did not specify any nationality for the head of the Greek army. Papandreou therefore appointed Scobie Commander of the Greek Brigade serving on the Rimini front, formed out of the remains of the two Middle East Brigades when they had been purged of all non-monarchist elements. Thus there was no longer any question of outside interference.

Everything was ready for Scobie to march into Athens at the head of the Greek army, supported by the British detachment whose role would be to carry out Operation Manna. To reach this point it had been necessary to stage the Middle East mutiny, partly to facilitate the recruiting of a praetorian force and partly to place Papandreou in a position of strength for the Lebanon negotiations. Two years of provocations, of undermining the Resistance, had gone into maintaining the apple of discord which would now 'justify' the fraudulent presence of a foreign peace-keeping force. The Trojan Horse was the Papandreou government. In its belly lurked Scobie and his troops.

There were still one or two details to be settled. Sarafis had been summoned to Caserta so that ELAS could be brought finally to heel. Scobie, head of the British force and the Rimini Brigade, must also take command of the partisan forces. Until now, EAM-ELAS policy had not budged an inch on this issue. But in Caserta there was nothing Sarafis could do but drain the Lebanese cup to its dregs. From the moment of his arrival he protested bitterly against the granting of such wide powers to Scobie, and he tried to get a Greek entrusted with the maintenance of law and order in Athens. It was too late. Zervas was sitting at the same conference table, sneering at him and interrupting: 'My word! You do seem to have got tangled up. . . .'

Papandreou listened for appearance's sake before pronouncing a sentence decided much earlier. Karageorgis later observed, with some truth: 'Caserta was the military's Lebanon.' EAM was still on trial.

Papandreou knew how far he could go. EAM-ELAS was fighting an uphill battle, and it was not going to be allowed back into the running at Caserta. The game was now being played by political rules and Sarafis, who represented far the largest military force, had to bow to the decisions of a committee of extras:

The Government of National Union delegates General Scobie to command the Greek Armed Forces and the Mountain organizations.

The leaders of the last-named organizations undertake not to attempt to seize power. Any manoeuvre in this direction will be regarded as criminal and punished as an attack on State security. The andartes are called upon to cease hostilities among themselves.

No operation will be undertaken in the Athens region without the express orders of General Scobie.

The Security Battalions are declared to be unlawful and will be treated as enemy forces unless they surrender as soon as they are called upon to do so.

Zervas will act against the Germans on the territory allotted to him under the Plaka agreements.

General Sarafis will do the same in the rest of Greece, with the exception of Attica (the region around Athens), the Peloponnese (where it was necessary to undo Aris's good work) and Thrace (including Salonika), all of which provinces will be entrusted to Commanders named by the Government of National Union in agreement with the British.[1]

Every paragraph in this document gave rise to violent arguments. Zevgos tried to get Bakirjis given the Salonika command, but in vain. Papandreou knew that the ELAS delegates were in no position to threaten to break off the negotiations, and he would not give an inch.

The regional commands of Athens and Salonika were given to two notorious fascists: Colonel Spiliotopoulos, former Chief of Gendarmerie under the Tsolakoglou government, and Colonel Papageorgiou, ex-leader of the PAO which ELAS had disbanded at the very beginning of the Resistance for its ambiguous activities. An agreement was signed on

---

[1] Quoted in Loverdo, op. cit., p. 339.

26 September by the partisans' representatives on one side, and Papandreou, Wilson and Macmillan on the other.

At the same time, ELAS was treading hard on the Germans' heels. Partisans entered Filiates and Arta, in Epirus, liberated Navpaktos, then went on to Tripolis, in the heart of the Peloponnese. Before long the whole of Greece would be administered by PEEA and controlled by ELAS. Every one of its victories was already touched by the Caserta agreement, embroidered in advance as if by a fungus.

Papandreou saw Churchill in Rome at the end of September when he stopped there on the way to Moscow. Papandreou would not disclose either the tenor or the results of this meeting to any member of his government, despite their unanimous clamouring.

Churchill landed in Moscow on 9 October and met Stalin the same evening, in the presence of Molotov and Eden. The atmosphere was cordial.

The moment was apt for business, so I said: 'Let us settle about our affairs in the Balkans. Your armies are in Roumania and Bulgaria. We have interests, missions, and agents there. Don't let us get at cross-purposes in small ways. So far as Britain and Russia are concerned, how would it do for you to have ninety per cent predominance in Roumania, for us to have ninety per cent of the say in Greece, and go fifty-fifty about Yugoslavia?' While this was being translated I wrote out on a half-sheet of paper:

Roumania
    Russia 90%
    The others 10%
Greece
    Great Britain (in accord with USA) 90%
    Russia 10%
Yugoslavia 50-50%
Hungary 50-50%
Bulgaria
    Russia 75%
    The others 25%

I pushed this across to Stalin, who had by then heard the translation. There was a slight pause. Then he took his blue pencil and made a large tick upon it, and passed it back to us. It was all settled in no more time than it takes to set down.[1]

[1] Churchill, op. cit., vol. VI, pp. 198 ff.

Alea jacta est. Churchill went on with a formal scruple or two:

Of course we had long and anxiously considered our point, and were only dealing with immediate war-time arrangements. . . .

After this there was a long silence. The pencilled paper lay in the centre of the table. At length I said: 'Might it not be thought rather cynical if it seemed that we had disposed of these issues, so fateful to millions of people, in such an off-hand manner? Let us burn the paper.' 'No, you keep it,' said Stalin.[1]

[1] Churchill, op. cit., vol. VI, pp. 198 ff.

Part Two
Stolen Victory
1944-1946

Liberation

The Moscow deal weighed on the future like an order of destiny. Hindsight enables us to work out the sequence of events; at the time, however, although the air was thick with speculation, nobody in PEEA or ELAS either in Athens or in the mountains had the faintest inkling of the exchange of contracts between Churchill and Stalin. The cryptic advice passed to Rousos by the Soviet ambassador in Cairo, to Bakirjis by Chernichev and above all to Siantos by Popov was certainly a great deal less explicit than the report Papandreou received from Churchill. The Prime Minister may have been guilty of underestimating ELAS strength both subjectively and objectively, but his ideas were very clear indeed on the twin subjects of British determination and Soviet indifference.

Not only were the PEEA and KKE leaderships excluded from the secrets of the gods, but they were also having difficulty in keeping their rank and file members up to date on the scraps of information that did reach them by devious routes. The committed Bolsheviks of the Central Committee could hardly broadcast the presumed defection of their great Revolutionary ally Russia; on the other hand, the combatants had to be made to swallow the Caserta agreement.

Unable to justify the measures that had been taken, ELAS HQ were reduced to imposing a kind of censorship by omission: they broke up the pattern. No unit head, not a single regional HQ, received a full report on the decisions reached at Caserta. Each was informed exclusively of the arrangements concerning his own region.

In Macedonia, Markos and Bakirjis protested when they received the laconic order to keep out of Salonika. The local organization made its arrangements and vigorously opposed the appointment of the collaborator Papageorgiou as commander of regional forces. Had the kapetanios and the fighting officers got wind of the full import of the new arrangements, ELAS HQ would probably have had other, and greater, difficulties in controlling its troops.

An ELAS Regiment stationed near the town of Florina and led by a Macedonian autonomist called Gotsev rebelled against the Caserta agreement and decided to go over to Yugoslavia. The Macedonian leadership was ordered to intervene and Markos, torn apart, obeyed orders and disbanded the unit. Later on, this would be the only ELAS action to receive government recognition, and certain officers who had taken part in the expedition would be integrated into the regular army on the strength of it.

Aris was recalled from the Peloponnese in accordance with British wishes. For the last few weeks he had been letting himself go completely, trying to reach the point of no return and secure an irreversible ELAS victory on the terrain. He had no time for the fraudulent agreements of the Lebanon and Caserta, and knew far too much about the activities of British agents to doubt that a confrontation was on the way. His recall from the Peloponnese brought him back to HQ, where he was still hoping to get someone to listen to him.

An uprising in Athens was to plunge the Germans into irreversible chaos during the second half of September. For the moment the Reich's services were feverishly trying to organize a hand-over of power to the British and cover for their own withdrawal from the capital. An order from Hitler recommended the destruction of all the vital installations in Greece. The SS General Shimans interpreted it very sweepingly and wanted to destroy the town and exterminate all the political detainees. He had explosive charges placed in the Piraeus port installations and the Marathon Lake dam which supplied the whole capital with water. He was suddenly recalled to Berlin, and General Felmy took over his command. Felmy was no fool. He was looking for Greek contacts, and to show goodwill dismantled the Haidari camp, freeing the leaders of the old liberal parties, Themistocles Sofoulis, George Kafandaris and Stylianos Gonatas.

Sofoulis had hardly drawn his first breath of free air when he was approached on Felmy's behalf by the Abwehr officer Hampe: Felmy wanted to discuss his withdrawal with PEEA representatives.[1] Sofoulis was out of touch and advised him to see Archbishop Damaskinos.

The Archbishop's career was advancing nicely. His candidature for the Regency had been considerably reinforced by his impeccable behaviour in standing up for victims of the occupation and by his connections with the British Intelligence agent Frank Macaskie (nicknamed the Scarlet Pimpernel of Athens after a series of extravagant adventures which he only survived thanks to a last-minute arrangement between the Germans and the British).

[1] Roland Hampe, *Die Rettung Athens*, Wiesbaden, 1951, pp. 17ff.

Though he had no real influence over ELAS, Damaskinos undertook to persuade the partisans to take a 'reasonable attitude' to the retreating German troops. In exchange, Felmy disarmed and removed the explosive charges honeycombing the Marathon dam.

Damaskinos's faith in the efficacy of the Caserta agreements was really very limited, and he feared an ELAS victory in the streets of Athens almost as much as the Germans did. It would not take a great deal to provoke the Athenians into invading the sanctuary reserved for Papandreou and his team of trusties.

The buffeting was intense even in the bosom of the EAM Central Committee. In the early part of October Ioannidis the orthodox, Aris's deadly adversary, was also trying to bring about a *fait accompli*, preparing his own kind of coup d'état.

Endless convoys of Germans were pulling out of Athens and the South of Greece. Amfissa, at the foot of Mt Parnassus, was a crucial staging post for the smooth operation of the retreat. Through Colonel Tsamakos, Ioannidis ordered ten battalions (4,000 men) to gather at the exit of the town.

Minor skirmishes between patrols had been going on there since 1 October, and the arrangements were completed within a few days, but the order to attack did not arrive. German convoys filed past on the road below under the partisans' yearning noses. A little squeeze on a single trigger could start the broadside that would bring the procession to an untidy halt.

Captain Grigoriadis watched the cohorts of lorries passing, two by two, stuffed with troops, arms and munitions. The andartes were holding themselves in check, assuming that their General Staff was waiting for a particularly juicy convoy before giving the order to attack. While they waited, incredible quantities of booty were slipping through their fingers. The exasperating, unconsummated ambush lasted eleven days. Eleven days in which the partisans had nothing to do but count the game wriggling through their lines.

In the evening of 12 October a car from ELAS HQ drove up to the position: perhaps the signal to attack had arrived at last. Siantos climbed out of the car. The Russian Popov and General Mandakas were with him. Popov gazed impassively around as eager officers pressed forward.

The Old Man spoke soothingly, but brought no orders. A table was set up in honour of the visitors, who spent a tense meal playing dumb and dodging awkward questions. As dinner ended a clamour arose in the distance: all the church bells in Amfissa were ringing in unison. An over-excited messenger skidded to a stop: 'Athens is free!'

The news should have unleashed an explosion of joy, but all the faces round the table were frozen.

Athens free. There was nothing left to wait for; the last of the German convoys were flowing past on the road below. Grigoriadis leaned towards Siantos: 'What about Amfissa?'

The Old Man's face was bloodless.

'It's all over.'

The sound of the axe on the block. The words echoed in a stony silence. A puff of wind brought the sound of bells closer for a second or two.

'But now we're going to be able to enter Athens.'

'You're not going back to Athens,' Siantos replied harshly. 'Stay here and wait for orders from Staff.'

Behind him, Popov's motionless features.

Some time later, when the tragedy had happened and he was in exile, Grigoriadis met Major Makridis on the island of Naxos. The Major asked him why the attack had never been launched at Amfissa. When he heard that the order had been withheld, and that Siantos had come on the last evening to tell them not to move, he fell into a black rage. The battle of Amfissa had been part of his plan for taking Athens.

Later still, after the return of orthodoxy and bogus trials, the ultra-respectable Zachariadis made great play of accusing Siantos of having had an understanding with the British. But the contract had been drawn up by Churchill and Stalin; the objective agent of British policy, that day at Amfissa, was Popov, a colonel in the Soviet army. Could the Greek Resistance have gathered the fruits of its victories alone, without help from Stalin?

Siantos was waiting for the Kremlin's go-ahead. Perhaps Stalin assumed that ELAS would act on its own authority without compromising his diplomatic relations with his Occidental Allies. Obviously, Popov could not answer this question any more clearly than any other.

A monster traffic jam blocked all the exits from Athens. Under the jeers and catcalls of the population, the Germans were abandoning ship. Fighting erupted round the power station between Athens and Piraeus, which the Germans (Felmy's promises notwithstanding) were trying vainly to destroy before their departure. In general, however, the effect of the Caserta agreement was to protect the German retreat by hobbling ELAS.

The British, who wanted to prevent Athens from being burnt at all costs, wisely refrained from harassing the retreating troops. 'A single Allied aircraft,' wrote Hampe, 'could have turned this chaos into a disaster. But not one appeared in the sky.'[1] The German troops on their way out of Greece were earmarked for Tito and Stalin – a division of responsibilities. The Athenians could stay put no longer. From the morning of 12 October onward, the crowd began to spread through the streets to enjoy its freedom, despite the fact that the occupying forces had not finished leaving. Convoys of haggard soldiers were struggling slowly through the joyful crowd, which yelled its delight at their defeat and seemed almost to have forgotten the hatred of yesterday.

Hampe left Athens in the evening: 'We found the streets filled with a sea of humanity, so dense that our car could only pick its way through with difficulty. I have never seen men in the grip of such joy and enthusiasm.'[2] There was no question of reprisals now.

Depressed men, haunted already with fear of the long retreat through the maquis, were piled into the vehicles mixed higgledy-piggledy with kitbags, provisions and small livestock. More than one of these soldiers had a dreamy look in his eyes. Were they remembering their triumphal entry into the sunlit city, rich in ancient marbles, wearing the Parthenon like a victor's crown as it awaited the coming of the new Barbarians? Were they thinking of the ruin they had sown in every corner of Europe and which now awaited them in their own country, a sepulchre for their dead?

Their eyes were moist, uneasy, like the eyes of the sheep lying hobbled at their feet. . . .

The people jeered at this pathetic departure, waved their fists, sang the songs of ELAS and EAM, sang the 'Internationale'. In the suburbs, in Piraeus where the Germans were blowing up the port facilities, there was fighting. The sound of grenades, of dynamite ripping the wharves apart, could be heard dully in the centre of the city. The people responded to this sound, the last noise of battle, with delirious joy, an immense clamour of triumph. The abhorred enemy was leaving. . . .

Still more men, women and children swarmed through the public squares, hair flying, laughing, weeping. Hundreds of blue and white flags and red flags waved from the crown; suddenly the immense mass of people started to form ranks and move off. Thus began the endless procession, a procession such as the world had never seen. For three days and nights the people of Athens, broken by the trials of so many dark years, so much mourning and misery, hungry, sick people spitting blood, marched in the sunshine or by torchlight without sleeping, without

[1] Hampe, op. cit., p. 104. [2] Hampe, op. cit., p. 98

eating or drinking, kept going by a collective delirium, the immense joy of new-found freedom.[1]

The Athenian crowd, which had known famine, riots, suicidal attacks, suddenly exploded and let itself go in celebration of a victory just as real, and just as impalpable, as the light itself. EAM-ELAS had 20,000 men in the town. It would only take a signal for Athens to pass under their control. But standing orders were that legality must be respected; the KKE political bureau had addressed the following message to its troops on 6 October 1944:

The KKE, which has been in the front rank of the fight against fascist tyranny, calls upon all patriots to display discipline and sacrifice of the highest order. Maintaining law and order and ensuring a return to normal political life are national priorities. War criminals will be punished whoever they are, but this is a task for the National Government. Do not take the law into your own hands; avoid actions which might harm the ennobling work we have accomplished together. Communists, you have been the soul of the National Democratic Movement against the occupying forces; now become the builders of public order and the democratic liberties! Patriots, unite, with ELAS and our Allies, to achieve the Liberation of Greece under the aegis of a Government of National Union!

So ELAS refrained, on the night of 12 October, from taking over the liberated capital of a country it controlled virtually from one end to the other. For the next few days the KKE and other left-wing organizations hesitated. They were waiting for some evidence of goodwill on the part of the Papandreou government or the British. They were waiting for a sign from the Kremlin, for some show of encouragement from Tito. Churchill had certainly never hoped for so much when he was tracing the broad outlines of Operation Manna: 'You should note that time is more important than numbers. . . . It is highly desirable that we strike without warning and avoid any preliminary crisis. That is the best way to forestall EAM.'

The summit of Mt Parnis rises from the Athenian Plain about thirty kilometres from the centre of Athens, a rocky stronghold overlooking the Euripus channel and the Saronic Gulf from a height of over 4,000 feet. Orestis and the Second Attica Division had been established there for some considerable time; from their mountain top, it looked a simple matter to run down two abreast into the jubilant streets of the capital's suburbs.

[1] Kedros, *Peuple roi*, Paris, 1966, p. 225.

The andartes had helped the Germans on their way by taking part in a few skirmishes in the area. They had not fought any major actions. Now they were watching from afar as the population exploded with joy. Zevgos, a member of the KKE political bureau, climbed up to Kavasina accompanied by Hajibeis to explain why the andartes on Parnis had not been invited to the party.

'The agreements signed at Caserta are perfectly correct. You must stay on Parnis and keep out of Athens.'

Orestis took him aside.

'It's impossible. The men have been dreaming about nothing but Athens for the last two years.'

'It's the Line.'

'We'll have to find a way round it. I'm going to take the brigade commanders and four andartes with me, find Spiliotopoulos (military commander of the Athens region) and explain the situation to him. Winter is coming. We can't stay here until the snow freezes us to this perch. I'm going to persuade him to let my brigades into the suburbs.'

Orestis brought his HQ down into the plain and installed it at Eleusis, the beginning of the Sacred Way of the Eleusinian Mysteries of antiquity, which leads to the Acropolis. It was out of bounds to ELAS fighting units. Orestis and his small delegation arrived to protest.

Spiliotopoulos formally refused permission for the Second Attica Division to enter the capital. Sarafis supported the request, but in vain: no ELAS unit was authorized to stay in Athens. There were not enough billets for the men. Orestis would not give up trying.

'It's very rough on my men. Furthermore, it looks pretty bad politically to try to keep partisans out of the town.'

In the end Spiliotopoulos agreed to let the Second Division into the suburbs on condition that the men arrived singly. Most of the troops would be scattered among different units of EP, the ELAS-based Civil Guard, and dispersed over a twenty-kilometre radius.

Operation Manna swung into action at the very beginning of October. On the 4th, six hundred British paratroops landed near Patras in the Peloponnese and began making their way towards the capital along the Gulf of Corinth. On the 13th, the day after the last of the occupants pulled out of Athens, a commando of thirty men landed at Megara airfield a dozen kilometres to the west of the capital and started clearing up in the port of Piraeus. On the 14th, the first airborne units marched into the town to the acclamations of the crowd. Troopships docked at Piraeus on the 15th and landed General Scobie and two British brigades. No sign or whisper came from the north where the Red Army was tiptoeing back up the Danube taking good care to keep off Churchill's flowerbeds.

Siantos felt almost certain that he could work on Papandreou on the spot, and he underestimated the British determination to intervene. He allowed Scobie's brigades to land and march past the Acropolis. Scobie's infantrymen received a frantic welcome; the words 'Welcome to our Great Allies' were inscribed on banners, walls, everywhere. The Russian Popov was trapped in his car by an exalted human tide; the car was lifted from the ground and carried on the crowd's shoulders like an enormous litter. 'Long live the Soviet Union! Long live Stalin!' Popov's face was inscrutable. Great Allies, shared Victory, Liberation, sovereign Greece: total confusion. It was a festival.

The Greek government had left Italy on board a British ship, but it landed on Greek soil from a Greek vessel, the old cruiser *Averof*. The Government of National Union had its share of the inexhaustible acclamations of free Athens as it trod the sacred Eleusinian Way into town. The government's triumphal march ended when it passed through the Propylaeum, and entered the perimeter of the Acropolis. Later a 'Te Deum' was sung in the cathedral, and Papandreou bent over Damaskinos's archiepiscopal ring. George II had agreed not to return to the country until after the elections; the huge archbishop, who already knew that he was going to become Regent, delivered his homily wearing a mitre that made him seem even more of a giant:

... O shades of dead heroes, O living people, O myriads of victims, O lines of tombs, and you who mourn in tears and serenity, give thanks to the Lord.

O mountain echoes, O laurels of the plains, O wind from the sea, O free breath of air, give thanks to the Lord.

O cohorts of victorious liberators, O clashing weapons, O bugles of glory, give thanks to the Lord.

O church bells resounding, O rippling flags of blue and white, O people enslaved but never defeated, give thanks to the good Lord with hymns and holy actions.

Lord God, bless our Nation, exchange the bitter thorns of martyrdom for laurel wreaths and crown the victors in honour and glory.[1]

Papandreou left the cathedral and headed for Constitution Square, where he was to speak. The square and all the roads leading to it were

[1] Loverdo, op. cit., p. 352.

jammed with people. The crowd in the middle was so dense that the little oranges in the trees would not have had room to fall to the ground. Papandreou climbed onto the rostrum opposite the Tomb of the Unknown Soldier.

'We believe . . .'

A chant rose from the crowd, drowning his voice:

'LA-O-KRA-TIA! LA-O-KRA-TIA! LA-O-KRA-TIA!'

Laokratia means people's power. The wave of sound rose and fell once, twice, three times, then died away. Papandreou resumed his leitmotiv: 'We believe . . .'

'LA-O-KRA-TIA! LA-O-KRA-TIA!'

The Prime Minister was rattled.

'Silence! I'm going to talk about *Laokratia*.'

But he did not. He eulogized the Resistance and the Greek Middle East Army. Then he moved on to Greek territorial claims: the evacuation of Thrace and Macedonia by the Bulgarians, the return to Greece of Northern Epirus and the Dodecanese islands. He steered clear of the Cyprus issue; the British flag was floating over the island. Finally he spoke about the future State, the reconstruction of the economy. . . .

'LA-O-KRA-TIA! . . .'

The chanting began once more. An enormous gulf separated the Prime Minister from this crowd which had come to acclaim him and was now trying to find out where he stood. For the moment, however, nobody could or would believe in a blatant return to the past. George II had stayed in London, submitting in the end with a very bad grace to Churchill's insistence that not even the heir apparent, Prince Paul, could be allowed back into the capital just yet. If there was to be a bloody settlement of accounts with ELAS the British Premier wanted to make quite sure that the monarchy would not be mixed up in it.

Papandreou's position was still very ambiguous. Facing him was a whole people and its popular army, which would not be able to live on evasions indefinitely. The whole town had come to listen to him in the square. Afterwards an endless homegoing crowd flooded down the wide University Avenue towards Concord Square. There was an eddy in the current outside the Hermes Hotel; the building was full of arrested collaborators, some of whom were leaning out of the windows and jeering at the crowd. Members of Grivas's X Organization appeared among these collaborators and informers; they were armed. A shot was fired into the air. The human tide paused, gathering its forces to attack the building. A

British officer rushed out of the entrance hall, flanked by an interpreter.

'Calm down! The prisoners are in our custody. We promise that those who fired will be dealt with.'

Men of the X Organization were seen to be operating in most areas during the days that followed. The British did not appear to have relieved them of their weapons. They were helping to keep 'order', an order that was already awakening the ghosts of yesterday. . . .

The arrest of collaborators and war criminals was not being carried out by the ordinary police force but by the Aliens Department in collaboration with the British services, under the pretext that most of these men were of interest to Allied Intelligence. In practice these agencies were less interested in gathering information than in protecting those who had rendered signal services in the war against Bolshevism.

On Liberation Day the quisling government's police chief, Evert, whose pro-Ally record had apparently made him as pure as driven snow, had the job of arresting the collaborationist Prime Minister, Rallis. In this confused atmosphere, with extreme right-wing groups on the loose, a frenzied settlement of accounts quickly became the order of the day. OPLA joined in, judging and condemning; the Civil Guard arrested numbers of individuals and delivered them to the Aliens Department which often let them out again by another door.

Thus Exarchos, one of the hooded informers of the Athens raids, was delivered to the authorities by the Civil Guard and was seen the next day walking about Concord Square in complete freedom. The British had given him a 'pass'. The collaborators imprisoned in Averof jail lived on in scandalous comfort, protected by prison walls whose main function was to frustrate the anger of the people.

The Athenians had lived through three years of terror and famine, and the physical misery of the survivors was terrible. Things were a little better in the Kolonaki district, which is not exactly of Athens although situated in it. Kolonaki is a residential quarter at the foot of Lycabettus, a sort of reservation reminiscent of a colonial consular enclave. It also came to be called 'Scobia'. The district was inhabited by colonists who were not foreigners exactly; they carried Greek passports, although their money somehow found its way into foreign banks and their fleets sailed under the most exotic flags. They sometimes spoke Greek but normally expressed themselves better in French or English. The miseries of Athens were barely perceptible from Kolonaki, whose houses, cellars and larders were opened wide to give a monster party for the British officers. Hellenic hospitality is justly legendary, but the parties that took place in Kolonaki in autumn 1944 were too sumptuous to be truly Greek. So shameless was the display that many British officers were deeply shocked and Reginald Leeper, the British ambassador, felt obliged to intervene.

It goes almost without saying that the officers and diplomats who attended these soirées were first softened up and then initiated to a Greece which had precious little contact with reality, in which the unwashed ELAS 'bandits' were depicted in the gloomiest colours.

The promised purge had not yet taken place; it was not due to happen for a long, long time. It was written into the Caserta agreement that 'the Security Battalions will be regarded as enemy organizations, and will be treated accordingly except where they give themselves up on the orders of the Military Command of Allied forces in Greece.' For the time being they were left pretty much alone in the capital.

Scobie's orders to Spiliotopoulos, Military Commander of the Athens region, had been extremely indulgent towards them: 'When the Germans withdraw or surrender, you will instruct the Battalions to desert to their homes (and hide) or to surrender to our forces.'

Scobie had no hesitation in nursing the former pro-German militia with an eye to recruiting them for the coming civil war. The Security Battalions which surrendered to the British were regrouped in the Peloponnese and Chalcidice, where they were not only not disarmed but trained by British instructors in the handling of modern weapons.

As the *feldgrau* tide ebbed away to the north, the British were preoccupied with preventing a resurgence of ELAS activity, and no operations on any large scale were mounted to transform the precipitate withdrawal of the Reich's soldiers into a fully-fledged rout. Hampe noted during the retreat that his column was frequently flown over but never attacked by British aircraft. On the road it met various EDES units accompanied by British officers. Everyone would continue about their business with a courteous salute; it was more like a relief than a pursuit.

The last major town on the Germans' route out of Greece was Salonika, Greece's second city, a town of railwaymen and tobacco workers; Jewish Salonika. The Jewish quarter had been a desert for eighteen months. 68,000 men, women and children had been spirited away in airless trucks 'to colonize the spaces of the East'. Of those who left in this way, only 2,000 were to survive. The liberation of Athens made Salonika restless, and the itchy population began taking to the streets. The German retreat began on 16 October.

The extreme right-wing groups led by Poulos and Papadopoulos were overcome with panic. On the morning of the 16th the Security Battalions attacked the working-class district of Neapolis. The militia were not expecting serious resistance as most of the men of arms-bearing age were in the mountains with Markos, Bakirjis and Kikitsas. There were very few weapons in the suburb, perhaps ten submachine-guns and a few ornamental pieces. What the fascists had not expected was the determination of the populace: EPON, the EAM youth movement, exacted a very high price for every inch of pavement and, as in Athens at the height of the big demonstrations, the people formed themselves into a human wall. Bullets tore into the multitude but the wall swept forward to attack. *Aera!*

The armed men fled before this ferocious determination, before this rage yelled from thousands of throats. Women grabbed the slowest fugitives with their bare hands and dragged them into the crowd. Once started, the wave kept growing and it swept down on the Pavlos Melas camp for Yugoslav prisoners. The sentries fled to avoid getting trampled underfoot. The prisoners were released; the camp armouries contained enough rifles to arm the quarter, plus three Fiat machine-guns. These were kept until the very end, carried to any critical point like the holy sacrament in a procession. Neither the Caserta agreement nor orders from Athens could prevent the town from rising. The Germans controlled their own main axis of retreat; the rest of the town belonged to EAM.

On 26 October, newly installed at Kokova in Pieria, Markos, Bakirjis and Kikitsas received new instructions from Athens. The order was laconic, containing only the relevant local details from the Caserta agreement: ELAS must not enter Salonika but must stay on the other side of the Axios river.

The kapetanios Markos and Kikitsas, and the soldier Bakirjis, decided to cross the river anyway, ignoring the protests of the political commissar Stringos. The first detachment crossed the Gulf of Salonika from Methoni on board twenty-eight small boats belonging to ELAN, the naval section of ELAS, while two others marched round by the north. Markos directed operations while Bakirjis stayed at his HQ in Pieria.

ELAS Tenth Division and part of the Ninth Division marched into Salonika on 28 October. The town celebrated its liberation with the combatants. Markos was crowned with a laurel wreath. The next day a small commando of eleven English who had parachuted onto the Chalcidice peninsula arrived at Salonika. An EAM delegation went out to meet them and made it clear that the town had been able to manage without their help and was in partisan hands. On 4 November Bakirjis arrived in Salonika with the rest of the partisans from Pieria.

ELAS HQ at Lamia was presented with a *fait accompli.* ELAS had occupied Salonika in violation of the Caserta agreement. The KKE leadership, which would never be able to forgive Markos for this initiative, sent him a stinging reprimand. This may well be the reason why some days later, when Aris urged him to throw over the official line and join him in imposing kapetanios decisions, he maintained a rigid Communist discipline, refusing to carry his challenge through to its conclusion.

Meanwhile Markos decided to attack the extreme right-wing groups led by Anton Tsaous which were still roaming Thrace. The British major Miller, who was attached to Tsaous's organization, managed to escape just before the last bands were dissolved. The whole of Greece was now liberated with the exception of the Chania region of Crete and the Dodecanese islands.

The Red Army was only a few kilometres away, across the frontier in Bulgarian territory. A few Soviet officers were invited to a party in Greece at which they were the guests of honour; they left before dawn and prudently returned to Bulgarian soil. Stalin always abided by his agreements.

Belgrade had been liberated since 18 October. There was total solidarity between the Yugoslav Communist Party and the People's Liberation Front, and the conquerors were making the law. Mihailović's right-wing resistance groups had lost their British support after the Teheran agreements; the fifty-percent share of influence in Yugoslavia which Stalin had granted the British with a stroke of his blue pencil had evaporated into thin air. From now on the Soviets were to find it just as difficult to impose their own tutelage. Tito had played a lone hand.

In Athens, Papandreou was hastily throwing together a 'National Guard' from divers elements including men from the Security Battalions. Its main function was to impose legality on the ELAS Civil Guard, but it was also supposed to hunt war criminals when it had nothing better to do. On 25 October Spiliotopoulos was replaced at the head of the armed forces in the Attica region by Brigadier-General Katsotas, Commander of Free Greek Forces in the Middle East. The Liberation Festival was over and disappointment was gaining a hold over the population. On 4 November an enormous crowd took to the streets to demand the proper observance of all the various treaties. It was wasting its time, for Churchill had no real intention of calming the situation down; to his mind, there was only one sure way to disarm ELAS and secure Greece as his own protectorate: armed confrontation.

While the KKE Central Committee, still hoping for instructions which would never arrive, muddled along with a seesaw policy alternating a tentative legalism with shows of strength (and even this strength would not last much longer), Churchill was gaining time and issuing orders.

Prime Minister to Foreign Secretary. 7 November 1944

In my opinion, having paid the price we have to Russia for freedom of action in Greece, we should not hesitate to use British troops to support the Royal Hellenic Government under M. Papandreou.

2. This implies that British troops should definitely intervene to check acts of lawlessness. Surely M. Papandreou can close down EAM newspapers if they call a newspaper strike.

3. I hope the Greek Brigade will soon arrive, and will not hesitate to shoot when necessary. Why is only one Indian brigade of the Indian Division being sent in? We need another eight or ten thousand foot-soldiers to hold the capital and Salonika for the present Government. Later on we must consider extending the Greek authority. I fully expect a clash with EAM, and we must not shrink from it provided the ground is well chosen.[1]

Three weeks after the liberation of Athens, EAM, which had suffered three years of furious combat and enjoyed the support of the great majority of the Greek nation, was suddenly the declared enemy of Churchill's Greece. . . . In writing: 'I fully expect a clash with EAM', he was not speculating but giving expression to a wish, a settled objective which was to be the outcome of three years of systematic manipulation.

The Rimini Brigade landed at Piraeus on 10 November. At Salonika the Fourth Indian Division, which had been circling the heavily-mined entrance to the bay since the day before, finally approached the town in the evening. But the British kept out of Salonika itself; Markos and Bakirjis were holding the town, and the Indian division tactfully installed itself a few kilometres away in Karabournou camp. The forces were deployed. Each busied itself calculating the determination of its adversary.

[1] Churchill, op. cit., vol. VI, p. 250.

The Lamia Congress

When Aris arrived at Lamia after his return from the Peloponnese, an uninterrupted running volley lasting more than an hour saluted him as the first hero of the living Resistance legend. Lamia was also the site of ELAS HQ. The peremptory epithets of orthodoxy had been coming back into fashion there during 1944. From the moment of his arrival Aris the adventurist, Aris the ultra-leftist, struggled to convince the leadership that a confrontation with the English was imminent. He knew no more than anyone else about the dealings between Churchill and Stalin. He knew nothing of the British Premier's recent instructions to his diplomats and generals. But the cynicism with which the National Liberation Army's legitimacy was being denied and concealed after three years of struggle, the fraudulent government of nonentities, the continuing influx of British intervention forces, all strengthened his conviction that the British meant to spark off a civil war.

In the streets of Lamia Aris was carried about in triumph, but in the minds of those whom he had to convince both in the Central Committee and at HQ he carried the stigmata of a non-conformist. He might just as well have been preaching in the desert. Only one solution remained to him: to unite his peers, the kapetanios, the popular chiefs, behind some sort of coup d'état within the Revolution. It was perhaps ELAS's last chance of harvesting the victory it deserved.

On 11 November, in response to Aris's summons, the kapetanios poured into Lamia from all parts of Greece: Markos, Kikitsas, Nikiforos, Ypsilantis, Lassanis, Orestis, Kalynos, Troyanos, Karas, Blanas, Morias. They had not followed the Party's bureaucratic *cursus honorum*, but they represented a considerable weight of authority. Before the meeting Aris met Orestis and took a short walk with him.

'You've noticed what's happening to us?'

'What?' replied Orestis.

'We're going to be handed to the British on a plate.'

'Not us, just our guns.'

Aris closed one eye and scanned Orestis with the other as if taking aim at him: 'How are we going to survive without rifles? How will we get what we want?'

'We'll be what we are, that's all.'

Aris remembered a conversation from a year earlier, over the matter of some uniforms and who was supposed to get them. On that occasion it had been Orestis who wanted the kapetanios to take power, while he, Aris, *dilosias* and renegade, had been reluctant to flout Party law. Now he was more disposed to risk damnation: 'Listen. We shouldn't hand over our arms until all outstanding issues have been settled.'

'Supposing we're ordered to?'

'There are the mountains. We know the way there.'

Orestis no longer believed in that.

'Aris, there are more spies than mules in your outfit. You're only alive now because it's the Party's will. The power of the kapetanios is no more than folklore these days. It's too late.'

The kapetanios had no voice; the guerilla chiefs had no authority recognized by the Party statutes. Aris knew that most of the men he was going to address felt the same anguish in their hearts as he did himself, but how far would he have to go to persuade them to take the step, to set themselves against the Party?

They had raised battalions of montagnards, they reigned over citadels of sharp stones; they were klephts, popular chieftains, strong and intractable. What law would be able to wrench the weapons from their grasp?

'*Synagonistes* (fellow warriors, combatants in the full sense of the word, comrades) . . . I was in the Peloponnese when the Caserta agreements opened the way to the British landing in Greece. We were presented with a *fait accompli*. Now, after all that we have done, I believe that we are going to be obliged to fight the British if we want our national independence. We should prepare ourselves for it.'

Whatever deep echoes these words may have awakened in the minds of his listeners, the haunting fear of provocation was too strong for them. Aris paused for a few moments; he was seeking contact with his audience, a supporting conviction from some of those present, so that he could get them to express their anxiety and build up some resonance from each man's repressed anger. But the room did not react; only one man stood up, Ilias Karas: 'Tell me, Aris, are you ready to assume all the responsibilities your position implies? We ought to know whether you're expressing your own personal opinions or the Party line.'

Karas had hit it exactly. Once, Aris had signed, sinned, suffered discipline for the transgression. Everyone else present was terrified of meeting the same fate. A single interruption in Aris's favour might have been enough to reverse the balance, but everyone was waiting for someone else to take the initiative. Aris drew back from the edge.

'It's not an official position. I'm expressing my own opinion, as a kapetanios.'

It was Markos's turn to stand up: Markos who was responsible for ELAS entering Salonika, who had violated the Caserta agreement and openly thrown Central Committee orders in the fire. He had no stomach for another revolutionary sacrilege so soon after the first.

'Comrade, the kapetanios have no means of enforcing their decisions. I don't see any sense in this meeting; I can't see why you asked us to come here just to listen to you expressing an opinion that commits nobody but yourself.'

Aris was blocked. It was he who had taken the initiative of organizing the meeting, and it was for him to carry the provocation through to its conclusion. But he was alone; he did not dare to dare for everyone. To the surprise and disappointment of almost everyone present, he adjourned the session. Three years later in the course of a new struggle, Markos was to incarnate the Mountain's aspirations in his own way. He would in his turn be alone among silent allies, tragically hemmed in by the pack-ice of dogma.

Some of those present at the meeting hung about in the school court-yard where it had been held in the hope of establishing a contact or discerning some sign of encouragement, but suspicion won the day. It was a fiasco. Aris thought it useless to continue the discussion. The kapetanios would march in step until their legend had been violated and their conquests stolen from them. The next day the soldier Sarafis came to Aris's rescue by expressing his own anxieties. He suggested formulating a contingency plan for a clash with the British as a simple precautionary measure. But it was all over after the experience of the previous day; everyone was paralysed with fear of police infiltration. The dialogue foundered and everyone returned to his unit. Not only did the kapetanios fail to marshal their convictions, not only would they never make their united voice heard in the Central Committee, but no overall plan to deal with the fighting to come was ever formulated.

Athens

As British reinforcements flowed into Athens and the remains of the Middle East Army, royalist to a man, paraded through the streets behind a flag recently blooded at Rimini, the Party and the EAM Central Committee were dancing to a measure usually associated with the French gentry: one step forward, two steps back. One day the Red Flag would be waved to make an impression; the next day's demonstrations would return to the familiar blue-and-white of National Union.

On 7 November, a feast-day in the Bolshevik calendar, the order was to deploy the masses as a giant revolutionary banner. Every piece of material, every last scrap of fabric scrounged from the attics of Athens was dyed by any means that came to hand and took on the colour of blood. Athens was red from dawn to dusk: scarves, ties, shirts, trousers, hats. A scarlet mob swarmed through the streets. It was enough to give Scobie a sleepless night or two. The respectable districts were petrified. They came to life three days later, though, to welcome the Rimini Brigade. 10 November: the Bankers' and Shipowners' International thronged the pavements of Kolonaki to acclaim the saviours of the fatherland.

There were popular demonstrations in response, but this time it was felt that it would be tactless to protest in red: 'EAM isn't exclusively communist after all. We mustn't frighten the bourgeoisie.' The blue-and-white waved over the lines of demonstrators. These chameleon-like colour switches reflected the Central Committee's indecision, but also showed to what extent the base was prepared to follow instructions.

More British were landing every day in an increasingly heavy atmosphere. 'The Greeks are curious people,' wrote a British officer. 'They acclaimed us in 1941 when we were fleeing from their territory pursued by Hitler's troops. When we returned as victors in 1944 they met us with hostility.'

The Security Battalions were still going strong. Not only were men arrested by the Civil Guard released by Papandreou's police, but 668 notorious collaborators and war criminals managed to escape from Syngrou jail in circumstances that can only be described as unusual, after overcoming the symbolic resistance of their warders.

OPLA and EAM's special services began a systematic search of every district. Every section of the official police was covered by a Civil Guard unit carrying the same number and code letter, which helped to keep the regular force up to the mark. General Scobie and ambassador Leeper called in the three communist members of the government and asked them to issue a public statement denouncing the 'illegal arrests' being carried out by EAM.

The conference that started the next day was supposed to end in the creation of a new national army and, more specifically, in the dissolution of ELAS. The British proposed that a 'mixed' division should be set up for an initial period, comprising an ELAS brigade, an EDES battalion, elements of the Free Greek forces (the Rimini Brigade and the Sacred Battalion) and a few conscripts from the most recent age groups.

The ELAS representatives felt that the Middle East units should be disbanded in the same way as the others with a view to individual recruitment into the new army, but Papandreou wanted to maintain his praetorian guard as an organic entity. The talks bogged down. The situation in the city continued to deteriorate.

Athens was living through a period of schemes and deception; an atmosphere of uncertainty and impatience pervaded the streets. Every boulevard, square, street and café terrace became a seething market-place for rumours; the endless wait for a gesture or decision gave rise to minutely detailed fantasies and speculations, vanishing in a moment to be replaced by others. EAM and the Party channelled the discontent into sporadic demonstrations. The base was still disciplined, but how far would the legalistic game get Siantos when the government was protecting collaborators, arming the militia and engaging in organized provocation? Jilted by the Soviets, the Old Man had not been able to find the courage to embark ELAS on a solitary adventure in the second half of October. Time was still working against him. Tito had entered Belgrade alone, without diplomatic or military support.

The Central Committee was beginning to wonder – not before time – whether the right formula might not be found in the Yugoslav direction. A month after the liberation of Athens the Party leadership decided to send another delegation to see Tito. Tzimas had been there throughout and was still sending his reports from Belgrade. He had good reason to think that a conflict in Greece would serve Tito's interests by keeping the British intervention forces in the Balkans fully occupied, thus forcing Churchill to abandon his last hope of winning the race to Vienna against the Red Army by landing on the Dalmatian coast. Quite apart from this, the Yugoslav war effort was concentrated on Trieste, and Tito was in no position to lend any substantial support to a Greek uprising. Siantos was not convinced and wanted to take another sounding. The delegation was led by Rousos and met Tito in Belgrade in the presence of Tzimas.

'Are you disposed to guarantee us your support if a conflict breaks out with the British?'

Tito replied without a moment's hesitation: 'Yugoslavia will support you.'

Tzimas bounded to his feet.

'How can you say you're going to help us when you're not in a position to send a single rifle?'

Rousos had already heard Tzimas's opinions on the subject. He had come to Yugoslavia to hear the reply from Tito's own lips.

Certain elements, probably starting with the KKE Central Committee, wanted to read into Tito's remarks the authority of a sort of neo-Comintern, but this too was a misunderstanding; Tito was playing a lone game. But the KKE leadership, getting more and more cornered by provocations every day, was incapable of taking the initiative and seemed to be searching desperately for orders.

Like a pendulum, the Central Committee was swinging between two poles: the need to organize for combat by seeking outside support, and the hope of progressing along the legal path without succumbing to the provocation.

A few embryonic battle plans were outlined, while those units of the Second Attica Division which had not been absorbed by the Civil Guard were ordered to let through all traffic bound for Athens. Arms destined for the Security Battalions and the National Guard poured into the capital in uninterrupted convoys.

EAM was holding back until events should force it to react; the city was swarming with British agents, and any effective preparation for the struggle would now be tantamount to provocation. Every day, little by little, the Resistance was being overtaken by History.

The negotiations with Papandreou and Scobie for setting up a national army gave rise to frenzied bargaining. The government had not relinquished an inch of ground. On the contrary, it was trying to provoke a rupture by imposing leonine conditions and pressing for a series of capitulations to which it was not entitled. In the words of William Hardy McNeill:

It is easy to sympathize with EAM's position. They had risen to supremacy in Greece during the years of occupation through hard work, danger and suffering. They saw no reason why they should of their own will relinquish the power which they had won, and give to the Right a chance to organize itself in the countryside and challenge their supremacy in the land.[1]

History is not always fair, however. It was the British who held power in Athens.

Papandreou insisted on setting up a mixed division in which ELAS would be placed in a weak position. All unintegrated partisan units were to be disbanded before 10 December. The Civil Guard must vanish by 1 December.

The legal path continued a line traced from the Lebanon agreements through those reached at Caserta. EAM could only follow it by capitulating all along the line.

On 26 November Zevgos announced on EAM's behalf that it was ready to discuss the project of the mixed division, on condition that forces of ELAS origin should equal such units as the Rimini Brigade and the Sacred Battalion not only in numbers but also in firepower, as these units had plenty of heavy weapons. The next day, although nothing had been signed yet, Papandreou released the news to the press.

Siantos, Ioannidis and the EAM Central Committee found themselves once again in a Lebanese half-nelson: backed into a corner as a result of trying to stay legal. The line of least resistance led straight as an arrow to the outcome desired by their enemies: the dissolution of ELAS without any political recompense. The alternative choice would be complete rupture which, after four months of continuous concessions, after letting their opportunity to seize power in October slip from their grasp, and in a steadily worsening military situation, would be bordering on adventurism.

On the evening of 27 November Siantos and Ioannidis had a long argument in the Stadium Street headquarters of the KKE. Relying on Tito's go-ahead, Ioannidis was trying to convince the Old Man that they should refuse this final capitulation and break with the Papandreou government.

Tzimas had left Belgrade after the meeting between Tito and the KKE delegation. He was heading for Athens as fast as he could travel in the hope of getting there in time to give the Central Committee a more realistic idea of the international situation as he had been able to analyse it from Belgrade. He was still on the way when Siantos succumbed to Ioannidis' arguments and decided, not to throw all ELAS forces into the

---

[1] William Hardy McNeill, *The Greek Dilemma*, London, 1947, p. 130.

battle for Athens, but nevertheless to refuse the final concession and if necessary to go into opposition.

On the 29th, Zevgos stormed out of Papandreou's office and slammed the door. He had just demanded the dissolution of the Sacred Battalion and the Rimini Brigade as a precondition for disarming ELAS. There was nothing extravagant about the request, but Papandreou knew how far Churchill would go in his support and saw no need to make concessions. Also on 29 November, the EAM Central Committee met in Athens. Siantos was able to persuade the KKE's partners, in particular Tsirimokos and Svolos, that they should go into opposition.

Almost at the same moment Scobie issued a proclamation addressed to ELAS andartes, ordering them to lay down their arms and disperse before the 10 December deadline already laid down by Papandreou. When the base was consulted, the decision at cell-level was unanimously opposed to unilateral disarmament.

The Papandreou government's Ministerial Council met on 1 December. None of the EAM members were present. The rupture had come.

EAM's precautionary arrangements were incredible. They were based on a tragic underestimate of the British will to intervene, totally unfounded illusions about the possibility of political support from Russia or the US, and a great anxiety to keep the Mountain and its guerillas well out of the way during the decisive period.

The Line, if even the embryo of a concerted plan could be said to exist, was as follows: Avoid any confrontation with the British, which meant letting them occupy all strategic points in Athens. Prepare to neutralize units of the right-wing organizations, the Security Battalions, the militia and Zervas troops. It was more a matter of making a show of force than of seizing power, and it was noted that the widely dispersed objectives enabled elements judged unorthodox by the guardians of dogma to be sent out of the capital.

On 2 December the command of ELAS was divided up and Resistance unity sacrificed to the petty-minded control of bureaucrats. ELAS Central Committee, whose functions had been taken over by HQ, was reconstituted. It was placed in control of the entire south: Athens ELAS, the Second Attica Division, the Third Peloponnese Division and the Thirteenth Roumeli Division, altogether some 25,000 men, were placed under the direct command of Siantos and another ageing figure, General Mandakas.

Unsound and 'competitive' elements, that is to say almost the whole of the former HQ including Makridis, the former Athens leader and author of the only military plan to envisage taking the capital, found themselves at HQ with Aris and Sarafis in command of the Eighth Epirus Division, the First Thessalian Division, the Cavalry Brigade and the four Macedonian Divisions (Sixth, Ninth, Tenth and Eleventh), almost 23,000 men altogether. Their job was to prevent the remains of Zervas's forces from marching on the capital. What had really happened was that the kapetanios, the very heart of that prodigious popular wave – the Mountain – who had threatened to submerge a rigid, paralysed system, had been removed from the vital point and diverted into tasks of secondary importance. The formation of PEEA had relegated Aris and Sarafis from the first to the second level; now they were being removed to the third.

Once again a demonstration had been mounted instead of an attack. Churchill had been trying to engineer a collision since 7 November but ELAS was still hoping to win the political battle by showing its teeth. Scobie issued more proclamations. On 2 December aircraft showered the capital with leaflets: 'I am going to protect you and your government against any attempt at a coup d'état and against unconstitutional acts of violence.' The Communist Party and EAM retaliated by calling a general strike for the next day. Athenians were asked to demonstrate in the streets on Sunday, 3 December.

Blood

The winter of 1944 was cold. It had been raining for several days, and the flooded drains at the top of Stournara Street in the Museum quarter had overflowed. There was a gaping fissure in the pavement outside the Asfalia, the Athens CID, from which emerged from time to time some ghastly evidence of the butcheries carried out by the mercenaries of order: hands, whole limbs, chunks of human flesh tortured and flushed away into the sewers.

The temperature had dropped with the coming of the rain but now the sky had cleared again. Early on the morning of 3 December the low, pale sun of an Indian summer flooded into Constitution Square, shining obliquely across the Tomb of the Unknown Soldier onto the columns of the former Royal Palace. On the left, on the other side of Queen Sophia Avenue, stood the Ministry of the Interior and next to it the Hotel Great Britain which in keeping with its cosmopolitan tradition housed the foreign press and the three military missions, British, American and Soviet.

A distant murmur, growing louder as it approached from all directions, eroded the silence of the big sunlit rectangle. Processions were converging on the Square, along Queen Sophia Avenue from the north, along Syngrou Avenue and from the Acropolis, along Hermes Street. The demonstration had not been forbidden; to what extent had the events that followed been deliberately planned?

The first procession from the suburbs marched into the square behind an immense banner of the red lion of Kaisariani with all his claws out: LONG LIVE KAISARIANI, CRADLE OF PARTISANS AND REVOLUTIONARIES. Another, further back: WHEN TYRANNY THREATENS, THE PEOPLE MUST CHOOSE BETWEEN CHAINS AND ARMS. Many demonstrators carried a shorter slogan: THE GERMANS ARE BACK.

The procession arrived in a solid mass at the Tomb of the Unknown Soldier. A youth surged from the front ranks and, encouraged by the yells of the crowd, began a wild dance. He leapt high in the air once, twice. Suddenly, he doubled up and fell to the ground, his chest covered with blood. An automatic weapon was barking somewhere. It was a machine-gun, spitting death from the roof of Police HQ on Constitution Square. Each burst chopped into a densely-packed crowd and few bullets were wasted. Another had opened up from the roof of the Royal Palace. For several minutes, each one an eternity, the firing continued. The crowd tried to climb over the railings into the royal gardens. People flattened themselves behind the low wall surrounding the Tomb of the Unknown Soldier. Some were trying to hide behind a big hoarding wrenched from the railings; it carried a photograph of Roosevelt underlined by the words: *Welcome to our Great Liberators.* The square continued to fill up as the machine-guns rattled; from the distant suburbs, from Faleros, Kokkinia, Kaisariani, Pankrati, the unsuspecting sea of humanity flowed forward, hearing nothing but its own murmur. Horrified journalists witnessed the massacre from the windows of the Hotel Great Britain. It lasted two or three minutes. Twenty-eight were killed and more than a hundred injured.[1]

It is quite unthinkable that machine-gun nests could have been set up on the roofs of public buildings in the heart of Athens without the

[1] See, for this incident, W. Byford-Jones, *The Greek Trilogy*, London, 1945.

authorities getting wind of it. 'British troops,' wrote Leeper, 'had been standing by in the neighbourhood of Constitution Square in case the situation got out of hand, but they were not needed.'[1]

Whatever the specific contribution made to this incident by the authorities, whether it was by virtue of direct responsibility or through more or less deliberate negligence, it is quite clear that the government's refusal to purge extreme right-wing groups had led to a situation which made some kind of confrontation absolutely inevitable. The collision anticipated by Churchill in his 7 November dispatch to Eden had been engineered in the most monstrous manner.

When the firing stopped, a leaden stupor settled on the crowds in Constitution Square. Some people soaked their handkerchiefs in the blood of victims and went to wave them in the faces of the journalists. Numerous policemen mingled with the demonstrators as they shouted their indignation at the elaborate façade of the Hotel Great Britain. Popov's motionless profile could be seen in one of its windows. Processions were still arriving in the square. Nobody was armed; the formal order of the day was to stage a demonstration which must not even begin to look like a riot. But now the crowd was so determined that it might just as well have been armed with rifles.

The next day's general strike was unanimous and paralysed the whole country. In Athens, the people took to the streets in the early morning and converged on Constitution Square. Hundreds of thousands of Athenians invaded the centre of their city. There was not a single British uniform to be seen. The coffins of the previous day's victims arrived, carried on the shoulders of demonstrators. The partisans' Funeral March swelled from the crowd, echoed and multiplied in all the neighbouring streets, loud, grave and menacing. When it ended, between four and five hundred thousand people knelt together, solemnly, and observed several seconds' silence. It seemed to last for ever, a solid silence pressing against the walls of the Hotel Great Britain, dense as stone, stifling.

The crowd filled all the town's open spaces as it moved off slowly towards the cemetery. A slow march for the dead. The cortège seemed endless but it broke up at last; the tide ebbed and the human sea drained back towards the central districts. The avenues were still swarming; outside the Hermes Hotel, where members of the X Organization and the militia had been holed up for the last month, University Avenue was black with people. An incident had occurred there three weeks before, on the

[1] Reginald Leeper, *When Greek Meets Greek*, London, 1950, p. 104.

day of Papandreou's speech. This time it was more serious. A volley of shots suddenly poured from all the hotel's windows; despite all the British promises, the 'prisoners' had not been disarmed. More blood; the crowd rushed to attack the hotel and was mown down a second time. A hundred dead and wounded.

After this new provocation Scobie declared martial law and issued a new ultimatum to ELAS. If partisan units had not left Athens before the day after next, 6 December, they would be regarded as enemy forces. The authors of this text, which was posted on every wall, did not shrink from any means of intimidation. Athens could remember the winter of 1941–42, when 300,000 of its inhabitants had starved to death; the ultimatum threatened to suspend food supplies until ELAS left the capital.

In Piraeus, a man holding a can of food from the UNRRA relief operation was reading Scobie's proclamation. On the other side of the road stood a British sentry, outside the Naval College. When he finished reading the poster, the man crossed the road slowly and placed the can of food at the sentry's feet. Men, women and children emerged from the houses nearby and copied his gesture; they went back and forth, piling all their provisions around the British soldier.

The EP (Civil Guard) groups which had been shadowing the different police detachments came on duty armed. A few last bombs were being manufactured, traditional in design but nicknamed 'Scobie Preserves' for this campaign. They were made by packing empty food tins with old nails and bits of scrap iron around a core of two sticks of dynamite or 'loukoumia' (turkish delight): the nail soup of people's war.

The men wore white scarves for identification, like Botzaris's fighters against the Turks. The password was a combination of the names of two heroines of the Resistance and the struggle of Klephts and pirates: Elektra-Bouboulina.

The attack was launched at midnight in every quarter. The first section to fall was the 15th. Opposite the building housing the 8th section was a school containing a Security Battalion 'imprisoned' by the government. At the first shots, the 'prisoners' opened fire with everything they had; not one cartridge had been taken from them. Fortunately, the police were equipped with Polish grenades which only worked one time out of three . . . the attackers' 'Scobie Preserves' guaranteed their overall technical superiority.

Even so, it was not until the next morning that the ELAS group was able to take the police station by blowing a hole in the wall with dynamite. Inside, they found about ten policemen behind bars, where they had been imprisoned by their colleagues for wanting to join the insurgents. The partisans used the windows of the police building to provide covering fire for a new attack on the school held by the Security Battalion, which fell after a few minutes. All the police stations in Athens were in ELAS hands.

In the Filopapou district, near the Theseion, the Grivas organization was defending the building it had occupied since the Liberation. These people specialized in hunting democrats, and had done so with some success under every regime. They were unanimously loathed by the Athenian population. The assailants swept towards the building, attacking with terrible violence. They were suddenly stopped in their tracks by the appearance of British tanks.

Firing on the British was formally forbidden, and the firing ceased immediately. Grivas's men emerged from cover, clambered onto the tanks and were almost all driven away clustered round their turrets. The andartes' guns were muzzled by the order not to open fire on the 'Great Liberators of Greece'.

The Asfalia, sinister headquarters of the Athens CID, was a symbol which had to be destroyed. It was attacked during the night from the entrance to an Underground station which opened onto the pavement a few yards from the building. The first attack was mounted by the young communists of an EPON group; adolescents aged between thirteen and sixteen, carrying submachine-guns or brandishing Scobie Preserves, fell to the defenders' volleys. A second wave gained a few more yards. The defenders waved a white flag and negotiations began. At that moment a British tank and a half-track drew up between the two sides, as they had in Filopapou. Through an interpreter, the captain commanding the detachment spoke to the attackers: 'You have to let us take these men away. They are our prisoners.'

On the evening of 4 December, perceiving that events had progressed to a stage where no intimidation would be able to contain them, Papandreou resigned, or rather tendered his resignation. The final decision was Churchill's.

The ELAS Central Committee was still hoping that the affair could be settled between Greeks. At 4.50 a.m. on 5 December, after a long discussion with Eden, Churchill cabled:

Prime Minister to General Scobie (Athens). Repeated to General Wilson (Italy).
1. I have given instructions to General Wilson to make sure that all possible forces are left with you and all possible reinforcements are sent to you.

2. You are responsible for maintaining order in Athens and for neutralizing or destroying all EAM-ELAS bands approaching the city. You may make any arrangements you like for the strict control of the streets or for the rounding up of any number of truculent persons. Naturally ELAS will try to put women and children in the van where shooting may occur. You must be clever about this and avoid mistakes. But do not hesitate to fire at any armed male in Athens who assails the British authority or the Greek authority with which we are working. It would be well of course if your command were reinforced by the authority of some Greek government, and Papandreou is being told by Leeper to stop and help. *Do not however hesitate to act as if you were in a conquered city where a local rebellion is in progress.*

3. With regard to ELAS bands approaching from the outside, you should surely be able with your armour to give some of these a lesson which will make others unlikely to try. You may count upon my support in all reasonable and sensible action taken on this basis. *We have to hold and dominate Athens. It would be a great thing for you to succeed in this without bloodshed if possible, but also with bloodshed if necessary.*[1]

Later in the day he telegraphed Leeper:

1. This is no time to dabble in Greek politics or to imagine that Greek politicians of varying shades can affect the situation. You should not worry about Greek government compositions. The matter is one of life and death.

2. You must urge Papandreou to stand to his duty, and assure him he will be supported by all our forces if he does so. The day has long gone past when any particular group of Greek politicians can influence this mob rising. His only chance is to come through with us . . . .

Churchill had no illusions about Papandreou's legitimacy as a representative of the Greek nation, nor about any of the alternative politicians. There remained the 'mob', i.e. Greece; to be precise, it was Greece he was trying to bring under control. He continued:

3. I have put the whole question of the defence of Athens and the maintenance of law and order in the hands of General Scobie, and have assured him that he will be supported in the use of whatever force is necessary. Henceforward you and Papandreou will conform to his directions in all matters affecting public order and security. You should both support Scobie in every possible way, and

---

[1] Churchill, op. cit., vol. VI, p. 252 (italics in original).

you should suggest to him any means which occur to you of making his action more vigorous and decisive.

Every good wish.[1]

While Churchill was suggesting a last attempt at intimidation for the sake of form, but at the same time echoing Balfour's dictum: 'Do not hesitate to fire', the ELAS Central Committee, still underestimating the British willingness to intervene, was dispersing its own forces and allowing British troops to circulate freely.

Sarafis and Aris deployed their forces along the edge of Epirus. There was nobody in Athens to counterbalance the Central Committee's authority, now vested in two ageing men, Mandakas and Hajimichalis, who were in formal command of military forces in Attica. Half of ELAS's forces had been removed from the nerve-centre. What of the other half?

On 2 December the ELAS units stationed in the Peloponnese received the Central Committee's order to march on the capital. Hermes, whom Aris had left behind in the peninsula, crossed the Corinth canal with 1,500 men and started along the coast road to Athens. His detachment, which was on foot, was overtaken by a convoy of British trucks. The commanding officer's jeep drew up beside the kapetanios: 'You have no right to march on Athens.'

Hermes waved an order signed by Colonel Papastamatiadis, ELAS commander in the Peloponnese, and continued on his way. He watched the lorries drive by, every one loaded with armed men in British uniform. They were Greeks from the Security Battalions, collaborators with whom he had been locked in furious combat only two months earlier.

Hermes handed the detachment over to his second-in-command, commandeered a horse and galloped at the maximum speed of which the beast was capable to the ELAS Central Committee headquarters near Eleusis. Just before he reached it a British tank appeared and another officer stuck his head out of the turret.

'What are you doing here? Don't you know you're not supposed to be here?'

'I've got my orders, I'm carrying them out.'

'Where are you going?'

'I'm looking for Siantos.'

They parted in their different directions. Hermes reached Staff HQ and rushed in to see Siantos.

[1] Churchill, op. cit., vol. VI, p. 253.

'I'm on my way with 1,500 men. Two British officers have tried to stop me. They were taking a convoy of militiamen to Athens; they're armed. What should we do?'

'You know the British are our allies,' answered Siantos. 'We absolutely must avoid any clash with them. Unless they attack us first, that is.'

Hermes was shouting: 'But it's a trap! They're bringing in the militia. They are in trucks and my men are on foot; I'm going to arrive two days later than them. Next time I see a convoy I'll ambush it. I'm going to blow up the bridges.'

Siantos interrupted: 'Calm down. Don't cut the road. Leave well alone and do as you're told.'

Hermes did as he was told. His column was breathing the dust of British convoys all the way to Athens. All the Security Battalions from the Peloponnese drove past under his nose and reached Athens before him. When he reached the capital he found his way to the HQ of Colonel Pyriochos, commander of the Athens Third Army Corps. ELAS Third Army Corps existed only on paper; its armed men hardly added up to a division. Hermes was greeted by the enormous Bartzotas, who took him in to see Pyriochos.

'Great to see you, you've arrived on the dot. How many are you?'

'Fifteen hundred,' Hermes answered.

'Good, good. You're to put 200 men at the disposal of the 2nd Brigade . . ., etc.'

Hermes exploded again: 'Impossible! We shouldn't scatter our forces. My men are used to fighting together – this is no time to be reorganizing the army. . . . We've worked out a plan which I'd like you to have a look at. . . .'

Pyriochos swiftly scribbled an order on a sheet of paper, which he handed to Hermes: 'Do as you're told.'

Hermes's plan was not the only one to be rejected out of hand; the Makridis plan, worked out even before the Caserta agreement had been signed, fared no better. While the British were busy occupying all the strategic points in the city, the ELAS Central Committee's main concern seemed to be with restructuring the people's army in Athens, diluting the authority of the kapetanios and the Mountain's military leaders by scattering their units. They were more interested in taking a small section of ELAS in hand than in taking the capital with the Liberation Army that had emerged from the struggle against the occupant.

Scobie did not wait until 6 December to start treating ELAS units in and around the capital as 'enemy formations'. On the night of 4–5 December a battalion of Nikiforos's Second Attica Division bivouacked its men behind the fuchsias and bougainvilleas of the hippodrome at Filothei. They were neither vigilant nor suspicious enough to prevent themselves from being captured by the British a few minutes before sunrise.

On the 5th ELAS held virtually the whole of Athens with the exception of the sacred triangle in the heart of the city. The andartes had abandoned the Acropolis after a British delegation had insisted that the sacred hill remain neutral out of respect for Greece's cultural heritage, held in trust for all mankind. The ELAS members had hardly left the steps of the Parthenon before a British artillery unit was in position behind the ancient ramparts.

Stretching away from Concord Square, on the edge of the triangle ELAS never occupied, is the Patisia quarter. It was here that the British liaison officer Hills, who had made no secret of his pro-ELAS sympathies, had been struck down by a solitary sniper. The culprit was never found but certain witnesses claimed to have glimpsed an Englishman at a window.

Marnis Street was barricaded with two sulphur-yellow buses and two tramcars lying across the road. A partisan was perched on the side of an overturned bus, singing.

> The girls who went out with the Germans,
> Kamerad.
> The girls who went out with the Italians,
> Signorina.
> Now they go out with the English
> wearing khaki shorts,
> followed by regiments of Indians, of Africans . . .
> Tell me, woman, whose are my children?
> One says ja ja,
> The other says yes yes,
> Tell me, woman, whose are my children?

A Patton tank had arrived, the clattering of its tracks drowning the last few words. It rooted about, clawing at the cobbles, and stopped facing the barricade. A British officer emerged from the turret and signalled for an interpreter.

'If you haven't abandoned your position and handed us your weapons by 6 o'clock, we're opening fire.'

There was no reply, but four men went into a nearby building and came out with a white sheet folded over their arms. The British officer was expecting a surrender signal. A woman appeared, framed in a window. She threw the men the nearest thing to red paint that she had been able to find, a tin of tomato concentrate. When the white sheet was hung over the barricade the British could read Epaminondas's message of defiance at Thermopylae, spelt out in red:

IF YOU WANT MY WEAPONS, COME AND GET THEM.

Silence. Then a faint whine as the tank's turret pivoted slowly, deliberately into firing position. The men flatted themselves on the ground behind the yellow rampart of overturned buses. With an earsplitting roar the tank's 80mm loosed the first British shell to be fired at the people of Athens.

The most violent fighting took place around the hill of Ardittos, which the Rimini Brigade, supported by the RAF and British tanks, tried unsuccessfully to take from ELAS. The andartes stood firm, but the price was high. British aircraft began bombing the working-class districts on which the hill's defenders were relying for supplies and reinforcements. Most of the British soldiers could no longer make out what war they were supposed to be fighting. The Greeks were beginning to count their victims all over again.

On 6 December all the public buildings in the centre of Athens were guarded by British detachments. Scobie had five brigades at his disposal, counting the Rimini Brigade; ELAS numbered at least two divisions, perhaps 8,000 men supported by thousands of reservists. The British forces were widely scattered about Athens and Piraeus; an action concentrated on the centre of the town would have had every chance of success, despite Scobie's armoured brigade. But the Central Committee did not want to escalate the conflict. Siantos was trying to rewrite history, to return to the period before the Lebanon agreement and negotiate on his own ground after liquidating the extreme right-wing organizations. He was making a show of strength. To attack the centre of Athens and occupy Constitution Square, the Parliament building and the principal Ministries would come close to overturning institutions, and the neophyte Central Committee maintained a clumsy and ill-advised respect for symbols in keeping with its attempts to attain power by the legalist road. Now that the bulk of ELAS forces were dispersed across the length and breadth of Greece, the Athenian forces were being squandered on secondary objectives. To quote Stalin: 'One victory every day, however limited.' But no decisive assault. Churchill was unlikely to allow himself to be intimidated by that sort of thing, and arranged for reinforcements to be sent to Athens.

Units from the Fourth Indian Division were stationed in the suburbs of Salonika, near the Alatini mill, surrounded by an ELAS detachment under Kikitsas's command. There were no instructions from the capital; the last communiqué from the Central Committee had merely stated that 'the Athens incident is of a local nature and will soon be settled'. Markos and Bakirjis had decided to nail the English to the spot on their own initiative and without consulting anyone. The Indian Division did make one tentative bid to get out, but Kikitsas fired a few ranging shots as a warning and the British did not persist. They were neutralized for the time being.

In a session of the ELAS Pan-Macedonian Committee, someone raised the question of going even further, attacking the British at Alatini mill and then marching on Athens. The political commissar, Leonidas Stringos, first backed the idea and then changed his mind. He had no up-to-date instructions from the EAM Central Committee or from the KKE.

Markos and Kikitsas were in favour of immediate action. They were supported by the EAM secretary Dilaveris, Papadimitris, a member of AKE (the Agrarian Party) and Aristotelis Bouras, secretary of the Macedonian branch of the KKE. Stringos did not know how to justify his opposition and could be heard muttering offstage: 'What can we do when they don't send us any orders?'

Bakirjis was in a more complicated position; as a career officer, he felt that he could only act to violate the Caserta agreement on formal instructions from ELAS High Command. Two other members of the Committee, the Socialist Charitantis and an agrarian group's delegate called Hajiasteriou, were violently opposed to any conflict with the British on the grounds that they wished to 'avoid bloodshed'. They resigned from EAM and left for Athens under British escort.

While the Pan-Macedonian Committee hesitated, the Fourth Indian Division took advantage of EAM's internal conflicts and withdrew to Kassandra, where it embarked on warships and sailed for Athens. Karageorgis, stationed further south in Thessaly, was less hesitant. He attacked the British, who withdrew precipitately by sea from Volos, abandoning a hundred lorries which would later be used to carry northern forces to Athens. But it was an isolated initiative without much future; had it been followed by other commanders it could have formed the basis for a united front stretching as far as the south of Olympus, when Churchill himself had confessed that the British were not equipped to operate outside Attica.

Since 5 December, the Thirteenth Roumeli and the Third Peloponnese Divisions, restructured by Athens Command which had dispersed the units under the pretext of counting them, had been fighting on all fronts in the capital. The British clung to the Navy HQ in Piraeus, which commanded the main road to Athens. ELAS concentrated a large part of the Roumeli Division on this objective and took it in a few hours. This placed the whole of the road from Athens to the port in insurgent hands.

The British were now locked into the centre of the town, with only two rather insecure channels for retreat or reinforcement: one leading north to the Tatoi airstrip near Kifisia, the other leading south to Megara. Scobie's military position was extremely precarious. On the political level, Churchill was being violently attacked by the Americans from the outside, while at home he had to face a difficult debate in the Commons between the 5th and the 8th.

... The vast majority of the American Press violently condemned our action which they declared falsified the cause for which they had gone to war. . . . The State Department, in the charge of Mr Stettinius, issued a markedly critical pronouncement, which they in their turn were to regret, or at least reverse, in after-years. In England there was much perturbation. *The Times* and the *Manchester Guardian* pronounced their censures on what they considered our reactionary policy. Stalin however adhered strictly and faithfully to our agreement of October, and during all the long weeks of fighting the Communists in the streets of Athens not one word of reproach came from *Pravda* or *Izvestia*.

In the House of Commons there was a great stir. I accepted willingly the challenge flung at us in an amendment moved by Sir Richard Acland, the leader and sole member in Parliament of the Commonwealth Party, supported by Mr Shinwell and Mr Aneurin Bevan. There was a strong current of vague opinion, and even passion, of which these and other similar figures felt themselves the exponents. Here again any Government which had rested on a less solid foundation than the National Coalition might well have been shaken to pieces. But the War Cabinet stood like a rock against which all the waves and winds might beat in vain.[1]

The Commons debate was a very stormy one. Churchill was interrupted several times by Seymour Cocks as he freely interpreted the

[1] Churchill, op. cit., vol. VI, p. 255.

defection of the two Pan-Macedonian Committee members to support his contention that EAM had been infiltrated by totalitarians and was on the point of disintegrating. He went on to deliver an impassioned homily on Liberty, of a kind which might have to be imposed on the rest of the world by England from time to time. . . .

. . . One must have some respect for democracy and not use the word too lightly. The last thing which resembles democracy is mob law, with bands of gangsters, armed with deadly weapons, forcing their way into great cities, seizing the police stations and key points of government, endeavouring to introduce a totalitarian regime with an iron hand . . . .[1]

'The mob' and 'bands of gangsters' are usefully vague concepts which in this case are used to describe a nation and its popular army.

. . . Democracy is no harlot to be picked up in the street by a man with a tommy gun. I trust the people, the mass of the people, in almost any country, but I like to make sure that it is the people and not a gang of bandits who think that by violence they can overturn constituted authority, in some cases ancient Parliaments, Governments and States . . . .[2]

On 8 December, the very same day that Churchill was hypnotizing the Commons into a state of acquiesence, the Athens 'totalitarians', who on the strategic level were stuck in booby-trapped back alleys of legality, sent Scobie an offer of a truce. The British military situation was catastrophic, but Churchill, encouraged by his political victory, was eager to make a practical application of his democratic theories:

Prime Minister to Mr Leeper (Athens) 9 Dec. 1944
Do not be at all disquieted by criticisms made from divers quarters in the House of Commons. No one knows better than I the difficulties you have had to contend with. I do not yield to a passing clamour, and will always stand with those who execute their instructions with courage and precision. In Athens as everywhere else our maxim is: 'No peace without victory'.[3]

Churchill was still pulling troops out of the Italian Front. He cabled Scobie on the same day:

. . . The clear objective is the defeat of EAM. The ending of the fighting is subsidiary to this. I am ordering large reinforcements to come to Athens, and Field-Marshal Alexander will probably be with you in a few days. Firmness and sobriety are what is needed now, and not eager embraces, while the real quarrel is unsettled.[4]

[1] Churchill, op. cit., vol. VI, p. 256. [2] Churchill, op. cit., vol. VI, p. 257.
[3] Churchill, op. cit., vol. VI, p. 258. [4] Churchill, op. cit., vol. VI, p. 254.

On 11 December Alexander, who was to be promoted a week later to command all Allied forces in the Mediterranean, landed with Macmillan at Megara airport, which was held by British paratroops. Alexander discovered a disastrous military situation. He cabled Churchill that 'The British forces are in fact beleaguered in the heart of the city'. They had only six days' food and three days' ammunition. All the British positions in Piraeus were insecure, and it was impossible to get ships into the port to land reinforcements. All the roads to Athens were effectively controlled by ELAS. On the same day, the text of Churchill's bloodthirsty 5 December telegram to Scobie was leaked to the American press. This caused such a public outcry that Roosevelt telegraphed to London:

As anxious as I am to be of the greatest help to you in this trying situation, there are limitations, imposed in part by the traditional policies of the United States and in part by the mounting adverse reaction of public opinion in this country. . . .

Roosevelt went on to give one or two pieces of advice which, under the circumstances, must have seemed very forthright to Churchill.

. . . I of course lack full details and am at a great distance from the scene, but it has seemed to me that a basic reason – excuse perhaps – for the EAM attitude has been distrust regarding the intentions of King George II. I wonder if Macmillan's efforts might not be greatly facilitated if the King himself would approve the establishment of a Regency in Greece and would make a public declaration of his intention not to return unless called for by popular plebiscite.

Only the day before Churchill had told Alexander and Macmillan that the king of Greece would not hear of the establishment of a Regency. It is highly improbable, as events were soon to show, that the king was in any position to refuse an insistent request by Churchill. The British Premier was practising politics at their very worst. The king's job was to lend his name and status to the enterprise, and he had said no because Churchill did not want to give an inch. Roosevelt's second piece of advice added up to the EAM platform that Scobie had rejected as exorbitant on 30 November:

. . . Meanwhile might it not be possible to secure general agreement on the disarmament and dissolution of all the armed groups now in the country, including the Mountain (Rimini) Brigade and the Sacred Squadron. . . ?[1]

Churchill limited himself to observing: 'This however did not give me any practical help.'

[1] Churchill, op. cit., vol. VI, p. 254.

Meanwhile Admiral King ordered Admiral Hewitt, C-in-C of the American Fleet in the Mediterranean, to withold further help in transporting British intervention units to Greece.

On the 13th, the Trades Union Congress met in England and, by an overwhelming majority (2,455,000 votes to 137,000), expressed its 'regret' over the Government's policy in Greece.

Given all this, the 'political' victory the EAM Central Committee was seeking to achieve by armed pressure did not seem so very inaccessible; but only if one underestimated the tenacity of Churchill who, defying American public opinion and strong internal opposition, meant to show how he could struggle for democracy against all totalitarian assaults on it.

In mid December the ELAS Central Committee was still marking time. Scobie and Alexander were clamouring urgently for reinforcements, but the final assault was not launched. Rockets were exploding in the working-class districts but attacks on the Sacred Triangle were still taboo. The town was without electricity and water was beginning to run short. On the 12th, Porfyrogenis called on the trapped Scobie with an armistice proposal.

The Englishman knew that the Fourth Indian Division was on its way to Piraeus. Churchill's formal order had been repeated by Alexander and Macmillan: No peace without victory. He therefore continued to demand the same unacceptable conditions: ELAS had been placed under his command by the Caserta agreement, and he was ordering it to evacuate Attica. All andarte units must cease fighting and hand over their weapons. The Central Committee's reaction was to organize another show of force. General Mandakas trimmed the Sacred Triangle that very afternoon by storming the Athens town hall. Yet again, however, it was only a baring of teeth, and the operation went no further. The EAM leadership had only a few hours left before the arrival of another wave of British reinforcements, but despite mounting pressure from the rank-and-file and the provincial commanders, Siantos refused to avail himself of this last opportunity. The rest of the country, which was almost exclusively under ELAS control, awaited the order to march on the capital, singing:

> The British are in Athens,
> They won't be there a month.
> The British are in Volos,
> They lost their trousers there.

But the order to march did not come.

In Macedonia, Stringo's embarrassment ended on 9 December. The orders had arrived at last. They were not the instructions everyone was expecting, to concentrate all forces on Athens. The First, Eighth and Ninth Divisions were being sent to Epirus to reinforce Aris and Sarafis, who already had more troops than they needed. After all the Pan-Macedonian Committee's heart-searchings, the two regiments of the Tenth Division (an elite corps of 6,000 men), which had stayed in Pieria and at Yannitsa, was ordered to Salonika to reinforce the single regiment Markos had stationed there and, if necessary, help him to disarm the British. When the Division reached Kindos, ten kilometres outside Salonika, it received a Central Committee order countermanding the first: the Division was to be dismantled. One regiment, the Thirtieth, was dispatched straight to Metsovo to reinforce the reserves still further, while the other, the Sixteenth, was sent to the same destination by a longer route, along the northern frontier.

Markos was left in Salonika with only the Fiftieth Regiment at his disposal, a force insufficient to contain the British. This gave the Fourth Indian Division the opportunity to leave Alatini mill for Kassandra, where they embarked for Athens. The Macedonian forces had been fragmented and removed from both Salonika and the capital.

When the Thirtieth Regiment reached Metsovo it received yet another order: to cross the country again, from west to east this time, to Volos. It was there that it finally got the order, when everything was over, to march on Athens via Thebes, where in the event it fought a last victorious (but absurd) battle against the British. The British lorries Karageorgis had captured at Volos would not be enough to accomplish a miracle. A motorized artillery unit which was still stationed in Macedonia was ordered to travel south at about the same time, leaving Salonika virtually defenceless.

Poised between Salonika and Athens, the ELAS forces in Thessaly circled impatiently on the slopes of Olympus, ready to dash to either town at a signal. The kapetanios Vratsanos, one of the Resistance's master dynamiters, had retrieved an enormous number of anti-tank weapons from the wreckage of the innumerable German trucks his men had pushed over all the precipices in the region, and was feverishly training his men in their use. But the orders did not come. The ELAS Central Committee was still hoping to achieve a settlement negotiated under pressure from its street fighters. Its political objective thus throttled its military activity, while at the same time every shot fired by the partisans provided their enemies with a permanent alibi for their own acts of violence.

Siantos was still hovering between a legality that rejected him and an armed struggle that he could barely keep under control. While he hesitated, Churchill was pulling reinforcements out of the Ardennes and the Italian Front and rushing them to Greece.

To hamper the passage of British armoured vehicles around the Sacred Triangle, ELAS made the crossroads impassable by dynamiting most of the corner buildings. The combatants were ill-equipped in every respect but were particularly short of anti-tank weapons. They sent tramcars stuffed with explosives careering down the sloping streets of Piraeus; they fought furiously from house to house, and even in the Underground at Concord Square. If they had no personal weapon they attacked with molotov cocktails and Scobie Preserves. Very young adolescents were involved in this fighting.

The Red quarters of the town were strafed regularly by British aircraft. Papandreou insisted that the Greek Squadron should not be sent on these missions, which shows clearly on whose behalf the British were fighting. The wood and plaster walls of the suburban houses were shattered by rockets and offered no resistance to heavy-calibre machine-gun bullets, which did their deadly work even inside people's homes. But the tanks were kept at a distance and the working-class districts of the city and suburbs remained impenetrable.

Porfyrogenis was therefore in a position of strength when he called on Scobie on the 17th with new proposals for a negotiated settlement. EAM's demands were virtually the same as the 'reasonable' proposals made to Churchill by Roosevelt: it offered to withdraw its formations from Athens and Piraeus on condition that the Rimini Brigade was withdrawn from Athens and sent to the islands, the gendarmerie would be dissolved and British troops would limit their activities to the missions planned at Caserta. The final condition was that a Government of National Union be set up. Woodhouse and Byford-Jones, who were both present at the meeting, both wrote in their memoirs that these were 'conciliatory' proposals. This was not Scobie's view. He declared the conditions 'unacceptable' and called on ELAS to disarm unconditionally.

Churchill cabled Roosevelt the same day:

... Our immediate task is to secure control of Athens and the Piraeus. According to the latest reports, ELAS may agree to depart. This will give us a firm basis from which to negotiate the best settlement possible between the warring Greek factions. It will certainly have to provide for the disarming of the guerilla forces. The disarmament of the Greek Mountain Brigade, who took Rimini, and the Sacred Squadron, who have fought so well at the side of British and American troops, would seriously weaken our forces, and in any case we could not abandon them to massacre. *They may however be moved elsewhere as part of a general settlement*.[1]

Between 15 and 20 December, 1,650 transport aircraft ferried into the Athens region some 4,373,000 lb. of arms and equipment, two full English divisions, another brigade of the Fourth Indian Division and divers other units of colonial infantry. Despite this impressive deployment of men and metal, General Tsakalotas (Commander of the Mountain Brigade) wrote in his memoirs that the British Staff were envisaging a general withdrawal to Faliron and the Megara airstrip, where it was felt the British troops would be better able to resist with the support of naval artillery belonging to the ships anchored in the Bay of Faliron.

Alexander warned Churchill that it seemed to him to be a matter of urgency to settle things by installing Damaskinos as Regent:

Otherwise ... I fear if rebel resistance continues at the same intensity as at present I shall have to send further large reinforcements from the Italian front to make sure of clearing the whole of Piraeus-Athens, which is fifty square miles of houses.[2]

Churchill had been subjected to violent new attacks in the Commons and was getting a little worried. He cabled Alexander on the 17th:

The ELAS advance towards the centre of Athens seems to me a very serious feature, and I should like your appreciation of whether, with the reinforcements now arriving, we are likely to hold our own in the centre of the city and defeat the enemy. ... Is there now any danger of a mass surrender of British troops cooped up in the city of Athens, followed by a massacre of Greeks who sided with us? The War Cabinet desire your report on the military situation in this respect. ...

... The King of Greece has refused categorically in a long and powerfully reasoned letter to appoint a Regent, and especially to appoint the Archbishop, of whom he has personal distrust. ... We have not yet decided whether or in what way to overcome the King's resistance. If this cannot be overcome there will be no constitutional foundation other than an act of violence, to which we must become parties. ...

[1] Churchill, op. cit., vol. VI, p. 265.
[2] Churchill, op. cit., vol. VI, p. 267.

Personally I feel that our military predominance should be plainly established before we make terms, and in any case I should not like to make terms on grounds of weakness rather than of strength. Of course if you tell me it is impossible for us to be in control of Attica within a reasonable time the situation presents difficulties, but not such as should daunt us after all the others we have overcome.[1]

Churchill had in fact decided not to let himself be intimidated by anyone. In the Commons, Arthur Greenwood had threatened to withdraw the Labour Party from the Coalition Government, and Lords Faringdon and Strabolgi had violently attacked the Athens intervention in the House of Lords. Although Churchill was contemplating leaving constitutional ground to 'become party to an act of violence', he was very emphatic in his answers to the House on the point that ELAS's march on Athens had been 'a deliberate attack on the institutions'. American reactions were just as turbulent. Harry Hopkins had cabled Downing Street on 16 December:

Public opinion here is deteriorating rapidly because of Greek situation and your statement in Parliament about the United States and Poland.

With the battle joined as it is in Europe and Asia, with every energy required on everyone's part to defeat the enemy, I confess I find myself greatly disturbed at the diplomatic turn of events, which throw into the public gaze our several difficulties.

I do not know what the President or Stettinius may have to say publicly, but it may well be that one or both of them must state in unequivocal terms our determination to do all that we can to seek a free and secure world.[2]

Churchill needed to gain time, and therefore sent Alexander another telegram on the 19th:

The Cabinet feel it better to let the military operations to clear Athens and Attica run for a while rather than embark all our fortunes on the character of the Archbishop....

... We are waiting here till the scene clears a little more, after which we shall give all the necessary directions.[3]

Alexander's reply, dated 21 December, is wry to put it mildly:

In answer to your signal of December 19, I am most concerned that you should know exactly what the true situation is and what we can do and cannot do. This

---

[1] Churchill, op. cit., vol. VI, pp. 267–8.
[2] Churchill, op. cit., vol. VI, pp. 263–4.   [3] Churchill, op. cit., vol. VI, p. 268.

is my duty. You would know the strength of British forces in Greece, and what additions I can send from Italian front if forced by circumstances to do so.

Assuming that ELAS continues to fight, I estimate that it will be possible to clear the Athens-Piraeus area and thereafter to hold it securely, but this will not defeat ELAS and force them to surrender. We are not strong enough to go beyond this and undertake operations on the Greek mainland. During the German occupation they maintained between six and seven divisions on the mainland, in addition to the equivalent of four in the Greek islands. Even so they were unable to keep their communications open all the time, and I doubt if we will meet less strength and determination than they encountered.

The German intentions on the Italian front require careful watching. Recent events in the West and the disappearance and silence of 16th SS Division opposite Fifth US Army indicates some surprise move which we must guard against. I mention these factors to make the military situation clear to you, and to emphasize that it is my opinion that the Greek problem cannot be solved by military measures. The answer must be found in the political field.

Finally, I think you know that you can always rely on me to do everything in my power to carry out your wishes, but I earnestly hope that you will be able to find a political solution to the Greek problem, as I am convinced that further military action after we have cleared the Athens-Piraeus area is beyond our present strength.[1]

But it was the capital that the Athens Central Committee had chosen as its battle-ground. The Soviet revolutionary model was cited in support of an idea whose origins were obscure and in which Alexander, to name one expert observer, had no faith whatsoever: the notion that to hold Athens was to control Greece.

Sarafis and Aris were still receiving new detachments of troops. Aris exploded anew every time another regiment arrived; it was evident that the Central Committee was trying to take as many units as possible out of Athens and Salonika. The two undisputed military authorities of ELAS were being diverted into a task of secondary importance. In the final analysis the only diversion they created was inside ELAS itself, while the bureaucrats and military dotards fiddled about in Athens.

The order to finish EDES off reached Aris and Sarafis on the 18th. Hurrying to get the job finished quickly, they crossed the snowed-up Metsovo and Makrinoros passes at night, bore down on Epirus and swept right through it as far as the Levkas peninsula. Their three divisions smashed Zervas's forces completely, and EDES survivors fled, in a general *sauve-qui-peut*, aboard Royal Navy ships which ferried them to Corfu.

[1] Churchill, op. cit., vol. VI, p. 269.

Zervas was among them. The whole battle lasted about two and a half days, or about the length of time it takes to cover the territory at a full run. But weeks had been wasted, and it was going to take another to get back to Attica. Aris kept the men marching at a hellish pace.

In Athens, meanwhile, the Central Committee gave its answer to Scobie's ultimatum, the most recent act in the British campaign of escalation. On 16 December there was extremely violent fighting between andartes and the Rimini Brigade, entrenched in their cantonments at Goudi. On the 18th, ELAS attacked Kifisia airstrip and the Averof prison, where 640 notorious collaborators were waiting for a more merciful system of justice to be established. The first attack on the airstrip was repelled, but a second wave launched the next day breached the last defences and took 350 British prisoners.

Averof jail was defended by 150 British soldiers and 150 gendarmes, shooting through loopholes in the walls. An ELAS battalion overran the outermost defences and blasted a breach in the wall with dynamite. At the moment of the explosion a concrete pill-box broke free from the gable of the building and came down like a lift, settling intact on the ground. A detachment of British armoured cars rushed up, broke through the prison gates and withdrew the garrison under cover of smoke bombs.

To protect their prisoners, the British resorted to a most original procedure. They released them 'on parole' and asked them to rendezvous outside the combat zone. Rallis, former head of the quisling government, and most of the others as well, evidently never appeared at the appointed time and place. A few of them were arrested later in the homes of friends, but all the others vanished into nature for good.

More troops were landing at Piraeus covered by the Indian Division which had managed to regain its foothold in the Naval School, although the whole port remained exposed to ELAS fire.

On the 20th Scobie, now considerably reinforced, moved over to the offensive to clear his access and supply routes. He announced to the civilian population that he intended to shoot anything that moved in the combat zones. RAF rockets rained down on the working-class districts.

The escalation of violence was reaching new levels. OPLA, the KKE's secret police, had begun arresting hostages. When the greater part of the people's army was still being kept out of the conflict and the Athenians were fighting desperately in the streets, the specialists in revolutionary order decided the time had come for the great washing of dirty linen recommended by all the Stalinist precepts. They hunted down Mensheviks, Trotskyists and 'social traitors' with as much zeal as they expended on collaborators and war criminals. They represented the abstract revolution eating at the vitals of the Greek revolution like a tapeworm.

Protected, like the Turks a century earlier, by the untouchable Temple of Athena, the British artillery on the Acropolis pounded the Filopapou quarter and supported the advance of the newly landed troops beating a path for themselves into Athens. The Ardittos heights fell into British hands. Andartes fiercely defended the Stadium, that immense U of white marble open to the sky, but had to abandon it in its turn.

The whole southern half of the city, the seaward side, fell under British control. ELAS was still giving a good account of itself in the northern half. A commando consisting mainly of women armed with Scobie Preserves stormed RAF HQ at Psychiko, disarming 47 officers and 538 other ranks. But Scobie was gaining ground on all fronts. Kaisariani's last defenders ran out of ammunition and had to take refuge behind Mount Hymettus, abandoning the suburb. And everywhere, on the heels of the British troops, were appearing gendarmes and National Guard policemen, setting to with a will and shooting people down in the streets. Thousands of Athenians were denounced as partisans or ELAS sympathizers, arrested and hurried off to the prison camps in Libya, crammed into the overcrowded holds of cargo ships.

OPLA was still busy. To its recent record, culminating in a hurried settlement of internal accounts at the height of the battle, it had now added the mass arrest of thousands of useless and inconvenient hostages.

Churchill on the Powder-keg

On Olympus, Vratsanos was still waiting for the moment when he could take his bazookas into action. At last a message arrived from Athens, but nobody seemed to be interested in his anti-tank teams. He was simply asked to supply three experienced dynamiters to participate in a sabotage of major importance.

Preparations for a possible showdown were advancing alongside the mounting intimidation, and the Central Committee had just taken a midstream decision to transfer to a more spirited beast. It was proposing to place a giant bomb in the foundations of that temple of the foreign presence in Greece, the Hotel Great Britain, situated right in the middle of the Sacred Triangle. Engineers had studied plans of the city's drainage system and come up with two alternative routes to the objective. The shorter one started at Monastiraki and passed under Hermes Street; the other, longer but less cramped, started at the Church of the Prophet Daniel, passed under St Constantine Avenue and Concord Square, and reached the Hotel Great Britain by way of University Avenue sewer, a total distance of some two and a half kilometres.

The first route was chosen. The charges were to be placed on the night of 23-24 December. The electrical firing mechanism was installed in a house near the sewer outlet. But just as the explosives arrived and before they could be taken underground, the British launched a violent offensive in the quarter, which led to the attempt being delayed until the next day. The alternative route was chosen for the second attempt. Even now, nobody can assess the full consequences of that day's delay.

At 9 p.m., on the 24th, Vratsanos's men and four ELAS technicians lowered themselves into the sewer outlet behind the Church of the Prophet Daniel. They found themselves standing in icy water up to their calves, but at the beginning their route took them through comparatively wide and recently-built passages. After an hour and a half they reached the glaucous labyrinth under Concord Square, and the rest of their route led through narrow, decayed conduits whose walls gave off an unbearable stench; the weather had been dry and there was little water in the system.

The tunnel walls were festooned with telephone cables, hooked over metal supports which projected from the sides and made the passage even narrower. The dynamiters were escorted by fifteen armed men; behind them, about sixty partisans of both sexes were beginning to bring in detonators, wires and explosives. 750 kilograms of penthrite: enough to obliterate Constitution Square. The bags of explosive tended to catch on the metal telephone-line supports, and those carrying them were sometimes forced to lie flat in the garbage, pushing their burdens in front of them. When they reached the hotel's foundations the men set off in the reverse direction, uncoiling the wires as they went. The subterranean coming and going lasted all night; the last partisans to emerge, six men and a woman, left the Church of the Prophet Daniel on foot at seven o'clock in the morning on the 25th. They were half-frozen and haggard.

The British Staff, the American and Russian missions, most of the diplomatic corps and a number of politicians, slumbered on above 750 kilos of penthrite and its detonators, all connected and ready to go. Among them was a Greek notable who had arrived in a British submarine on the 18th at Papandreou's invitation: General Plastiras.

Plastiras, who had been nominal head of EDES, was returning to Greece after eleven years of exile spent in Nice. It was he who had sent Pyromaglou to Greece in 1941 with a warning not to trust Zervas. His earlier career and his long exile had given him a reputation for intransigent republicanism. In 1922 he had marched on Athens to force King Constantine to abdicate, and he had been responsible for executing six monarchist politicians. George II was not exactly eager to make him his Prime Minister, but Papandreou's authority had never recovered from the events of 5 December in Constitution Square. Churchill was looking for a new man, untainted by the quarrels of recent months and possessing some semblance of a democratic aura.

Plastiras had given a press conference in the hotel lounge on his arrival. He did not know much about Resistance matters, and had been in no position to follow the upheavals which had taken place during the dark years of occupation, but he did not hesitate to deliver the customary – almost obligatory – attack on the extreme Left, EAM and ELAS. 'Though ill-informed, rugged and unsophisticated, Plastiras was treated as a future head of state from the word go by the British authorities and the journalists present. It was in this role that the elderly general addressed a prompt appeal to ELAS to lay down its arms.'[1]

Scobie was on the advance everywhere in Athens and Piraeus. Mandakas had summoned the ELAS reinforcements too late, and they were still a long way from the city. Though reassured on the military level for the time being, Churchill still had to consolidate his political position, even if it meant organizing another rigged conference to provide him with an alibi before international opinion. He knew no better way of dealing with the situation than that of hurling himself physically into the fray.

Late on Christmas Eve, therefore, he dragged Eden from his family Christmas tree and into a Skymaster which was waiting on the runway at Northolt to fly them to Athens via Naples. They landed at Megara airstrip, encircled for the occasion by 2,000 airmen at the alert, at midday on the 25th. Field-Marshal Alexander, ambassador Leeper, and Macmillan boarded the aircraft as soon as it landed and gave Churchill their

[1] Kedros, *La Résistance Grecque*, Paris, 1966, p. 499.

reports on the situation. In the normal course of events Churchill and his entourage should have installed themselves in the Hotel Great Britain, where the Staff was going about its duties in blissful ignorance of the infernal device beneath its feet, primed and ready to blow the whole lot to kingdom come.

The road to Athens was not quite secure, however, and at the last moment the British Premier decided to spend the night on board the light cruiser *Ajax*, which was lying in Piraeus Bay. Thus Churchill avoided by a hairsbreadth installing himself on top of a volcano, or would have done if the Athens ELAS HQ had not disarmed the bomb at the news of Churchill's arrival; the British Premier was expected at the Hotel Great Britain at any moment, and the firing mechanism was disconnected in the expectation of peace proposals.

During the day Vratsanos's men, led by Christos Milonis, went back into the sewers to check the condition of the charges and the wires leading to them. Long before they reached their objective, somewhere in the neighbourhood of Concord Square, they were spotted by a British patrol, which dropped grenades on them through manholes in the pavement above. Fortunately the rubbish which had collected in the drains deadened the explosions, and all the men managed to get away. The bomb stayed in place, an enormous buried threat whose existence was suspected by nobody.

Churchill boarded the *Ajax* at nightfall. He had decided to take a personal look at the candidate for Regent, and Archbishop Damaskinos was expected.

It is one of the traditions of the Royal Navy that on Christmas Day the men dress up and produce an impromptu pantomime for their officers. When Damaskinos set foot on the *Ajax*'s gangway this carnival was at its height, and his ecclesiastical robes, mitre, chignon and beard were warmly applauded. A sailor advanced and put out a hand to pull the archepiscopal beard, but the officer of the watch arrived in the nick of time and averted a diplomatic incident.

The Archbishop's style and bearing made the best possible impression on Churchill, who was reassured still further by his anti-EAM pronouncements. Damaskinos passed his interview with flying colours; it only remained for Churchill to convince King George II, if not to inspire him with his own enthusiasm. In the meantime, Churchill was getting ready to preside over a conference which would gather in one room representatives of all the forces engaged on both sides, together with Greek politicians from before the deluge who had been resurrected for the occasion. During the night he cabled the Government in London:

On our arrival at airport at Athens Foreign Secretary and I held a conference with Field-Marshal Alexander, Mr Macmillan and Mr Leeper.

2. Field-Marshal Alexander gave an encouraging account of present military situation, which had been grave a fortnight ago but was now much better. The Field-Marshal however had formed the decided view that behind the ELAS units there was a stubborn core of resistance, Communist in character, which was stronger than we had thought and would be very difficult to eradicate. If we were successful in pushing the ELAS force outside the boundaries of Athens we should still be faced with a tremendous task if we tried to eliminate them altogether.

3. Mr Macmillan and Mr Leeper informed us they had been considering the summoning of a conference of all the political leaders, which ELAS would be invited to attend. We felt that the convening of such a conference, with the declared object of putting an end to fratricidal strife in Greece, would, even if ELAS refused the invitation, ensure that our intentions would have been made clear to the world. We also agreed it would be a good move that the Archbishop should be chairman of the conference. At our meeting (in the aeroplane) we drew up the text of a public statement which Messrs Macmillan and Leeper were to show to the Greek Prime Minister and the Archbishop, text of which has already been telegraphed to you.

4. We expressed our wishes that the conference should rapidly become a conference among Greeks, though we would stay there as long as it was helpful. When the time came to put this to the Archbishop we had been informed beforehand that he would be willing to play his part. When he came to see us (on board the Ajax) he spoke with great bitterness against the atrocities of ELAS and the dark, sinister hand behind EAM. . . . He is a magnificent figure, and he immediately accepted the proposal of being chairman of the conference. We are asking the US and Soviet representatives in Athens to be present as observers. The conference is fixed for 4 p.m. on December 26.

5. . . . It may be of course that ELAS will refuse the invitation. If they do so they will be shown before the world as making an unbridled bid for power. If they do accept I do not rate the chances of forming a united government high. . . .[1]

The path of legality was thus virtually blocked at the start. EAM would be confronted with unacceptable conditions once again. Churchill's calculation was that EAM had two alternatives: either to refuse to take part, thus making an 'unbridled bid for power', or to sit down at a

[1] Churchill, op. cit., vol. VI, pp. 272–3.

conference table without the slightest hope of reaching a reasonable settlement. In the first part of his telegram the British Premier had admitted that the communist element in ELAS was limited to 'a stubborn core of resistance', but there was no need for him to spell out the impossibility of dialogue with the 'dark, sinister hand behind EAM'. Another fake conference. . . . Churchill flying to Athens on Christmas day, landing on the powder-keg and conferring with 'gangsters' to sound-effect of distant artillery fire. . . . The whole trip may have been a charade, but it was carried out with such style and panache that it stood a good chance of making a favourable impression on British and international opinion.

Churchill was about to make his way to the Hotel Great Britain on the morning of 26 December when he learned that the security services had discovered the 750 kilos of penthrite in the hotel foundations during the night. The detonators had been removed, but he decided to change his destination to the British Embassy all the same.

As he set foot on shore, shells threw up several columns of water a few yards from the *Ajax*. Violent fighting was still going on in Piraeus. The road to the capital was exposed to artillery fire. Churchill boarded an armoured car and arrived without incident at the British Embassy in Queen Sophia Avenue, where bullets were whistling in all directions. He held another meeting with Damaskinos. 'I was already convinced,' he wrote later, 'that he was the outstanding figure in this Greek turmoil.'[1] For obvious reasons the afternoon's conference, which originally had been planned to take place in the Hotel Great Britain, was finally held in the Greek Foreign Ministry.

The first session began at six o'clock in the evening in a large chamber decorated in neo-Ionic style, dark and freezing cold. The EAM delegates were not there on time, as they were misinformed about the location of the meeting and delayed still further passing through the lines. While waiting for them to arrive – or perhaps hoping that they would not turn up at all – the Archbishop gave an opening address. Churchill and Eden sat on his right, Field-Marshal Alexander on his left. All of the invited foreign representatives were present: US ambassador Lincoln MacVeagh, French plenipotentiary Jean Baelen, and the deadpan Lt-Colonel Grigory Popov, head of the Soviet Military Mission. Representatives of all the old Greek political parties, from the extreme Right to the liberal Left, were also squeezed into the room. Tsaldaris and the notorious collaborator Gonatas represented the most reactionary tendency, Sofianopoulos and

[1] Churchill, op. cit., vol. VI, p. 274.

Maximos the most liberal; the centre and the more or less liberal right were represented by Sofoulis, Kafandaris, Dragoumis, Kanellopoulos, Rallis (no relation of the collaborationist prime minister), Stefanopoulos, Alexandris and Theotokis. The man of the future was Plastiras. Papandreou had run his race.

Churchill insisted, however, when he rose to speak after the Archbishop, that the reigning Prime Minister had approved the conference project. He announced that the British were going to withdraw and leave the Greeks to fight it out among themselves, and mentioned in passing that the British had come to Greece 'with the full approval of President Roosevelt and Marshal Stalin'. Needless to say Popov did not turn a hair. The EAM delegation arrived at the end of Churchill's discourse, just in time to hear a new version of his intervention from an interpreter. The delegation consisted of Siantos, Partsalidis and Mandakas

Alexander spoke next and delivered a eulogy of the British troops. After listening to Maximos and Papandreou, Partsalidis stood up in his turn and affirmed EAM's desire to reach a negotiated settlement. Finally, in a short concluding speech, Eden credited Churchill with the whole idea of the conference. The curtain had now been raised. Churchill left the conference room, followed by all the foreign observers. He returned to the Embassy, huddled over a paraffin stove and telegraphed his wife:

... The conference at Greek Foreign Office was intensely dramatic. All those haggard Greek faces round the table, and the Archbishop with his enormous hat, making him, I should think, seven feet high, whom we got to preside....

... After some consideration, I shook ELAS delegate's hand, and it was clear from their response that they were gratified. They are the very top ones. We have now left them together, as it was a Greek show....[1]

The first issue raised at the conference table was that of the Regency. Although the EAM delegation did not oppose the idea in a systematic way the conversation soon ran into difficulties, and the talks were adjourned until the next day.

Propartisan opinion had been gathering force abroad, and Churchill had been forced to go to Athens in person under pressure of more and more violent criticism. This gave EAM the illusion that it was in a position of strength, and the delegation, led this time by Siantos himself, had every intention of standing firm. It should be remembered that at this time Churchill's principal role in the eyes of the world was that of Liberator

[1] Churchill, op. cit., vol. VI, p. 276.

and champion in the struggle against fascism; the partisans were willing to accept his arbitration. But on e again the dice were loaded; Churchill, acting through the Archbishop, still intended to wield legality as a dagger. His sudden departure for Athens and the conference initiative were signs not of weakness, but of his desire to construct an alibi for himself so that he could continue with the same policy, strip an entire people of its victory and its very sovereignty, and impose the rulers of his choice on Greece.

Damaskinos, chosen peacemaker of the day, knew perfectly well that his patrons were no more inclined to favour Greek independence than they were to honour those fighting to achieve it.

On 27 December Siantos submitted a six-point draft agreement to the conference:

1. EAM to comprise 40–50% of the government.

2. EAM portfolios to include the Ministries of the Interior and of Justice and the Secretariats of State for War and Foreign Affairs.

3. Gendarmerie to be dissolved and collaborators punished.

4. The Mountain Brigade, the Sacred Battalion and the National Guard units set up in the British-controlled sectors to be dissolved.

5. A plebiscite to decide on the form of the future regime to take place on the first Sunday in February.

6. Elections for a Constituent Assembly to take place in April.

This was only intended as a basis for discussion, but the memory of the total defeats suffered in the Lebanon and at Caserta made Siantos present it in the form of an advanced platform. A less rigid set of initial proposals would, in all probability, have served only to prolong the talks by several hours.

As soon as EAM's six points had been read out Plastiras, who was already behaving like the Head of State, stood up and rejected them out of hand. The delegates from the Populist Party, a monarchist formation, rose and left the room in protest. Things were going from bad to worse, and within a few minutes the two factions were separated by an unbridgeable gulf. True dialogue became impossible as argument edged over into gross polemic. Every word uttered by Siantos or Partsalidis was drowned in the indignant vituperations of a roomful of insubstantial political mercenaries.

The EAM delegation had responded to Churchill's peace overture in good faith, and could not give up its illusions. It clung to the belief that the British Premier was genuinely seeking a compromise solution but was being thwarted by the intransigence of his Greek representatives. The delegation walked out of the Foreign Ministry and sent him a letter asking for a personal meeting.

At that moment Churchill was giving a press conference for the foreign correspondents, judging that he could now supply world opinion with ample proofs of his goodwill. He did not need to wait for the conference to end before announcing that his efforts to achieve a negotiated solution had been foiled by ELAS intransigence. In the afternoon he received a visit from Damaskinos which was to his entire satisfaction.

As the result of his conversations [*sic*] with the ELAS delegates it was agreed that I should ask the King of Greece to make him Regent. He would set about forming a new Government without any Communist members. We undertook to carry on the fighting in full vigour until either ELAS accepted a truce or the Athens area was clear of them. I told him that we could not undertake any military task beyond Athens and Attica, but that we would try to keep British forces in Greece until the Greek National Army was formed.

Just before this talk I had received a letter from the Communist delegates asking for a private meeting with me. The Archbishop begged me not to assent to this. I replied that as the conference was fully Greek in character I did not feel justified in agreeing to their request.[1]

As for Papandreou, he quietly left the stage after playing a difficult supporting role in the last scene of Act I in the British masque.

I had no chance to say good-bye to M. Papandreou before leaving. He was about to resign and was a serious loser by the whole business. I asked our Ambassador to keep in friendly touch with him.[2]

Then Churchill returned to more serious matters and cabled the Chief of Staff, ordering two more brigades to be sent to Athens.

The street fighting had continued throughout. On the 29 December, two days after the conference, the partisans suddenly found themselves face to face with Destiny in the form of a decision reached by the Big Three.

Vishinsky summoned Politis, the Greek Ambassador in Moscow, to his office and announced officially that Sergeyev had been appointed Soviet Ambassador to Athens.

This was the first public result of the Churchill-Stalin agreement. EAM-ELAS had not been able to understand in time that its true destiny could only be found in Greece itself through force of arms; the news came

---

[1] Churchill, op. cit., vol. VI, pp. 276–7.   [2] Churchill, op. cit., vol. VI, p. 277.

as a dramatic betrayal. Churchill was back in London, and that day he received the Greek sovereign at Downing Street. It was a stormy interview, but Churchill had more than one argument at his disposal. George II, King of Greece by grace of the British, was persuaded to name a Regent.

This has been a very painful task to me [wrote Churchill]. I had to tell the King that if he did not agree the matter would be settled without him and that we should recognize the new Government instead of him.

George II finally gave in at 4.30 in the morning and signed a proclamation:

We George II, King of the Hellenes, having deeply considered the terrible situation into which our well-loved people have fallen through circumstances alike unprecedented and uncontrollable, and being ourselves resolved not to return to Greece unless summoned by a free and fair expression of the national will, and having full confidence in your loyalty and devotion, do now by this declaration appoint you, Archbishop Damaskinos, to be our Regent during this period of emergency; and we accordingly authorize and require you to take all steps necessary to restore order and tranquillity throughout our Kingdom....[1]

On 3 January 1945 Damaskinos formed the new government, headed by the 'republican' Plastiras.

In the first few days after the aborted conference, EAM policy continued to balance uneasily between OPLA's acts of violence and repeated peace overtures. On 1 January Churchill had received another message from the ELAS leadership, informing him that the conditions required by Scobie, notably the departure of ELAS from the Attica region, were about to be observed. This was in fact nothing more than a pathetic closing speech for the defence; EAM had been reduced to pleading for clemency. Churchill's Athenian escapade had cleaned up his image in international opinion, and his only thought now was to extract the maximum advantage from the military intervention. He did not even bother to reply.

TERROR

The governmental terror and the mass escape from Averof jail provided OPLA with an excuse for letting itself go. The Stalinist clique which controlled the revolutionary police started purging for all it was worth; giving free rein to its atavistic distrust of the 'allies of socialism', it struck

[1] Churchill, op. cit., vol. VI, p. 279.

out in all directions. 'Red atrocities' were manufactured by the Greek police and were presented to a British Commission under Walter Citrine who accepted them at their face value.

ELAS had lost 5,000 men since the demonstration on 3 December. Every day the innumerable civilian victims of street fighting, snipers and 'settlements of accounts' were buried in the improvised cemeteries which had sprung up on vacant lots all over the town. The bodies of combatants were collected in the Zapeion Gardens. Here is one scene from among many, reported by a witness:

One evening, a member of the governmental police contacted a young Greek who was not averse to being forgiven for certain transgressions of the law: 'I've got a job for you. Keep your mouth shut and we'll never forget it, we'll always look out for you and your family. Mention it to anyone and you'll disappear.'

The recruit joined a small group after nightfall, at a fire station. The team boarded a lorry, drove to Zapeion and collected a load of bodies which they took to the garden of a private house. There, other individuals set to work: they worked the corpses over, mutilating them artistically and mass-producing victims of Red torturers. A whole bucket of eyes was carried out of this nightmare workshop and was much photographed and reported by the international press the next day.

It usually happened that when a man disappeared a relative, wife or friend would go to the Zapeion morgue to look for his body. Like a lot of others, a certain woman arrived there one day to have her worst fears confirmed: her husband's corpse was lying in a row of others on the edge of a lawn, the blue smudge of a bullet-hole marking his temple. The situation in Athens made it impossible for the woman to have the body taken away. Two days later she was summoned by the police, who led her to an improvized morgue and showed her a tattered, horribly mutilated body. Outraged and nauseated by the spectacle, she protested that she had identified her husband's body two days before and that it had then been intact. The embalmers of terror had been in such a hurry to fill their quota that they had slipped up on the most elementary precaution, that of setting aside bodies which had been identified.

Many of the accusations made against OPLA were, of course, well-founded. In the cellars of certain houses in Peristeri the exponents of Stalinist order were undergoing an intensive apprenticeship that was to stand them in good stead a year later, when they turned their talents to purging their own Party with almost undiminished enthusiasm. On the other side of the scale, units of National Guards thrown hastily together from ex-collaborationist elements were advancing on the heels of Scobie's troops. They were not idle.

The government services had not yet reached their peak in this orgy of violence: soon they would be offering a reward of several golden sovereigns to anyone bringing them an andarte's severed head. A photograph of one of these bounty hunters, arriving to collect with the heads of several women tied to his horse's saddle by their hair, was published in the British press at a later date and gave international opinion its due frisson of horror.

The End

The fighting in Athens was drawing to a close, and was now being maintained only to cover the withdrawal from the city of the hostages and the last ELAS units. However, in the provinces most of the forces were still intact. Churchill and Alexander had both become convinced that ELAS controlled the country as a whole and could not be dislodged from it.

Sarafis came back from Metsovo and ordered the units in Thessaly to mine all the railway lines and main roads. The Mountain men, violently resentful over their exclusion from the decisive battle in the streets of Athens, felt that they were not involved in the Central Committee's defeat. Markos and Bakirjis were still occupying Salonika, where their implacable policy in dealing with collaborators won the grudging respect of a British observer, Capell. Aris and Sarafis had five divisions at their disposal. Thessaly was in the hands of Karageorgis and Boukouvalas. But they had been kept away at the decisive moment and now it was too late for them to intervene in the capital. Piraeus fell entirely into Scobie's hands on 7 January, and the British were controlling the whole length of the road between Piraeus and Athens by the end of the next day. House-to-house mopping up began in the working-class districts.

The same day an ELAS delegation called on Scobie to tell him that the andartes would accept the ceasefire conditions. ELAS would withdraw its troops to a distance of 150 kilometres from Athens, to the north and west, and would evacuate Salonika, the Peloponnese and most of the islands.

Prisoners would be exchanged on a one-to-one basis. If all these conditions were fulfilled hostilities would cease at midnight on 15 January.

The dismantling of the forces controlling the interior began with the evacuation of Salonika and the Peloponnese. The leadership resorted to the methods it had used after the Caserta agreement: unit commanders received limited orders pertaining to their own sectors and were kept in the dark about what was going on generally.

The Central Committees of EAM and the KKE had been out-manoeuvred by Churchill; now they had to take their own turn at manipulating, if they wanted their own troops to accept the terms of an armistice which they did not feel to be necessary.

During the night of 4–5 January an ELAS battalion came to the relief of a completely decimated student unit which was trying to hold out in the Exarchia quarter. It was preparing to attack Lycabettus when an order to fall back reached it; its role was to cover the forces' withdrawal from Athens, nothing more.

The general retreat began on the 5th. The militants were preceded by a vast number of hostages: some 15,000 of them, drawn mainly from the Athens bourgeoisie, were herded over the mountains in the north of Attica to the Trikkala region. Food was scarce and the weather harsh. British aircraft strafed anyone who appeared to be armed but dropped containers of food and DDT for the columns of prisoners.

In the suburbs, especially Peristeri, people's tribunals were working day and night in a last-minute rush to see justice done while the machinery was still in place. OPLA chose this moment to revive an old ideological quarrel and, with scant political realism, executed several Social-Democrat trade union leaders. The last ELAS fighting units to leave Athens were gone by the morning of 6 January.

An extraordinary calm reigned over Athens. The British suddenly found themselves in a silent town. The last andartes were approaching Tatoi and Kifisia, about fifteen kilometres north of the capital, where the summer residences of rich Athenians were thick on the ground. An EPON group attacked the Tatoi palace in passing; it was a symbolic capture which gave them the sour satisfaction of stealing a few bottles of the best vintages from the royal cellars.

British aircraft appeared at daybreak, circling in the sky and machine-gunning the columns. The roads were still under very accurate fire from naval artillery and from the battery on the Acropolis. The partisans had not organized any system of defence against aerial attack. The ditches were heaped with the wreckage of supply vehicles which had been shot up on the two previous days. All the villages on their route were in ELAS hands, and the men were able to snatch a few hours' rest in them. But the British were hard on their heels, trying to reach Thebes in time to capture the mobile artillery unit from Salonika, which had been sent for too late and had only just reached the town.

Early in the morning on 7 January, after a night's march, a rumour spread to the effect that some units were going to position themselves for a rearguard action. It was quickly followed by an order: 'There's no question of stopping, you must get to the armistice line at Lamia as quickly as possible.' Only Boukouvalas's Cavalry Brigade went into action, harrying the British and slowing their advance.

On its way north the ELAS column crossed the main Thebes road. A group had just crossed the road and started across an open field of winter-sodden clay, when British armoured cars appeared and opened fire like a line of sportsmen at a shoot. Stumbling in slow motion through ankle-deep mud, the men presented easy silhouetted targets like the cardboard cut-outs on a firing range, and the machine-guns struck them down at leisure.

The retreat went on throughout the next night. Dawn broke, and sent a last hope muttering its way through the ranks: We'll soon be at Thermopylae. We're going to make a stand at Thermopylae.

They reached the historic pass and stopped beside the hot springs to await orders. The city-dwellers among the men were suffering from severely blistered feet after the long forced-march in poor footwear. After rendering a stumbling homage to the scene of a legendary act of resistance, they collapsed beside the springs, took off their shoes and bathed their swollen feet in the hot water. They believed the situation was going to change, that they would be ordered to hold the pass. Daylight, and the first aircraft droning overhead. The orders arrived at last: Carry on. No battle in the pass. The men got wearily to their feet to carry on retreating. Their feet were so swollen from the hot springs that they could not get their shoes back on.

It was a ragged procession of exhausted automata that finally crossed the Lamia bridge and walked zombie-like across the armistice line.

Lamia. Walled city, cradle of the Mountain resistance. The newly-arrived troops from the capital, sweaty, worried and depressed, suddenly found themselves in a different universe. The last sheep were being cooked with immense care over charcoal fires, and the men were urged to renew their acquaintance with the earth and forest taste of resinated wine. They were welcomed not as a vanquished army but as warriors who would soon be going into battle.

At Staff Headquarters, Major Makridis felt that, in the absence of any outside help, an attempt to continue the struggle in the provinces would be doomed to fail midway through its course. There were political arguments too: Ioannidis said later: 'There were millions of us in EAM and 450,000 in the Communist Party – too many for everyone to be a good communist. If we'd had 100,000 real militants we'd have been able to seize power.' To turn to the Mountain now, when the 'revolutionary elite' – through no fault of its own – had been partially discredited, would be to reinforce a nonconformist current and to elevate the recognized guerilla leaders to the top echelons of the Party. On the one hand, the party leadership had accepted the political cards dealt by Churchill; on the other, it had proved (by reconstituting the ELAS Central Committee) that it was absolutely committed to pursuing an orthodox revolutionary struggle in the capital. The conclusion of this particular logic was that since Athens had fallen into Scobie's hands the armed struggle was virtually over. The leadership's main problem in the immediate future was going to be to persuade EAM and the people's army to swallow the consequences of a defeat which was the leadership's, not theirs. Neither Alexander nor Churchill expected the Mountain forces to relinquish their positions. The shock caused by the final withdrawal of Soviet support, evidently much more serious among the Stalinist bureaucrats than among the guerillas, may have had something to do with it.

Aris, and most of the other kapetanios, refused to consider themselves beaten after a battle in which they had played no part. In Lamia five weeks earlier Aris had not been able to find anyone, in an audience which basically shared his feelings, who would dare to support him in public. He had now been proved right by events. The majority of the Mountain's forces were intact. Aris distrusted the Central Committee's policy and wanted to carry on with the struggle. He was too closely watched to be able to organize another conference, but he sent a sealed letter to every kapetanios in the country with formal orders not to open it or to destroy it without express instructions from him.

The ELAS forces which had been pulled out of Athens gathered at Trikkala where a Staff HQ was set up during the second half of January.

The exchange of prisoners was begun under the terms of the armistice agreement. Tzimas had been back from Yugoslavia since 15 December. He was feeling restless; time seemed to have congealed, everything was suspended in mid-air after the armistice and before the fumblings and hesitations to come.

Two American officers arrived at the Trikkala HQ to negotiate the exchange of British airmen captured at Tatoi by ELAS Second Division.

The resolute attitude of the rank and file, and the presence of a majority of the popular leaders in Trikkala, gave the leadership every reason to fear the birth of an organized opposition within the ranks of ELAS. Aris's Black Bonnets, still hungry after their lightning defeat of Zervas, were letting the townspeople know what they thought of the battle of Athens when they rode by on their horses. But OPLA had joined the retreat in full force, and nobody was quite safe from a denunciation. Secret police were insinuating themselves into the ranks of ELAS in the hope of keeping some sort of order, a fact which alone gives some idea of the Central Committee's confidence in its following.

Tzimas did not support the continuation of armed struggle, but the Mountain's men were beginning to be affected by strong centrifugal currents. Whatever the reason, Siantos decided to send Tzimas away again, and dispatched him to Athens to negotiate the exchange of prisoners with Scobie.

Tzimas did not want the job; he had been a *bête noire* of the Foreign Office since the first military mission had arrived in the mountains.

'You know quite well what the British think of me. It's absurd; why don't you send someone else?'

The Old Man refused to discuss the matter. Tzimas set off for Athens with a lawyer called Kostas and the two Americans, crossing the zone ELAS had evacuated a few days earlier. A heavy, stifling calm reigned there, presaging a storm in the future. When they passed through Levadia the two ELAS men were summoned to the British Officers' Mess where their reception was far from cordial.

'You are nothing but bandits. But we are curious to know how the Russians managed to cover 400 kilometres in a single stage during their advance on Berlin.'

This was news to Tzimas; he was delighted to hear it. Much as ELAS wanted the support of Moscow's famous 'hand' it had not succeeded in getting it, nor indeed any special sources of information. That was all his questioners wanted to know, since they were simply trying to determine how much help and guidance the Greek partisans were getting from the Soviets. But although Stalin was winning the race to Berlin, he was not trying any funny business with the Moscow agreements.

When Tzimas and Kostas reached Athens they presented themselves at Scobie's HQ. The General had not been told that they were coming, and handed them over to Major Matthews, who was already known to the EAM delegates to the Cairo conference.

'Mr Tzimas, you have crossed the armistice line without authorization and are therefore under arrest.'

Tzimas was shut in a small room on the fourth floor. On the wall was a map of Europe, the same as the one in Levadia mess, bristling with little flags that illustrated the movements of the Russian front.

Tzimas had been sent on official business to organize the exchange of prisoners in accordance with the armistice, and could not help noticing that members of ELAS were still being treated as gangsters. He protested vigorously and began a hunger strike.

He only missed one dinner. The next morning Matthews and General Scobie whisked him out of his cell and started the negotiations. Everything was settled in three hours and when Tzimas left Scobie's HQ that afternoon it was with a most imposing escort: two cars and three armoured vehicles. The roads were not safe. The governmental enclave was swarming with extreme right-wing bands which were beginning to plunder the population. A figure called Sourlas was opening a new, intensive and very well-paid Red-hunt.

Meanwhile Walter Citrine was keeping up the good work of collecting evidence of the Red Terror. The conditions under which the 15,000 hostages were living provided ELAS's enemies with easy ammunition and enabled them to adjust the background of the recent negotiations to suit their taste.

While Tzimas was away the Central Committee kept looking for outside support, and sent a note to Bulgaria. Dimitrov's reply must have stripped it of most of its remaining illusions:

'. . . Any support from Bulgaria and Yugoslavia which involved them in fighting the British armed forces beside ELAS would be of little immediate use to the Greek comrades but might well harm Yugoslavia and Bulgaria. Our Greek friends should bear all this in mind. ELAS and the Greeks must direct their steps *away* from this situation, which is dangerous for them. They should not wish to pull too hard on the rope, but on the contrary should try to manifest an exceptional resilience and freedom of manoeuvre with a view to conserving their strength as far as possible, and awaiting a more favourable moment for putting their democratic programme into effect.'

This unambiguous, terribly explicit rejection by a neighbouring country forced the Central Committee to compromise. Once again, the reasons dictating its retreat could not be admitted to the rank and file.

EAM controlled all the provinces and was certainly not defenceless on the political level. It could bring a formidable record of struggle against the Third Reich to bear on the balance of any negotiation: the cutting of Rommel's umbilical cord at Gorgopotamos; the tying down in Greece of considerable enemy forces (i.e., before September 1943, the German Fifth Army, the Italian Eleventh Army and two Bulgarian Army Corps – somewhere near 300,000 men who had never been able to subdue the country or even protect their own main communications); and, after September 1943, the diversion of 180,000 soldiers from other tasks (some ten German and three Bulgarian divisions which had left 22,000 of their own dead behind them). Last but not least was the blood shed by the whole population, which despite all its sacrifices had always been ready with unlimited support for the andartes, and had very rarely betrayed them. This amounted to 500,000 dead, including the 260,000 victims of the Athens famine, in other words, nearly seven per cent of the population in a country of 7,300,000 souls.

This balance-sheet of the struggle against the occupation, with its enormous blood-letting, nevertheless constituted a victory for which ELAS was undeniably mainly responsible.

Scobie, for his part, could produce the following forces: representatives of former political organizations which, apart from EDES, had played no notable part in the resistance struggle; a praetorian army supported by British armoured cars; the pious indignation of political bit-players over the excesses of the Red repression – 13,500 victims counting the Security Battalions defeated in the field. Not a negligible figure, certainly, but where is the scandal to compare with the outrageous indulgence of Scobie's recruiters towards the imposition of an unrepresentative government, or the dirt and discredit heaped on a heroic and glorious Resistance?

On one side stood an armed people – armed but not shooting – which had lost all hope of any outside support, suffering the bitterness of a stolen victory, a wound deeper than any defeat, and with a will taut and ready to explode at any moment. On the other were the seasoned professionals of wheeling and dealing, and the blessing of the Great Surveyors, now converging on Yalta in early February 1945.

Varkiza

The EAM delegation – including Partsalidis, Tsirimokos and Siantos (the latter as chief delegate) – arrived at Varkiza on 2 February 1945. Varkiza lies between Athens and Cape Sounion. The negotiations took place in a white villa at the end of a long grove of pines, the property of Kanellopoulos.

At Varkiza, Siantos's pursuit of legality sent him straight back into the ambush set up in the Lebanon. He had an army of 75,000 men behind him and controlled four-fifths of the country – twenty-seven of the thirty-one regions – but he had been so thoroughly demoralized by Dimitrov's brush-off that he could not stand up politically to opponents who resumed the trial of ELAS from the word go.

What happened in that house in Attica over the next nine days seems incomprehensible. EAM's whole future rested on the bowed shoulders of an old man who regarded legality as a sort of unattainable holy sacrament and who, pursuing the path laid down during earlier negotiations, was moving from multiple concessions to a sellout on the grand scale. Disowned by Moscow, the old militant felt himself to be cornered from the start, although his adversaries were under some pressure themselves to reach a negotiated solution in view of the impending Yalta conference.

Siantos did not know how to use his armed force to intimidate, but he allowed himself to be intimidated by 'legality'. In the final analysis, he was too anxious to preserve the KKE's orthodox skeleton to be able to play the ELAS card properly; he was incapable of grasping its potential value to him. It is probably true to say that nobody at the conference underestimated the power of the partisans as much as he did. In preparing for the future, his first concern was to save a venerable revolutionary apparatus.

The only real debate was on the question of amnesty. The government representatives would not hear of a general amnesty and began setting up machinery that would later permit them to prosecute the great majority of partisans for infractions of common law. Since he had forsworn ELAS,

Siantos could only bring pressure to bear on the situation through the 15,000 hostages who, by making the totalitarian scarecrow loom immeasurably larger, finally turned out to be yet more grist to his adversaries' mill.

The Varkiza talks were still going on when, on 5 February, the biggest auction in history opened at Yalta.

During the sitting that took place on 8 February, Stalin said that he 'would like to ask what was going on in Greece', quickly adding that 'he had not the slightest intention of criticizing what the British were doing in Greece, but would simply like to have some information'.

Churchill replied that negotiations were well under way, and seized the opportunity to thank Marshal Stalin for 'not taking too close an interest in Greek affairs'. Stalin ended the exchange of civilities by repeating that he did not wish to criticize the British over any aspect of their intervention in Greece and that he had no intention of interfering in the matter.

All the same, the next day Churchill invited Stalin to send an observer to Greece, knowing that this would deal another blow to EAM's morale. With a creaking smile, Stalin replied that the idea seemed to him a dangerous one, as the British had never allowed any forces but their own into Greece. This was, of course, a joke, and he ended on the official note thought more appropriate to subjects of this kind: 'I have every confidence in British policy on Greece.'

Siantos was giving ground under the Varkiza pines. The asking-price of legality was exorbitant, but it was too late for him to change his tack. He understood neither his own strong position nor the true value of the 'legality' for which he was prepared to sacrifice so much, and he was ready to pay. The British were in a hurry to reach some compromise and intervened in favour of a general amnesty; but Plastiras's ministers could feel things going their way and kept pressing for total capitulation. The outgunned EAM delegation gave up the whole idea of a general amnesty, abandoning its militants to a ferocious repression or condemning them to exile, but it managed to obtain a deformed, limited amnesty which expressly excluded a very wide range of common-law crimes and in the final analysis only protected important Party cadres. Siantos had failed to build anything on the existing foundations; all he had managed to do was to buy time for an arthritic revolutionary machine and to avoid posing any diplomatic problems for Stalin. On the evening of 11 February he held an international press conference at the Greek Foreign Ministry.

'The Great Allies decided that it would be useful to have the British army present in Greece, and in that respect its presence is a good thing. We believe that the conflict between the British and ELAS is the result of a regrettable misunderstanding which we hope will soon be forgotten.'

The Yalta agreements would be respected. Those reached at Varkiza were simply to hand ELAS over to its enemies: the first holocaust dedicated to the establishment of Stalin's socialist bastion.

On the night of 11–12 February, Siantos hesitated for a long time before signing the document that disarmed the Liberation Army and excluded EAM from all the ministries in order to safeguard the Party's legal status. He was a haunted man, his torment making quite clear to his interlocutors the atmosphere in which the agreement had been extorted from him, an untidy agreement that brought four years of implacable struggle to a furtive conclusion.

... Siantos [wrote Leeper], in British battle dress and gum boots, was stalking up and down the room saying that he had no intention of signing tonight, that he was much too tired and his head was not clear enough. Various attempts were made to persuade him to sign, but he was by this time too obstinate to agree.

Macmillan and I sat there with nothing to drink but water and nothing to eat but one meat sandwich, waiting like two policemen until we got our bit of paper signed. Finally at 4 a.m. Siantos said that, though he could not sign the full agreement, he was prepared to sign a short provisional agreement.[1]

Parallel with these political negotiations Sarafis took part in a conference on the disarmament of the people's forces. ELAS was required to hand over before the end of the month 41,500 rifles and submachine-guns, 2,015 machine-guns and 32 pieces of assorted artillery.

Allied deliveries to the Resistance had amounted to about 3,000 rifles, 300 Sten (submachine) guns, 30 heavy machine-guns and 100 machine-rifles (Bren type), and 10 mortars. The rest of ELAS's armament – between eighty and ninety per cent of the total – consisted of war booty.

TRAUMA

Trikkala nestles at the foot of Mount Ardami, on the edge of the plains of Thessaly, close to the winding river Lithaios, the Lethe of antiquity. In the middle of the main square, a platform awaited the returning ELAS delegates. The streets were flooded with bright light; the winter was coming to an end. The rostrum, the square, the streets were all deserted. The whole town was waiting beside the Athens road, blackening the hill-

[1] Leeper, op. cit., pp. 147–8.

sides, craning their necks for the first glimpse of Siantos's car. Earlier, the people had been chattering with forced optimism, but a crushing presentiment stifled every attempt at conversation and the crowd had grown quieter and quieter. As time passed, the people became even more uneasy. All eyes were fixed on the place where the road emerged from the hills. The stony universe bristled with tense, impatient outlines. The delegation was six hours late.

Cars swept into sight along the curving line of the road, sending a new wave of disquiet sweeping through the waiting crowd. There was no noise, no cheering; the last few moments were sharp with expectation. The first car was slowing down between two walls of eager faces. Partsalidis was leaning out of the window. The dumb entreaty he read in the faces was unbearable. He tried to say something, and managed to force out in a strangled voice: 'It's all right. It's all right.'

The muffled syllables cleared the air suddenly, like a detonator. They set off an explosion of feverish joy, as if good news had just been pronounced. The crowd escorted the cars to the main square, their chests unloading six hours of oppression in a few minutes of fragile euphoria supported by nothing but cheers. Stiff and expressionless, Partsalidis climbed onto the rostrum. A few last cheers were still trying to exorcize whatever was coming, to push reality away.

'We have been obliged . . .'

It was like a thunderbolt. There was no cheering now. In a leaden silence, Partsalidis recited the clauses of the Varkiza agreement from beginning to end. When he reached the end, someone slowly intoned the ELAS anthem and it was taken up shakily by hundreds of constricted throats.

> With my rifle on my shoulder,
> In town, on mountainside and field,
> I'm clearing a path for Liberty,
> Strewing palms for her advancing feet.
> Forward, ELAS, for Greece,
> Justice and Liberty.
> On the mountain-tops and in the valleys
> Leaping, fight with all your heart.

Then silence again, as if after a violent explosion. Overwhelmed by the consequences of his actions and deeply upset, Siantos refused to move into the hotel room reserved for him and went instead to spend the night at his mother's tiny house in the town.

Members of the Central Committee and the Political Bureau met in

Ioannidis's quarters in the evening. Karageorgis and Zevgos made a violent attack on Siantos, who was in no condition to defend himself. Tzimas tried to call a halt: 'The time has passed. We can't force the British out now.'

He did not have the heart to exploit the Old Man's weakness. Probably for this reason, in addition to his ownership of a Soviet-made automatic carbine, Siantos chose to ignore their old quarrel and at midnight asked Tzimas to escort him home to his mother's house. Before going inside he said: 'It's not because I'm frightened that I asked you to come with me. I'm quite calm and tranquil. We have lost a battle but the Greek people is with us and, in the end, we will prevail.'

The effect on the Greek people was traumatic. Asked to lay down its arms by men in whom it had placed its trust, it obeyed, for the most part crushed and uncomprehending. It would perhaps have taken no more than the right signal to start a counter-movement, to make the people refuse to give up its arms, but discipline worked mechanically in the prevailing atmosphere of stunned dismay.

Officials began gathering the rifles the next day. A number of trusted teams were detailed to bury substantial quantities of modern weapons; to make up the weight for Scobie, blunderbusses and old Gras rifles were the first to go. Thus it proved possible to keep hidden a large part of the brand new arsenal captured from the Italians; but all of this work was done in secret, and most of the men had to part with the weapon they had carried through the Resistance, which in many cases was a battle-trophy. Most of the kapetanios could not bring themselves to explain the circumstances to their men, and they usually limited themselves to issuing a gruff order, which the men obeyed in tears. The same scene occurred in every unit: men kissing their rifles, reliving the years of suffering before giving up the weapon which symbolized their victory and guaranteed their personal security.

The psychological shock of those few days in February was to have incalculable effects; it was a tragic ending in the strict, literary sense of the word, describing heroes and destiny. Absurd orders and useless battles; victories squashed by a blind power from elsewhere, God knows where, turning everything to mockery. Today, more than twenty years later, not a single combatant, not one of the kapetanios exiled after the later Civil War to Tashkent, Bucharest, Prague, Sofia or Budapest can recall the childish misery of those men embracing their rifles without having to hold back his own tears.

Varkiza opened a shameful era animated by a mad ambition to rewrite history, to snatch back a stolen victory, to redress the 'scandal' of a people's triumph. Men versus Destiny: the Greek people versus the Great Allies who were dividing up whole continents. In addition, the fluid relationship between the orthodox revolutionary organization and the people's movement which had provided most of the manpower for the national resistance, which had arisen and been maintained in the heat of battle, was at last beginning to decompose. The peasants, who comprised most of ELAS's troops, were recognized in the National Liberation Army which had been more or less started by the KKE, but had no place in the commissars' revolution. Many of them had become Communists because Communism identified itself with their struggle; but they could see no reflection of themselves in the leaders and 'engineers of the soul' who had come from the city and auctioned off their victory. In their eyes, all the discredit which had been heaped upon the traditional politicians had re-bounded onto the revolutionary politicians who preached Revolution by the industrial proletariat in a bureaucratic jargon to which they were profoundly allergic. They had a strong feeling that they had been manipu-lated once again, this time by technicians who had sacrificed the natural progress of their struggle to a set of abstract models.

But they obeyed. They handed over their arms and went home to their villages, where they were exposed to acts of revenge by extreme right-wing bands armed by the government. The KKE had never gone the whole way with ELAS, but it had succeeded in forcing ELAS to share its own defeat.

Units which were not at Trikkala received three orders in rapid suc-cession. First they were told that ELAS fighters must return to their villages, taking their weapons with them; then they were told that only certain officers would be authorized to keep their personal armament; finally, they were all ordered to disarm.

Very few units were so annoyed by this crescendo as to refuse to obey. Tzavelas stayed on Olympus and Yannoulis refused to disband his unit, but such reactions remained isolated. Men who did not want to return to their villages were setting off for Albania and Yugoslavia, blazing a trail into exile that later was followed by many.

The Party leadership revived the old ELAS command-structure to dress up its ultimate proclamation:

16 February 1945

Officers, kapetanios and andartes of ELAS and EAM: our army's struggle is over and ELAS is dissolved. For nearly three years you fought hard against the invader

*in a confrontation notable for its sacrifice and heroism. . . . Our mountains and our
plains are covered with enemy graves and with wreckage abandoned by the fleeing
occupant. . . . Be proud of your achievement. You have done your duty to your
Country. When you return home, become good citizens and continue to pursue your
democratic ideals.*

*Let us kneel for a moment, reverently, for our heroic dead. Their memory will
live for ever in respect and glory.*

*In bidding you all farewell, after leading and following your many battles, we
would like to express our admiration and our gratitude. Your actions will decorate
the most brilliant pages of the glorious history of our beloved Greece.*

Long live our indomitable Nation!
Long live ELAS, its supreme manifestation!

Signed:
STEFANOS SARAFIS and ARIS VELOUCHIOTIS [1]

But whether he had really signed this proclamation or not, Aris refused to
bend to the conditions of the Varkiza sellout.

Aris's Calvary

The kapetanios to whom Aris had sent sealed letters were ordered to
destroy them a few days before the end of the negotiations. The tragic
events that followed suggest that a leak had somehow occurred. The order
to destroy the letters came not from Aris but from the Party leadership,
probably following a denunciation of Aris. In all probability the sealed
letter had contained a call to continue the struggle and plans for regrouping the army.

At the end of February Aris, who had not unclenched his teeth for the
past two weeks, declared that he was going to join his family and left
Trikkala for Lamia. All partisans returning to Athens would have to pass
through the town. With a hundred men, he installed himself a few kilometres away in the village of Sperchiada, where ELAS had made its first
appearance one winter's day in 1942. It may have been the rallying-point
mentioned in the destroyed letter. The news spread through the Lamia
region that Aris was asking andartes to join him and prepare for the 'third
round'. But most of the kapetanios were far away, and the call did not
reach them.

[1] Quoted in Loverdo, op. cit., pp. 362–3.

On 3 March, Ioannidis and Siantos heard of Aris's decision when they stopped at Lamia on their way to Athens. Ioannidis reacted violently and appointed a small delegation to take a stern message from the leadership to the Sperchios valley.

'Tell Aris that the Party *orders* him to come back to Athens. If he's afraid, we'll get him papers so that he can get out of the country.'

The messengers were recruited from among his oldest friends: Pericles, Grigoriadis and Nikiforos. Nikiforos was able to wriggle out of a painful task, refusing to go on the grounds that Aris had sworn to strangle him in a moment of anger when he heard of the capture of his sleeping battalion at the Filothei hippodrome on the first day of the Battle of Athens.

Aristotle Vassiliadis, Party Secretary for Roumeli, joined the group when it left for Sperchiada, but when it drew near the village Pericles urgently counselled him to stay in the background: 'If Aris sees a politico coming there'll be no holding him. Stay back or you'll be killed.'

But Aris and the Black Bonnets had left Sperchiada and installed themselves a little further away at Dilofon, which was easier to defend. The road was bad and covered in snow, and the three emissaries resumed their journey on foot. From the windows of the first house in Dilofon, men wearing caps of black fur were covering the approach to the village. Fivos Grigoriadis walked forward on his own; his arrival had been announced to Aris, who rushed headlong down the stairs and ran to meet him.

'Fivos, you're the first to arrive. Let me embrace you.'

Grigoriadis tried to extricate himself from the kapetanios's excited grasp.

'Aris. Aris. Keep your shirt on, you won't be so pleased to see me in three minutes' time.'

Aris released him and took a step back. He closed his right eye and fidgeted with his beard: 'You were sent here, then . . .'

'Yes,' Grigoriadis said. 'There are three of us.'

'Call them, they'll be all right.'

They went into a house, where Grigoriadis gave Aris Ioannidis's message.

'You have to go back to Athens, or go abroad.'

The indomitable, violent Aris was alone once more, facing the Machine and all its shackles. During these last days, when the weapons were being used to fire a final salute to the Resistance dead, it is certain that more than one kapetanios would have hurried to join him – if they had heard his call. But the letters had been destroyed, and Ioannidis had been the first to arrive at Lamia. Now the others were being watched, and Aris knew they would not be coming. He dictated a letter: 'I will go if the Party wants me to, on condition that I remain a combatant and that I am free to express my opinion, to Stalin himself if necessary. I am heading for the frontier. My men will not be disarmed. If you do not agree, send Bartsotas to speak to me in person; I will not trust any other messenger.'

The letter reached Athens hidden in Grigoriadis's boot and was given to Partsalidis. Aris left Dilofon. In Palaiokastro he met Ploumbidis, a political cadre with whom he was on friendly terms.

'It's all agreed. Carry on to Trikkala, and you'll be given a safe-conduct right through to Albania.'

Aris and his men, who had scorned the rules of secrecy throughout the occupation, shaved their beards, stripped the insignia from their uniforms and slunk off like pariahs to Trikkala, which the newly-disarmed ELAS had just vacated. There, the political commissar had received no instructions and sent him on to Yannina. From there Aris moved on to Konitza, then to Kastoria, a few kilometres from the frontier. There was still no word from Athens.

The kapetanios decided to send Pelopidas and one of his men into Albanian territory, to Koritsa. Tzimas had in fact just passed through the town on his way to Yugoslavia, but he was not up to date on this matter and had left no message or instructions.

While Pelopidas was away, a British unit from the Fourth Indian Division discovered that the detachment was in the region, and attacked it at the village of Kriapigi.

Aris managed to withdraw and crossed the frontier. One of his partisans, Hector, was killed in the exchange of fire. An Albanian border patrol refused to allow armed men into the country, and they were obliged to return to Greek soil, where their whereabouts were now widely known. Leaving three wounded in the care of the Albanians, they sneaked back across the frontier at night.

Pelopidas returned at the appointed time and gave Aris his negative report on the Koritza mission. For the next five days the detachment zig-zagged along the frontier, its footsteps dogged by the British every inch of the way, hoping to meet a delegate from the Party. No messenger appeared, but the headline news in *Rizopastis* on 11 April awakened a last, crazy hope not only in Aris but in thousands of other Greeks as well. Karageorgis had left for San Francisco as the paper's correspondent and picked up a fantastic snippet while in America: Nikos Zachariadis, former First Secretary of the KKE, had been found among the survivors of Dachau. Zachariadis: a trusted leader whose absence absolved him of all responsibility for the unpardonable errors of the last three years. Four years after his disappearance, he was being lauded again at every Party meeting:

> The people are victorious
> They snap their chains with ease
> For the leader of our Party
> Is Zachariadis. . . .

Zachariadis back! An end to political wanderings; the way out of the labyrinth! The good news revived an old personality cult, announced the coming of the saviour, dusted off as good as new the only revolutionary myth to have been left untarnished by the Varkiza agreements. A Stalinist myth to be sure, intact and formidable; but Aris, like many others, took new heart from it. He decided to go back to Athens.

The return journey was more dangerous than the journey north had been. Leaving Dilofon when the snow was still on the ground, Aris had not reached the Albanian frontier until the middle of spring. Now he was going to have to spend another month travelling through the Greek mountains. The country was infested with armed bands of the extreme right, either supported by the government or indulgently tolerated by it. The best-known of these bands were those of Sourlas (who had operated with German approval throughout the occupation), Tsantoulas, Kalabalikis, Velentsas and Manganas: thieves, murderers, mercenaries and head-hunters.

When he reached Trikkala, Aris learned that Zachariadis had arrived in Athens and had been welcomed by a monster demonstration in the stadium. He wrote to the town's political commissar: 'I am prepared to do whatever Zachariadis decides, even to return to Athens if he thinks it would be useful. If he cannot reply for some reason, he should send Bartsotas to me with further instructions.'

He went back into the mountains to await a reply, going to ground in the Tzoumerka region, former Zervas territory. Early in June he was located by a unit of the governmental army, which moved in to attack him. Aris managed to break out of the encirclement by employing the services of a former bandit called Drakos, who knew every inch of the territory and guided him through government lines.

He regrouped his partisans near the village of Mesounda. It was there,

in a mill beside the river Acheloös, that Drakos interrupted a reconnaissance trip to hold a long meeting with the region's political commissar and
another personality, afterwards returning to Aris with the suggestion that
they march south.

The column set off, preceded by a small group of scouts. Aris asked
Pelopidas to stay in the rear and look after a metal box containing his
personal files, including perhaps the key to the mystery of his famous
signature of the *dilosi*.

The leading group started along a wooded hillside, followed at a little
distance by the rest of the column. After a minute or two, the bushes suddenly began spitting fire; they had walked right into an ambush. Witnesses
affirmed the next day that Drakos and the political commissar had been
seen at the mill talking to an officer of the government army. Drakos's
later treatment at the hands of the authorities was, in fact, suspiciously
indulgent, and although Aris did not know it yet, he himself had been
condemned by Zachariadis, in a foul article which had just appeared in
Rizopastis: 'Aris Velouchiotis, Thanasis Klaras, Miserias, dilosias,
renegade . . .'

When he heard the first shots Aris sent Pelopidas and a few men to
reconnoitre the Mesounda bridge, which he had bypassed at the suggestion of the guides. The small advance guard managed to pass right
through the ambush to the other side. Aris leapt into the Acheloos and
swam across with about thirty partisans; the rest of his men, about fifty
in number, crossed over some distance away and the two groups lost
contact. During the retreat Pelopidas had had to abandon the file-box on
the other bank, and Aris was terribly worried about it: 'We're unarmed
without those documents.'

Two shepherds, father and son, came walking along the river-bank.
They had met the other group a little way downstream, to the north, and
the father offered to go and find them again while his son guided Aris's
detachment. The young shepherd held a newspaper out to the kapetanios,
Eleftheri Ellada of 12 June 1945.

The KKE chief Nicholas Zachariadis has made public a Central Committee
decision to denounce the activities of Aris Velouchiotis as those of an adventurist
and suspect person.

Velouchiotis's current activities are helping the forces of reaction to formulate
anti-KKE arguments, providing them with a pretext to claim that the Varkiza
agreements are being broken and to invoke the crimes Aris has committed
against the democratic world. . . .

Zachariadis the saviour had turned out to be orthodoxy's latest inquisitor. Aris was condemned without the right of appeal. He sat down on a rock, ordering the column to carry on without him but keeping Tzavelas at his side. A few minutes later, a grenade exploded.

There were no government soldiers at the Mesounda bridge, which should have been the column's most obvious crossing-point. This strongly suggests that the ambush was the result of a concerted plan. Pelopidas clearly heard the grenade explosion and the decrease in the intensity of the firing which immediately followed, as if the government forces knew that they had gained their objective.

It will never be known for certain whether Aris and Tzavelas committed suicide or whether Drakos seized the opportunity to unpin the grenade while they were alone behind the rest of the column. But everything seemed to have conspired to make the end of ELAS's first kapetanios as cruel and sordid as possible: Zachariadis's offhand condemnation and betrayal of a hunted man, the lost documents, Drakos's murky personality, and the Manichean zeal of the political commissar, who had known of Zachariadis's condemnation for several days.

The bodies of andartes who had been killed in the clash floated solemnly down the river Acheloos. They were intact, which in those days was abnormal; the staff of Justice Minister Rendis were not in the habit of handing out rewards without the presentation of . . . capital proof. Former ELAS partisans who fell into the hands of Sourlas or Voideros were always buried without their heads. On 18 June, however, the quarry was one head in particular, and if the pack ignored the small game it was because it already had the main trophy.

Pelopidas could hear the voices of Voideros's thugs calling up from the river: 'Give up, drop your guns. Your chief has been killed.' But Aris's men were already out of earshot. The head-hunters did not bother to chase them; their job was done.

After dispersing his men Pelopidas returned to the scene of the fighting, retrieved the metal box and buried it there. Two years later he returned to dig it up and hand it over to Gousias, Zachariadis's loyal man in Roumeli. He was killed a few weeks later; Aris's documents, whether pulped or thrown into the dusty *oubliettes* of orthodoxy, are lost for ever. That same evening Pelopidas called at the mill, where the miller assured him that the day before he had seen Drakos and the commissar talking to an officer of the government army.

At the same moment, on the spot in Trikkala's main square from which

Siantos had announced ELAS's capitulation in February, the severed heads of Aris and Tzavelas were being strung up on a double gibbet. Thus perished, on 18 June 1945, the first and last combatant figure of ELAS, victim of a perverse conspiracy between the orders of reaction and abstract revolution.

Part Three

Rewriting History

1946–1949

Legality

As Aris left Roumeli – abandoning his last chance of regrouping the partisans for the third round – and made his way towards the Albanian frontier, disarmed ELAS troops were drifting back to their towns and villages. At the end of February partisans of Athenian origin were returning to the capital on board British lorries, to a reception which showed how very quickly times were changing. Extreme right-wing commandos, often tipped off by the police and always tolerated by them, were waiting for the lorries when they arrived; the former resistance fighters had to stick together in groups for protection as they crossed the town, and the lynching and Red-hunting began as soon as the groups dispersed. The Varkiza agreement contained clauses on the punishment of collaborators, but they were not being applied. Monarchist commandos started to let themselves go all over the provinces.

Colonel Grivas's X Organization was making its own law in the capital while its collaborationist activities went unprosecuted. Sofianopoulos, a member of the government, observed later: 'Had I known that ELAS's honourable weapons were going to be given to those X people, I would never have signed the Varkiza agreement.' But his fine words did nothing to slow the accelerating slide to the Right, and the men who had been disarmed by the Varkiza agreement – resistants and conquerors – continued to be subjected to bloody reprisals.

Plastiras suited Churchill's short-term plans, as his republican façade and his total ignorance of contemporary Greek problems helped provide a suitably foggy alibi for a very ramshackle national unity. Zervas had called on him at the Hotel Great Britain when he reached Athens at the end of January.

'During the occupation we formed EDES in your name without receiving your formal consent. Similarly, we raised guerilla groups in your name, without your ever telling us whether you agreed.'

Plastiras had a thoroughly personal idea of the Greek realities, and had never felt any great esteem for his valiant disciple.

'You did well,' he replied, 'to set the political organization on its feet . . .

but the partisans have harmed Greece. It's because of them that all the villages have been destroyed.'

Zervas had come to have his efforts acknowledged, and was rather taken aback: 'We've harmed Greece?'

'You have burned villages just like all the others.'

'Yes, maybe, but if we hadn't existed you wouldn't be here as Prime Minister. Aris Velouchiotis would be sitting in that chair.'

'I am not of that opinion. With two battalions I could have liquidated ELAS throughout the country. I would have got them all out of Athens by issuing a proclamation.'

'It was Scobie's tanks that got them out of Athens,' said Zervas. 'Your proclamation might not have been quite so effective.'

Plastiras had no doubts, however: 'If there's one member of EAM left in Greece in a month's time, you can spit on me.'

'For Christ's sake don't say anything like that in public,' Zervas said, 'or you'll look ridiculous. You've been out of Greece for eleven years. You are ignorant about the present situation. You ought to do some homework.'

Plastiras would hardly have the time to learn anything. The White Terror was overtaking him on the right and the British were concentrating on one objective to the exclusion of all others: that of reducing political choice in Greece to two simple extremes, Communism or the Monarchy.

Plastiras had served his purpose when he signed the Varkiza agreement, just as Papandreou had manoeuvred himself out of a job a few months earlier by appointing Scobie Commander of the Greek army. The police were arresting former ELAS partisans on common-law charges as fast as they could, but this was still not enough. At the end of April the British leaked a letter Plastiras had written in 1941 to the extreme right-wing press:

'. . . War against a great power such as Italy can only have been started by the maladroitness of the Metaxas regime's foreign policy. . . . At the end of November I was informed that there was a chance of reaching a compromise with Italy through German intermediaries. I did everything I could to help Greece take advantage of this opportunity, but I came up against the hostility of the Metaxas government . . .', etc.

Collaborationist and right-wing circles waxed extremely indignant, and by 7 May 1945 these elements were turning towards the patriot Voulgaris, who will be remembered as the leader of the successful raid on the mutinous Greek ships in Alexandria harbour. Pyromaglou called on Sir Reginald Leeper, the British ambassador, and asked: 'Why produce this meaningless letter at this stage when you've known what was going on all along?'

'Mr Pyromaglou,' replied Leeper, 'understand that the British Government intends to bring the king back to Greece, with the agreement of the Regent Damaskinos.'

To Churchill, normalizing the Greek political situation meant restoring the traditional monarchist Right to power.

The legal KKE published *Rizospastis* and EAM published *Eleftheri Ellada* in Athens. Well-known Party leaders were not persecuted in any way, but the rank and file were subjected to coordinated repression by the police and informal 'direct action' groups, and selling the newspapers in the street was a risky business. It was in this atmosphere of revenge and para-legal violence the KKE began to find out what everyday 'legality' was like.

Meeting between 5 and 10 April, the Eleventh Plenum of the Central Committee laid down a Party line for the duration of the British intervention. It was to consist of 'gaining time, sapping the strength of the enemy and gathering strength for launching a counter-attack' (Stalin).

Greece's territorial claims on the Dodecanese, Cyprus and Northern Epirus were supported by an overwhelming majority of the population and, although the Northern Epirus problem directly involved Albania, the KKE refrained from adopting a clearly internationalist line and supported (though with some reservations) the national policy recommended by Siantos.

Eventually the Central Committee issued a proclamation urging 'all democrats to join the forces of democracy . . . for a democratic rebirth and the construction of a "People's Democracy".'

But the 'allies' of the past were abandoning ship. On 18 April, Svolos, Askoutsis, Stratis and Tsirimokos (whose personal Hesitation Waltz had begun with the formation of the Plastiras government) left EAM and founded a new party called ELD-SKE (Popular Democratic Union and Greek Socialist Party).

After the Varkiza capitulation, the revolutionary phenomenon of the Resistance was in danger of shrinking rapidly away to nothing. The ensuing repression was so intensive, however, that the former partisan movement retained its solidly Party structure. It became a force adrift, temporarily disoriented but ready to regroup at any moment, to crystallize around the first pole of attraction. Then, on 30 March, someone landed at Eleusis airstrip who, from the political void that the Party had become, looked like a revolutionary messiah.

A month earlier, Karageorgis's articles from the United States had announced Zachariadis's presence among the survivors of Dachau. He was brought to Greece from France by an RAF aircraft, but even before he reached Paris Zachariadis had been behaving as if he had never stopped being First Secretary of the KKE. He had declared in an interview that the KKE renounced all claim to the part of Northern Epirus administered by Albania. What orders had he been given so early?

He did not signal his arrival in Greece to anyone, and left the airport alone in the British uniform supplied to all freed prisoners. In a suburban newspaper kiosk he borrowed a copy of *Rizospastis* to check its office address, which was in Stadium Street in the heart of Athens. He boarded a tram to Constitution Square, and only remembered half-way through the journey that he had no money to pay for his ticket. He sidled off the tram without being noticed and a few minutes later was standing outside the *Rizospastis* office in crowded Stadium Street. Zachariadis had been in prison since 1936, and was breathing the air of freedom again: a freedom whose concealed hazards had not yet become apparent to him. The building was efficiently guarded and a sentry denied him access to the editorial offices; without revealing his identity, Zachariadis asked to see the chief editor, Karageorgis, and sat down to wait on a chair in the hall. It was some minutes before anyone recognized him, but when it came his welcome was delirious.

A special edition was hastily prepared, and the vendors scattered through the streets in the late afternoon, towards five o'clock. 'Zachariadis back!' shouted the vendors, braving the wrath of Grivas's heavies and selling the paper openly for the first time in two months.

Zachariadis was back. Suddenly the errors of the past, the terror in the streets, seemed to be no more than temporary mishaps. Zachariadis would rewrite history. Even Zachariadis himself, elated by his enthusiastic welcome and equipped with an arsenal of canonical certainties picked up in Stalin's universities, was not far from believing that his return would open a new and splendid era for the Revolution.

Nikos Zachariadis had a square profile and a massive head with crew-cut brown hair growing low on the forehead and temples. He was the leading Greek exponent of the Stalinist panacea. A Greek born in Asia

Minor, he had been a victim of the nationalistic 'Great Idea' of the twenties although he was not personally given to the national enthusiasms of most of his compatriots. Born in 1902 in Nicomedia, on the Black Sea, he was twenty by the time the Hellenic communities were repatriated *en masse*. He left for the USSR and received KUTV training until 1925. On his return to Salonika he became the leader of the unconditionally orthodox element within the Party, the Kutvists, who generally supported the claims of the Macedonian Slavic minorities throughout the Balkans.

He was arrested in 1926. He visited the Soviet Union again on his release, and when he came back to Greece in 1928 became the Comintern's man in the KKE, of which he became General Secretary in 1934. He was elected to parliament just before Metaxas took power in 1936 and imprisoned very shortly after the 4 August coup. He addressed a proclamation to communist militants from his cell, asking them to fight the invader alongside Metaxas's forces. The Germans found him in prison in Corfu in 1942 and rushed him off to Dachau.

The Zachariadis cult stayed alive during his three-year absence. Varkiza had been a traumatic shock, and partisans and militants who found it impossible to accept the fact that they had slipped through a hole in the fabric of history seized the opportunity to believe in Zachariadis; to believe in miracles. Aris was one of the thousands who wanted to believe that Zachariadis's return marked the beginning of a new era; by any 'realistic' standard his return to Athens in the face of his rejection by the Party had been suicidal. After all, Zachariadis had played no part in making the Greek revolution; he had returned to put it in some sort of order.

'The extreme centralism propounded by Lenin,' wrote Rosa Luxemburg, 'seems to us to be imbued, not with a positive and creative spirit, but on the contrary with a sterile, night-watchman's attitude. It would concentrate all effort on controlling Party activity rather than enriching it, on restricting the movement rather than developing it, on strangling it rather than unifying it. . . . From the historical point of view the errors committed by a genuinely revolutionary movement are incomparably more fertile and precious than the infallibility of the best Central Committee.'

But Zachariadis had been trained by Stalin. There could be no question of learning anything about revolution from the Greek reality – for him even less than for other members of the Central Committee, who had at least been present throughout. When he appeared in public for the first time, however, at a trade union meeting in Athens Stadium, he was welcomed with the quasi-mystical adulation reserved for carriers of the infallible Word.

The Athens stadium sits between the old royal palace and the Acropolis, an immense marble megaphone open to the sky. Thunderous cheers rose from the banks of seats, echoing off Lycabettus, ricochetting down the opulent streets of Kolonaki and awakening fears of new riots in the breast of Voulgaris's Greece. After the May Day meeting every event attracted enormous crowds which made the very air vibrate, despite the continuing terror which was beginning to worry not only the extreme left. At the beginning of June the centrist politicians Sofoulis, Kafandaris, Tsouderos and Plastiras signed a memo to Voulgaris who had become premier:

The campaign of terror instituted throughout the country by the extreme right after the events of last December is growing worse every day. Its nature and extent are now such as to make life impossible for non-royalist citizens, and preclude any thought of proceeding to a free plebiscite or to elections. The extreme right-wing terrorist organizations, of which the most important were partially armed by the Germans and collaborated with them in every way, have not only not been disarmed or prosecuted but are still collaborating openly with the forces of law and order to stifle every vestige of democratic thought.

British opinion was also growing uneasy over the turn Voulgaris's 'normalization' programme had taken. Woodhouse, who had done so much to further Churchill's Greek policies, could not stand by and allow the Resistance to be discredited by the despicable activities of the collaborators and former militiamen who were hunting partisans down as common criminals, lynching people in the street and head-hunting in the mountains. Supported by Sir Reginald Leeper – still British ambassador in Athens – and elements of the Labour Party, he tried to persuade the British authorities to form a Greek government which at least included non-communist resistance men and would proclaim a general amnesty applying to both right and left.

The Regent Damaskinos was called to London. After a few days his political secretary Georgakis resigned, declaring when he arrived in Athens: 'The Archbishop is betraying Greece. He's agreeing to all the Foreign Office demands.'

Voulgaris's hopeless search for a representative government had even led him to consult Pyromaglou.

'I'd like you to be my Minister of the Interior.'

'Why?' asked Pyromaglou.

'To chase the Communists.'

'D'you mean to neutralize the Communist threat or literally to chase the Communists?'

Voulgaris gave him to understand that there was to be no quarter. Pyromaglou turned the job down and Voulgaris pursued his liquidator's bent. By 20 July, when he asked Britain to send troops to deal with the increasingly anarchic situation in Epirus, the Foreign Office was desperately trying to set up a 'liberal' team which would be able to restore a convincing enough appearance of legality to permit elections to be held.

On 25 June the KKE Central Committee's Twelfth Plenum officially restored the title of General Secretary to Zachariadis. Siantos and Ioannidis retained their Secretary status. Partsalidis, Bartzotas and Chrysa Hajivasiliou – Rousos's wife – joined them in the Political Bureau.

Zachariadis laid down the new Party line. Though tortuous in conception, it was of course to be applied without the smallest deviation. On the international level it began with the two-pole theory:

Greece is situated at a sensitive and crucial spot in the British Empire's vital communication network. As long as there is a British Empire this artery will exist and Britain will do everything in its power to preserve it. A consistent Greek foreign policy should function between two poles: that of the European Balkans, with its centre in Soviet Russia, and that of the Mediterranean, with Great Britain as its centre.[1]

Unfortunately, the two poles had effectively neutralized one another since the Moscow deal between Churchill and Stalin, leaving Greece a singularly narrow margin of manoeuvre; its progress was limited to the agreed rhythm (90 per cent-10 per cent) of one timid step to the left for every nine resolute paces to the right.

In practical terms, the pole theory meant that the KKE would pursue its legalist policy while preparing itself for the revolution which was expected to break out if and when the balance of forces in the Balkans changed as a result of Soviet policy. This revolution, whose first stage had already been accomplished by the Resistance, 'will be socialist in character and will resolve at a stroke all the problems of bourgeois democracy which are being maintained by the existing foreign domination . . .'.[2]

Thus, KKE policy was doomed to oscillate inconclusively between the two international poles that dominated it: on one hand preparing for an abstract revolution copied from a canonical model totally foreign to

[1] Minutes of the Twelfth Plenum.   [2] Minutes of the Twelfth Plenum.

Greek revolutionary reality, on the other trying to pursue a ramshackle legalistic policy in the face of ceaseless provocations. To counter the growing terror, the Central Committee and the Political Bureau called on former partisans to organize themselves into self-defence groups. 'Democratic citizens should defend their lives and resist all fascist attacks by any means, beginning with a country-wide general strike.'

On 24 August Zachariadis declared to an audience of 150,000 in Salonika:

Unless the situation takes a rapid and fundamental turn towards normal democratic development, we will retaliate against monarcho-fascism in the towns, mountains and villages, using the same methods. . . . If the supreme interests of the people require it, the glorious ELAS marching song, 'Forward ELAS for Greece', will be heard again in the ravines and on the mountain-tops.[1]

These remarks aroused a hurricane of cheering, but Zachariadis was only sabre-rattling. The self-defence groups were ordered not to dig up the buried weapons. Numbers of former partisans were forced to take to the mountains again, to live hunted lives without adequate means of defending themselves. Many of them crossed the frontier either to Albania or, more often, to seek refuge in Yugoslavia.

Bulkes

Nearly 3,000 exiles had landed at Tetovo in Yugoslavia – not far from Skopje – immediately after the Varkiza agreement. This first wave of exiles – the first of many – stayed at Tetovo for a while in temporary accommodation while Tzimas searched for a more suitable site for establishing a long-term community. Most of the region's men had been killed in the struggle against the occupying forces, and the Greeks were welcomed warmly by the lonely Yugoslav women. When they left the town two hedgerows of widows and young girls saw them off with tears, flowers, fruit and food.

The next stopping place was Novis Iva, a village left abandoned by the German community which had built it up before the war to an enviable level of prosperity. The Greek partisans found the bourgeois furnishings of their temporary homes almost unbelievably luxurious, but they barely had time to pry into the tabernacle-like glass cupboards and make a rather awkward acquaintance with the marvels of mechanical civilization before they learned that they were to travel north once again. Tzimas had discovered the ideal place in Bulkes, in the Yugoslav loop of the Danube, above Belgrade. The lands around the village and its modest industrial installations seemed to promise an idyllic refuge from the bitterness of exile: but Bulkes was destined to remain a sovereign enclave of dogmas and became a utopia only for Zachariadis's police. OPLA's Grand Inquisitor Pechtasidis arrived to introduce the arbitrary and suspicious order of Stalinist orthodoxy, supervised by Ioannidis who installed himself in Belgrade.

The KKE had achieved a bourgeois revolution and it was now time to put the Twelfth Plenum's decisions into practice by moving on to the superior stage of socialism and the dictatorship of the proletariat. To Pechtasidis this meant quite simply that it was time to purge the revolutionary troops. Right from the start, the facilities of Bulkes were turned to account to inculcate the rank and file with the healthy notions taught in the KUTV catechism. Popular leaders, kapetanios and intellectuals were *a priori* suspected of petit-bourgeois romanticism, ultra-leftism and Trotskyist adventurism. Bulkes camp, through which many of the former ELAS leaders were destined to pass sooner or later, opened under the trademark of police terror. The slightest criticism, the most harmless request for clarification of the KKE's political line, was interpreted as treason. Many of the ELAS chiefs, who had never been subjected to this type of constraint during the war, responded by turning a deaf ear to the Managing Committee.

So that there would be absolutely no confusion about the new hierarchy, Party bureaucrats were accorded open privileges: they lived in the largest houses, took their meals in a sort of officers' mess and kept the best clothes for themselves, while the kapetanios and former partisans were penned in like prisoners. At one meeting a kapetanios stood up in the audience and asked: 'Why this inequality between the leadership and the rest of the camp? Why are Resistance heroes being treated with such suspicion and indifference?'

Pechtasidis stood up on the platform. 'The comrade ought to be expelled.'

The meeting rejected this proposal and was adjourned immediately. But some of the argumentative elements had been identified, and before long their names were heading the black-list of an insidious, often bloody persecution. The advancing stain of police infiltration poisoned personal relationships, sapped people's wills and ended by stifling all ideas of constructive criticism.

'Look, this guy has an anti-Party attitude and if you associate with him he'll drag you down. . . . If you're not careful we'll have to take measures against *you* as well. . . .' When this warning did not bear fruit, arguments of a more direct and practical nature were employed.

Pechtasidis organized his first purge at the end of the summer, using a complaint from the Yugoslav authorities as pretext. The kapetanios Mavros and twenty other hard cases were sent back across the frontier to run the gauntlet of the armed bands combing the Greek countryside for people like them. Most of them had been found guilty of disciplinary offences, to which were added the obligatory charges of treason and anti-Party activities.

When their indictments had been read out at a public meeting, edifyingly stage-managed with platform and music, Mavros and the twenty partisans were made to walk to the station between two lines of psychologically conditioned men, who waxed indignant on the count of three and spat at the outcasts. There were many who turned a blind eye to this spectacle, feeling that they had nothing to lose by waiting a little longer; they were the *skoulikia* or earthworms. After his expulsion by the bureaucrats, the 'traitor' Mavros survived long enough to raise new partisan groups, and died heroically two years later in the ranks of the Democratic Army.

Great Expectations

The situation in Voulgaris's Greece was deteriorating every day. Tens of thousands of former resistance fighters were on the run from the police. More than two thousand of them were condemned to death by courts martial, while extreme right-wing bands claimed hundreds of victims in an even more direct manner.

Menaced by the prevailing climate of terror, but in full (if paradoxical) legality, the KKE held its Seventh Congress at the beginning of October 1945 in the main auditorium of the Titania Theatre in Athens. The walls and balconies were draped with blue and white national flags alternating with the red flag of revolution. The stage was dwarfed by two huge portraits of Stalin and Zachariadis.

During his visit to Salonika Zachariadis had declared on 25 August: 'Macedonia is and will remain Greek.' The Congress now pronounced on Epirus, deciding that 'if a democratic majority favours the immediate military occupation of Northern Epirus by the Greek army, the Party will maintain its objections but will bow to the majority decision'.[1] Thus the 'national' line was dominant in foreign policy. For the rest, the Congress was content to give sweeping endorsement to the line which had been followed during the occupation and to the events of the previous December, and ratified the conclusions of the Twelfth Plenum.

Tzimas and Karageorgis were among the few dissenters: 'We might well have achieved victory if we had not committed certain distinct errors. The Central Committee delayed its departure to the Mountain until too late, and we pulled our punches on the orders of the British, who were thus able to prevent us from fighting some battles. Despite ELAS HQ's magnificent schemes the army was not sufficiently hardened for battle. The only way to resist the British would have been to fight the Germans as hard as possible until the very end. Finally, at the time of the Battle of Athens, the most experienced troops were kept right out of the operation; the reorganization of the army was a very bad move.'

The only effect of this statement was to blacken Tzimas's own case in the eyes of the leadership. The atmosphere of the Seventh Congress, dominated by Zachariadis's Stalinist personality, stifled all discussion. The assembly was not told the result of the secret ballot and had to be content with listening to the Central Committee's reports.

It seemed that the KKE's first objective was still the establishment of a 'People's Democracy' in Greece, and that the only thing holding this development back was the presence of British troops in the country. Finally Zachariadis criticized 'the tendency of certain comrades, who talk of peaceful transition, to see the future from only one angle. We should insist on the fact that the *possibility* of peaceful transition exists, but not the *certainty* . . . and we should remember that the possibility is receding with every day that passes.'[2]

Zachariadis was preparing a final assault to complete the 'bourgeois' revolution achieved by the Resistance, and this implied a heightened

[1] *Seventh Congress of the KKE*, Athens, 1945.
[2] ibid.

mistrust of political 'allies'. This model prevented him from making proper allowance for the different democratic forces in Greece and eventually turned out to be more useful to the British than to anyone else. It helped to create the split the Foreign Office wanted, by driving the more or less liberal and republican formations temporarily towards monarchism. Finally, in the opinion of some commissars, it brought seeds of decay into the ranks of the revolution itself.

Kanellopoulos was substituted for Voulgaris for a few weeks but there was no diminution of the terror. Damaskinos was quite unable to control the activities of right-wing bands in full cry. On 5 November 1945 a new government was constituted under the leadership of the liberal Sofoulis, whose principal task was to organize elections. An agreement signed with Hector McNeil three days earlier had recommended that a constitutional referendum be held in 1948. Pyromaglou was not invited to join the government – a result of pressures exercised by the same McNeil – but the cabinet included the principal signatories of the 5 June memo protesting against the right-wing terror: Kafandaris, Sofianopoulos, Kartalis, Tsouderos. Even so, there was little reduction for several months in the terrorism which affected every corner of Greece.

At the end of the year the Minister of Justice, Rendis, held a press conference to answer the questions of foreign journalists who had been outraged by the sheer brutality of this repression. One of the things he explained to them was that the policy of presenting severed heads at a window for payment, like rats' tails during a vermin drive, was a Balkan tradition which would only seem shocking to foreigners unused to the local customs. He also produced a memorandum which quantified the industriousness of the Greek police:

According to information collected by the Ministry of Justice, the total number of persons detained in prison has risen to 17,984. Of this total, 2,388 are serving legally imposed sentences and 15,596 are in preventive detention. The number of criminal cases under investigation has risen to 18,401. We have no up-to-date information on seventeen departments in which 48,956 individuals are being prosecuted as members of EAM-ELAS. We lack certain necessary information on fourteen other departments. The total number of individuals being prosecuted, including those in preventive detention, exceeds 80,000 according to our calculations.[1]

[1] *Eleftheri Ellada*, 11 December 1945.

In fact, the police were so overworked that it was considering the introduction of 'decongestion' measures, and Rendis added:

It is impossible to keep so many men in prison. It will take several years to deal with all their cases. We are also in danger of seeing the most guilty of them escape from justice. It is possible that the immense number of accused is the result of a deliberate manoeuvre on the part of the detained persons to over-burden the judicial system [*sic*]. As a result, in some cases a single crime will lead to fifty prosecutions. To facilitate the task of chastising the real culprits, the government has made the following decisions, to be applied to offences and crimes committed between 27 April 1941 and 12 February 1945:
   1) there will be no further judicial prosecutions except for cases of murder;
   2) prosecution will no longer apply to cases of incitement to murder;
   3) for the time being, no new complaints will be considered.

The argument that the accused had been throwing themselves into the arms of the police 'to overburden the judicial system' could hardly be taken seriously, and the Justice Minister's 'decongestion' scheme did very little to cool the ardour of his heavies, who continued to pack their victims into the camps and prisons like sardines.

As its strength increased from 30,000 to 75,000 men, the army began to count for more alongside the British intervention forces, which were still present in their entirety. In direct violation of all the past agreements, officers who had served in ELAS were systematically withdrawn from active service, while the 1,319 officers inherited from the pro-German militia were allowed to carry on with their careers under the new govern-ment's banner. Finally, the X Organization and divers bands of bounty-hunters continued to enjoy a growing prosperity.

On 6 January 1946 there was a monster meeting in the Panathenaic stadium, where 350,000 people gathered to protest against the repression. The KKE's trade union organization, ERGAS, controlled the Greek trade unions, whose secretary-elect, Paparigas, was a communist. Every show of strength by EAM or the Party was impressive, but it usually took place in a solemn legality which seemed eccentric by comparison with the acts of violence being perpetrated daily by the authorities.

Starting at the end of December 1945, EAM officials began touring the provinces to organize political resistance. They split the task up between them and scattered through every region. In Macedonia, the territory most violently treated by the forces of repression, a virtually identical scene took place in every town.

Two of these EAM representatives arrived in Kozani during the first week of 1946; they were Papadimitris, of the Agrarian Party, and General Neokosmos Grigoriadis, founder of the Left Liberal Party. On their arrival they presented themselves to the military authorities. Taken to see the Commandant of the Governmental Army garrison, they found a British officer sitting behind the desk while the Greek officer stood in a corner of the office.

Papadimitris addressed the Greek, but in vain: he kept pointing to the British officer. Grigoriadis and Papadimitris walked over and stood in front of the Commandant: 'We want to deal with a Greek.'

He eyed them with an ironic smile: 'Can't you see that even the cloth of my uniform is British?'

In the end the two EAM men had to turn to the British officer, whom they asked for permission to hold a meeting in the town.

'You're a legal organization. I have no objection to your holding this meeting.'

But there followed a series of questions which quickly began to sound like a police interrogation and finally became openly insolent. General Grigoriadis interrupted: 'I should perhaps inform you that I am a General in the regular army. I used to be a member of ELAS and I might add that the British never stopped trying to mislead me. I have decided to return the decorations your government awarded me in happier times.'

The old General actually did send his medals back to the King of England a few days later. The British officer brought his interrogation to an end and gave permission for the meeting.

Ten thousand people had already crowded into the town's stadium, and more kept on arriving despite the presence of a British unit which was watching all the entrances. When Grigoriadis and Papadimitris arrived at the entrance, ten men armed with cudgels appeared from nowhere and felled General Grigoriadis. Before the crowd had had time to react a jeep drew up containing the Greek Commandant, the British officer and the town attorney.

Grigoriadis was bleeding heavily from a head wound. Papadimitris, who was much bigger than the General and had been trying to protect him, screamed at the attorney: 'Can't you see what's happening? Do something! What are you playing at?'

The assailants had melted away. The attorney ground out between clenched teeth: 'What d'you expect me to do about it?'

Grigoriadis mounted the platform with blood all over his face and Papadimitris began to speak. After a minute or two he was interrupted by a volley of stones. Before EAM security officials had time to isolate the people throwing them, British troops began clearing the whole stadium, firing in the air.

The same week Partsalidis lost an eye at one of these meetings, in Verria, where the authorities played the same ambiguous role. So much for the legality that had now prevailed in Greece for over a year.

In many cases the people, sometimes even helped by members of the military, succeeded in containing the provocateurs. After six hundred citizens had been arrested there, Tzimas organized a meeting in Kastoria. Afterwards he went to spend the night in his family house a few kilometres away, in the village of Argos Orestikon. During the night the house was attacked by twenty men. There was a government army contingent in the village, most of whose members were Cretans. They spontaneously threw themselves on the assailants and drove them off. Tzimas, who was totally exhausted after a harassing day, did not even wake up. In the morning he noticed that the house was surrounded by ten soldiers; repressing his impulse to take flight, he discovered to his relief that they had been standing guard all night to protect him.

Despite the shock of the Varkiza agreement, a majority of the population was still loyal to EAM. At the beginning of 1946, the efforts of successive governments to strangle the Resistance spirit had failed dismally.

On the way back from one of these tours of the north Partsalidis, Kyrkos, Papadimitris and a few other EAM cadres, accompanied by an English journalist, boarded an old ship on the Salonika-Athens run, the *Korinthia*. A government army regiment was also on board. When the EAM men entered the dining-saloon for the first time they found the colonel of the regiment already seated with two of his officers, who immediately set up an offensive clamour. They signalled two orderlies and told them to expel Partsalidis and his group. There was a brief scuffle and the soldiers were repelled. The colonel stood up on his chair: 'Why don't you get out of the dining-room? You're not wanted here.'

He had hardly finished speaking when a delegation appeared to express the regiment's solidarity with the EAM members. The ship's captain followed suit, welcoming Partsalidis and his entourage on behalf of the crew. Such expressions of solidarity were as much a daily event as the provocations. The whole of Greece was creaking with the tension of a barely-controlled riot.

An honest election held at this time would almost certainly have given EAM substantial representation, but the British were pressing Sofoulis to hold it in mid-terror. Meanwhile Zachariadis fixed his gaze on the north and east, waiting for the sign permitting him to abandon the legalist line established by the Seventh Congress. The 'two poles' policy had placed the KKE's future squarely in Stalin's hands, and the consequent attitude of expectation removed all real meaning from the legalist alternative.

In the middle of December 1945 the Party had made contact with representatives of Tito and Dimitrov at Pietrich, on the Bulgarian frontier. The neighbouring countries had promised substantial aid in the event of an insurrection in Greece, and Tito had detailed Rankovitch to work out the terms and conditions of Yugoslav assistance. But no Soviet representative attended the meeting, which had to content itself with 'hoping' that Stalin would supply material aid.

The Soviet position in support of the Iranian Communist Tudeh Party's declaration of an autonomous government in Azerbaijan province, which was also adopted in mid-December, seemed a splendid sign to Zachariadis. The pro-Communist coalition sharing the government of Rumania with King Michael in an alliance of unheard-of promiscuity, and the regime that held sway in Sofia, also seemed to signal a Soviet advance towards the Eastern Mediterranean.

During December and January ERGAS called strikes in every town in Greece, and the strikes received wide support. All of these events received much more attention from the KKE General Secretary than either the parliamentary situation, on the one hand, or the establishment of the first self-defence groups in the mountains on the other.

At long last, on 21 January 1946, the day the Party published a manifesto accusing the British of responsibility for the carnage going on in Greece and demanding the immediate withdrawal of their troops, the head of the Soviet delegation to the UN addressed a note to the Security Council asking for a discussion of the Greek problem under Article 35 of the United Nations charter.

... The presence of British troops in Greece after the cessation of hostilities can no longer be justified by the need to protect the lines of communication of British troops occupying defeated countries. In other words, the British presence in Greece has become an instrument of political pressure, which reactionary elements have used continually against the democratic forces in the country. This situation ... has given birth to an extremely tense atmosphere charged with serious dangers not only for the Greek people but for the peace and security of the world.[1]

[1] Official transcripts of Security Council proceedings, Year 1, Supplement 1, annexe 3, p. 73.

Judging the circumstances to be extremely favourable, Zachariadis summoned the Central Committee elected at the Seventh Congress to its Second Plenum on 12 February. The policy of legal reconciliation remained the basis of the official Party line, but at the same time Zachariadis added that 'after examining internal factors and the Balkan and International situation, the Plenum should proceed with the organization of a new armed struggle against the monarcho-fascist orgy'.[1] In the end he did not put the most urgent problem forward for discussion at all, and imposed a resolution on the Plenum that left him in sole charge of 'legality's' future: 'The problem of our participation in the elections will be decided by the Political Bureau.'

During the next few days the Central Committee established a politico-military mission whose task, far from being the consolidation of the self-defence groups, was to examine the prospects for an immediate seizure of power in the major towns. Markos and most of the military leaders were violently opposed to this plan. Markos wrote later: 'It was more a question of a putsch than of a revolution. It was an adventure which would have ended with not only the putsch but also the people's movement being smashed.'[2]

Faced with such strong opposition, Zachariadis adjourned the discussion and asked the organizations simply to 'study the insurrectional and military prospects'. Secretly, however, he still believed that the time had come to start an insurrection; not a Mountain insurrection, based on the resurgence of ELAS which was taking place as a result of the terror and led by kapetanios who did not always march in step, but one carried out by the traditional, urban revolutionary forces.

The Political Bureau's power of decision over the matter of participating in the elections meant that he could bring the legalist interlude to an end whenever he wanted to. Certain Liberals seemed to be bent on goading him into it.

On 17 February 1946 *Rizospastis* announced the EAM Central Committee's decision to abstain from the elections until such time as the Greek government had 'restored public order, eliminated nazi collaborators and former members of the Security Battalions from the police, guaranteed a general political amnesty, removed the names of non-existent people from the electoral registers and shown itself amenable to the formation of a democratic government with EAM participation'.

[1] N. Zachariades, *New Situation, New Duties*, Nicosia, 1950, p. 38 (in Greek).
[2] *Seventh Plenum of the Central Committee*, 1957.

Meanwhile Partsalidis, who left for Moscow at the end of January, was meeting Molotov and various Soviet personalities. The Greek insurrectional projects were received with icy scepticism and the KKE was strongly advised to form a Democratic Front and take part in the elections. Partsalidis's report did not reach Athens until 20 February. On the 22nd *Rizopastis* published a more moderate declaration:

If genuine goodwill exists and British opposition ceases, the preconditions for a genuinely free election will have been achieved.

The advice lavished on Partsalidis in Moscow came from outside Greece; on the spot, however, events seemed to be following the course eagerly anticipated by Zachariadis. On 15 March, after Sofianopoulos's resignation from the government, Kafandaris, Mercouris, Kartalis and Papas also resigned, refusing to stand surety for the electoral parody that was being prepared. The danger of the KKE abstaining in isolation seemed to be receding. Three days later Prime Minister Sofoulis himself declared:

The Liberal Party has always favoured the holding of elections at the earliest date after the establishment of full public order. Today I am obliged to admit that, as far as the Liberal Party is concerned, these indispensable conditions for going ahead with the elections still do not exist. My information from every part of Greece confirms that there is no guarantee of our candidates' freedom of movement. Freedom of expression exists only for Monarchists.[1]

The forces of repression were building up an impressive score of victims. Between Varkiza in February 1945 and March 1946:

1,219 murdered
6,671 wounded
31,632 tortured
18,767 arrests with pillage
84,931 arrests
509 attempted murders
165 rapes and acts of violence against women.[2]

Sofoulis's Minister of Public Order, Mercouris, stated after resigning:

Armed bands rule the provinces. Unfortunately, these bands have been collaborating in many areas with all the State organizations responsible for public order, and where they have not collaborated they have always been treated

[1] *Eleftheri Ellada*, 19 March 1946.
[2] *The Truth about Greece*, a Blue Book edited by the Provisional Democratic Government, August 1948, p. 16.

considerately by the authorities. Until I was nominated Minister of Justice (November 1945) none of these bandits was prosecuted, despite their many crimes.[1]

Zachariadis left for Prague, feeling that events were definitely moving his way. Against the advice of Thorez and Togliatti in particular, but possibly in line with orders coming more directly from the Kremlin, he decided to boycott the elections. The non-Communist elements in EAM backed the decision. Whether or not the unanimous outburst of liberal indignation had been part of a manoeuvre, the British now had their opportunity to isolate EAM.

Sofoulis cabled Bevin, demanding that the elections be delayed until order had been restored. The British Foreign Secretary replied that, according to his information from the Athens embassy, circumstances were favourable to the organization of a poll, and insisted that the agreed date of 31 March be adhered to.

Sofoulis withdrew his objections, declaring: 'While it is true that circumstances are not favourable for holding elections, the problem has assumed an international significance which obliges us to go ahead as arranged.'

The KKE and the other EAM parties found themselves alone in their abstention, apart from a small group led by Kafandaris. All the other Socialists and Liberals put up candidates and prepared to go to the polls.

The electoral law required all candidatures to be deposited fifteen days before the election. On the day the lists were due to close, General Grigoriadis and Hajibeis were sitting in the office of their Left Liberal Party, which belonged to EAM. The old general, who had opposed the boycott from the very beginning, had bowed to the majority decision with an ill grace. EAM's isolation after the Liberals' *volte-face* made him gloomily fear the worst.

Towards 1 p.m. the telephone rang, summoning General Grigoriadis to a meeting of the KKE Central Committee. He was too depressed to go and sent Hajibeis in his place. Within half an hour the phone rang again. It was Hajibeis: 'Wait there, I'll be back in a minute.'

A few minutes later he rushed in, very excited: 'We're saved! The KKE's decided we should ask Sofoulis to delay the closing date by two days so that we can put our names down. The left-wing vote will go to our candidates.'

[1] *Vima*, 20 March 1946.

This was Siantos's decision; Zachariadis had not yet returned from Prague. Though the decision was fully justified by the sequence of events leading up to it, there can be little doubt that the Old Man had taken advantage of the General Secretary's absence to move things in the direction he had favoured all along. Grigoriadis asked Sofoulis for a meeting and was received at the end of the afternoon.

The Prime Minister hid behind the Regent: Damaskinos, it seemed, was opposed to any delay in closing the lists. It was too late. The Left would be alone in taking no part in the elections. The British had played a masterly game, and were now in a position to denounce the KKE and EAM for their refusal to work through the democratic institutions. Zachariadis had supplied them with some of their best arguments. He had not told anyone in the Central Committee about the warnings he had received from Thorez and Togliatti. He was instituting a personal policy which for years afterwards consisted basically of attempting to force the hand of Stalin and the fraternal Parties. After imposing the election boycott he dispatched an order to the KKE organization in Macedonia, telling it to make an armed attack on a target of its choice the day before the elections were scheduled to take place.

Markos and Kikitsas, of the Macedonian Committee, chose the town of Litochoron as their objective. It had close historical connections with the Klephtic resistance, and three EAM officials had been disembowelled there in the course of the last few weeks. An armed EAM group entered the town on 30 March 1946, the eve of the elections.

Twenty-nine of the thirty-three men who took part in the raid were native to Litochoron, including the leader Ypsilantis. The town was defended by a gendarmerie detachment, reinforced by an army platoon which had just arrived to help control the next day's election. The regular army platoon offered no resistance, and some of its men even joined the partisans, but the gendarmes would not lay down their arms. Their barracks was surrounded and set on fire. When they finally displayed a white flag they had lost twelve men; none of the attackers was scratched. When British armoured vehicles approached the town Ypsilantis ordered his men to retreat.

The isolated groups of partisans scattered about the country took this incident as the starting signal for the third round. They began digging up the buried weapons.

The results of the next day's election were everything that the British could wish. The number of registered electors remains something of an enigma but, assuming that the proportion of electors was roughly the same as in later consultations, the population of 7,232,543 would suggest a minimum electorate of about 2,200,000 (in 1951 there were 2,224,246 registered electors in a population of 7,395,219).

1,121,696 votes were cast: 705,000 went to the monarchist parties (Populist Party, Nationalists' Party, etc.) and 410,000 to the republican centre (Liberal Party, Venizelist Liberal Party, Social Democratic Party and Greek Agrarian Party).

Assuming that the figure of 2,200,000 electors is reasonably accurate, the abstention rate was of the order of forty-eight per cent. Twenty per cent seems to be regarded as a normal abstention rate; thus it can be estimated that twenty-eight per cent of the vote (more than 600,000 votes) would have gone to EAM and Kafandaris's group. These cautious calculations do not take into account the faked registers and other frauds which were undoubtedly practised in the heat of the moment by the legal authorities. In any case, it is certain that at least a million votes would have gone to republican formations.

These elections [wrote Jean Meynaud] had been placed under the control of an International Commission most of whose observers knew next to nothing about Greece and could not speak the language. This body declared that the consultation had been carried out honestly and estimated the level of abstention at fifteen per cent of the registered electorate. In view of the Commission's composition and frame of reference, it would be very naïve to see this certificate of good democratic behaviour as anything more than a move designed to reinforce the international standing of a government in pawn to the Anglo-Saxon powers.[1]

This massive abstention, which would later be denounced as 'a monstrous error' by the KKE and even by Zachariadis himself, logically opened the way to an armed uprising. In fact, however, it was the forces of repression that went on expanding and venting their fury, while Zachariadis quietly continued with his preparations for an abstract insurrection which had nothing to do with the resurgent people's movement. The andartes had laid down their arms when they were in a strong position; now they found themselves being forced to take to the mountains again to avoid being massacred.

[1] Jean Meynaud, *Les Forces politiques en Grèce*, Lausanne, 1965, p. 80.

The Pendulum

Zachariadis passed through Yugoslavia on his way back from Prague, and called at Bulkes camp, where Pechtasidis had been evolving the 'pure, hard order' which the General Secretary meant to apply to the whole Greek revolutionary movement.

The camp's governing Committee, which was composed exclusively of ex-members of OPLA, had set up an internal militia whose representatives, distinguished from the mass by armbands bearing the letters YTO, occupied themselves with tracking down intellectuals and kapetanios who might be guilty of 'petty-bourgeois Trotskyist tendencies' inherited from ELAS. This process was taking place within the hothouse atmosphere of the camp; there was no escape for the victims. The direction of this systematic purge, which was not practised fully in Greece itself until eighteen months later, brings Zachariadis's revolutionary ideas into sharp focus. The earthworms or *skoulikia* held up to collective opprobrium during public meetings were living in a climate of persecution and terror. One morning the Committee asked all those wishing to return to Athens to put their names down on a list.

'It was a ruse,' declared Pechtasidis a week later, 'to unveil *skoulikia* who are not happy here and want to go back and collaborate with the monarcho-fascists. When an organism is infected one is justified in using any means to extract the pus.'

Even the sexual activities of the camp's inhabitants were subjected to a system of marriage licences which could only be granted by the leadership. Women were in a very small minority, and the authorities did not hesitate to resolve rivalries in favour of 'right-thinking' men or those well up in the internal hierarchy. A certain Kalfas, a YTO leader, distinguished himself with a special erotic ardour which guaranteed him a disturbed future.

The partisans who, after fleeing their country to escape persecution by the government, now found themselves subjected to YTO's bullying, still refused for the most part to see their situation at Bulkes as anything other than an extraordinary but temporary interlude. They gave Zachariadis a delirious welcome, which reached its climax when the General Secretary announced from the platform: 'You will soon be returning to Greece to fight for liberty.'

The first result of the Greek election was not long in making itself felt. Extreme right-wing leaders such as Manganas, Sourlas, Kalabalikis, Vourlakis, Velentsas, and their gangs of head-hunters, began a period of frenetic activity. Spyros Theotokis, the new Minister of Public Order, answered all protests by saying: 'This is just an explosion of triumph following the election victory, the drunkenness of the conquering side, which in the nature of things is sure to be over before long. . . .'

Following the Litochoron attack and the election boycott, the partisans were preparing to launch the insurrection proper. There were many who had never concealed their opposition to the boycott, feeling that all the legal avenues should be explored before they took the plunge into a dubious adventure of that sort.

It was now evident that the KKE's abstention had done nothing to arouse international feeling and that the great powers could hardly wait to recognize the monarchist government formed by Tsaldaris at the beginning of May. Now that the boats of legality had been burned, now that the election results and the Litochoron expedition had unleashed a new wave of violence, the time had surely come to stop hesitating; it would be only logical to carry the thing through to the end, to try and rewrite history by organizing Zachariadis's famous insurrection. This in any case is what the regional organizations were forced to do from that time onward. They made their preparations without straying from the directives Zachariadis had issued in February at the end of the Second Plenum.

Ten months had passed since Aris's severed head had been displayed in the square at Trikkala, the head of a man disowned and betrayed by his Party because he had wanted to continue the struggle. Now Zachariadis's own policy was pressing the partisans inexorably back towards the mountains; but the Central Committee was still wavering.

At the beginning of May Zachariadis visited Salonika. The people's leader Markos Vafiadis, the kapetanios now destined to lead the armed struggle, told the General Secretary that the Macedonian organization could 'arm and train 25,000 fighters in the villages and major towns within two months', and asked for authority to 'arm the self-defence groups which are in the mountains already'.[1]

Zachariadis replied: 'You are not informed on all the Central Committee's decisions. What we did at Litochoron was a bluff intended to force the government to make concessions.'[1]

For several weeks longer Zachariadis, who was personally responsible

[1] Letter from Markos to the Central Committee, October 1957.

for unleashing the current drive by the monarchist bands and the police, clung to the pseudo-legal line in the hope of organizing the revolution along dogmatic lines. On 12 May, for example, he made a floundering speech to KOA (the Athens organization), explaining that the KKE must 'seek a political solution with the cooperation of all workers, even the most resolutely nationalistic . . . to ensure economic progress, liberty, democracy, and the independence and integrity of the nation'.

The truth of the matter is that Zachariadis had no confidence in the people's movement which his policies had forced to take refuge in the mountains. He had made it quite clear during the politico-military conference in February: what was being envisaged was an *urban* insurrection.

In March, the Greek TUC fell entirely under ERGAS control when the Communist Paparigas became General Secretary. But Zachariadis felt that this was only a partial success, and the Political Bureau asked ERGAS to harden its demands and organize a general strike. The Tsaldaris government did not allow this opportunity to pass: using 'technical competence' as a pretext, it annulled the union elections and imposed a new leadership on the TUC in the shape of the Makris crew, which is still in office today, twenty-five years later.

Despite everything, Zachariadis clung perversely to his canonical model, putting all his effort into the big-city proletariat and limiting the development of the new Mountain movement from the outset. His secondary objective, equally orthodox, was the creation of soviets in the army. Militants who were called up were forbidden to desert to the self-defence groups: the result, in a country whose police files had been growing for twenty years, was that activists and sympathizers were handed over to Security as soon as they showed their faces at a recruitment centre. Some 50,000 men followed this easy route into the government's concentration camps.

Sarafis and Bakirjis were placed under police surveillance in a camp near Athens, along with six hundred other former ELAS officers. At the end of May, Colonel Mousterakis was given leave to visit his family in Salonika, where he managed to arrange a discrete meeting with Markos. Both men were convinced of the urgent need to call all democratic officers to the mountains. Mousterakis and a few others had worked out an escape plan. When Zachariadis was consulted, however, he replied crushingly: 'It's absolute folly. It's a provocation which will compromise the Party's political line.'

Mousterakis and Kikitsas held a meeting with forty-five officers who were still in Salonika. They were all men who had followed the order to abstain from voting, and some had been involved in the Litochoron expedition; knowing themselves to be closely watched and needing only the right word to take to the mountains, they turned to Zachariadis once again.

'We know that certain andartes took up arms again after Litochoron. We observe that we are walking straight into another armed conflict. We are being called to Athens for isolation or dispersal. Should we submit to the government or join the partisans in the mountains? The movement is taking shape before our very eyes, but badly needs military leaders.'

Zachariadis answered: 'The Party has not taken the decision to go and organize a new Resistance. You must be disciplined, and present yourselves to the government when called upon to do so.'

Zachariadis had no more faith in former ELAS officers than he had in the new movement forming in the mountains; while the insurrection was starting to emerge spontaneously, he kept doggedly chasing his abstraction.

In September 1946 Generals Sarafis and Bakirjis, along with three hundred other officers, were arrested by the government and exiled to the islands of Aegina and Ikaria. This event put an end to the opportunity, and the shortage of trained officers in the mountains had disastrous consequences.

The experiences of his predecessors had taught Zachariadis nothing and made him forget nothing. His atavistic mistrust of revolutionary spontaneity and of Greek popular structures prevented him from doing anything but repeat and aggravate the errors of the past.

At about the same time as Colonel Mousterakis came to Markos with his escape plan, Tzimas, Partsalidis, and Kyrkos arrived at Verria, a former Turkish military colony whose clandestine chapels, hidden away in backyards, bear witness to the ineradicable nature of the Greek resistance spirit. About a hundred citizens had been arrested and tortured by the authorities there, with full collaboration from the local monarchist gangs.

The three men composed a formal protest to the government, dispatched it and called on the head of military Security. They passed through the unshadowed courtyard of a barracks where ten men were resting between interrogation sessions. As soon as they saw the EAM delegation the soldiers rushed forward to beat up its members, and Partsalidis was seriously injured in the ensuing mêlée. After taking him to a safe place, the other two visited the archbishop, the British and the Chief of Police in turn; each time, after voicing their protest, they were politely shown the door.

After Verria they went to Naousa, where the terror was raging with even greater violence. Tzimas and Kyrkos made an approach to the gendarmerie, who gave them an icy reception and began to show signs of irritation when the question of the support given to bandits by the police was raised. Tzimas and Kyrkos had to leave fast, and were astonished to find themselves intact when they reached the street.

On the way to Edessa they passed through territory which had been liberated by ELAS thirty months previously. Hearing gunfire not far from the road, the shots echoing and bouncing among the mountains, they stopped their car to try and locate the fighting. Presently two British jeeps appeared over the horizon and approached purposefully, apparently trying to cut off their retreat. Partsalidis made a rapid U-turn and drove back to Salonika.

The Party's political cadres could not take a step without a policeman breathing down their necks. Under these absurd conditions, and expecting to be arrested any moment, Partsalidis and Tzimas pursued their inquiry into the terror and sent protest after protest to Athens.

The police were closing in, but the Central Committee's orders were unchanged: Stay in the towns, no running away to the mountains. The inevitable finally happened at the beginning of July. This time nobody escaped being arrested. The Tsaldaris government attacked. It was only now, much too late and in the most half-hearted manner, that Zachariadis resolved to organize the self-defence groups.

The Resurgence of ELAS

Towards the middle of July, Zachariadis and Markos held a meeting; doctrinaires and kapetanios together, hardly a meeting of minds. Markos was ordered to leave the Macedonian organization in Bartzotas's hands and get in touch with a commission of the Political Bureau to examine the problems of organizing and arming the groups of andartes already established in the mountains. Zachariadis was insistent on certain points:

1. Recruitment must be undertaken exclusively on a voluntary basis.

2. Markos must accept only individual volunteers and refuse to accept any organized bodies from the governmental army which might express the intention of joining the andartes *en masse*.

3. Armed activity must be restricted to attacks on monarchist bands; the regular army must not be touched.

4. Only defensive actions would be permitted. No Party organization was to be set up within the partisan groups.

5. 'We are maintaining our "conciliatory" line and all our activity must contribute to this end. It is simply a matter of exercising pressure on the government.'[1]

A few days later Markos met the commission for the first time. His projects immediately aroused old suspicions about the Mountain.

'We can gather at least 20,000 partisans in the mountains before the spring of 1947; if the big Party organizations mobilize themselves in time to supply us with cadres, we might manage three times that number.'

There was a tense silence, broken at length by the sound of throat-clearing. The reply had the oily emptiness characteristic of those, either priest or commissar, who carry the infallible Word: 'Comrade Markos is in a hurry. He has not really understood the Party's political line . . . and he must be very careful if he wishes to avoid exposing the organization to grave dangers.'

Another kapetanios, Tanakaridis, was asked what size of force he was planning to organize. 'About 3,000 men.'

The custodians of wisdom greeted this with a smile: 'That's far too many. Try to keep down to 1,000.'[2]

So why the attack on Litochoron? Why the election boycott? Zachariadis was whiling away the time until the British intervention forces left by giving them a pretext to dig in. This was far from being his only inconsistency. The Political Bureau, which was still hoping to cut a fine legalistic figure, decided against all logic to take part in the referendum on the form of the future regime. Its political retreat, which was by now irreversible, was balanced only by a symbolic mobilization for armed struggle. The two alternatives were cancelling one another out instead of reinforcing each other.

Tsaldaris and the British were in luck. They did not waste any time. The embryonic activity of the first 'rebel' groups enabled the new parliament to pass a law concerning 'emergency measures for the

[1] Markos.   [2] Markos.

re-establishment of law and order'. It established martial law in areas where 'the situation was abnormal' – in other words, throughout almost the whole of Greece.

Former ELAS officers were being deported to the Aegean islands. There were more and more arrests. The British opened 400,000 police files which were used to eliminate suspects from the army and send them to rot on the island of Makronisos, opposite Cape Sounion.

The few officers who did manage to get back to the Mountain all went there of their own accord. Vratsanos, the dynamiter of Mount Olympus, had been called up by the governmental army in September 1945. He was assigned to a unit of Engineers, but when he arrived to take up his commission he found that his fame had preceded him: the men recognized him and greeted him with an ovation that brought his career as a regular officer to a sudden and premature end. He was placed on the B list, which meant that he was removed from active service and placed under permanent surveillance. Leave-passes were extremely rare and he was forbidden all contact with left-wing organizations. This isolation did, however, have one advantage: it prevented the politicos from persuading him not to rejoin the Mountain. After Litochoron, surveillance intensified and officers were required to sign themselves in twice a day. Vratsanos managed to get himself a governmental army officer's uniform and set off for Euboea in a lorryload of men going on leave. From there he went to Volos, where the terror made it extremely difficult to make any contacts. After hiding out for a week in the upturned boats in the harbour, he made his way back to Olympus and busied himself recovering weapons from the piles of German scrap-iron he had tipped into every ravine on the coast of Thessaly.

Kikitsas and Markos did not find travelling much easier. They sometimes had to shoot at the bloodhounds dogging their footsteps. Attempts had already been made to capture, then to kill, Kikitsas in the streets of Salonika, but so far the kapetanios's reflexes had proved quicker than those of his enemies.

When Markos first took over the self-defence groups, he had about 65 men on Mount Grammos under Yannoulis, 350 men on Vitsi under Ypsilantis, and about 1,200 men spread through the rest of Greece and led by Lassanis, Liakos, Bellis, Agrafiotis and other former ELAS kapetanios. Popular figures from the first 'andartiko' were making their way back to the mountains. Old Barba Kitsos, bearded like Chapaiev and accompanied by his wife in national costume and his flock of sheep, showed up one day on the heights of Verria. Women were already numerous in partisan ranks. The opposition consisted of 206 armed monarchist bands, each one numbering about a hundred men and safe in the support of the governmental army.

As the constitutional referendum drew nearer, Vidalis, the assistant chief editor of *Rizospastis*, decided to go and investigate the activities of monarchist bands in the provinces. From the moment of his departure he sensed the presence of a diffuse threat. Certain faces, glimpsed once in the train and again later in the streets of Trikkala, began to grow familiar; they seemed to pop up everywhere. Something hostile was closing in on him. The details began to fall into place and Vidalis telephoned Karageorgis to tell him about his anxiety. Karageorgis did not hesitate a second: 'Come back at once.'

The next day, 16 August, the train was puffing laboriously towards Athens when the clatter of its wheels was interrupted by the sound of gunfire. It ground slowly to a halt. Sourlas's men ordered all the passengers out and lined them up along the track. The man in charge walked straight up to Vidalis, flanked by a British officer. The rest of the passengers were held at gunpoint while Vidalis was pulled out of the line. The leader of the commando insulted him, struck him, flashed a knife-blade in the sun and began to torture him. It was a lengthy business; eyes, tongue. Women screamed. One passenger collapsed in the dust, his mind unhinged by the spectacle. The British officer remained impassive; when Vidalis's sufferings had exhausted his strength, he drew his pistol and finished him off. The train resumed its journey, carrying the same insupportable image graven on hundreds of brains.

A few days later Vidalis's wife Teti, who had been an EAM official at Trikkala at the time of the Liberation, appeared at Athens police headquarters. She was received by a British officer who listened to her with his feet on his desk. Teti managed to keep her voice steady as she demanded an inquiry into the affair.

'A man has been killed. What do you expect *me* to do about it?' answered the 'adviser'. '*We* certainly aren't responsible, and to be honest with you I can't make out what your compatriots are up to.'

The result of the constitutional referendum achieved the main objectives of the British intervention at the summer's end, but there was no sign of the intervention coming to an end. Zachariadis's conciliatory line, still careful even now everything seemed to be settled, to provide documented evidence of legalistic goodwill, required Communists and members of the

EAM organizations to take part in the plebiscite on the return of King George II on 1 September 1946.

The consultation took place in conditions of extremely poor political visibility. It was announced that sixty-eight per cent of the votes cast were in favour of the monarchy. The official results put the registered electorate at 1,921,725, a figure which sheds unexpected light on the declarations of the Control Commission after the March election, when it had calculated the abstention rate as fifteen per cent on a total vote of 1,100,000.

This time, no commission dared to guarantee the validity of the voting figures, of this monarchist sixty-eight per cent voicing the wishes of 'National Unity'. Systematic terror and para-legality had achieved an arguable figure on which the Glucksburg dynasty would now base its claim to the Greek throne. George II returned to Athens immediately. This was what the British had wanted; surely now they would be able to bow out gracefully?

No. The rebirth of the guerilla provided a marvellous pretext for flying to the aid of the Greek monarchy on the grounds that it was suffering 'aggression' at the hands of neighbouring socialist countries. On the other hand, however, the intervention was becoming rather a drain on the British exchequer. Attlee's Labour government had made no basic changes to Churchill's Greek policy but was beginning to jib at the Tsaldaris government's incessant demands.

Innumerable missions had sprung up in Athens, beginning with those whose task it was to rearrange, organize and train the security forces on behalf of the army and the gendarmerie. Greek agencies could not commit themselves to any expenditure without referring it to the British missions, which were accountable in their turn to the Treasury.

Visiting London in July in quest of further subsidies, Tsaldaris had been particularly emphatic in urging the Foreign Office to give the British ambassador and the head of the police mission a more comfortable margin of manoeuvre. At the same time Venizelos went to Washington to try and interest the American government in the economic reconstruction of the country. The renascent Mountain guerilla provided both men with an effective stanza or two in their grandiose appeals to Occidental solidarity. The British were running out of steam, but it did not look as if Anglo-Saxon interference in Greek affairs was going to end just yet. By baring his teeth before the British had left, Zachariadis had given them or their successors a residence permit which (with appropriate histrionics in the UN) would be renewable more or less indefinitely.

Though hampered by the Central Committee's political line, the guerilla forces began to attack. Units of thirty to forty andartes made their presence felt from September onwards, especially in Macedonia. Kikitsas visited Bulkes and returned to Greece with all the kapetanios he could lay hands on, leaving Pechtasidis a clear field for the methodical imposition of the infallible virtues of the revolutionary order on the 3,000-odd refugees left at the mercy of his conditioning enterprise.

More or less supervized by Markos but enjoying a wide margin of independence, the first armed groups were practising the guerilla principle: 'Strike where and when it suits us.' They were making surprise attacks on villages, disengaging as soon as reinforcements arrived, refusing to do battle with superior forces, harassing patrols and vulnerable units and then vanishing. Villages in almost every region were invaded for an hour or two by groups of a few dozen andartes, which would take new recruits with them when they left. The most successful of these swoops was carried out on the village of Deskati, at the foot of Mount Hassia in Thessaly, where Lasanis's andartes left with some fifty recruits at the end of September.

The hundred or so operations carried out during October announced the resumption of the struggle in no uncertain fashion. Four hundred andartes stormed the town of Naousa with the support of the population, totally destroying the National Guard garrison and capturing a considerable quantity of arms. By the time governmental reinforcements reached the town the andartes had vanished into the rocks.

The Athens government, reshuffled on 2 October but still led by Tsaldaris and supported by the parliamentary Right, was getting very uneasy and kept asking Great Britain for new supplies of arms. Instead of arms it received permission from the Attlee Labour government to use the governmental army alongside the National Guard in the struggle with the andartes.

It was now admitted that things had progressed well beyond a police operation against bandits and that what was happening was a civil war in the real sense of the word. The only reason the army had not been called in earlier was that, in spite of every precaution, it had never seemed entirely trustworthy to the government.

In the Kozani region, sixty men from the regular forces decided to join the insurgents, and wandered through the mountains for days trying to find them. The andartes knew they were looking for them, but the Political Bureau's standing orders were that mass desertions should not be encouraged, and they stayed out of sight. After a few days the deserters were caught by government forces and court-martialled; how could they have imagined that the partisans would have orders to avoid them?

At about this time Vlantas declared to a meeting in Piraeus: 'Those who want to take to the mountains are cowards, running away from the real revolutionary struggle in the towns and in the factories.' Even so, Markos managed to build his effective strength up to about 6,000 men by the end of October. He announced the creation of the Democratic Army on 28 October 1946.

The Democratic Army

After sounding the call to arms the Democratic Army's HQ turned back to the Party leadership.

'Send political cadres into the mountains, members of the Central Committee. Order the Party organizations to support the guerillas by sending supplies, fighting men and cadres into the mountains.'[1]

These were the demands Tzimas had been making at the beginning of 1943. The Mountain was being isolated once again from the Party's 'revolutionary elite'. The Salonika Bureau, which was run by Bartsotas, replied: 'We will support you with the means at our disposal. But the essential thing is the day to day struggle of the proletariat and the people to supply their own needs. Above all, we must never forget that we are struggling for reconciliation.'[1]

At about this time the governmental army made its first big offensive in the Olympus region and eastern Thessaly, but all its sweeps closed in on empty space. The andartes evaded each pincer movement, re-formed in the enemy's rear, struck and disappeared. In the middle of November the government admitted that it had lost control of the Olympus region. Further to the north, partisans entered the town of Skra, near the Yugoslav frontier, and held it for several days. The Democratic Army's strength reached 7,000 at the end of November, according to government estimates.

The time had come to call EAM militants to arms: now or never. But

[1] Markos.

Zachariadis was busy organizing the 'day to day struggle of the proletariat', and kept the infallible phalanx under wraps for the final assault.

On 30 November 1946 the Greek government ini iated a line of argument in the UN which seemed likely to have considerable mileage in the
context of the steadily mounting cold war. It suggested that the established order in the country was being threatened, not by the Democratic
Army, but by 'the aggression of countries to the north'.

Citing articles 34 and 35 of the UN Charter, Tsaldaris protested against
interference by Yugoslavia, Albania and Bulgaria. Thus Greece's Anglo-
Saxon allies could keep their troops in the country to confront the external
threat.

The Security Council had been called on to deal with Greek affairs on
two previous occasions: once in January 1946, after a Soviet complaint,
and again in August, following a note from the Ukrainian Foreign
Minister accusing the Greek government of fomenting a situation in the
Balkans which threatened international peace. On both occasions a
majority of delegates had voted against an inquiry. In response to
Tsaldaris's appeal, however, the Security Council decided unanimously
at the beginning of December to set up a special commission on the
Balkans (UNSCOB), on which each of the Security Council's eleven
members would be represented, including the USSR.

For the time being, the British were given the benefit of the doubt and
allowed to keep their 16,000 men on Greek soil. But the cost of all this was
exorbitant, and the Labourites wanted certain formalities to be respected;
it was on this condition that they agreed to extend their military aid to
Greece for another three months, until March.

The Tsaldaris government fell on 2 January 1947. Harassed by press
and parliamentary criticism, the British Foreign Minister Bevin obtained
a few months' respite by installing a team representing a wider spectrum
of Greek parliamentary opinion. Maximos, a monarchist, formed the
government of the 'seven chiefs', with Kanellopoulos, Venizelos, Kartalis,
Papandreou as Minister of the Interior, and Zervas in charge of Public
Order.

The British had only granted Maximos three months' relief; after that,
Greece would have to bear its own military expenses and straighten itself
out economically. Colonel Sheppard, a member of the British Economic
Mission to Northern Greece, reported that 'out of a ten-million-dollar
loan granted to the Greek government in 1946, it was ascertained by the
Exchange Control Commission, composed of British, American and

Greek members, that 40 per cent of the money had been spent on six hundred 'missions' sent abroad by the Tsaldaris government for the most improbable reasons. Dollars were also wasted in other ways, notably on imports of perfumes, jewellery, ties and coloured scarves.'[1]

Foodstuffs sent to Greece by UNRRA were invariably hoarded by speculators. From time to time the supplies went bad in the warehouse and had to be dumped in the sea. Greece was an emaciated country where the concept of rarity was anything but an economist's abstraction, but scandals of this sort were a daily occurrence. Homer Bigart wrote in the *New York Herald*: 'Athens today is a kingdom of intrigue, hatred, wickedness and corruption challenging the standards of the Middle Ages. . . .'

Financial order was not going to be achieved overnight, but on 13 January 1947 an American economic mission led by Paul Porter arrived in Athens to prepare a report on the country's needs for President Truman.

Under the pretext of solving the problem of right-wing banditism the government formed its own self-defence groups in the villages, the anti-communist MAY. It killed two birds with one stone by dissolving the para-legal bands and reconstituting them with the same men under the governmental banner. Added to the National Guard, the MAY groups raised the government's fighting strength to 160,000 men. Their new name did not deter the bands from using well-tried methods; terrorism was organized systematically. It was all laid down in a little 38-page manual intended for training the gendarmerie:

Soldiers will approach dead bandits in groups of three. One will hold his weapon in readiness while the other two cautiously examine the bodies to ensure that they are not simulating death and holding grenades or other weapons in their hands. By using this method our soldiers will be able to avoid possible surprise attacks. The bodies should be searched minutely. They should not be left until all weapons and identification have been removed. They should then be decapitated and their heads placed in a bag and taken to the nearest command post for public exposure.

Other methods, less spectacular but every bit as dangerous to the Democratic Army, were beginning to come into operation. The government forces' major strategic innovation was the systematic evacuation of village populations, which began in the winter of 1946–47. While Markos was still waiting for the Central Committee to grant him the means for recruiting on a large scale, the British Mission under General Rawlings was

[1] Colonel A. W. Sheppard, *Britain in Greece*, London, 1947.

busy draining the substance out of the mountains. 'Refugee camps' sprang up around the major garrisons. The partisans were in danger of finding themselves in control of a desert in which food would be as difficult to find as recruits. The system was perfected later by the American General Livesey, supported and advised by Under-Secretary of State Lovett.

By the beginning of January 1947 Markos, who was positive that he could raise fifty thousand men if only the Party leadership would give the signal, could see that his best opportunities for building up his strength would slip away if he had to wait much longer. He approached the Political Bureau once again: 'Does the Party contemplate seizing power? If not, what are our prospects for the future?'

The reply was as evasive as ever: 'For the time being we are not raising the power question. Perhaps in 1948. . . .'[1]

So the Democratic Army organized itself as best it could on the severely restricted basis allowed it by the political leadership. An officers' school was established close to the mobile General Headquarters to train on the spot the cadres the leadership had refused to supply from the towns. Repeated small-scale raids kept the government army on the defensive and supplied a trickle of recruits.

Yugoslav and Albanian assistance was limited almost exclusively to supplies and care of the wounded. Even in the opinion of a British observer, 'General Markos had placed high hopes on the Soviet Union providing food and material for his campaign, but despite vague promises Stalin sent nothing at all.'[2]

This did not prevent the UN Commission which was operating in Greece from mid-January onward from amassing evidence of foreign aggression. Partly to make the Commission's task more difficult and partly to spread the governmental army's effort as thin as possible, the Democratic Army developed its activities at the other end of Greece, the Parnon and Taygetos mountains in the southern Peloponnese, the home territory of Grivas's X Organization. A savage attack enabled the partisans to occupy Sparta for several hours.

In Thessaly and Macedonia Markos took over about a hundred villages. It was an extremely severe winter and the ill-equipped andartes suffered cruelly from the cold, but the snow-storms covered their tracks and made their eyries even more inaccessible to governmental units. Eventually the entire north-western sector of the country, near the meeting-point of the Greek, Albanian and Yugoslav frontiers and just below the big Lake

[1] Markos.   [2] Edgar O'Ballance, *The Greek Civil War*, London, 1966, p. 131.

Prespa, fell under Democratic Army control. The precipitous region around the Grammos and Vitsi mountains, consisting almost entirely of bare stone, offered choice positions provided they could avoid being cut off there. A new Free Greece was beginning to make its appearance in the countryside. The garrisons, which were in a permanent state of alert, controlled the towns, but the roads and the hinterland fell under the sporadic control of the Democratic Army.

Guerilla units were extremely mobile, rarely numbering more than a hundred men. They were controlled from four mobile HQs: one in Western Macedonia, one in Eastern Macedonia and Thessaly (where Markos's GHQ was based), one in Roumeli and one in the Peloponnese. The units in Roumeli, where Aris's legend was still very much alive, were subjected to the orders of one Gousias, a Zachariadis man, one of the few members of the orthodox elite to have been sent into the mountains. He had, in fact, been sent there specifically to counterbalance the kapetanios legend in the area where it had been born. But the kapetanios, the ELAS people's leaders, led the struggle in every other region.

YAFKA, a clandestine EAM organization operating in the villages, supplied the guerillas with recruits, information and food. By March the Democratic Army had armed about 13,000 combatants. Most of them were very young, and from this time onwards about twenty per cent of the troops were women.

Markos's personal legend was beginning to overshadow the Zachariadis cult. Inside the features of the head of the Democratic Army, the Central Committee began to see the shadowy face of someone it had already sentenced to death: Aris, the *bête noire* of the bureaucratic centralists. The name had changed, but the battle-song was the same:

> Markos, what mountain ridge are you treading
> Now? In what town is your swift step heard?
> On what hill, what high pass do you pause for breath?

At the Lamia meeting before the battle of Athens, Markos had opposed Aris in the name of Party discipline. It would not be long before he had his own experience of isolation, of the politicians' scorn and distrust of popular leaders.

Aris had died rejected by the Party; Sarafis, the second most important figure in ELAS, was stagnating on an Aegean island. Samariniotis had been deported as well; first of all Tzimas had urged the KKE to take part in the elections and then, when it had abstained against his advice, he had exhorted it to join forces with the Mountain and not to repeat the dogmatic error that split the Resistance forces in 1944. Karageorgis was kept in Athens by his journalistic activities. Events seemed to be repeating themselves, but in an atmosphere deadened by the weight of accumulated suffering and fatigue. Only dogma lived on unchanged, timeless, inhuman and cut off from reality, embodied in the Central Committee's continued functioning in a legality it had sabotaged itself.

Despite everything – despite, that is, the governmental forces and the Party leadership – the Democratic Army kept up its development during the early part of 1947. The three months' grace that the British had given the Maximos government to take the situation in hand and find another source for its military expenses had profited nobody but Markos.

The deadline was approaching. On 20 February the British dropped hints in Athens to the effect that the Treasury was opposed to any resumption of aid to Greece. The Greek government turned to the US on 3 March 1947, asking for economic and military assistance. America, which had sent the Porter mission to Greece to prepare for this moment, got ready to relieve the British Empire in Greece and took the first official step along the path which took it, from one intervention to another, as far as Vietnam. The scenery was all in place: the Communist menace, 'external' aggression against an allied country run by a mercenary gang, a slide to the Right, military missions, escalation. . . .

America's Ides of March

12 March 1947: President Truman made a speech to Congress in which he spoke of the United States's 'unreserved interest in Greece' and asked that it be granted 'all possible economic aid for the reconstruction of its ruined economy'. He added the warning that 'without financial aid from America, Greece will fall under Communist domination within twenty-four hours', and asked for an initial grant of three hundred million dollars.

The hundred-million-dollar grant which he obtained for Turkey during the same session clearly illustrates America's strategic interest in the bridge between Europe and Asia. The decision to aid Greece had been taken on 27 February, at the end of a secret conference at the White House between the President, General Marshall and representatives of the Democratic and Republican parties. According to United Press, 'the matter was clearly presented to the parliamentary delegation as being of greater importance than anything which had happened since the end of the Second World War'.[1]

In fact American economic assistance to Greece had surpassed British aid ever since the liberation. 'According to Hugh Dalton, Chancellor of the Exchequer, British expenditure over the last two years had risen to £87m.; American aid in the same period had been $497m., of which $334m. had been channelled through UNRRA.'[2]

The time had now come, however, for the United States to take full charge of supporting the pro-Western Greek government. Under what was already being called the 'Truman Doctrine', Greece became subject to the draconian control of the divers missions already ensconced in Athens and others which were now hurrying to the spot.

An American trade union representative, Mr Brown, had been working since January with the Makris gang which the Tsaldaris government had placed in control of the Greek TUC. 'Mr Marshall,' wrote a *New York Post* commentator, 'has asked the State Department to find reliable and experienced American union leaders to work for us in the Balkans. Mr Marshall's advisers believe that US trade union leaders, having led the struggle against Communism in our country, will be able to adopt an effective strategy elsewhere. The first to leave will be Klin Golden, lately nominated Vice-President of the CIO Steelworkers' Union. He is to lead the American Labour Mission in Greece.'

'It was interesting,' Meynaud wrote, 'to compare the behaviour of American envoys in foreign countries with that of their British counterparts. . . . The Americans are much less skilled than the British in managing the confidential approach or the indirect intervention. . . .'[3]

All Greek expenditure was subject to the direct approval of the American missions; every investment brought with it an intensification of political control, influencing the composition of governments, dictating the choice of senior civil servants infiltrating the security and intelligence services, governing the military staff.

The application of the Truman Doctrine was leading towards the creation in August of another government led by Tsaldaris. In the meantime as Minister of Foreign Affairs he was giving his aid and blessing to the total takeover of Greek political and economic life by official – and unofficial – American missions. To quote the *Washington Post*: 'Diplo-

[1] *Le Monde*, 19 March 1947.
[2] J. Meynaud, op. cit., p. 400.   [3] J. Meynaud, op. cit., p. 400.

matic observers in Washington have been unable to find anything in contemporary history to compare with the eagerness with which this small, independent country has hastened to place the management of its internal affairs in the hands of another country.'

An immediate result of Truman's declaration was that the Maximos government took new heart from it and provided instant proof of its gratitude and goodwill. Six hundred EAM sympathizers were arrested in Athens in a single night.

The Western members of the UN Commission on the Balkans (UNSCOB) were working away meanwhile to amass evidence that would show that foreign intervention in Greece originated from the socialist countries to the North rather than from the Anglo-Saxon powers. The Soviets, for their part, were not as uncooperative as might have been expected; they were anxious to cut the existing diplomatic links between Tito and the West, and to limit the centrifugal tendency appearing in the Balkans, which seemed to derive much of its energy from Belgrade.

UNSCOB

The Commission of Inquiry seldom ventured down any perilous byways; in general, it contented itself with hearing the witnesses produced by the Athens government. One day the security services came up with a particularly choice penitent, a former KKE political cadre called Kondopanos who wanted to make a full confession. He asserted that Yugoslav and Albanian units had participated in the raid on the town of Skra. After conducting their own little inquiry among his associates, the Yugoslav delegates finally produced his own sister, who (despite the risk) stated: 'An American colonel named Muller visits my brother every day. His food comes in a car from the US embassy, and his dirty linen goes there to be washed.'

This kind of testimony and counter-testimony abounded in the UNSCOB files. Nothing useful ever emerged from this mish-mash, either in the Security Council or in the UN General Assembly, but as long as the inquiry was still going on the Anglo-Saxon intervention was assumed to be justified in the absence of any hard evidence to the contrary. What emerges most forcibly from the mass of reports is the courage of the prisoners condemned to death by courts martial. Every last one of them refused to buy his life by playing the government's game and alleging interference by the countries to the North. To save their necks, it would have been sufficient simply to say that they had seen a Yugoslav submachine-gun (and there had been quite a few of these weapons lying about). But they refused to talk.

The Commission had nevertheless to listen to the EAM officials in Athens, and tossed a memorandum from Partsalidis into the file. It was also obliged to meet Markos, or at least to let it be understood that it had *tried* to meet him. A meeting was arranged.

The governmental army had started its spring offensive, and the Commission's movements were so indiscrete that it was necessary to take certain minimal precautions in any dealings with it. The hearing was supposed to take place in the Siatista region, near Fardikambo, the scene of one of ELAS's first major battles. Lieutenant-Colonel Delvoie, head of the sub-commission detailed for the job, gave the following account of his curious odyssey:

Group B left Salonika at daybreak on Wednesday 12 March 1947. Following an agreed programme it made its way to Siatista by way of Kozani, where Colonel Lund was supposed to meet one of Markos's agents. Beyond this locality we had been given no precise directions. No contact could be established, but several peasants had told us that there were andartes at Yermas. A jeep carrying Messrs Zafaridis and Ryan was sent to Yermas to investigate; we actually did meet some andartes in the area. Our convoy was told to be at a road junction a kilometre south-east of Argos Orestikon, on the road to Vogatsikon, at 4 p.m. From there, one jeep had to cross the Aliakmon and go to Ammoundara, a place in the middle of no man's land. The jeep soon returned and it was decided that three other jeeps would carry our luggage to Ammoundara, where we would have to find mules. The journey across mountainous country to Nestorion could be covered in four hours' march and took us along mountain tracks, fording streams and scrambling up and down precipitous slopes. The conditions led to the column's becoming somewhat scattered, and darkness added to the difficulties of the journey. There were one or two incidents: one of our number suffered a slight sprain, and it took twenty minutes to free one of the mules, which got bogged down. What with one thing and another we did not reach Nestorion until nearly 9 p.m., and we were told on our arrival that we would have to travel through the mountains for another two hours to reach the place where we expected to meet Markos. In view of the late hour and the danger of taking tracks along the edge of precipices in the dark, I decided to delay our departure until the next morning, thinking that there would be time to record Markos's statements in the course of the day. Towards 9.30 the next morning we reached Kastanofiton, which is about twenty kilometres from the Albanian border as the crow flies.

The chief andarte of the region asked to speak to me personally. He said that we still had five hours' march ahead of us before reaching Markos, and that even then we could not be sure of finding Markos himself, although we would certainly be contacted by one of his liaison agents. I held a meeting of the group. A majority of the members felt that we had done enough walking and that it would be reasonable to expect Markos, who had asked to be heard and had even told us when to leave Salonika, to come to us, especially as we were in the middle of territory under his control. I asked the local chief how long it would take Markos to get to us. He replied: 'I am going to contact him by messenger, telephone and radio; as soon as I get an answer I'll pass it on to you. Markos could be here tomorrow, Saturday 15th, in the early afternoon, or some time tomorrow night.' But we had had no reply from Markos by the next day.

At a meeting held that evening, most of our group expressed astonishment at this silence. Various opinions were aired; some wanted to leave for Salonika immediately, some wanted to wait until Saturday night and others felt that there were grounds for prolonging the wait even further. The United States and British delegates both said that they required half a day's hearing, including translation time. It was going to be necessary, therefore, to spend a long day with Markos. Taking the group's other tasks into account, and the time available for Markos, it was going to be impossible to prolong the wait indefinitely. As president I struggled to arrive at a working formula, but without success, as the delegate from the USSR was determined to wait for Markos however long it took him to arrive. When the Syrian delegate invited his colleagues to abide by the decision of the majority, the USSR delegate declined and made it clear that he intended to stay put. I pointed out to this delegate that any testimony gathered by him alone would not have the same value as testimony heard by the whole commission. It was finally decided by six votes to two, the president abstaining, that if Markos should arrive by Saturday midday the sub-commission would meet instantly to hear him; if not, the group would go back to Salonika. The next day, just as we were about to leave, the andartes' leader gave me a message which had arrived by courier, which Mr Zafaridis translated. It was from Markos, who said that he would arrive on Sunday or Monday. Since he had not arrived before Saturday midday, the group set off at the appointed hour. As we were leaving the Polish delegate handed me a document which I have passed on to the principal secretary; the USSR delegate protested formally against the majority decision; and the Albanian, Yugoslav and Bulgarian liaison officers came to tell me that they would not be coming with the delegation. I replied to these latter that they did not have full delegate status and that according to the Security Council's instructions their duty was to 'help the Commission (in this case the sub-commission) in its functions', which clearly meant that they should conform to the wishes of the majority. They persisted in their refusal.

Before we left Markos-controlled territory Mr Zafaridis handed me a document stating that he was joining the andartes' side.[1]

[1] *Le Monde*, 20–21 September 1947.

It is difficult to imagine what more urgent task obliged the delegates to return to Salonika in such a hurry. Although its problems were described in what might seem to be excessive detail, the commission refused to include in its dossier the interview obtained from Markos a couple of days later, on 20 March, the date mentioned in the only message which had come direct from the head of the Democratic Army. Its report did not dwell on the reasons which had driven Safaridis to take to and stay in the mountains after working alongside the commission for two months.

Markos had been held up by urgent dispatches from the Peloponnese, where governmental forces had started a series of operations. When he arrived he found himself talking to the remains of a sub-commission which no longer represented anything. He was accompanied by General Kikitsas and two political cadres and escorted by about fifty andartes. Markos was wearing boots, an officer's tunic and a roll-neck sweater. He had a montagnard's head: a klepht's moustache, leathery features and an intense expression always on the point of mutating into a smile which narrowed and lengthened his blue eyes and made his cheekbones stand out over deeply furrowed cheeks.

The remaining delegates knew as well as Markos just what kind of aid the Democratic Army was getting from the socialist countries. They knew that the projected Balkan Headquarters had alarmed Stalin as much as it did the Western powers. They knew how suspicious Stalin was of the victorious Tito, and the results of the partisans' appeals for arms: food, a trickle of weapons (less than 0.5 per cent of the andartes total armament) and, whatever happened, no direct intervention.

Markos's answers to their questions could only repeat the basic argument of EAM's memorandum. They were based on a body of evidence which it was UNSCOB's specific purpose to obscure.

'Why was the Democratic Army created?'

'The reasons for the formation of the Democratic Army are of an exclusively internal nature, far removed from the reasons given by the British occupants and the monarcho-fascists, who claim that the civil war in Greece had been provoked by the democratic Balkan countries. The freedom of the Greek people and the country's territorial integrity are threatened only by British interventions and by the monarcho-fascists, who have sold their country to British imperialism and are now preparing to sell it to American imperialism. Thus the creation of the Democratic Army answers a need: it is the full expression of the aspirations of our freedom- and independence-loving people. It was born during, and out of, the monarchist orgy directed and managed by the British. . . .'

It was like a litany, but since the partisans were not through with taking up arms to liberate their country, he had no alternative but to preach these arguments to the converted, although the refusal of the other delegates to stay and listen had deprived the commission of its representative status. Markos proceeded:

'It has not been possible to give a full account, in the memorandum we are giving you, of the drama Greece has lived through during the last two years. The monarcho-fascists have had only one aim: to smash the people's movement so as to be able to subject the country to their stated or unstated wishes. The events which occurred in December 1944 were stage-managed by the British with the intention of turning Greece into an anti-Soviet bastion and a centre for activities directed against neighbouring democratic countries. This policy culminated in the monarcho-fascists appealing to the Security Council, feeling that the time was ripe for a vigorous anti-Soviet, anti-Balkan action. To guarantee the fullest possible support they have changed masters and accepted the help of American imperialism.

'The Greek people hates all occupants, whoever they are, and opposes any threat to the country's liberty, independence or integrity. It has turned to the fraternal Balkan peoples which, full of sympathy for its cause, have granted it their moral support. . . .'

Next came the arms question. Two or three old Soviet rifles, captured from white units during the Resistance and found later in villages, constituted virtually the only exhibits for the Commission. Its members knew better than most people what it could and could not believe, and they also knew that certain arms had been buried after Varkiza. Markos went on:

'Until the middle of 1946 members of ELAS and EAM were in hiding in the mountains, and also in the towns. Our first armed detachment succeeded in capturing some arms in February 1946, by making a surprise attack on a monarchist group stationed in the village of Fitis. These arms were the nucleus of our arsenal. Actions of this sort were carried out subsequently in large numbers. Little by little, small skirmishes have given way to major battles thanks to the heavy equipment we have succeeded in capturing. While we are on the subject of arms, we have in our possession a letter from the British embassy in Athens concerning equipment delivered to monarcho-fascist bands. We have been able to take possession of part of this armament by means of repeated raids.

'At the time of the struggle being waged by ELAS we did, in fact, have some arms of Soviet origin. They had been brought to us by former Russian prisoners of war – mainly Tartars – who, after fighting for the Germans, ended by joining ELAS units. When these units were disarmed by the British all their equipment was seized, including the Soviet-made stuff. This gave birth to the story that our arms came from the Soviets.'

Markos opened the briefcase in front of him and took out some documents.

'In response to energetic protests about the monarcho-fascist bands, the British embassy was forced to produce a list of the organized bandit groups in Greece. This list was displayed at the British embassy to prove that the number of bandits who had been supplied with arms was smaller than people claimed. [Markos waved another sheet.] While putting the Varkiza agreement into effect, among other things I surrendered 22,000 rifles and forty machine-guns to the British. This document proves that fascist bands began to appear immediately after the Varkiza agreement – at a time when all the bands armed by the Germans had been disarmed by us. This indicates that the arms handed in by ELAS were redistributed to them.'

There followed some letters concerning a certain Themistocles Markis, asking local authorities to support him in his patriotic activities; letters and orders from leaders of bands, including Nikolis, Theos and Sourlas; and a letter provided by Bishop Ambrosios of Lamia, the writer of which, a certain Vourlakis, addressed the bishop as an 'Eamo-Bulgar' and threatened to chop his head off unless he would appoint candidates put forward by the bands as priests. The secretary recorded Markos's statements word for word. He noted the next question: 'How is the civil power organized in territory controlled by the Democratic Army?'

'We have retained those officials who have not collaborated with the monarcho-fascists, but we do not forgive those who *have* collaborated. Communes are run by a president, a vice-president and a counsellor. The leaders of certain communes have fled, and some of them have been shot by us – in such cases we were dealing with thieves and criminals, men who had stolen UNRRA goods and terrorized democratic elements. Where this has happened we have organized elections with all the villagers free to vote, to elect local committees to look after the peasants' interests. We have also set up 'reconciliation committees', in which all the opposition parties are represented, to arbitrate any conflicts that might arise. Women have the vote and sometimes sit on committees.'

'What are the aims of the Democratic Army?'

'The Democratic Army is fighting, and will continue to fight, for independence and for the people's rights. It is against all foreign interference in Greek internal affairs, since it wishes the people to be master of its own destiny and to have the right to decide for itself on the nature of its institutions.'

'How can the Greek problem be solved?'

'EAM outlined a very specific programme. The British must leave Greece and the Americans must not be allowed to take their place. Further, the measures announced for the rooting out of fascism must actually be put into practice; in the same way, the principles protecting the people's rights have to be respected. We believe that when all foreign intervention ceases, the reconciliation of the Greek people will come about automatically.'

All Markos's answers were based on the current platform of the Democratic Army, a set of principles that the partisans were taking up arms to defend.

NOF, the movement grouping the Slavic minorities of Macedonia, was supporting the Democratic Army. This had given the government useful support for its claims that Greece was being threatened by pan-Slavic aggression.

'During the German occupation, the great majority of Macedonian Slavs joined the Greek people in its struggle against the occupants. . . . When EAM was in power there *was* no Macedonian problem. In accordance with the principle of equality for all citizens, the Macedonian Slavs were permitted to speak their language freely, to publish newspapers in it and teach it in their schools. . . .

'. . . Monarcho-fascist claims that NOF is an organization whose aim is to detach Macedonia from the rest of Greece serve only to obscure their own crimes against the Macedonian people . . . one more pretext for persecuting the Macedonians by making them out to be bandits and "Eamo-Bulgars".'

Finally, someone raised the question of frontier incidents. Markos replied: 'I am convinced that these incidents have been and still are being organized by British Intelligence with the intention of discrediting the People's Republics in the Balkans. In this connection, I can mention the Dimchev case: this war criminal kept in touch with the British when he was thrown in jail. Somehow or other – the details are of course obscure – he found himself back in Bulgaria one fine day, organizing armed bands whose only purpose seems to be to start incidents between Bulgaria and Greece. . . .'

Markos concluded with a remark which, addressed to men who understood the Democratic Army's needs better than almost anyone, was a declaration of principle with polemical overtones: 'If only the Yugoslav Federal Republic would supply us with useful quantities of arms, we could bring this struggle to an end.'

Although he had been speaking to socialist delegates Markos had been preaching in the desert. His interview did not get into the UN report. He returned to his Hassia HQ, which was about to be attacked by governmental forces, at the same time as the sub-commission reached Salonika.

Zevgos, a Salonika political cadre, had arranged to meet certain members of the commission on the afternoon of 23 March. Towards 1.30 p.m., as he left a restaurant near the municipal theatre, a man approached and shot him twice from in front at about six feet range, then twice in the back before running away. Zevgos sprawled, dying, in the hollow of a wall; like Markos, he would never be heard by the full Commission.

With Siantos, Tzimas, Partsalidis, Karageorgis and Chrysa Hajivasiliou, Zevgos belonged to the tendency within the Party which was most fiercely opposed to the election boycott. After 31 March, when the legal path had been severed, he had continued to oppose Zachariadis by favouring the sending of urban militants into the mountains. Now Zevgos lay murdered in a Salonika street. Thousands of former resistance fighters were being arrested in the city because they had not been given permission to join Markos.

Bulkes II

The partisans at Bulkes camp had to submit to an entirely different concept of order. Most of the former kapetanios had gone back to fight in Greece, but various deviationist elements, 'earthworms' – *skoulikia* – and undiscovered traitors remained at Bulkes under the iron rule of Pechtasidis who worked night and day to unmask and either redeem or destroy them. The Anglo-Saxons had named the camp as the insurrectionary HQ and a main base for attacks by the pan-Slavic hordes, but in reality there were hardly any combatants left there.

The village had begun to resemble a laboratory experiment: the crude caricature of a certain police state was already taking shape in (as it were) a small dish of bacterial culture. It was a place where good militants – not vicious, not clinically paranoid, not bloodthirsty, but hard-working, obedient, conscientious pragmatists, gentle but determined – found themselves practising an elaborate system of mistrust in the name of the revolution.

At the first mention of a possible visit from the UN Commission they did away with 150 refugees who were thought too 'insecure' to be allowed to stay in the camp. The remaining 3,000 or so, by no means cleared of all suspicion, were subjected to an unprecedented system of supervision. The five-man cell or *pendada*, which had long been the basic unit of the KKE's underground organization, was adopted in the camp itself among men who had crossed the frontier specifically to escape from the obligation to stay underground; its function at Bulkes was to subject everyone, partisan and exile alike, to an insane mutual surveillance.

The complex hierarchy of suspicion was reflected in every cell: the most 'secure' man would be the secretary, there was a security officer, a press officer, and two persons with no official title. These two were of course the main suspects, but the others were also more or less under suspicion on their various levels, and everyone was watching everyone else.

The individual was compelled to live his whole life within the cell; visits and conversations could only take place between one complete cell and another. Dissidents and *skoulikia* were dispersed and could not keep in touch with one another. The supposed imminent arrival of the UN observers raised the rule of the *pendada* to a truly Kafkaesque level. Pechtasidis loved discipline and would organize his groups into marching order at the drop of a hat. Eventually, the cell had to line up to go anywhere at all, childish and grotesque as a row of tin soldiers. It was thought likely that the UN observer would appear suddenly in the street, so the secretary, the cell's 'secure' man, walked on the outside covering the group's exposed flank. It was possible, on the other hand, that the dreaded observer would emerge from a house just as the cell drew level with the door; the security officer was therefore instructed to walk close to the walls at all times. The other three had to walk shoulder to shoulder in between, with the chief suspect in the middle, the second suspect between him and the security officer and the press officer next to the secretary, ready to do his official duty of answering questions.

This unbelievable system, which nipped any human contact in the bud and subjected every step, every second of the day, to a clanking apparatus of suspicion, did not have to be endured for just a few days; men were marching about five abreast, spying on one another, eating and sleeping together, for more than three months. If a man, a partisan, wanted to go to the lavatory at night, he had to wake his neighbour and ask him to go too. After a good deal of extremely violent argument and in a crushing atmosphere, the men eventually managed to get permission to urinate by themselves.

The whole sinister charade is revealing of the extent to which the Party cadres had always trusted ELAS and now trusted its former partisans. Naturally the Yugoslav government had emphasized the need for security; but who could have imagined that a handful of men obsessed with discipline would be able to carry their ludicrous zeal to such an extreme?

This whole system, and the extensive purges which came later, were organized solely to prevent anyone from telling the UN observers that Bulkes was a military training camp. What happened at Bulkes is only one example of the abyss separating a certain kind of revolutionary abstraction from the Greek people, and from harsh reality. The real military school was in the mountains near Markos's HQ, where the prevailing value system was not based on suspicion.

The Government's First Major Offensives

Zervas had not allowed his martial tendencies to be blunted by the muted grandeur of the ministries. The new Minister of Public Order 'returned to active service' in the southern Peloponnese, among the stones of Parnon and Taygetos. Before the start of the big spring offensive announced by the government, he proclaimed his intention of clearing the Peloponnese, with a noble impartiality, of all Democratic Army units and all elements of the X Organization. If the UN appeal was to have some semblance of plausibility, it was very important that the Democratic Army be prevented from developing at the opposite end of the country from the sector where 'Pan-Slavic aggression' was supposed to be taking place.

Zervas began by arresting five hundred EAM sympathizers suspected of provisioning the Democratic Army and recruiting on its behalf. His clashes with partisan units, which melted away and reappeared at will, achieved no decisive results. The Democratic Army's future in the peninsula was certainly limited, owing to its geographical isolation, but Zervas was guilty of some slight overstatement when he declared on his return to Athens that 'from now on the region is clear of all terrorist activity'. His actions against X and other right-wing terrorists had of course been limited to a few formal sweeps; the aid flowing to the terrorists through other government agencies more than compensated for the little that Zervas *did* do, and the health of General Grivas's militiamen was hardly threatened.

King George II died on 1 April 1947 to be succeeded by his brother Paul. Paul was married to Princess Frederika of Brunswick, grand-daughter of Kaiser Wilhelm II, and an ex-leader of the Hitler Youth. The new queen was ambitious and had for many years employed her sharp intelligence in the service of a lively nostalgia for the extreme autocracies of the past. Through the intermediary of the Ankara offices she was rumoured to have kept in touch with the German services throughout the war. The Danish King Paul was more flexible, more or less prepared to bend to the requirements of his puppet role without complaining exces-sively, but his court, dominated by the queen's energy, always tended to push him towards uncompromising positions. A week after the accession of the new royal couple, the government began its major spring offensive, first unwisely declaring that its failure would 'imperil the regime's very existence' and naming it 'Operation Terminus'.

On 9 April 1947, 15,000 men taken from the Second Army Corps at Larisa marched on the Pindus range, occupying strategic roads and bridges and thrusting towards the Democratic Army's strongholds. Two divisions set out from Karpenisi, one marching north and the other west; a third division came directly from Larisa.

In the mountains the offensive was signalled by the appearance of a wave of aircraft, long before any troops were in sight. Tons of leaflets showered from the sky, calling on the andartes to surrender to regular forces. Almost at once a second wave arrived carrying more convincing arguments in the form of volleys of rockets which they fired at the mountain-tops. Each burst of explosions was multiplied by a deadly blast of rock splinters. The snow and the freezing wind blowing across the peaks caused far greater suffering to the partisans than to the far better equipped government troops: more than a hundred and fifty andartes died of cold during the operation. But the small Democratic Army units were extremely mobile and usually kept out of reach. On the evening of

17 April, however, the government forces managed to locate a major concentration of the democratic resistance near Agrafa, and began to concentrate troops there. They had found the position occupied by Markos himself. He was backed by his Staff, a hundred cadets from the military school and a Democratic Army battalion.

The government troops were slow-moving. When aircraft appeared in the sky, the regular forces moved in to attack a position the andartes had already abandoned; they had broken out of the encirclement without raising the slightest alarm. The chase began. By making forced marches of fifteen or twenty hours' duration Markos managed to slip between government lines every time. Finally he came back down to the plains near the village of Viniani. Three partisans were sent towards the town to reconnoitre. When it saw a guard post controlling the road, the patrol approached, thinking that it was dealing with a Democratic Army unit, and was greeted with a sudden burst of machine-gun fire which wounded one of the scouts. The alarm had been given, and seven government battalions emerged from Viniani.

The Democratic Army battalion was two hours' march away and Markos only had the hundred officer cadets to repel the attack with. The battle started at nine in the morning. The Democratic Army battalion managed to reach Markos at 1 p.m., and at the end of the afternoon another hundred men showed up to help. Ammunition was running very low; a midnight check showed that there were only eighty rounds left for each machine-gun and only six or seven for every rifle. Markos decided that there was nothing for it but to wriggle through the enemy lines yet again. A two-hour march, carried out in cat-like silence, took all the partisans out of the government's encirclement.

At sunrise, about 5 a.m., a new wave of aircraft appeared in the sky. They circled mount Kafki, which the partisans had just abandoned, and peeled off one by one, howling like banshees, to swoop on the mountain and rain down their tons of bombs. Stones flew, but there was nobody there to get hurt. While Markos was enjoying the fireworks from a safe distance a group of peasants appeared from Viniani, pushing two captives in front of them. The government units, thinking that they were dealing with greatly superior forces, had evacuated the village at dawn, leaving twenty dead and forty wounded behind them. Picking over the battleground with a fine toothcomb, Markos retrieved 2,000 rounds of ammunition, four Thomson submachine-guns and a wireless transmitter, not to mention a few sleeping bags.

The theatre of operations moved northward, into the area between Grevena and Mount Olympus. This time the government forces were harried at all times, and never managed to pin the partisans down; on the contrary, the small guerilla units were able to move back and forth at will through the large meshes of the governmental net. The first phase of the spring offensive ended at the end of April. The government did not publish any victorious communiqués, but Foreign Minister Tsaldaris declared, during an address to the population of Salonika: 'The nation will settle accounts fully and finally with the rebellion.'

King Paul had taken the oath before parliament on 22 April 1947. After the customary hundred-gun salute, he addressed the nation to condemn the insurrection and announce the start of new clearance operations.

While Zachariadis awaited a green light from the Soviet Union and toured foreign capitals looking for further support, the urban militants were still waiting for permission to join Markos's units and meanwhile being arrested in droves every day. The spring offensive had enabled the Democratic Army to increase its effective strength from 13,000 to about 18,000 partisans. Every failed attack by the government army reinforced the Democratic Army by providing it with captured or abandoned arms.

Generally speaking, official communiqués from Athens presented the guerillas' tactical withdrawals as defeats. This standard propaganda practice did not prevent the government and the military mission from making more objective reports in the right quarters, however. A few alarming noises would serve very well to prime the dollar-pump which was due to start operating in May.

On 14 May, thirty Members of Parliament, led by the Vice-Premier Gonatas, submitted to the Assembly a bill banning the Communist Party. The American embassy intervened in the corridors in the name of Democracy, pointing out that a *clandestine* KKE would have no alternative but to support the Democratic Army, thus strengthening the insurrection. The bill was duly thrown out the next day. A few days later leaflets rained down on the mountains, promising amnesty to any partisans surrendering to the governmental forces. At a time when the UN Commission's report was sinking slowly into the ground in Geneva, convincing nobody and provoking a Soviet veto in the Security Council, this amnesty offer was nothing but a gesture; a gesture, moreover, which could not conceal the preparations for a new police action.

In the final analysis Zachariadis's policy was objectively more useful to the Americans than to anyone else. He was paying a very high price for a legality which did not bring him the slightest advantage; the revolutionary concepts on which he based his strategy were such as to prevent him from forging even the most tenuous alliances with centre-left forces. On the one hand, therefore, there were no revolutionary allies outside the KKE; on the other, the Democratic Army was not considered to be a revolutionary army but simply an instrument for exercising enough pressure on the regime to expose its rottenness. Thus Zachariadis could only benefit from this 'legality' by waiting for the right moment to launch the urban insurrection. These hopeful visions were totally invalidated by everyday reality.

On 20 April 1947, Siantos died of a heart attack in the clinic of Dr Kokkalis, future Minister of Health in the Provisional Government. With his death the Central Committee lost the First Violin of legality, the most influential supporter of an effective policy of parliamentary opposition.

In the big towns the police continued stuffing the prisons to bursting point, while mountainous regions which were not controlled by the Democratic Army were being methodically emptied of their inhabitants; the ugly shanty-towns known as 'refugee camps' were growing like mould on the edges of all major settlements. By the end of the spring of 1947 it was estimated that 200,000 peasants had been uprooted, and this was only the beginning.

Back in the mountains, Markos was uncomfortably aware that time was against the insurrection as long as the Central Committee insisted on keeping its troops and cadres in Athens and Salonika. If the Democratic Army was to develop, it must make its effort now or never; late spring, 1947, was its last chance to grow dramatically.

While Zachariadis was being acclaimed as the Messiah by Pechtasidis's welcoming committee at Bulkes, American equipment was flowing into Greece, the countryside was being emptied and there were more arrests every day. Markos did what he could with the 18,000 men at his disposal. If he achieved no spectacular victories during May and June, he at least managed to retain the initiative in the north of Greece and to keep the government forces trapped in their garrisons.

The basic guerilla units of seventy to a hundred men sometimes combined into battalions and even when necessary into brigades, depending on the size of the target. On 28 May, a Democratic Army force of 650 men marched on the town of Florina, situated at the meeting point of three frontiers. The town was defended by a governmental unit of about five hundred men. Four hundred people had been arrested only a few days earlier, and the disorganized population was in no position to provide the inside support the partisans were expecting. After a preliminary mortar bombardment the Democratic Army launched several infantry assaults. Government aircraft retaliated and the insurgents had to withdraw. The Democratic Army returned to the attack four days later. By this time government forces had been reinforced and it was impossible to take the town, but the garrison was trapped there for the rest of the summer.

During June the Democratic Army launched major attacks on Konitsa, Kastoria and Grevena in western Macedonia, on Kilkis to the north of Salonika and on Alexandroupolis in Thrace. The leadership of the little guerilla units was sometimes out of its depth trying to run operations involving as many as 2,500 men, but the record for the early part of the summer was, broadly speaking, a positive one. Every attack made further recruitment possible, and the effective strength rose to 25,000. Soon the countryside around Florina, Grevena and Konitsa was entirely controlled by Markos.

Government units could only venture abroad under the protection of an armoured escort. The big tanks supplied by the British kept the roads open but were useless on the broken terrain comprising most of the land area of Greece. The government troops were shut into the towns in a permanent state of alert, cut off from one another and frozen on the defensive. The free Greece of the mountains, the klephts' natural fortress where half the inhabitants of every village, men and women alike, were partisans, rose once again from the arid rocky soil. But the signs for the future were not encouraging. There was fatigue; the millstone of dogma; ruthless opponents were turning the country into a desert. The Democratic Army – fifteen-year-old freedom fighters, armed women – needed aid from fraternal countries and reinforcements from the towns.

Escalation

The KKE was allowed to remain legal for a while longer, for appearance's sake, while Zervas launched an enormous police offensive. The pretext was that Democratic Army Headquarters were continually asking EAM to mobilize and send it some reinforcements; this was quite true, although EAM was not doing anything about it.

There was no organization in Athens for ferrying militants into the mountains. Anyone who wanted to disobey orders and join Markos had to approach freelance guides who, for a consideration of ten gold pounds, were as likely as not to turn them over to the police. At the end of June Karageorgis, feeling the net closing in around him, left on his own authority and managed to join the Democratic Army. If he had left it a day or two longer he would have been arrested along with Partsalidis, EAM General Secretary, and most of the journalistic staff of *Rizospastis*.

Salonika, 8 July 1947. Hot night air scented with basil and retsina. At dawn, the noise of banging on doors and a sleepy murmuring. Each door is opened on a soldier and a policeman. Three hundred arrests, another three hundred at Kavalla. On the 10th, a good number of Athenians did not even go home to bed, judging it safer to walk the sweltering streets all night. Despite these precautions there were 2,613 arrests in the course of the day. The police kept at it all the next day, and the next: workers, union officials, writers, journalists, high-school students and artisans were all taken in sweeping monster raids.

By the 15th there had been 7,000 arrests in Athens alone. Other raids followed all over the country, continuing until 10 August. There were more than 3,000 arrests in Salonika and perhaps 20,000 in the whole of Greece. This was just the beginning, but there was no change in KKE standing orders: 'Only cowards want to go and join the Mountain.'

Zachariadis and Porfyrogenis passed through France at the end of June during the Eleventh Congress of the French Communist Party, which was held in Strasbourg from 25 to 28 June. Porfyrogenis, who spoke French, introduced a romantic note into the dreary proceedings by announcing that the partisans meant to set up a Greek Revolutionary Government. His speech received an ovation which was much prolonged by the measured rhythmic handclapping of the comrades present. On his return to Greece Zachariadis made copious use of this warm reception, never mentioning Duclos' vigorous protest to the effect that the KKE delegate should not have raised the matter before the Congress without first reaching an understanding with the French party leadership. *L'Humanité* of 28 June did not mention the Provisional Government and blandly reported:

'Porfyrogenis, President of the Control Commission of the Greek

Communist Party, received very emotional applause from the delegates when he greeted the Congress on behalf of the heroic Greek people, who are in the forefront of the struggle against imperialism. To further applause from the Congress, Gaston Auguet affirmed the French people's complete solidarity with the heroic Greek people.'

While Zachariadis took the bow in Strasbourg on the Democratic Army's behalf, Markos pursued his uphill struggle with the KKE.

Tito had been trying to lay the foundations of a Balkan federation for a year now. At the beginning of July representatives of Yugoslavia, Albania and Bulgaria met at Bled in Yugoslavia. The Bulgarian and Yugoslav delegates clashed over the Macedonian question: Tito regarded Macedonia as an autonomous state within the Yugoslav federation, while Dimitrov wanted to preserve Bulgaria's existing frontiers and administrative arrangements. It was becoming absolutely clear that Stalin no longer tolerated Tito's attempts to carve out an empire within the Empire. The conference produced nothing new in the way of aid to the Greeks, but probably succeeded in jaundicing Stalin's view of the Democratic Army a little more.

Meanwhile the government forces were speeding up their campaign to depopulate the countryside, and Markos found himself racing against time to build up his armed strength. His men raided villages and ambushed small government units in every district, procuring a constant trickle of new arms and recruits.

Aris's old companions-in-arms Diamantis and Hermes almost pulled off a coup that would certainly have won Aris's approval: they tried to kidnap Scobie. They learned that Scobie was hunting with some of his officers near Levadia, in Roumeli, and that though heavily guarded they were expecting smaller game than andartes. Leading a small commando, Diamantis and Hermes slipped into a village where the hunters were said to be spending the night. Unfortunately, Scobie had had to return to Athens the night before, taking most of his officers with him. Not wishing to leave empty-handed, the andartes took an old deputy called Koutsopetalos who had stayed behind in the village.

When the authorities heard of Koutsopetalos's capture they launched in pursuit the governmental army unit stationed at Arachova on Mount Parnassus, and this unit occupied the andartes' hideout before they reached it.

Diamantis and Hermes knew every inch of the ground and decided to give battle there and then, despite the fatigue of their own men. As the sun burst over the jagged eastern skyline they launched their first attack, and within an hour they had not only recaptured their stronghold but won an appreciable booty as well.

This victory brought an unexpected bonus in its wake. The hostage Koutsopetalos was deeply impressed by the conduct of the andartes – many of whom were little more than children – in battle. The next day he was placed on a mule and taken to Roumeli HQ, near Dadi. The partisans kept him there for a week, then hurried him to Gravia and let him go.

Back in Athens, Koutsopetalos made a very poor martyr. It was not just that he failed to complain about his treatment at the hands of the bandits; he worried his colleagues by making the most flattering remarks about the Democratic Army in parliament. Markos's army reached an effective size of 35,000 at the end of the summer. From now on, recruitment would be virtually impossible.

On 29 August the Maximos government was replaced for several weeks by an exclusively monarchist cabinet led, once again, by Tsaldaris.

Athens

Times had changed, and with them the time-honoured British methods for controlling the Greek economy. Gone for ever were the days when the unfrocked English parson Balfour had presided courteously over sessions of the Greek parliament; the American economic mission under Griswold used more brutal and direct methods of control and intervention. The Marshall Plan's contribution to the crusade against communist ideology was supposed to work in two ways: by instilling its beneficiaries with the virtues of Anglo-Saxon enterprise and by promoting a euphoric vision of the future of capitalism.

Applied to Greece, however, the dollar panacea was far from achieving the desired results. Capital was being moved about by private banks, which charged phenomenal commissions for their trouble. Import licences had somehow been obtained for the flood of late-model Chryslers that glided over the potholed roads of Kolonaki. The population, which was needy in every way, was supplied with a plethora of celluloid combs, soft drinks, packaged peanuts – many Athenians at this time lived exclusively on packaged peanuts. Imports of wheat and cereals, on the other hand, were impeded by the strict regulations in force. Rice, sugar and edible pastes had disappeared from the shops and were freely available on the black market at astronomical prices. Since Truman's declaration in March, the currency in circulation had increased from 537 to 970 thousand million drachmas, and inflation had been of the order of fifty per cent. Despite the twelve age classifications that had been called up by the services, despite the thousands imprisoned or exiled, more than 100,000 unemployed were hanging about Athens, unable even to take to the mountains. The original 300 million dollars of American aid had been increased by 50 million dollars, but military expenses absorbed the greater part of the budget earmarked for reconstruction, which was reduced from 150 to 82 million dollars. A substantial part of this was spent on restoring the airports in the northern towns, widening the roads from seven to nine metres to make room for armoured units, and on other improvements to the infrastructure dictated by defence requirements. The remainder was available for speculation and mammoth embezzlement schemes, which proved ample to maintain the 'traditional elegance' of the capital's desirable residential districts.

The results of an inquiry into imports during 1946 are recorded in a letter to the Governor of the Bank of Greece from M. Varvaressos, a Greek economist: 'More than 150 million dollars were allocated for imports in 1946, but only 58 million dollars' worth of goods actually entered the country. The rest of the money was transferred abroad by means of false payments and stretched invoices.' The most resounding event of 1947 was the allocation of 109 Liberty Ships to twenty-three shipowning families and ten companies by the Minister of Merchant Shipping, Avraam, in circumstances which the whole American press described as an 'unparalleled scandal'.

Foreign capital, on the other hand, was often protected by being attached to specific operations, and therefore remained idle. In July 1947 the *Daily Mirror* reported that a gift of £20,000 made several months previously by the Lord Mayor of London to the town of Salonika, for restoring the town's central hospital and founding a nursing school, had been withdrawn because the appropriate authorities had not made any use of it.

The 'Amerikani', scandalized by all this, continued to extend their control over Greek affairs. Porter, head of the first American economic mission, wrote in *Collier's* in September:

From what I have seen, the government's only practical policy has been to make constant demands for foreign aid, both to keep itself in power and to safeguard the privileges of the small clique of businessmen and bankers which constitutes the invisible power in Greece. . . .

. . . This clique has decided to defend its own economic interests at all costs, without any concern for the possible effects on the economic health of the country. The members of this clique want to maintain a fiscal system which favours them personally to a truly scandalous extent. They oppose exchange controls, because these would prevent them from exporting their profits to banks in Cairo or the Argentine. They have never considered investing their profits in their own country to help its economic recovery.

. . . Shipping interests have also been run in a scandalous manner. The Greek merchant navy is now flourishing and shipowners are making immense profits, but the bankrupt Greek State gets nothing out of it. The sailors' wages return to Greece, but the shipowners send most of their profits to safety in foreign banks.

Every enterprise should pay a substantial contribution to the State under whose protection it operates. This is doubly true of the Greek shipowners, whose biggest profits are earned by the 'Libertys' that were allocated to them by the American Shipping Commission under guarantee by the Greek State.

Most of these shipowners are very charming people who speak good English. They are always eager to do anything at all for the American mission. But behind all that lies their wish to use the American mission to further their own interests. I still remember a sumptuous banquet in the Athens villa of one of the leading bankers. There were three liveried servants; a selection of fine wines was served with the magnificently prepared dishes. During the meal, a member of this clique spent some time singing the praises of life by the seaside, with digressions on the beauties of the aristocratic sports.

What was really terrible was the contrast between that meal and the streets of Athens, where children were still dying of hunger. . . .

Contact with the civic virtues of the traditional Right made the Americans willing to use almost any means to impose a coalition which would open the government to liberals. It was a vicious circle: to establish a regime which they hoped would prove less corrupt, they had to interfere even more directly in Greek internal affairs. With a clumsiness which was in no way lessened by the high principles involved, they manoeuvred the old Liberal Sofoulis into the government; the methods they used were such that, like his predecessors, Sofoulis would only be able to play a walk-on part.

Sofoulis and Tsaldaris were implacable enemies. To get them to cooperate, the American services ended up threatening to cut off Greece's fuel supplies – oil, petrol and coal. The two antagonists finally reached a working agreement in a town deprived of electric light and threatened with grinding to a complete halt: on 7 September 1947, the Liberal Sofoulis became President of the Council, with the monarchist Tsaldaris smiling at his side in the role of Vice-President. The nationalist paper *Ethnikos Kyryx* commented the same day:

'The Americans produced this whole event. Ambassadors were present throughout, high-up administrators, specially delegated politico-diplomatic senior civil servants. These people were following the crisis, in fact they were taking part in it. They were everywhere: interfering, arranging, pressuring, insisting, imposing.

'As if by accident, the ships bringing much-needed fuel to Greece have been stuck in Italy for the last few days. . . .'

Some American observers were panic-stricken by this sequence of events; they glimpsed a future in which intervention would follow intervention, always designed to set up a responsible government but somehow always resulting in a puppet regime. George Petler wrote to the President of the Congressional Control Commission:

'The events of the past week clearly illustrate the dangers and excesses of the "Truman Doctrine" and the "Marshall Plan". Despite the fact that Mr Truman has paid out 300 million dollars to maintain the weak and corrupt royalist regime in power, the regime has not even been able to win the support of the moderate parties. The efforts made in the last few days, in line with Mr Truman's policy, to impose the new Prime Minister on his colleagues have exposed the extent of American involvement in Greek internal affairs before the entire world.'

Under these conditions the Liberal Sofoulis did not have a hope of achieving anything resembling national unity; he will go down in history as Prime Minister of the Civil War.

The American Military Mission, under General Livesey, Admiral Snackenberg and Colonel Scott, was also taking a more and more direct hand in Greek Staff decisions. It decided that it was necessary to increase the size of the governmental army to 200,000 men. Twelve age classifications were all called up at once. This time, recruitment was not selective, but postings were of two kinds: either to barracks or to a concentration camp. Suspect recruits were sent to political indoctrination camps, where well-proven methods were used, combining physical and moral forms of torture. Recruits were considered redeemed when they recanted publicly. 'Extremists who did not respond,' wrote O'Ballance delicately, 'were sent to island corrective camps where more serious attempts were made to wean them from their political convictions.'[1] Most of these men, whom Zachariadis had not wanted to mix with the Democratic Army, were doomed from this time on to a moral form of resistance which was at once heroic, agonizing and ineffectual. A whole generation of Greeks, the generation of famine, stolen victory, booby-trapped peace and a struggle that could be adjourned but never seemed to end; a victorious generation doomed to impotence and jail.

The Mountain

On 10 September 1947 Markos declared in a statement sent to and printed in *The Times*: 'We are always prepared to come to an understanding and compromise provided it is honest, based on equality, and democratic. The people's basic demand today is for peace and reconciliation.'

By this time the prisons and concentration camps contained 50,000 militants and sympathizers, including 12,000 soldiers. To show goodwill, Sofoulis set up a Commission with the task of 'releasing all those who are not guilty of crimes against the State'. However much or little might be expected to result from this initiative, it was at least a beginning.

It was at this precise moment that Zachariadis chose to declare: 'We will not negotiate with the monarcho-fascists until Tsaldaris has been tried for treason and war crimes.'

Just as things seemed to be easing a little, when the Democratic Army had assimilated all the available recruits, the General Secretary pulled off a sort of coup d'état within the KKE. Between 12 and 15 September he held the Third Plenum of the Central Committee, with six of the statutory twenty-five members present. After noisily parading some rather unlikely messages of support from abroad, Zachariadis got down to business and dictated the new political line to the Central Committee:

We have decided to shift the centre of gravity of Party activities towards the politico-military sector, with a view to turning the Democratic Army into a force that will ensure the establishment of a Free Greece in the shortest possible time, starting with all the northern regions.[2]

[1] O'Ballance, op. cit., p. 155.
[2] *Neos Kosmos*, no. 8, August 1950, p. 478.

Zachariadis had refused to mobilize all the Party's forces for armed struggle at the end of 1946 and the beginning of 1947, when the time was favourable: now he was falling back on the Democratic Army whose development he had hindered so consistently. But even now he was not making any doctrinal concessions; recruitment problems had become insoluble, but he was unconcernedly preparing to group all the forces in the north, to squeeze guerilla units into the canonical mould of Stalin's regular army, to occupy the towns and fight a positional war.

Taking the People's Army in hand in this manner opened the way for a real purge of kapetanios, which would leave the doctrinaires a clear field for imposing their tight political control on the centralized framework of army corps and divisions. Order on the Bulkes pattern had reached the Mountain.

Markos disagreed violently with Zachariadis, and refused to report to a Central Committee shorn of three-quarters of its members. This was the beginning of his fall into disfavour and the beginning of the end for the Democratic Army. The stony resistance to Tzimas's appeals during the occupation, the atrocious way Aris had been treated, the way the Democratic Army had been first isolated and then suddenly taken over, all arose from the same idiotic dogmatism. It was not just that the prodigious revolutionary lesson of ELAS had borne no fruit; the Central Committee had thrown away all the urban support it could have provided for the Democratic Army and was now settling in a more abstract attitude than ever. With the dogged, mournful zeal of Stalinist theorists, the Central Committee was preparing to let its 'human engineers' loose on the Democratic Army. Zachariadis had failed to wield either 'legality' or the partisan struggle at the appropriate moment; his visions of urban insurrection, of establishing soviets in the army, had withered away in the Athens police files. It only remained for him to mutilate the Democratic Army and apply the strategy used by the Red Army in the plains of the Don to Greek mountain conditions, before the drama could end; before another defeat could pay for the omnipotence of orthodoxy.

On 8 October *Rizospastis* published a résumé of the decisions taken by the Third Plenum. Ten days later both the communist *Rizospastis* and the EAM *Eleftheri Ellada* were banned by the government. Zachariadis and Ioannidis had come to the Mountain.

In the absence of any encouragement from the socialist countries, Zachariadis found his long-awaited signal in the reorganization of the Communist International. The Communist Parties of the USSR,

Yugoslavia, Poland, Hungary, Czechoslovakia, Bulgaria, France and Italy decided in October to resurrect the Comintern, dissolved since 1943, in the form of an information bureau. As a sign, this was a good deal less promising for Greece than Zachariadis might have imagined. The Cominform had not been set up to nourish marginal revolutions which were not of immediate strategic use to the 'bastion'.

Markos versus Zachariadis

Markos took no active part in the first meeting of the new General Staff at Grammos; he was saving his explanations for the Political Bureau. Ioannidis, in whose presence hardened unit commanders were afraid to twitch an eyelid, mumbled his way through a paper on strategy cribbed from a 1930 instruction manual. To Zachariadis and his faithful officers Gousias, Vlantas and Bartzotas – all now either Generals or Colonels – the slightest sign of disagreement was equivalent to treason. Discussion was undisciplined, a divisive activity. These were founder-members of the Revolution, executives and executioners; nothing could stop them in their draconian application of dogma.

The last operations genuinely planned and run by Markos took place in the Metsovo region at the beginning of November, before the first snowfall. Four hundred men of the Democratic Army entered the town of Grevena, where they seized a substantial arsenal and recruited a hundred more men. Small guerilla units successfully harassed the governmental forces for a month. Markos's last practical demonstration was a brilliant success, but it was Zachariadis who had the final say. On 2 December 1947 he briefed the Political Bureau on his plan for applying the decisions of the Third Plenum.

'The Democratic Army must establish a strategic reserve of 15,000 men before March, and prepare to occupy and hold a number of large towns.'[1]

Markos knew that if he ever had to be convincing in his life, now was the moment. There was something mobile and alive about him, something alien to the impassiveness of the doctrinaires and the brutal certainty of Zachariadis.

'Personally, I don't see the problem in quite the same terms as comrade

[1] Markos.

Zachariadis. My immediate thought is that if the Democratic Army is to establish a 15,000-man reserve in the Grammos region, it will have to abandon other regions; it's not a question of reserves but of transferring existing active troops.'[1]

Markos thought he could discern an encouraging gleam in the eyes of Karageorgis, Partsalidis and Chrysa Hajivasiliou. Apart from them the room was beginning to feel like a court-room. He continued: 'The Third Plenum decided that we must increase our effective strength to 65,000 men, and the task of finding them can now only be performed by the Democratic Army. You must understand that if we abandon the regions in which we are now operating, we throw away our chances of recruiting at the same time. If we concentrate all our troops on Grammos, moreover, we release a large part of the enemy's troops from their present tasks and enable him to concentrate the bulk of them round our 25,000 men. The strength of the governmental army is now 170,000.'

'This is defeatism!'

'But you're playing the enemy's game. . . .'

Losing his priestly detachment, Zachariadis fell back on a few fashionable epithets: 'The comrade is clinging to an adventurist, petty-bourgeois conception of strategy.'

'. . . the enemy's plan,' Markos pursued doggedly, 'consists precisely of trying to force us to do that, to concentrate our troops so that he can undertake a decisive action against us. We must do the opposite, *decentralize* our forces. We have to enter towns to deal with our recruitment problem, but we should take them by surprise; we should not attack them frontally or try to hold them. A year ago we were able to muster 65,000 men, but the Central Committee. . .'

'Treason!'

Zachariadis interrupted, grossly insulting Markos in front of his expressionless coadjutors. The head of the Democratic Army was left with no alternative but to listen and obey.

'We will establish a strategic reserve of 15,000 men without abandoning any region. Our army is already a regular army, provided we can eradicate the results of incorrect conceptions. Through its good offices, we will be in power in Macedonia in 1948.'[2]

No reality, however pressing, would ever be taken into account by Zachariadis if it seemed to be a *heretical* reality. A regular army is politically controllable, while small guerilla units led by kapetanios are always

[1] Markos.　　　　　[2] Markos.

liable to produce deviations. In these circumstances the bureaucrat has no alternative but to 'pass to a higher stage' by placing the power in the hands of bureaucrats.

A distrust of guerilla troops is deeply ingrained in orthodox strategy. There are, however, some eloquent historical precedents: Chou En-lai and Mao Tse-tung were in conflict over this issue in 1931.

The situation was even more unfavourable to Mao Tse-tung within the Party hierarchy. The First Party Congress of the Soviet Area, in November 1931, contented itself with denouncing his policies in virtually every domain, with particular emphasis placed on shortcomings in military matters: the persistence of guerilla tactics, and the stubborn refusal to enlarge and consolidate the Central Soviet Area by linking up with the other bases in neighbouring provinces. The following August, at the Ningtu conference of the party, Mao was not merely criticized but began to lose his authority over the Red Army, which passed to Chou En-lai. The process found its culmination in May 1933, when Chou, who strongly supported the military line of the 'Twenty-Eight Bolsheviks', was appointed political commissar of the entire Red Army.

Mao's loss of control over the army was doubly grave because it occurred in the midst of the struggles to save the Kiangsi Soviet Area in the face of Chiang Kai-shek's campaigns of encirclement and annihilation; indeed it opened the door to the rigid tactics which ultimately led to defeat.[1]

This conflict is far from being settled even today.

On 11 November 1947 the *Daily Mirror* published a news photograph of horsemen going to collect their bounty-money, swinging the severed heads of woman partisans by the hair. This was hardly a new practice, but public opinion is cyclical in nature and blessed with short memory. Suddenly noticing Greece and its problems, people were horrified by 'the excesses still being committed by the army and gendarmerie after three years of British military training'. The Foreign Office was obliged to order an inquiry, and Sir Clifford Norton, the British ambassador to Athens, was asked to 'look into this story about so-called atrocities'. He approached Rendis, the Minister of Justice, who told him simply: 'It is an old custom for bandits on whom the State has put a price to be decapitated and have their heads exposed to the public.'

While the right-wing bands incorporated into the government army carried out their duties in this picturesquely traditional manner, Zachariadis and his lieutenants were preparing to purge the Democratic Army.

[1] Stuart Schramm, *Mao Tse-tung*, Harmondsworth, 1966, p. 155.

The Greek people, trapped between these two Orders, produced heroes and martyrs but could not be said to be controlling its destiny.

Since 18 November the government army's operations had been directed by a joint Greek-American headquarters. The American Military Mission had expanded to ninety officers and eighty other ranks. 50,000 tons of equipment were unloaded at Piraeus, Salonika, Volos and Patras. The British were still responsible for training government army officers.

On 23 November, thirty-five Communists were executed in various Greek prisons, bringing the number of people killed since the beginning of the Civil War to an estimated 45,214.

The Provisional Government

At the beginning of December the Athens government made strikes illegal. All the KKE's activities were being attacked with new laws and decrees, but the Party itself was not banned by law until the 28th.

On 24 December 1947 the rebel radio announced officially that a Provisional Greek Democratic Government had been formed in the mountains. Zachariadis, who was planning to capture a town and make it the capital of Democratic Greece in order to obtain diplomatic recognition from friendly countries, did not figure among the ministers. Markos, on the other hand, despite his energetic opposition to the Third Plenum line, was coopted as Prime Minister and Minister of Defence for the sake of the public image. Although he accepted, perhaps hoping that this role would help to get his point of view more widely understood, Markos was only a figurehead. The real decisions on methods and objectives were to be taken by Zachariadis and other grey eminences of the Central Committee.

Ioannidis was made Vice-Premier and Minister of the Interior; Rousos, Foreign Minister; Bartzotas, Minister of Finance; Vlantas, Minister of Agriculture; and Stringos, Minister of National Education and Minister of Supply. These Zachariadis men were partially counterbalanced by Porfyrogenis (who had been General Secretary of EAM since Partsalidis's arrest) as Minister of Justice and Kokkalis (the only non-KKE member in the government) as Minister of Public Health. The new government's broad programme was the following:

1. Mobilization of all people's forces for the liberation of Greece;

2. Installation of people's justice;
3. Nationalization of foreign-owned property and of heavy industry;
4. Agrarian reforms;
5. Reconcilation between Greeks;
6. Reorganization of the country on a democratic basis;
7. Establishment of friendly relations with the People's Democracies;
8. Equal rights for ethnic minorities;
9. Organization of armed forces to resist external aggression;
10. Organization of new elections.

The government police reacted immediately, arresting five hundred people in Athens on Christmas Day. For the moment, however, the Central Committee was occupied with the more immediate problem of seizing a capital city for the infant Democratic Greece.

On 25 December the Democratic Army's Macedonian headquarters, newly revised and corrected by Zachariadis, launched a major attack on Konitsa, twenty kilometres from the Albanian frontier. 2,000 men grouped in regular formations advanced on the town from the foothills of Mt Grammos to the north, while diversionary operations broke out in Thessaly and Epirus. The Democratic Army positioned itself on high ground outside the town and captured the bridge at Borazini, over the river Aoös, which controlled the vulnerable southern approaches.

The insurgents used all their meagre artillery in the battle: two mountain batteries, three 105-mm guns, a few old 55-pounders, and every available mortar signalled each attack with a preliminary barrage. The town was defended by a 1,200-man garrison, which repelled every attack.

Andartes' HQ was set up in the village of Kastaniani, a few kilometres away. When the first assault fails, correct guerilla tactics favour withdrawal before enemy reinforcements can reach the spot. But Zachariadis's new Staff was determined to hold onto the positions it had won and maintain the siege. For the time being, the weather was helping the Democratic Army; governmental reinforcements were toiling uphill from Yannina along a road which had been turned into a waterfall by torrential rain. This respite only lasted a few days, however, and government forces reached the partisans, and began surrounding them, on the 30th. Governmental attacks were supported effectively by aircraft, which were able to function more precisely once the weather had cleared. Democratic Army Command ordered the first withdrawals on the night of 31 December–1 January. By 4 January the artillery had been pulled out and the government army controlled all the approaches to the town. Zachariadis's new tactics had bestowed an unexpected victory on the government forces, which exploited the situation to the full.

Before the end of the fighting, which went on until 15 January in the neighbouring hills, Queen Frederika visited the town in person. The victory was celebrated to the greater glory of the Monarchy. The international press was flooded with pictures of the Sovereign being triumphantly chaired by the faithful subjects so recently rescued from the Pan-Slavic hordes. These warlike images, reinforced perhaps by the high quality of their new American equipment, had a beneficial effect on the regular army's morale.

The democratic forces managed to hang on to the village of Kastaniani, but the Provisional Government still had to conquer itself a capital city. Its baptism of fire had cost it 650 men, dead and wounded.

On 15 January Zachariadis called a meeting of the Party's political and military cadres. Markos turned his analysis of the Konitsa battle into yet another attempt to uphold the principles of guerilla warfare.

'Our organization, the means available to us, the possibilities open to us, are all those of a guerilla army. We are not a regular army, and we are in no position at the moment to operate seriously against urban centres.'[1]

Zachariadis interrupted: 'Markos is a great fighter and is good at looking at problems from a tactical point of view, but he does not seem able to grasp strategic problems.'

That evening Zachariadis called a meeting of the Central Committee, without bothering to go through the correct form of a vote by the Political Bureau. He immediately asked for a vote of confidence: 'Are the Third Plenum resolutions correct?'

The sycophants murmured their usual agreement, but Markos was the real target; Zachariadis turned and looked him in the eye.

'What's *your* view, Markos? Are the resolutions correct?'

To insist on his difference would have meant exposing himself to accusations, to the whole liturgical arsenal of criticism, dissociation, even expulsion. Markos was head of the Provisional Government on paper and uncontested spiritual leader of the Democratic Army, but he had to stay in the Political Bureau if he wanted the 'Mountain tendency' to be represented there at all. His mouth was dry.

'Yes.'

The session was adjourned.

[1] Markos.

On the announcement of the Provisional Government's creation UNSCOB had circularized the world's governments urging them not to recognize the rebels. From the Communist world's point of view Greek affairs were bound up with the Balkan problem. The independent airs which Tito was giving himself in Belgrade were becoming more and more distasteful to Stalin. On 22 January *Pravda* published a violent attack on 'any attempt to set up a Balkan or Danube Confederation including Poland, Czechoslovakia and Greece'. On 10 February Stalin received representatives of the Yugoslav and Bulgarian Parties. He strongly advised them to forget the Balkan Confederation and, according to Milovan Djilas, then turned to the Yugoslavs and said without beating about the bush: 'The Greek revolution should be stopped immediately.'

Zachariadis of course knew nothing of this and was still certain that some exploit by the Democratic Army, the capture of a major town for example, would force Stalin's hand. The battle of Konitsa, that ill-starred initiation ceremony for the new Democratic Army, had taught him absolutely nothing. He was more determined than ever to persevere with the Third Plenum line. Any defeat could always be explained by unmasking a few 'traitors' and having them shot.

At the end of 1947, Anna Pauker had succeeded in dropping Rumania right in Stalin's lap. Zachariadis was convinced that he could achieve the same by clamping a doctrinaire yoke on the Democratic Army – something that could only be done by stifling the very spirit of the insurrection.

By now there were 500,000 peasants encamped around the towns. The Americans, eager as always to finish the job properly, began experimenting with new incendiary and chemical devices (known these days as defoliants). The coastline of Thessaly and the northern mountains were reduced to a sort of lunar desert in which the Democratic Army had some difficulty finding anything to eat.

Following the decisions Zachariadis had dictated to the Political Bureau, HQ decided to concentrate its forces on Grammos and also, despite all the odds, to send out recruiting parties during the winter. Very few people were ever forced to enrol in the Democratic Army, although it was usual for recruits to pretend that they were joining under duress so as to minimize governmental reprisals against their families; winter recruiting would do little to improve the Democratic Army's image, and would produce very little in the way of recruits.

Democratic Army HQ launched two big recruitment operations across the north of Greece from snowbound Vitsi. Triandafyllou was recalled from Roumeli (where Zachariadis never liked to see too many of Aris's kapetanios gathered at one time) and sent along the frontier with a brigade. Another brigade under Paleologos, 1,500 partisans including fifty women, went looking for recruits a little further south, in the region of Pieria and Katerini. Leaving Mt Smolika, the partisans plunged into a frozen no man's land. They passed through silent ghost villages separated by long marches through the snow, sometimes travelling for days at a time without seeing a living soul. After a week of this they surprised a government company near the village of Deskati. It was a very short engagement; after a few shots had been exchanged the 1,500 andartes rose on the skyline, and the whole government company, captain included, laid down its arms: 150 rifles, two machine-guns and a few Brens. Paleologos sprang a few ambushes on the main road between Kozani and Larisa, increasing the size of his booty; arms were piling up, but the recruitment position was still rather weak. The detachment entered a number of villages around Pieria and continued its course towards Katerini, clashing more frequently with government forces as it descended towards the plains. Two days after leaving Pieria, the andartes had just succeeded in breaking through the scattered enemy positions when Paleologos received a message that a thousand unarmed men had arrived from the south to join the maquis and were waiting for him on Pieria.

The detachment retraced its steps and sought out the survivors of Zachariadis's 'Long March'. After more than fifteen days' travel on foot, many of them without shoes, they were exhausted and many were suffering from frostbite. Paleologos gave them arms and ammunition, managed to find warm clothes for the sickest of them and shared out the last of the food.

All this delay and moving back and forth gave the government forces time to join up with one another and surround the mountain. Aircraft entered the scene with daylight every morning. General Van Fleet had replaced Livesey at the head of the American military mission, announcing on his arrival in Athens: 'Greece is our laboratory experiment.' Now the partisans on Pieria became guinea-pigs for perfecting the latest technique in air warfare, napalm.

Huge areas of rock were plastered with blazing jelly, but all the government attacks were repulsed. It was only half successful; the enemy managed to keep the partisans trapped where they were for a week, while government reinforcements kept flowing in. All the food on the mountain was exhausted and the last mules had been eaten five days before: more people succumbed to hunger and cold than to the napalm. The combatants, both men and women, clutched their rifles in numb hands and saved their last energy for scrutinizing the rocks for enemy infantry. To break out of the encirclement would mean abandoning the sick and wounded.

On the evening of 11 March 1948, half-buried in the snow that was draining their lives out bit by bit, the partisans heard an announcement by Athens radio: '3,000 bandits are surrounded on Pieria. They will be exterminated tomorrow morning.'

During the night Paleologos decided to hide 130 immovable wounded in a cave and leave them the rest of the food. Thirty of them knew that they were mortally wounded and asked for arms so that they could resist the government forces to the last breath. They were installed in another cave. The sky was overcast and the retreat began in dense darkness. The partisans slipped through the night. Just after dawn, the first flashes of napalm painted the heights of Pieria with their russet glare. The thirty fighting wounded kept firing until the end; the government army launched its final attack on an enclave of dead and dying.

Paleologos weighed seventy kilos at the beginning of the expedition; he weighed forty when, after another week on the march, he regained Hassia. He had set out with 1,500 men on a recruiting expedition. He had met another 1,000 en route. He came back with 1,200. Of the 1,300 missing, four-fifths had died of hunger and cold. The expedition along the frontier fared about the same. Triandafyllou, and half his brigade, never returned.

While some of the Roumeliot andartes were on their 'Long March' towards Grammos, others were ordered south to Athens, to open a route for partisans wishing to leave the capital. Diamantis and Hermes went to see Gousias to protest: 'It's too late. This operation is doomed in advance. It's a suicide mission.'

Gousias did not tolerate argument from kapetanios. He formed an elite company of two hundred men and sent it to Athens. There was not a single survivor.

Now and later there were plenty of protests; people demanded explanations. But the new leadership never ran short of arguments. 'Traitors' had infiltrated the Democratic Army and caused the massacre. Thirty-five of the most argumentative partisans vanished without trial.

ELAS on Trial Again

Just as Zachariadis was, in all probability, ignorant of Stalin's real attitude to the Greek revolution, so the grass-roots partisans knew nothing about the conflict between the First Secretary and the kapetanios. The orders they were given originated from the *éminences grises* of the Provisional Government, but bore the signature of Prime Minister Markos in the regular way. The new politico-military leadership was taking over from the guerilla cadres, but slowly, little by little. Officials who refused to swallow the new strategy were removed from their units one by one: now one, now another. The Party press launched a smear campaign against the ghost of ELAS: in March 1948 the third issue of the Democratic Army newspaper *Demokratikos Stratos* carried an editorial entitled 'Learning to Fight':

... The Democratic Army's basic weakness stems from the fact that, although it is a revolutionary army committed to achieving the democratic reconstruction of our country, in the tactical sphere it is still enslaved by the foreign concepts and bourgeois traditions inherited, for the most part, from ELAS. Our task is to forge the Democratic Army into a force which will really become a people's revolutionary army, not only in the ideological sense but in its organization, leadership structure, combat techniques and effectiveness. ...

This is the essential point: many of the obstacles we are facing are caused by our lack of military experience and by our copying the organization and tactical methods of the bourgeois army and of the negative side of the ELAS tradition.

All this literature could only have been intended to absolve the Party of responsibility for its past errors in trying to suppress every spontaneous manifestation of the Greek revolutionary spirit. For doctrinal reasons the legendary Mountain guerilla was said to have been tainted with 'foreign techniques', while the positional warfare evolved in the Crimea by nineteenth-century imperialism was granted the stamp of revolutionary orthodoxy. The Democratic Army intoxicated itself with résumés of 1930s Russian strategy manuals, while the Americans happily went on colonizing Athens.

The next issue of *Demokratikos Stratos* contained another article on the same subject, this time signed by Zachariadis himself. After running over the evidence for the moral and doctrinal superiority of the Democratic Army, he continued:

... Only if it can develop this superiority to the fullest extent will the Democratic Army be victorious. This is its real 'secret weapon'. Thus it is a gross error, almost a 'mortal sin', to cling to the anti-popular traditions and foreign influences which have come to us from the negative side of the ELAS heritage. Those who do so are forgetting or underestimating this most irresistible of the Democratic Army's weapons, the very basis of our superiority.

On 25 December 1947, the day of the attack on Konitsa, a dozen or so party cadres, including Partsalidis and Tzimas, managed to escape from the island of Ikaria. Many partisans were surprised when Tzimas failed to turn up immediately at the Vitsi HQ. Kikitsas had been plaguing Ioannidis and Zachariadis about him: 'Why don't you send for Tzimas? He's a walking map of Greece, knows every inch of it, and the men trust him completely.'

Aris was dead. Sarafis was still in exile. Tzimas/Samariniotis was the only free, living representative of the legendary ELAS triumvirate. He was too popular to be eliminated in a straightforward manner; what Zachariadis did was to stage a moral execution.

Tzimas arrived at the HQ at the beginning of April. He had been receiving treatment for violent attacks of migraine, and was not fully cured. He was exhausted by his captivity and much weakened by the treatment he had been receiving, but was quite well aware that he was being drawn into a trap. He wandered about HQ in a distinctly substandard condition for about three weeks; Zachariadis wanted to exhibit him, to add substance to the suggestion that he had lost his reason. Tzimas was too weak to fight back but could sense the trap closing in on him. One night, he disappeared. Friends with whom he had spent the evening were called to HQ. The elephantine Bartzotas was sitting behind a desk, Markos restlessly pacing about behind him.

'I know we ought to have told you sooner,' Bartzotas began, 'but Tzimas is extremely ill. He has disappeared. Do you know where he's gone?'

Markos walked nervously up and down, his face pallid. The others scented an ambush.

'If he's as ill as all that, why did you bring him here?'

Bartzotas cleared his throat: 'It was an error ... but we have to find him, we're afraid he may drown himself. He could also be capable of walking towards the enemy. He'll be killed or captured.'

Markos came to a halt facing Bartzotas.

'I know Andreas very well. He'd never "walk towards the enemy" even if he *is* as sick as you claim he is.'

Bartzotas waved his arm evasively. The discussion was over. When Tzimas's friends returned the next morning to see if there was any news of him, Bartzotas greeted them with a Buddha-like smile.

'Don't worry, we've found Tzimas.'

'Where?'

'He's quite an operator. He slipped through everybody's security and got into Yugoslavia.'

Even if an attempt had been made to liquidate Tzimas on the quiet, he had managed to escape in time. He had sidestepped the Vitsi trap. But the Party's arm was long; Ioannidis was installed in Belgrade. He arranged for Tzimas to enter a clinic where he continued to receive 'treatment' for his migraine. Later on he was sent to Bulkes and made to do the most arduous work. He escaped and made for Hungary, landing back in the world of clinics with barred windows, of pills which make you dizzy and bring back memories of childhood. . . . Eight years later, in 1956, the Soviet Twentieth Congress cured him at a stroke by opening the door of his cell.

While Zachariadis was purging the Democratic Army, the Athens government was busy doing the same thing with its own forces. To speed up the re-education and redemption of those detained in the camp for army conscripts on the island of Makronisos, a series of prearranged 'mutinies' exploded and urged the forces of law and order into action. What follows is a prisoner's account.

It was just after daybreak on Sunday, 29 February 1948. After morning roll-call the detainees were ordered to assemble in a ravine shaped like an amphitheatre, which was sometimes used for religious services. When they got there the detainees saw that instead of a priest there were soldiers of the Guard lined up on the slopes of the ravine. This had never happened before.

The police were then ordered to arrest two soldiers from among the detainees, allegedly for questioning. Suspecting that they were to be killed, the soldiers refused to go. The police began beating them with clubs. Other detainees surrounded Second Lieutenant Kardaras and begged him to stop this arbitrary action. The Guard soldiers began shouting: 'Let the Second Lieutenant go!'

The detainees did, in fact, stand off from him and let him go. He started to walk away and after a few steps gave the order to open fire (Kardaras had been in the pro-German militia during the occupation). The Guard soldiers began firing at the assembled detainees – 4,500 men – at a range varying from 15 to 40 yards, using both rifles and automatic weapons. Six were killed and eleven wounded.

When they saw what was happening, some prisoners bared their chests, shouting: 'Aim here!' At that moment, however, Commandant Karabekos, director of Makronisos military jail, appeared shouting: 'Cease fire!'

The next morning Bairaktaris, a colonel from the camp HQ, arrived in a great hurry and began shouting over the loudspeaker system: 'Do not align yourselves with the communists. Men wishing to join the Government Army should assemble on the 7th Company parade ground. You have a quarter of an hour. Anyone who has not appeared in that time will be considered an enemy and chastised without pity.'

Only four men went to the appointed place; the rest stayed in their tents. The attack started almost before the fifteen minutes were up, with guards going into the tents and killing the detainees there and then. Some, who left their tents and headed for the kitchens, were shot at longer range. The bodies began piling up, one on top of another.

When this happened the detainees stopped and began singing the national anthem. A little later, when they were filing along the seashore, a coastal launch anchored nearby suddenly opened fire on them.

They were ordered to sit on the ground. They were beaten into unconsciousness. Guards danced on their chests. Several were taken away in lorries never to be seen again. Three airmen died as a result of their beating just as the lorries were leaving. Their corpses were thrown in the sea and it was claimed that they had drowned themselves.

From end to end, from the Peloponnese to Macedonia, Greece was in a state of siege. All the towns and villages held by the government forces were bristling with barbed wire and surrounded by a depopulated countryside in which the Democratic Army found subsistence virtually impossible. American Under-Secretary of State Lovett announced at a press conference that the number of refugees had nearly reached the half-million mark.

In addition to its own provisioning problems, the Democratic Army had to try and ensure the survival of those elements of the civilian population which had managed to slip through the governmental net. The endless exodus from the villages had been followed by air raids and attacks by government forces. The climate in which the survivors, including thousands of children, were forced to live, was one of dramatic danger and unpleasantness.

The Greek Children

On 3 March, during a Belgrade Youth Conference, the Cominform countries took the decision to offer refuge to Greek children between the ages of three and fourteen who were living in particularly exposed districts. By the end of the year, according to Red Cross reports, there were 23,693 of them: 10,000 in Yugoslavia, 3,801 in Rumania, 3,000 in Hungary, 2,660 in Bulgaria, 2,235 in Czechoslovakia and 2,000 in Albania.

After the collapse of its original report, the UN Inquiry Commission had been reconvened in October of the previous year, this time without Soviet participation. Seizing the opportunity, it began compiling a dossier on the 'kidnapping of Greek children'. These unhappy victims, torn from their families and forced to absorb Slavic ideology by intensive brainwashing, would surely illustrate the true extent of pan-Slavic intervention in Greece.

All the correspondents in Athens at this time were in agreement on the incredible misery reigning in the government-controlled zones; entire regions had been reduced to desert by the removal of their populations and the systematic destruction of crops. Under the circumstances, to try to arouse international indignation over the 'kidnapping' of Greek children could only be the shabbiest of masquerades.

The Inquiry Commission had no trouble accumulating a few statements supporting the idea that the children had been removed by force. When interviewed by the Greek security services, parents showed a natural reluctance to boast of having chosen to send their children to the People's Democracies rather than to Queen Frederika's camps. The extreme youth of most of the Democratic Army's combatants helped to add substance to the fantasy that children were being kidnapped, conditioned and in-doctrinated abroad and then rushed back into battle by their kidnappers. The campaign certainly stirred up a few eddies in international opinion, but contradictory views also began to be heard.

Propaganda never sinks so low [wrote Colonel A. W. Sheppard, former chief of the British economic mission in Northern Greece] as when it seeks to exploit the natural affection which everyone feels for children. In some weeks the UN delegates were literally bombarded with published material emanating either from the Athens Ministry of Information or from one of its direct or indirect agencies. This propaganda was cooked up by organizations which were either in the pay of, or unequivocally loyal to, certain governments. . . .

It is certainly unnecessary to make a case for the principle of evacuating children from war-affected regions, whatever the causes of the war and whoever may be responsible for it. Was the British Government wrong to send its children to Australia, New Zealand, the United States and Canada to prevent them from being killed by German and Italian bombs? And is the Greek Provisional Government wrong to evacuate the children from the regions it controls to save them from the British and American bombs used by the Royal Hellenic Air Force?

All war is cruel, civil war especially so. Mr Tsaldaris has admitted that the Athens government was in the habit of exposing severed heads in village squares. In reply to representations made at the beginning of this year by the British Government . . . , Mr Tsaldaris explained that this was an old Greek custom, but that he would do what he could to prevent it being done with women's heads in the future. Whether the heads are men's or women's, should we not do every-thing in our power to spare children's eyes from such sights?

Like Bigart [an American journalist investigating the same business] and quite unlike all the propagandists who have made pronouncements on this issue, I have seen both sides of the question. . . . I should perhaps mention here everyone who has seen both sides is unanimous in rejecting the stories put out by the government in Athens. I chatted recently with Mrs Levinsohn of the Save The Children organization in Stockholm. Although I have not had time to obtain her express permission, I am sure she will not mind if I quote her here: after carrying out searching inquiries among the mothers and children of the children's camps in Hungary, she is convinced that they all left Greece with their parents' consent and that they are being looked after in a way that leaves nothing to be desired. Mrs Levinsohn said all this to her country's press when she returned from Hungary, but although the Swedish press has a fair reputation for objectivity it seems that in this case agents of the Athens government had enough influence to prevent the publication of all, or very nearly all, Mrs Levinsohn's personal statements.

. . . One of the Athens government's allegations has been refuted by the BBC correspondent Kenneth Matthews: 'No attempt is being made to instil these children with Slavic culture. They are so completely surrounded by Greeks that it would be impossible in the very nature of things for them to learn a single word of Bulgarian.'

. . . My own experience confirms Matthews' opinion. In Hungary and Czecho-slovakia, where Greek is not widely spoken, officials attached to the children's camps are supplied with small Greek primers to enable them to communicate with their charges. I even had an argument on the subject with the Greek camp inspector in Czechoslovakia: I was of the opinion that the rule forbidding the children from learning foreign languages ought to be relaxed so that youngsters of outstanding ability could attend courses at local technical schools, but he insisted that it could not be done, as the Athens propaganda machine would get hold of it and distort the truth so as to be able to complain to the world at large that Greek children were being prevented from learning their mother tongue.

It would be possible to go on for ever in this vein, citing the opinions of investigators and foreign journalists. Neither the UN Commission's reports, nor the discussions they stimulated, allowed anyone to get at the reality behind the 'abduction' of these children. In the meantime, however, the confusion was such that the issue provided a comfortable excuse for continuing American aid. Back in the United States, the experts had set all sentiment aside and were beginning to pore over their account books.

Escalation

Early in the Spring of 1948 Glen H. Taylor, a Democratic Senator, calculated that according to President Truman's report American spending on the Greek civil war had reached an average of '$8,600 for every ragged, ill-fed partisan holding the mountains. This is,' he added, 'one of the costliest, most extravagant military operations in history, in which our wastefulness has only been equalled by our inefficiency.'

To bring a little more order to the Staff, to increase the forces' effectiveness in the field, JUSMAPG (the Joint US Military Advisory and Planning Group) had to impose even tighter control than previously. The number of American officers involved in day-to-day decision-making rose to 250, fifty of them attached directly to operational government units. New deliveries of American machines had been strengthening the governmental air force since the beginning of February. Twenty-five million dollars' worth of old German equipment and 35,000 British rifles were landed at Piraeus in the same month.

A regular army of 136,000 men, equipped with artillery and armour and supported by 50,000 National Guards, had been letting the 25,000 partisans of the Democratic Army, who had neither armour nor aircraft, slip repeatedly through its fingers. Now the governmental Staff, reshuffled and placed under the command of General Ventiris, was preparing a new wave of operations to appease its senior partners.

Zachariadis, facing them, was preparing for the mass suicide of the democratic forces by gathering his troops on Mt Grammos. Gousias arrived from the south after an exhausting 'long march', but not before leaving more than a tuft of feathers on the ground outside Karpenisi. The recruiting operations had achieved nothing. Roumeli was now held by a mere 2,500 partisans under Diamantis and Hermes.

On 15 April the new governmental Staff poured 20,000 men into the region. Operation Dawn was launched from the north in three successive waves to prevent any partisans from wriggling through the government lines. The Gulf of Corinth shut off their escape to the south; naval vessels prevented any retreat by sea and shelled the mountains with their artillery.

A violent snowstorm was not making things any easier for the andartes on the peaks. The LOK governmental mountain commandos carried out their first operations with a measure of success. Regular units had learned to move much more rapidly than they had in the past; they travelled at night and launched surprise attacks on new objectives in the morning. The partisans evaded successive pincer movements but were harder and harder pressed. The chase went on for a month.

While it was going on, the government First Army emptied the last villages and isolated the democratic forces in the snow. Finally, after very bitter fighting in the Mornos valley and around the town of Artotina, the last partisans managed to slip into the Agrafa valley, and part of Roumeli passed into governmental hands. The regular army was beginning to make effective use of the continuous flow of American equipment. At the same time, Zachariadis's determination to group all his reserves on Grammos disastrously weakened the mountains of central Greece while providing the Athens Staff with a single target on which it would soon be able to concentrate all its forces.

Operation Dawn marked a turning-point in the war. 1,368 partisans were disarmed in the course of it; 641 others were less fortunate and paid with their lives for the trial of strength between the West's tanks and Zachariadis's orthodox principles. Anglo-Saxon empiricism had adapted itself to the terrain much more thoroughly than the Central Committee's dogma.

By using guerilla methods, the relatively weak Democratic Army forces in the Peloponnese were managing to keep the regular army in a state of confusion, and had actually taken over several villages. On 14 April 1948 a mine laid by andartes blew up the commandant of the Second Motorized Gendarmerie Company, based on Sparta.

That evening there was a 'mutiny' in the Sparta garrison. Extreme right-wing elements seized a Bren-gun carrier, raided the town prison and there murdered twenty-six political detainees. This was a foretaste of something that would soon be happening with the full backing of the law; the time was almost ripe and the police were only waiting for a pretext. They did not have to wait very long, although the pretext was in no way commensurate with what followed it. On 1 May an Athenian called Evstathios, according to the Greek government a member of OPLA, made a successful attempt on the life of the Justice Minister, Christos Ladas. The whole country was immediately placed under martial law and the government ordered a mass execution of those condemned to death for offences committed before 1944.

238 former resistance fighters were shot between 1 May and 3 May 1948; the victims were scattered through every town in Greece. The Ministry of Justice issued orders to speed up court proceedings so that all the condemned could be shot before the middle of the month; according to the same note there were 2,961 of them. This sudden haste on the part of the government and the American missions aroused a storm of international protest. Soon after the executions, on 6 May, the *Manchester Guardian* commented:

Whatever one's feelings of horror at the assassination on May Day of Mr Christos Ladas, the Greek Minister of Justice, the Greek Government's decision to execute 151 Communist prisoners by way of reprisal fills one with shame and dismay.

The same day's *Times* echoed this indignation:

The Greek government has harmed its cause in Western eyes by ordering the execution of 152 Communists long held in prison. Its cause will suffer still more if sentences are carried out against many of the other 800 Communists....

In an editorial on 7 May the *Daily Herald* published its own warning to the Athens leadership:

Very sincerely we urge the Greek Government to reconsider its policy in relation to these people. The fact that they have endured imprisonment for so long under the shadow of death is in itself obnoxious to 'decent opinion'. If they are now to be executed in hundreds, what can be the effect except to intensify the passions which already divide the Greek nation, and to provide the Communist enemies of Greek freedom with invaluable propaganda?

The crimes committed by the imprisoned Communists were committed during a Civil War in which there were ferocious excesses on both sides. After four years, is it wise or right to stimulate hatred by acts of judicial slaughter which to many people will look very like political revenge?

... If the Greek Government persists in the mass executions it will deeply shock world opinion and further harm the prospects of unity at home.

This upsurge of worthy sentiment did have a short-term effect. The Soviet Union addressed an official protest to Athens and the Western embassies showered the Greek government with tight-lipped notes. The reprisals were discontinued for a while to give international opinion time to move on to other amusements.

The press had played an important part in this affair, though without shaking America's extremely indulgent attitude to its protégés. The Greek and American services were quite keen to give the papers a chance to wax indignant in the other direction: to show, if possible, how the 'totalitarians' treated these pressmen who were always so quick to point at minor ups and downs in the administration of law and order.

An American journalist and CBS correspondent called George Polk had been trying for some time to get into Markos's territory. On 8 May he wrote to his colleague Edward Marlow that he had heard of two guides in Salonika who might take him into Free Greece. He met these two persons that evening near the Luxembourg Casino: a rendezvous was arranged for the next day, Thursday, 9 May, at a beach in the Thermaic Gulf, where a boat was to pick him up for the journey to Pieria. Polk kept the appointment and was never seen alive again.

All his friends in Athens knew that he had gone to Salonika to try and contact Markos. On Monday the 13th a journalist's identity card was delivered to Salonika 3rd Precinct police station by 'persons unknown'. A file was opened, and a rumour that Polk had been murdered in the mountains began to gain currency. A month later, however, his bound corpse, the neck broken by a pistol bullet, was disgorged by the sea. Put together with the identity card allegedly found in the mountains, the body from the sea hardly clarified the situation, but the police went on asserting under increasing pressure that the journalist had been killed by the Communists and the culprits would be arrested. The American Union of Journalists smelt a rat and, despite the objects of Under-Secretary Draper, insisted on conducting an on-the-spot inquiry.

General Donovan, the Union's president, arrived at Athens in person. He wanted to talk to Hajiargyris, an American journalist of Greek origin who had been a friend of Polk's, but despite all his efforts he never managed to see him except in the Salonika CID building. After a few days of setbacks and irritations he accused the Greek government of setting up obstacles in a systematic attempt to obscure the whole affair. The foreign press began dragging the names of the American Secret Service and British Intelligence into their coverage.

The Salonika police were still promising to produce the killers, but months passed before they could organize a trial which, when it came, merely added to the confusion. A chance combination of undersea currents had prevented international opinion from being manipulated exactly as planned; despite its ambiguities, however, the affair had caused enough uproar to make the mass executions of early May recede in the public memory.

On 31 May the rebel radio broadcast a peace proposal signed by Markos.

... The Provisional Democratic Government is still prepared to accept and encourage any initiative, from any of the parties involved, which could help Greece to return to a state of peace.

Tsaldaris published a first, unofficial response in an Athens newspaper:

No negotiation is possible with the rebels. We can only offer them the choice between unconditional surrender and obliteration.

Two days later the Vice-Premier officially denied this statement. The international press gave itself up completely to byzantine speculations. The Sofoulis government sent an emissary to Grammos, but Zachariadis was no more serious than Tsaldaris about reconciliation. Not for the first time, he answered: 'We will not entertain discussions until the members of the Athens government are put on trial as war criminals.'

Meanwhile Griswold had sent a reassuring memo to Washington: the Greek regular army, he affirmed, was now in a position to bring the rebellion to an end before the end of the autumn. The argument immediately bore fruit; Tsaldaris on the one side, Zachariadis on the other, both proclaimed that they had dug the grave of their adversary.

On 15 June the government army launched 90,000 men at Grammos in an attempt to encircle the democratic forces gathered there by Zachariadis. While government aircraft dumped napalm over the heights of western

Macedonia, another kind of bomb was about to go off in Belgrade. After rejecting every attempt to start a Balkan Federation, Stalin decided to put an end once and for all to Tito's attempts at independent action. He revived the project under his own supervision as a new federation under the authority of Dimitrov.

The two Josephs were at war.

Tito's Excommunication

The Soviets had sent their first scolding message to the Yugoslav Central Committee on 17 March 1948 after Tito had signed an agreement with the Albanians. Two others followed, on 4 and 22 May. Tito had no wish to conduct the debate on an ideological level; his first reply went to the Soviet Foreign Minister, Molotov, and on 20 May he turned directly to Stalin.

The Soviets wanted to settle the dispute with an ideological debate in front of Cominform delegates. This form of procedure would have resembled a tribunal, and Tito refused to have anything to do with it. He suggested instead that the Russians send a mission to Belgrade to thrash out their grievances and work out the basis for a settlement. But the conflict had already reached the point of no return. Soviet 'specialists' had insinuated themselves into the Yugoslav administration on every level. Tito, who knew Stalin's methods of old, had no compunction in keeping a very close watch on the 'specialists' and, when necessary, having them arrested or done away with altogether. From Stalin's point of view, the emergence of Titoism, of aspirations to independence within the socialist bloc, was an evil which must be dealt with at all costs. The definitive rupture came on 28 June, when the Cominform condemned Yugoslav policy.

The 'Tito-Kardelj-Djilas-Ranković clique' was accused of every crime in the calendar. It had betrayed Marxism-Leninism; it was carrying out an anti-USSR policy by slandering the Soviet specialists; it had taken a false road in its agrarian policy by failing to nationalize the land; it was liquidating the Party in favour of the Popular Front; it was persecuting good Communists; it was proposing the 'extremist' measure of nationalizing small businesses; it refused to hold proper discussions with the fraternal

Parties; it was leaning towards nationalism and making concessions to the imperialists.

The break between Tito and Stalin placed the Greek revolutionary movement in an extremely delicate position. Zachariadis's dearest wish was to force Stalin to recognize him, but he was in no position to do without Yugoslav aid. The dissension between Markos and Zachariadis has often been explained by analogy with the Tito-Stalin split. This is rather a simple-minded view. As chief of partisans, Markos certainly saw Tito as an influential ally, if not as an incontestable model. He knew enough about the agents of orthodoxy to be able to form a good idea of the value of the epithets the bureaucrats hurled at him; they were not slow to accuse him of Titoism. Orthodoxy had to get its terminology from somewhere; in reality the Tito/Markos collusion went no further than that. Zachariadis, for his part, was only controlled from Moscow up to a point, though he longed to throw himself into Stalin's arms; he favoured the expansion of the struggle, while the Soviets wanted to drain the Greek abscess. The real conflict between the Democratic Army chief and the General Secretary of the KKE was over strategy. At the beginning of the summer of 1948 the crisis was about to break out into the open. It was not so much the Cominform resolution as a divergence of opinion over the battle of Grammos that kept the dispute going. Markos was not removed as a Titoist agent, and it was not Stalin, in all probability, who asked Zachariadis to move on to the 'higher stage' of strategy.

The KKE held its Fourth Plenum a few days after Moscow's curse on its ungrateful children, in the middle of the battle of Grammos. It refrained from taking an open position, supporting the Cominform decision in secret but not criticizing Yugoslavia publicly. Seven months later the Fifth Plenum voted a new resolution, but just as discretely. It was only much later, when the consequences of the KKE's policies had to be explained away, that Stalin tried to make Tito the scapegoat for the Greek tragedy. It cannot be said that in doing so he was motivated primarily by his love of truth.

Meanwhile, the Greek partisans continued to get more useful support from the Yugoslavs than from any of the other fraternal countries. The last act in the Markos-Zachariadis confrontation was played out in the livid glare of napalm, among the fused and blackened rocks of Mount Grammos.

From Grammos to Vitsi

'We are marching on the Grammos mountains to obliterate Slavo-Communism. May the Grammos range become Slavo-Communism's gravestone.' 15 July 1948: the governmental army's order of the day signalled the start of Operation Coronis. General Van Fleet personally supervised the troop movements.

A first wave of 70,000 regular troops converged on the north-western corner of Greece. They faced 12,000 partisans. Partisans versus draftees; the qualitative superiority of the convinced would be the partisans' only advantage against superior numbers, aircraft, armour and the latest products of the destruction industry.

One claw of the governmental pincer tried to infiltrate along the frontier, while the other was supposed to sweep from East to West. The partisans had been ordered to stand firm at all costs. Only a few groups of saboteurs were using guerilla tactics, manoeuvring in the enemy's rear. Where the earth was too rocky for their mines to be buried, they booby-trapped the trees or sent bundles of high explosives rolling down from the heights.

Every peak overlooking the Aliakmon valley was fried in napalm, splintered by salvoes of rockets and used as a target for endless ranging fire: the opulence of America at war. But the andartes kept surging from their holes in the scorched rubble. Wave after wave of governmental assault troops were mown down on the bare slopes. Sometimes, when the last crags of a particular hill were surrounded, the surviving defenders would follow the old klephtic tradition and hurl themselves into the void rather than fall into the hands of the enemy. Kleftis, Smolikas, Vasilitsa, Agios Nikolaos Boliana, Pyrgos, Marjia Golio, Steno Ondria, Orlia, Kopantze, Volia, Amouda, Grammos; peaks where every inch of rock cost its weight in blood.

All observers were fascinated by the determination of the Democratic Army's combatants, men, women and adolescents. Once again, Greece was producing heroes: but what for? Why were the revolutionary forces clinging to untenable positions? Why were they making no use of their principal strength, their mobility and intimate knowledge of the terrain? Yannoulis, a reserve officer and former lawyer who had reorganized the Macedonian underground after Litochoron, had been ordered to hold the heights of Batras to the death. When he saw that all was lost, he decided to withdraw his wounded and the rest of his brigade; Yannoulis was a kapetanios and mountain man, and disobeyed orders. He managed to reach Kamenik and joined another veteran kapetanios, Ypsilantis. He had done what he could against the government attacks, held out to the extreme limit of his unit's ability, and then managed to save the lives of fifty men. When the dead came to be counted, people would be looking round for scapegoats. Yannoulis filled the bill very nicely. His trial would serve to educate the kapetanios on the 'petty-bourgeois descent of ELAS methods'.

The battle of Grammos was supposed to annihilate Slavo-Communism in two weeks; it lasted eight. Throughout the battle the government poured in reinforcements to compensate for its heavy losses. The courage and determination of the rank-and-file partisans never wavered; they were the instrument and they had faith. They obeyed orders and died at their posts. But closer to the leadership, on the decision-making level, many were sceptical about the infallibility of Zachariadis's methods. The way things had developed gave Markos ample opportunity to confirm the dictum that 'the defensive is the tomb of the revolution'. Orders were always signed with his name, but all his suggestions were scornfully swept aside by the academics.

FOURTH PLENUM

The Cominform's indictment of Tito on 28 June 1948 justified the holding of another Plenum, which Zachariadis used to bring the kapetanios back into step. The battle of Grammos was raging a few kilometres away.

Markos insisted that the Third Plenum line be re-examined and a new strategy adopted for the battle under way. He outlined his criticisms of the most recent military operations during a preparatory meeting on 2 July, and was interrupted by Zachariadis: 'If the Third Plenum's objectives have not been achieved, it is because bad Communists have failed in their duty.'[1]

Nobody dared risk an internal crisis in the middle of a crucial battle. The introductory report and the Plenum's resolution were both written by Zachariadis, but it was Markos, the oppositionist, who had to read them out to the ten cadres present (eleven others were absent). Once again, for the last time, Markos agreed to bend for the sake of Party unity. Past errors were summarily justified and the final resolution even went as

[1] Markos.

far as proclaiming that 'Monarcho-fascism has a wooden leg' and that 'its final end is closer than ever'.

It was a serious abuse of trust. The fighters being barbecued in napalm at that very moment believed that in selling their lives for knockdown prices they were making the final sacrifice before victory. Many of them were women and many were very young adolescents, almost children; they all resisted the regular troops with incredible, furious determination. Courage has never been lacking in the mountains; Greece is not afraid to bleed. It is the exploitation and abuse of this nobility, the inexhaustible generosity of Greece, that gives the Greek tragedy its peculiar poignancy.

THE CORONIS CAMPAIGN

The partisans on Fourka heights were using bomb craters as trenches. The wounded crouched in the last shelters nursing phosphorus burns that pushed their pain under the skin and smouldered on in the flesh. There was no real cover left; the shelling and bombing of the last few days had pounded the crags to rubble and cleared the peaks.

An aircraft circled like a buzzard. Its engine note rose to a siren wail as it turned and dived at the position. The andartes flattened themselves on the hard ground, pressing their faces to the pebbles so as to show no outline. Only one of them remained standing, a young woman; she was facing the aircraft, holding a Bren gun at her hip. She emptied a magazine at the plane as it flashed overhead. The girl's name was Anna Dossa. She was twenty-five years old and commanded thirty-three montagnards. The aircraft dived again; Anna stayed on her feet and emptied another magazine. It was a duel between the girl on the rocks and the pilot. When the aircraft came in for the third time Anna had the range. Black smoke began to trail from the engine; this time, the plane did not pull out of its dive but keeled over and curved into the foot of the mountain.

Against armour, planes and artillery the andartes used anything and everything: they rolled improvised mines downhill onto the enemy, they left booby-trapped mules wandering the slopes, they started landslides, they consciously sought out opportunities to use cold steel at close quarters.

The governmental attack made little progress until the end of July. Kleftis, which overlooks Konitsa from a height of over 6,000 feet, fell on 1 August after forty-five days of fighting. In the twenty-four hours preceding the final assault more than 20,000 shells pounded the top of the mountain. The king, the queen, Marshal Papagos, General Van Fleet and the cabinet all came out personally to inspect the rear positions and raise the morale of their troops.

General Kalogeropoulos was replaced by General Kitrilakis at the head of the regular forces, while General Tsakalotas marched north-west with all the available reserves.

Klephtis was the main natural obstacle barring the way to Grammos, and when it was finally abandoned the democratic forces fell back to the north. Golio, Gardari and Steno held out until 6 and 7 August, Kamenik until the 17th. After eight weeks of fighting the democratic forces found themselves trapped at the top of Grammos itself: 9,000 partisans besieged by 90,000 soldiers. The losses were enormous. Government sources gave their own casualty figures as 801 killed and 5,000 wounded, with 3,128 killed and 589 prisoners (no wounded) among the andartes. The Democratic Army supplied the following figures for government losses: 5,125 killed, 16,000 wounded, 1,737 prisoners or deserters, and 35 aircraft and 18 tanks destroyed. The latter set of figures is probably closer to the truth. All the foreign correspondents who witnessed the battle were horrified by the cost in human lives of the government army's assault waves, ordered uphill towards the peaks across exposed ground and followed by other waves to prevent them from retreating.

The hard soil and bitter fighting around Klephtis prevented the governmental side from burying its dead for several days. In high summer the spectacle was not for the squeamish. On 19 August the government army regrouped itself and prepared to launch the final attack on Grammos.

At Democratic Army headquarters the strategic conflict between Markos and Zachariadis exploded. Markos wanted to try and break through the enemy encirclement to the north and then disperse his forces to harass governmental units. Zachariadis, who had by now been forced to admit that their position on Grammos was untenable, grudgingly agreed to the evacuation plan, but wanted the Democratic Army to fall back on Vitsi and dig in with its back to the Yugoslav frontier. Is it possible that Zachariadis, realizing how desperate the situation had become, was trying to arrange for the Democratic Army's defeat to be blamed on Tito's deviationism?

More immediately, the decision to withdraw from Grammos as soon as possible made it necessary to re-examine the Central Committee's recommendation to fight a positional war. Zachariadis did not change his convictions noticeably; he simply named the culprits. Yannoulis, who had founded the partisan movement in the region, was held responsible for the deaths and charged with all kinds of sins. It was said that Klephtis and Kamenik had fallen because 'bad Communists' had betrayed them by taking untoward initiatives. On 20 August a made-to-measure indictment was brought against Yannoulis. He was accused of having belonged in 1942 to a resistance movement called IVE which (after he had left it and joined ELAS) had gone over to the right. After a parody of a trial Gousias ordered his execution personally:

'Confirmation of the sentence is on the way from HQ. No point in waiting; shoot him now.'

'Despite its great strength', then, the Democratic Army was forced to leave Grammos by the machinations of a traitor. In another violent quarrel, Markos accused Zachariadis of trying to liquidate the revolution. It was going to be difficult for Zachariadis to deal with the leading light of the Democratic Army in the same way as Yannoulis; but Markos was in a dangerous situation for all that.

THE ATTEMPT ON MARKOS'S LIFE

On the night of 20–21 August the Democratic Army counter-attacked in the Slimnitza region to the north of Grammos. The enemy lines were breached and all the democratic forces managed to drain out through the gap during the night. The last wounded were evacuated at 10 a.m. on the 21st and were led off towards Lake Prespa.

The Agence France Presse correspondent cabled: 'General Markos has always managed to disengage with great skill at the last possible moment, covering the retreat of the main body of his troops with a thin screen of men picked for the purpose.'

In reality, the split between Markos and Headquarters had become irrevocable. As the Democratic Army left Grammos the commissars went into action; while the battle-weary democratic forces travelled up the frontier towards Vitsi, Markos was ordered to Albania following his final quarrel with Zachariadis.

When the democratic forces slipped through the gap in the governmental lines on the night of the 20th, Markos separated from the main body of partisans and set off in a westerly direction, escorted by ten men. His associates had been shaken by the Yannoulis affair and the party was on its guard, expecting the worst. Markos plunged rapidly into the mountainous border country. He was not mistaken in sensing the approach of danger; he had hardly left Headquarters before another detachment left in hot pursuit. It was commanded by a certain Polydoras, whose skill in whisking contentious elements out of sight was well known. His orders were to simulate a border incident. His men were not sentimentalists. They were used to punitive expeditions. Even so, there was a feeling among them that this business of ambushing Markos was a different matter, that it would take them outside the normal scope of their duties. All the time they hesitated Markos was travelling at full speed, and Polydoros only managed to catch up with him after he had crossed the frontier. The first shots alerted an Albanian detachment that happened to be patrolling nearby, and Markos was able to disengage and withdraw under the covering fire of Enver Hoxha's frontier guards. The Soviet Mission in Albania took him under its wing and guaranteed his protection.

Following Aris's death and Zachariadis's campaign to discredit ELAS, Markos's removal from the centre of things, and the attempt to murder him, put a final end to the influence of the guerilla approach to the struggle, and once again veiled the true, living face of Greece. There remained the partisans, those women and children digging in on Vitsi with the same determination and selflessness, the same generosity that they had shown throughout; there remained the Revolution, manipulated, paying without counting the cost and subject, in the final analysis, to a fate determined from outside.

To the combatants, Markos was still the unquestioned chief of the Democratic Army. Orders from HQ continued to bear his name. In the interval between the botched assassination and the inevitable indictment, the leadership decided to tell the troops that their general was suffering from a serious illness.

Kikitsas was called to the new Vitsi HQ on 25 August. The message was signed with Markos's name, but when he arrived he found Zachariadis and Gousias waiting for him. A vague unease had been weighing on the kapetanios for some time, and he was surprised to find Markos absent: 'Where's Markos? He sent for me.'

Zachariadis was sitting with his elbows on the table. He rested his chin on his hands and stared Kikitsas in the eye: 'Markos is gravely ill. We think he's going to die.'

Something in Zachariadis's manner or in this declaration alerted Kikitsas. His scalp crawled. He had known Markos a long time; they had fought side by side since the Resistance. The last time he had seen him, two weeks earlier, he had not seemed a sick man. Kikitsas remembered the rumours surrounding Tzimas's departure. The same thing was happening again. They were trying to do away with Markos. Zachariadis met his look with a limpid, unflinching gaze: 'Markos's health makes it impossible for him to lead the Democratic Army any longer. You're first in line for the command.'

Liquidate Markos and give the first walk-on part to his second-in-command. Kikitsas had no intention of fronting for the *éminences grises* of the abstract revolution.

'I know Markos. I'm certain that if he's ill, he'll recover in no time. It seems a bit premature to talk about his successor.'

Zachariadis did not insist. By refusing to fulfil his allotted role in the commissars' carnival, Kikitsas had shot his name to the top of the black-list. He had commanded the withdrawal from Grammos, and his prestige and authority would be difficult to dispute even through an obedient tribunal; he would have to be eased out indirectly. On the 28th, three days after his little chat with Zachariadis, he was sent to the People's Democracies in the platonic role of roving ambassador.

The last veils were torn away. As it dug in on Vitsi the Democratic Army passed under the direct command of a Supreme War Council totally obedient to Zachariadis. The kapetanios, who were not for the most part convinced of the infallibility of trench warfare, followed Kikitsas into limbo to perform the thankless task of peddling the Greek revolution. Ypsilantis, Alevras, Barbalas; and presently Hermes, Lambros, Hajis and Lasanis, at one time the popular chiefs of ELAS, went to join the extras on the banks of the Danube.

The andartes dug their foxholes in the rubble of Vitsi. Stalin, for whom the Greek troubles represented a useful argument in the international arena, probably wanted nothing better. For Russia to become openly involved in Greece would be to risk generalizing the conflict, but now there were seven Soviet divisions massed along the Yugoslav frontier; they would go no further, provided the Greek guerillas did nothing to strengthen centrifugal currents in the Balkans. What is not clear is whether Zachariadis could still reasonably expect a Soviet intervention, or whether on the other hand he was liquidating the Greek revolution to order, to adjust Stalin's diplomatic scales for him.

Though threatened, Tito went on supporting the Greek partisans at the risk of keeping Cominform agents on his territory. How far could he go?

The very choice of the Vitsi stronghold, its back to the Yugoslav frontier, left the question open. It positioned the pieces on the board in such a way that Stalin would be able a few months later to accuse Tito of stabbing the Greek revolution in the back; it made this so inevitable, in fact, that it is impossible to ignore the suggestion that Zachariadis was engaged in a criminal plot. Either way – whether the Central Committee was showing zeal in the hope of forcing Stalin's recognition, or whether it was preparing to sacrifice the Greek revolution on his orders – from now on the Democratic Army gathered in the north-west corner of Greece could only expect an outside intervention in its favour if a miracle happened, while government attacks were absolutely certain to be resumed with redoubled violence.

Witnesses claim to have overheard one evening a conversation between Gousias and a political commissar. Gousias, a trusted lieutenant of Zachariadis's, was saying:

'. . . It's all over already, but we've got to hang on at Vitsi for a while longer. . . .'

This did not prevent Zachariadis from declaring on 29 August after a meeting of the Political Bureau: 'Our strength is the people's trust, and until the rights of the people finally prevail our slogan will remain: Everyone to arms, all for victory.'

The partisans still had no idea that Markos had been sacked. They were assured repeatedly that international brigades would soon come rushing to their support, that they had never been so close to victory. Zachariadis was right on one point: the partisans of the Democratic Army were unstinting in their faith. It makes their betrayal all the more criminal.

VITSI

After a week of indecision the governmental army hurled itself at Vitsi on 29 August. One assault wave after another broke against the andartes' defences for ten solid days. Most of the governmental forces were grouped around the mountain of Mali Madi, whose slopes were carpeted with corpses decomposing in the September heat. The governmental forces were getting tired; on 9 September the partisans counterattacked in force. From all the heights of Vitsi, from Koule, from Yamata, 10,000 men rolled down on a large but exhausted regular army, which gave ground. The democratic forces were also at the end of their tether. The fighting ended on 20 September, when a Democratic Army attack on the town of

Kastoria was repelled. Zachariadis, lord of Vitsi, set his troops to digging trenches and building fortifications.

The regular forces had not annihilated communism by the end of the autumn. Van Fleet admitted in a statement that the army 'had suffered unprecedented losses'. But the pieces were in place for the return game. The Democratic Army was concentrated in one spot from which it could do nothing to recoup its losses; from now on it would be a stationary target, and the government conscripted 30,000 new recruits to help deal with it. On the international level, the UN Inquiry Commission's reports were quietly foundering in Geneva, Tito was on the tightrope and Stalin himself was busy with Berlin, where Ernst Reuter had secured Western aid for the defence of the 'front-line city in the Cold War'. The situation was hardening generally, but marginal Greece remained a pawn, kept in reserve on the secondary level.

With the approach of winter it became clear that the civil war was going to last another year. The Americans were annoyed. On 22 October Secretary of State Marshall in person arrived in Athens. He inspected the government forces and severely criticized the Staff for hesitating after Grammos and ending operations too early. Portfolios and commands changed hands in the customary minuet. A new cabinet was formed on 13 November, still led by Sofoulis and Tsaldaris but with wider participation by the populist Right. Venizelos and some of the Liberals went into opposition. The main purpose of all this was to reassure the Americans about the government's efficiency, and the reshuffle made no difference to the policies being applied from Athens.

Zachariadis's Army

Zachariadis was not through with his task of setting the Democratic Army in order. The failure of the attack on Kastoria gave him a pretext for another purge or two. Vlantas said at a meeting: 'We have known cases where orders were not carried out at times when the High Command was in great difficulties. One example is the case of a battalion commander at Mali Madi, who allowed the enemy to escape by failing to execute the turning movement which had been calculated to block his retreat. . . .'

From now on, in fact, every operation was led by Zachariadis's men, but whenever there was a failure a few dissidents were eliminated from among the former kapetanios.

Though he had been driven from the centre of things and his life had been menaced, Markos still wanted his voice to be heard. At the beginning of November he sent a long letter to the KKE Political Bureau: by supplying the prosecution with the text of what would be described two months later as 'Markos's opportunist platform', he was helping to lend weight to the case against him.

By tradition, internal democracy is lacking in our Party, and none of the successive leaderships has made an autocritique and admitted their failings. . . . Instead of showing the way to full and courageous reflection, the Party leaderships kill all thought. The result of this is that our cadres do not express their opinions clearly. They do not dare to ask basic questions which might suggest criticism of the leadership's theories. This regime has caused a decline in militancy and thoughtfulness in the Party. Senior cadres force themselves to keep silent and tolerant as the price of their privileges. In this way we have built up a toadies' regime, in which people are only concerned with enshrining the deeds and gestures of the leadership. This has led the Party into grave errors; the case of the Third and Fourth Plenums of 1947 and 1948 is typical. Since the Eighth Congress in 1945 there have been extremely serious developments. Our Party's policies have been severely tested. The Party's members and cadres, and its hundreds of thousands of sympathizers, had every right to expect a clear explanation of these events. None was forthcoming. Neither during the Third nor the Fourth Plenum has the leadership even touched on the problem of its own errors; it has not even deigned to consider that it *could* have committed any errors.

Markos went on to analyse the Party's political line since the Varkiza agreement and to repeat the criticisms he had been making all along. First of all, the abstention from the 1946 elections:

. . . We can state that this was exactly what the Anglo-Americans and the reactionaries wanted; they were seeking an opportunity to strike a decisive blow against the revolutionary movement and succeeded, thanks to our decision to abstain, in creating a climate propitious to their plans.

Next, the beginning of the armed struggle:

. . . The Party did not join the people's armed struggle with much conviction, still less in the intention of carrying it through to victory. It wanted to use armed struggle as a form of blackmail to deal with the situation which had arisen after Varkiza and the elections. . . . Until June 1947, no effort whatsoever was made to encourage big-city militants and cadres to leave for the mountains.

The manpower problem came next.

. . . Events have shown that, firstly, we lacked the recruitment pool necessary to reach the Third Plenum's figure of 50,000–60,000 men, and secondly, we were in no position to hold urban centres until the spring, as the Plenum had decided we should.

Finally, Markos sketched his analysis of the current situation and the prospects for the struggle:

Supported mainly by American imperialism, which is well on the way to occupying our country and certainly constitutes foreign domination of it, the monarcho-fascists have succeeded (despite their pathetic efforts at economic management and the squabbling between the various cliques involved) in establishing a relative degree of political and military stability, reflected in the following: (1) Purging of the State apparatus and establishment of a regime based on fascist force; (2) Maintenance of the Sofoulis-Tsaldaris government in power for a whole year to block the people's democratic insurrection; (3) The fact that the monarcho-fascist army, despite its inability to finish the Democratic Army off, has been fighting for two years without experiencing any major mutinies, cases of mass desertion to the Democratic Army, widespread desertions back to civilian life or other events of that sort. Monarcho-fascism is not only able to make good any military losses, but can increase its fighting strength still further as soon as the Americans provide the means; (4) Monarcho-fascism controls all the urban centres, both large and small, most of the communication routes and some major support centres in the countryside; (5) It has taken over all the trade union organizations by force, and is thus in a position to stifle any sign of a strike or any protest the workers might try to make about their miserable economic situation. It has outlawed all the mass political organizations and democratic parties (EPON, Democratic Leagues, KKE, etc.) and, in the towns and the rural districts under its control, it has succeeded in reducing sympathizers with the people's democratic movement to silence or to passive acceptance of the regime by means of executions and widespread persecution.

The people's movement, which today expresses itself almost entirely through armed struggle, has also attained some degree of stability; this is due to the successful defence of Grammos, the Democratic Army's activities in other regions, the justice of the people's cause and the devotion and self-sacrifice characteristic of Party members and cadres. . . . Nevertheless, this stability cannot compare with that achieved by the monarcho-fascists, and offers us no chance of overthrowing them in the immediate future. At the moment the Democratic Army's strength is about [23,000][1] combatants, against the Government Army's 300,000 men. If the Democratic Army is to be able to undertake offensive actions to liberate whole major regions, thus gaining the supply base

[1] Figure missing in text.

necessary to carry out the kind of operations it will take to overthrow monarcho-fascism once and for all, it will have to increase its strength to 65 or 70,000 men between October and March. Looking for a moment at the interval between the Third and Fourth Plenums, we observe that we were only able to recruit 15,000 combatants in a period of almost a year, and that under conditions which were far better from our point of view than those prevailing now. It follows that, simply in terms of recruitment, it is impossible to realize the performance envisaged in the resolutions of the Fourth Plenum. I am not even taking into consideration the possibility of an intensified American intervention, or the increase of 70,000 effectives that the monarcho-fascists have been demanding from the Americans. Apart from all this, the state of our urban organizations is such that we cannot expect the Democratic Army's offensive effort to be supported by coordinated strikes, let alone insurrections. This is all the more true as long as the Democratic Army cannot even attack the surrounding areas in a serious manner, which is an indispensable precondition for an insurrection inside the town. Taking into account the existing balance of forces and the means and possibilities open to us, one is led to the conclusion that the Democratic Army is not in a position to overthrow monarcho-fascism by itself in the immediate future; it might be able to do it with direct military aid, which could follow the recognition of the Provisional Democratic Government by friendly countries. This aid does not, however, seem very likely to materialize, as the Democratic Army has not managed to create the necessary conditions and the international situation does not appear to favour such a development, at least for the moment.

There are two possibilities: (1) Our Party can propose a democratic pact with a view to working out a peaceful solution to the Greek problem. There is absolutely no chance of this succeeding under present conditions. (2) We can continue the armed struggle in the form of intensive guerilla activity throughout the country. Through this form of action the Democratic Army can seriously hinder the fulfilment of American plans for Greece, by preventing them from turning the country into a launching-pad for war against the Soviet Union and the People's Democracies. Since there is no third alternative, the only way for us must remain the pursuit of armed struggle.

In this way, then, by engaging in intense guerilla activity which will cause a continuous drain on the military and economic resources of the Americans and the monarcho-fascists, we can help to create a climate of growing political instability; in view of the miserable economic situation of Greek workers, it should be possible to exploit these conditions to strengthen the urban movement, which would in its turn enable the Democratic Army to strike combination blows of increasing power.

The maintenance of the regular army formations which we set up, as stipulated by our resolutions, to overthrow monarcho-fascism, constrains us whether we like it or not to a defensive state of mind and to a static posture facing settled enemy positions. It prevents us from intensifying our guerilla activities and consequently from reaping the benefits of doing so. From this point of view it can be seen that centralizing the army into divisional commands was over-hasty. We should distribute our artillery and heavy weapons to a very small number of specialized units, freeing all our other units from their useless weight and making them ultra-mobile, with light armament, so that they can fight where it is profitable to do so rather than where the enemy wants them to. We should also organize a larger number of saboteur and sniper units.

MARKOS VAFIADIS[1]

Only Chrysa Hajivasiliou supported Markos's platform openly; Karageorgis kept his mouth firmly shut for the moment, while everyone else learned by heart a prose-poem composed by Zachariadis:

During the battle of Grammos, Markos had a psychological crisis which reduced his ability to carry out his duties. The Political Bureau sent him away to recover, shelving the problem of his future until after his recovery. At the time of his breakdown, however, the Political Bureau decided that Vafiadis could never again be entrusted with his former responsibilities, and created the Supreme War Council to replace him. Markos Vafiadis was perfectly well aware of all this.

Vafiadis has now come up with a political platform alleging that the Grammos incidents were due not only to a passing confusion but also to a deeply rooted political crisis.

This deed forces the KKE Political Bureau to re-examine the early political career of Markos Vafiadis and uncover the roots of his present anti-Party position.

Markos Vafiadis has had a series of breakdowns, beginning when he was a Young Communist and continuing through his career as a partisan; the most serious of them occurred in prison, on Aegina and at Acronauplion. Basically, these successive withdrawals from people and from reality have been caused by his manifest anti-Party feelings and his frustrated personal ambition, characteristics which have finally driven him into opposing the Party. Within Markos Vafiadis there has always been a neurotic conviction that he is undervalued and persecuted by the Party. . . .

This masterpiece was kept entirely under wraps for the time being. On paper and in the partisans' minds Markos was still head of the Democratic Army, whose ranks of sacrificial victims were hardly aware of the havoc wrought by successive inquisitions. Zachariadis announced that the Vitsi positions were impregnable and, free at last from most of the 'bad Communists' who had been degrading that victorious incarnation of

[1] *Neos Kosmos.*

dogma, he threw the Democratic Army once again into the task of conquering a capital.

Things were moving very fast. The partisans were conducting a positional war and attacking urban centres. They would experience more purges before the shifting fortunes of the Cold War put them out of their misery, crowning all their other sacrifices with the offhand sentence of the Great Allies.

ZACHARIADIS'S CAMPAIGNS

While the Political Bureau was reading Markos's letter, the Democratic Army Eighteenth Brigade was attacking the town of Siatista, which it held for twenty-four hours. At about the same time a big consignment of arms was sent to the Peloponnese to help the peninsula's andartes to move to the 'higher stage' as recommended by the Central Committee. The caïque carrying them was intercepted by a government Navy vessel; one month later its 1,500 rifles, 100 machine-guns, its thousand anti-tank mines and large supplies of explosives, would be sorely missed by 3,000 partisans trapped between Mani and Olympia.

On 1 December a wave of 1,000 andartes was stopped in the outskirts of Serres by a deluge of napalm. They withdrew leaving 183 dead.

Zachariadis was busy rewriting History once again, and wanted his revenge. The formation of the first Provisional Government had been marked by the failed attempt to take Konitsa. The new Democratic Army would expunge the shameful memory: on 11 December – almost the anniversary – 2,000 partisans descended on Karditsa. All the approaches likely to be used by governmental reinforcements were blocked and the bridge on the Trikkala-Larisa road destroyed. The Democratic Army entered the town and managed to hold it for two days. When a governmental brigade managed to dislodge them after an eighteen-hour battle, the democratic forces retreated along the Agrafa, pushing five hundred new recruits in front of them.

On the night of 22 December 1948 three Democratic Army brigades besieged Edessa and Naousa, on the road between Florina and Salonika. Edessa held out, but the partisans occupied Naousa for three days. They left again on the 26th with sixty recruits, food supplies and a large quantity of medical supplies taken from the local hospital's stores. Encouraged by this success, Zachariadis ordered another attack on the town on the night of 11–12 January 1949. Democratic forces recaptured the town and held it for another three days. They retreated in good order at dawn on the 15th, through an opportune blizzard that obliterated their tracks; this time, some six hundred recruits accompanied them more or less willingly along the Mountain road.

The government army had by now launched Operation Pigeon in the Peloponnese; the democratic forces at Erymanthos and Chelmos suffered the first attacks on 3 January, but managed to avoid a direct confrontation until 20 January, when they were trapped on Parnon. The government forces secured the surrounding district and sent for their special mountain units. The tissue of the insurrection had been stretched very thin by the successive northward concentrations of partisan forces in Central Greece; the isolated Peloponnese Democratic Army had not received its arms shipment from the north. The small units which managed to find their way through the government net round Parnon had no alternative but to vanish into the landscape and do their best to defend themselves until the end of April.

In the north, Zachariadis's Supreme War Council was jubilant over the double victory at Naousa, for which all the credit went to Major-General Vlantas. Zachariadis and his men were carried away by recent developments.

The democratic forces of Roumeli found themselves at the gates of Karpenisi once again. After a violent attack, launched on the night of 19–20 January and lasting until the morning of the 21st, they took the town and held it for eighteen days.

THE FIFTH PLENUM

The moment had come for Zachariadis to come out into the open with the principles he had been imposing from behind the scenes for more than a year. The Fifth Plenum, which met from 30 January onward at the top of Vitsi, was totally dominated by his personality and the zeal of his followers.

Zachariadis, Ioannidis and Vlantas had been in Sofia for the last week in January, attending the Fifth Congress of the Bulgarian Communist Party. Since Tito's condemnation by the Cominform, Zachariadis had been preparing to make pledges to Dimitrov which were almost certain to revive one of the KKE's oldest internal conflicts. The Kutvists of the thirties, fresh from Stalin's universities, had ended by abandoning the Comintern's revolutionary line on the Balkans, which held that the KKE should support the national claims of the Macedonian Slavic minorities:

not only had the policy clashed with Greek national feeling, but it would also have had little chance of winning decisive support from a province inhabited by 1,500,000 Greeks and only 80,000 Slavs. The problem therefore remained in the shadows until January 1949, when Zachariadis dusted off the old banner brought back from Moscow twenty years earlier. Now that Tito was suddenly infected with every kind of ideological pestilence, the revival of Macedonian claims which lent themselves so exactly to the furtherance of Bulgarian ambitions could only be an offering to Dimitrov. On another level it suggested a return to a lost orthodoxy, with which Zachariadis still hoped, perhaps, to seduce the high priests of the Kremlin. Lastly, the new line meant that NOF (the Macedonian Autonomist Movement in Greece), which was supporting the insurrection, could expect wider representation in the leadership structures. Zachariadis wrote later: 'This change made it possible for us to mobilize the Macedonian Slavs and put a stop to Tito's efforts at division and subversion.'[1] In reality, however, the mobilization of the Slav-speaking Macedonians simply stirred up certain spectres from the past which had never brought the KKE anything but bad luck.

The Fifth Plenum was notable for restoring an antediluvian orthodoxy to its full youthful vigour. Zachariadis used strange, spell-like formulae to exorcize the whole of the country's recent history. Dogma triumphed all along the line. During the talks it was casually announced that Markos and Chrysa Hajivasiliou had retired for health reasons. Chrysa, who was married to Rousos, was in fact suffering from leukaemia. A leader of the Athens underground organization, she had often been the only member of the Political Bureau to stand up against Zachariadis's brutal authoritarianism; she now began her long agony in total isolation. Ioannidis replaced Markos as head of the Provisional Government. There was nobody left but Karageorgis to oppose Zachariadis's strategic principles, which were forcibly reaffirmed during the Plenum:

... Firstly: to continue waging a war of attrition without respite ..., to carry the war into the towns and settlements as part of an overall strategy of large-scale offensive operations, partisan attacks and raids ..., to solve the manpower problem by increasing recruitment and cutting losses ..., to improve the efficiency of both cadres and fighters by means of intensive training and political education. Secondly: to smash the enemy's offensives in the Peloponnese, Roumeli and Thessaly, to make a bloody riposte to the enemy's forthcoming attack on Grammos and Vitsi, follow this up with a strategic counteroffensive to

[1] Zachariadis.

push the enemy back still further, and mount a broad manoeuvre to re-invade and liberate Epirus.

All these glowing visions were endorsed unanimously by the righteous chorus. On 8 February the insurgent radio and the KKE press informed the fighting troops of Markos's departure for health reasons, a whole year after Zachariadis had first gagged him. The following announcement was attributed to him:

My state of health, which has deteriorated since the battle of Mount Grammos, has forced me to give up my duties as President of the Government of Free Greece and Commander-in-Chief of the Democratic Army. . . . Our enemies will seek to exploit my resignation, but they will be silenced by the victories that lie ahead of us.

Latching onto a matter whose broad outlines had been apparent for some considerable time, the international press began gossiping about the rumours that Markos had been executed after Grammos. Under the headline 'Moscow does not want another Tito in Greece', *Le Monde* concluded: 'With Markos liquidated and the Stalinists firmly in control of the rebellion, it is most unlikely that Tito, who has already refused to allow a representative of the Greek Communists to attend the Skopje Congress, will maintain a benevolent or even neutral attitude.'

For the moment, however, the KKE's line on Yugoslavia remained secret, and Tito made no radical changes to his position on the Democratic Army.

Zachariadis had his eye on Bulkes: it was time to put the camp in some sort of order. Pechtasidis, who had served him unwisely and only too well, was becoming rather an inconvenient witness, a fine example of the man who knew too much. Pechtasidis sensed the threat and let it be known that he might, if pressed, inform Stalin of one or two juicy items concerning Zachariadis and Ioannidis. It was not a prudent move; at the end of February the Political Bureau sent a squad of five men, led by a certain Spourchitis, to terminate his career. More than five hundred partisans are thought to have been liquidated on the islands of the Danube during Pechtasidis's tenure of office. It sometimes happens that political zeal as exceptional as that shown by Pechtasidis is similarly poorly rewarded.

THE LAST WINTER

On 8 February, as the insurgent radio announced Markos's retirement, governmental reinforcements were entering Karpenisi. The Democratic

Army brigade which had occupied the town for the past eighteen days disappeared into the mountains. Regular forces followed hard on its heels, beginning a chase that lasted three months.

The Government Army also spent the latter half of the winter in reorganizing. On 25 February, the American Mission put an end to the hesitation and squabbling of rival persons, coteries and pressure groups, by imposing General Papagos as Commander-in-Chief. The National Defence Council was at last reduced to a reasonable size, and immediately found itself less directly influenced by the Byzantine political intrigues which had always sapped its powers of decision. Papagos, who had followed the 1948 campaign as an observer, reorganized unit commands from top to bottom in preparation for carrying out coordinated operations in specific predetermined sectors, without the distraction of time limits: no zone would be considered secure until it had been completely evacuated, sewn up with a double or treble military garrison strategically placed, and finally 'cleared' by the LOK. Papagos's new methods were first systematically applied in the Peloponnese, with Operation Pigeon.

FLORINA

Zachariadis, very full of himself after the military success at Naousa and his total political victory in the Fifth Plenum, was preparing a crushing, irrefutable demonstration.

On the night of 11-12 February 3,500 partisans attacked the town of Florina, the first step on the road to Salonika: Florina, Edessa, Yannitsa, Salonika, steps to the conquest of northern Greece through the masterly application of theory.

Using almost all of its artillery, the Democratic Army laid down a preparatory fire from 3 a.m. until dawn. The first infantry assault captured the southern part of the town, but the Democratic Army could get no further. Florina was the headquarters of an Army Corps, and the governmental army had stationed a large number of auxiliaries there in addition to the regular troops: Zachariadis had underestimated the strength of these auxiliaries, who played an active part in the town's defence. All the surrounding high ground was in the hands of a second brigade of partisans. The approach of government reinforcements was delayed by continuous snowfall, but aircraft arrived at once and voided tons of napalm over the attackers' positions.

The Democratic Army held on to the southern part of the town for the whole of the next day but could make no further progress. On the third day, as reinforcements formed up in their rear, the partisans made no attempt to push forward but simply held their existing positions. The units posted on the surrounding high ground began to give way. Vlantas, who was running the whole operation on the infallible principles of the new strategy, was gradually losing control of his units. On the fourth day the offensive collapsed and the partisans began to pull out; small commandos of saboteurs carried out a few last diversionary operations to cover the general withdrawal.

One of these commandos was led by Dimitris Flogas. It penetrated the enemy lines and then, owing to poor coordination and the fluid situation, lost contact with the main body of the democratic forces: the government forces closed in around Flogas and his men. Most of his men managed to break out of the trap by splitting up into small groups, but Flogas, who had been hit in the belly and was bleeding heavily, stayed behind until they had nearly all reached safety. When it was his turn to leave, he discovered that his legs would not carry him. He had six crates of explosives and some rockets placed around him and then, doubled up in a pool of blood, covered the retreat of the last of his men with a machine rifle.

Flogas was alone with his crates in a deserted square. A moment of silence. Soldiers appeared, fifteen of them, edging towards him, gaining confidence, walking across the open space towards him. When they were a few yards away Flogas picked up a mortar shell, primed it, rose to his feet for the last time and flung the shell at one of the crates. Everything moving in the square was blasted to shreds. A big, bloody star spread across the dust.

The Democratic Army retreated along the Pisoderi valley, leaving 743 dead behind it. Operation Pigeon was drawing to a close in the Peloponnese. The governmental forces were uncontested masters of the peninsula by 25 March. At the Vitsi HQ discipline was tightened following the defeat. Officials wandered about looking for scapegoats and arranging for 'traitors' to be chastised. New purges were in the air. Since the Yannoulis affair, certain of the legal cadres had been refusing to march in step, and the Supreme War Council decided to do something about it. A few days after Florina, Beloyanis, commandant of the Ninth Division, received a telephone call from General Vlantas, and a few minutes later rushed agitatedly into the divisional attorney's office.

'HQ just phoned. Comrade Katsaros is to be arrested, court-martialled and shot. They say he tried to kiss a girl.'

Katsaros was a jurist who felt strongly about certain basic principles and believed in the independence of the law. He had had occasion to read one or two files whose contents were not in strict accordance with the spirit of the law, and had not restrained himself from letting people know what he thought of them. Beloyanis was extremely reluctant to court-martial a man over a trifle just because HQ had condemned him in advance. He asked the attorney for his advice: 'What do you think of it, as a jurist?'

'It's a ridiculous story. He hasn't even committed any offense. I suppose we could reprimand him.'

'Try to straighten it out. Why don't you go and see this girl.'

The victim was twenty years old. She would not have behaved any differently if she had been acting under orders. She snarled with Eumenidean fury: 'This Katsaros needs a lesson. He tried to kiss me by force.'

'We'll give him a good talking-to,' answered the attorney soothingly.

'Too easy. He deserves to be court-martialled.'

Beloyanis decided to do nothing for the time being and let things cool down. Three days later HQ phoned again; it was Vlantas.

'I thought I ordered you to deal with Katsaros? I've just heard that he's still under arrest. Try to hurry it up.'

Beloyanis and the magistrate called at the jail. The criminal was unwell and incapable of organizing his defence. The next communication from the Staff was a written order: 'You will try Katsaros before a court martial within two days.'

It would not have been prudent to delay any longer. Katsaros's last chance was to be properly tried and defended. An old lawyer called Zakas was asked to head the tribunal. The legal cadre tried a last visit to the plaintiff.

'Courts martial pass very severe sentences, you know. Won't you forgive him?'

'No, out of the question.'

Katsaros was sentenced to ten years in prison. Two days later the divisional attorney passed Vlantas's jeep in the street. The General ordered the vehicle to stop.

'How come Katsaros only got ten years?'

'Nothing to do with me, it was the court's decision.'

Vlantas leapt out of the jeep waving a pistol.

'If you don't order his execution immediately I'll kill *you*, right here.'

The official kept calm.

'Kill me, then. I'm not going to order Katsaros shot over that piece of nonsense.'

Vlantas uttered a few more threats and departed. The next day the whole of the Ninth Division's legal service was dismantled. Its members were dispersed and singled out for persecution. They were replaced by a team obedient to the Supreme War Council, which was charged with liquidating the 'traitors' responsible for the defeats of Edessa and Florina. Two men, Skotidas and Giorgiadis, had dared to speak out against the Council's plan during the briefing before the attack on the town.

Skotidas was dismissed. Giorgiadis paid a higher price to satisfy his accusers; he was a former ELAS kapetanios, a reserve officer who knew guerilla ways, the very incarnation of a mentality that had to be stamped out. The court martial accused him of losing a battle planned by the Supreme War Council, convicted him of treason and had him executed without a moment's delay.

Neither the members of the Provisional Government, nor any of the assemblies, had any part in these decisions. Three men, Zachariadis, Vlantas and Bartzotas, constituted the nucleus of the Supreme Council and kept the power to themselves. The partisans were simply presented with the fait accompli. They still trusted the Party leadership.

ROUMELI

After the retreat from Karpenisi, the Democratic Army's Second Division, 1,500 partisans under Hermes, made its way towards the north through the mountains of Roumeli, followed every step of the way by government forces. Zachariadis's men were on a long march for the second winter running. When it reached Metsovo, the detachment found itself practically surrounded, with only the narrowest of corridors through which 1,500 men, women and children had to tiptoe during the night. So close were the enemy positions that they had to make no more noise than a fifteen-man commando preparing a surprise attack. The whole column was mortally threatened by the fragile but potentially disastrous presence of a baby, the child of a captain and a woman andarte. The infant was crying, after the manner of its kind, and refusing to go to sleep. As the column approached the most critical point on its route the unfortunate parents saw themselves faced with the choice of staying behind and falling into the closing governmental trap, or abandoning their child. During a short rest, an unspoken question showed in every face. Nobody dared look at the parents struggling with their impossible decision. Suddenly, as inexplicably as they had started, the child's wails stopped. The column moved forward again, stretching out into single file and walking along a stream whose gentle babbling drowned the small sounds of feet on pebbles.

When most of the troop had passed, Hermes took the sleeping child in his arms and brought up the rear. The small creature slept on his shoulder, sensitive and unpredictable as a rusty bomb: a sudden jolt, a nightmare, would be enough to set it off and unleash a massacre. For two hours the 1,500 andartes slipped through the meshes of the enemy net. The bomb did not go off. The trek had started in mid-January. The column did not reach Grammos until the end of March.

Diamantis was operating further south with the remains of the Second Division. He avoided every attempt at encirclement until the end of June, when he was finally trapped on a peak and died in the last battle the Democratic Army fought in Roumeli.

For the time being Zachariadis was having better luck in the north, where he was busy organizing the reconquest of Grammos. Despite everything, he was preparing to carry out from there, for the second time, his infallible positional strategy, ensuring that the governmental forces would find the Democratic Army waiting for them, all present and correct, when they arrived at Grammos and Vitsi for the big summer rendezvous.

THE NEW PROVISIONAL GOVERNMENT

The NOF Second Congress met on Grammos on 25 March 1949. In accordance with the decisions of the KKE Fifth Plenum, the Macedonian movement called on all militants to support the Democratic Army's struggle. On 3 April the Provisional Government was reshuffled.

Partsalidis got the job of Prime Minister and Ioannidis the Vice-Premiership. Petros Rousos became Foreign Minister; Vlantas, Minister of War; Bartzotas, the Interior; Stringos, Economics; Karageorgis, War Supply; Papadimitris (Agrarian Party), Agriculture; Savidis (Agrarian Party), Cooperatives; Porfyrogenis, Justice; Avdelidis (Agrarian Party), the National Economy; Kokkalis (Independent), Health and Education; Tsapakidis (Agrarian Party), National Assistance; Mitrovski (President of NOF), Supply; Vournas (Agrarian Party), Transport; and Gotsev (NOF) was made Under-Secretary for National Minorities.

It was a paper government. In practice it was the Supreme War Council that made the law. At its head were Zachariadis, Ioannidis, Bartzotas, Vlantas and Gousias. Karageorgis was kept on the Council for the sake of form, along with Koliyannis, Gouzelis, Loulis and Erythriadis; Gotsev was brought in to represent the NOF. The new Provisional Government's first statement proclaimed:

... Anglo-American Imperialism needs Greece as a bridgehead and an operational base for the new massacre of humanity which it is now preparing. On the one hand, it is sub-contracting Greece to its Greek lackeys, especially the northern regions which it has already plundered, while on the other it is conducting a lying campaign against us, based on the alleged danger to Macedonia in our present cooperation with NOF...

Our victory is the victory of freedom and independence, the victory of peace and economic recovery, the victory of people's democracy and of socialism.

Everyone to arms! All for victory!

Any meaning in this stirring piece of rhetoric crumbled to nothing against the realities of the situation. The KKE's new Macedonian policy served only to isolate the Democratic Army in public opinion and to ensure that the final battles would be limited to the Vitsi/Grammos region.

Everyone knew that the approaching summer would bring a new governmental offensive, and that the spring clearing operations in the Peloponnese, Roumeli and Thessaly had left only one major target; the Democratic Army was nevertheless gradually returning to its former positions on Grammos. Zachariadis went on repeating that the partisans entrenched on impregnable Vitsi, soon to become the graveyard of monarcho-fascism, were within rifle range of victory.

All these pious utterances now seem to have been woven into a monstrous plot. The movement which the isolated Tito had been supporting through fair weather and foul was now revealing itself more clearly every day as a pawn of the Cominform; obviously Tito could not continue indefinitely to run useless risks for Zachariadis's insurrection. An event which even the most elementary logic would have seen to be inevitable was soon to be presented as an act of betrayal, a 'stab in the back' inflicted on a triumphant revolution by Tito.

The Berlin crisis came to an end without provoking the hardening of Soviet foreign policy which might have brought some diplomatic support to the Greek partisans. Zachariadis, apparently indifferent to such nuances, went on preparing grimly for battle – or for the final liquidation of the revolution – from the two last strongholds of orthodoxy, Grammos and Vitsi.

ATHENS

At the beginning of April 1949 another ministerial reshuffle purged the Sofoulis government of various characters who had been involved in embezzlement scandals or inconvenienced the American services in other ways. The death sentence passed on Manolis Glezos, the national hero famous for tearing the German flag down from the Acropolis at the very beginning of the Resistance, aroused noisy but short-lived international protests. A few days later the Trade Union leader Paparigas was found hanging in his prison cell. The government, which scented victory and was not in a conciliatory mood, handed out heavy sentences on all sides. There was, however, some sign of change on the international scene. On 3 May the Provisional Government issued a peace proposal, the twenty-first to emerge from the Mountain since 1946. Gromyko discussed the Greek problem with McNeil just before the opening in Paris of the Big Four conference on Germany. The *Neue Züricher Zeitung* wrote: 'He (McNeil) found that his interlocutor, though still unwilling to admit that the guerillas could be made to see reason with no more than a word from Moscow, has the backing of two top-level mediators, Dr Evatt and Mr Trygve Lie, both of whom have been struggling for some years to establish the basis for a settlement.'

Porfyrogenis, now Foreign Minister in the Provisional Government, wrote to Dr Evatt (President of the UN General Assembly) as follows:

We learn with great joy that you have renewed your efforts to establish peace in Greece. We always have been, and still are, ready to cooperate with all our strength in ending the war in our country. We beg you to let us know what preconditions you believe to be necessary to ensure peace in Greece, and also the measures most likely, in your opinion, to help your initiative to succeed.

We ask you to accept this assurance that we will do everything possible to achieve a satisfactory outcome.

The Sofoulis-Tsaldaris government violently condemned Porfyrogenis's 'manoeuvre', rejecting 'what it calls foreign interference in Greek internal affairs with a haughty pride which seems a little threadbare in view of the American Mission's role in Athens' (*Le Monde*).

Some rumours, which were later given a great deal of exposure, suggested that an earlier overture made by Tito had been wrecked by the Tsaldaris government. Walter Lippmann wrote in the *New York Times*:

This is not the first attempt to resolve the Greek civil war by diplomatic means, but the second. The previous round of secret negotiations, between Marshal Tito and Mr Tsaldaris, was broken off when the latter leaked some information to the London *Daily Mail* – nobody seems to know for certain whether the leak was calculated or merely stupid. Tito, who is in a delicate situation, could not risk an additional quarrel with his own more extreme Communist supporters, and was forced to withdraw. It now seems that Dr Clementis (the Czechoslovakian Foreign Minister), who still has some influence in Communist circles, could have picked up the ball that Tito dropped, thus allowing Mr Porfyrogenis back into the race, no doubt with Vyshinsky's approval. It would appear from all this that the Kremlin would like to be credited with the relaxation in the atmosphere of the Foreign Ministers' Conference which would follow a peaceful settlement in Greece.

All this achieved nothing, in the final analysis, except a further strengthening of the Cominform's case against Tito, while the Soviet overtures ran up against the sovereign indignation of the Athens government.

General Plastiras, seeing that the government had no intention of adopting a more constructive attitude, announced that he was going to Paris to do what he could on the fringes of the Conference. The Athens authorities refused him a passport and placed him under house arrest.

The Last Act

The scene was set for the last act, with the Democratic Army wiped out in the Peloponnese, the Second Division dissolving in Roumeli and the First Division retreating northways through Thessaly. No aid could be expected from the Soviets, who by now were openly in favour of lancing the Greek abscess. Tito, whose mind was occupied with Trieste and who had the Cominform baying at his heels, was in no position to increase his commitment. The Macedonian policy laid down at the KKE's Sixth Plenum was creating new divisions among the Greeks (it had been hatched solely to cut the ground from under Tito's feet, but had failed completely to modify the Soviet posture at the Paris Conference).

In an isolation resembling quarantine, the Greek partisans doggedly

went on with the job of reconquering Grammos. They were gathering for
the slaughter. The apparent successes of May and June, won while the
governmental forces were concentrating their ponderous strength on the
final target, were helping to sustain a costly illusion: on the spot, people
were seized with euphoria. The general enthusiasm overwhelmed foreign
visitors and inspired poets and singers, whose lyricism further inflated the
price of an acre of stones, payable in blood before autumn.

Simone Théry, a member of the French Communist Party, had returned
from the mountains in 1948 with voluminous, admiring notes on Markos.
Shortly after her book appeared its hero was suddenly afflicted with all
kinds of ideological scabs and the whole edition was pulped by the watch-
dogs of orthodoxy.

At the end of May 1949 Paul Eluard, Yves Farge, Jean-Maurice Herman
and Bassis all passed through Free Greece on their way to Prague. On
Grammos they witnessed some of the victories of this army of adolescents;
they were carried away by the experience of seeing twenty-five year old
women leading battalions of montagnards into combat, and began to
believe in the reality of victory. Wearing a forage cap with earmuffs,
something between a Phrygian cap and a shepherd's bonnet, Eluard put
his lips to a microphone and delivered an impassioned appeal, echoed and
distorted by two hundred loudspeakers, to the governmental units
stationed at the foot of the mountain:

Sons of Greece,
I am speaking to you, the peasants, workers and intellectuals forced to serve
in the army of a government which does not represent you. Firstly, I have come
here to see it with my own eyes, prompted by no other consideration than my
personal concern for peace and my love of truth.

. . . I entreat you to consider, from where you stand on the side of the jailers
and hangmen, all these men who are paying with their blood for that justice
people are always talking about. I ask you to remember the horror of Makronisos, of your prisons in which thousands of patriots, sure of their eventual
victory, look forward daily to torture or death.

Everywhere here, both at the front and behind the lines, I have seen your
prisoners treated with the greatest respect for their humanity. They receive the
same food as soldiers of the Greek Democratic Army.

These prisoners, who are growing more numerous every day, are offered the
choice of returning home or joining the Democratic Army. Most of them choose
the second alternative.

This is the first time in modern history that an army has felt strong enough,
certain enough of victory, to show such confidence in Man.

It is also the first time that an army has sought peace the more eagerly as its forces have increased. The only victory it aspires to is unity for all its fellow-countrymen and an end to the miseries of a war imposed by the Anglo-Saxon Imperialists.

Throughout the entire world simple people are struggling for peace. The brave and glorious Greek people stands in the vanguard of this struggle.

Eluard had seen only the light shining from the partisans' eyes; like them, he was still blind to the other facet of reality. He visited the Democratic Army regiment commanded by Paleologos, somewhere high up on Grammos. The unit had just received from headquarters a decoration for one Andreas Giorgos, killed the previous day. Paleologos decided to present the medal to Eluard, and did so at an impromptu ceremony in front of his men. Eluard, deeply moved, declared as he accepted the decoration: 'This is an immense honour for me, and it is also a duty. The name Giorgos will be made known to every Frenchman; it will never be forgotten.'

Within a few weeks the entire world would be trying to forget Greece and a vast silence, maintained from every side, would descend crushingly on its history. Meanwhile Eluard moved on to the Prague Congress where the Communist parties of Czechoslovakia, Hungary and Poland heaped the customary epithets on Tito's head and decided to sever commercial relations with Yugoslavia.

Tito was completely isolated. In his Pola discourse of 10 July 1949 he announced his intention of progressively closing Yugoslavia's frontiers to the Greek partisans. The Cominform had found someone to carry the can at last, and washed its hands. The Athens Governmental Army launched Operation Torch.

ZACHARIADIS'S SUMMER RENDEZVOUS

Diamantis's death on 21 June had left Roumeli definitively 'cleared'. At the beginning of July, before approaching Vitsi and Grammos, the governmental forces launched an operation in the Kaimakchalan mountains, along the Yugoslav frontier to the east of Vitsi. 1,500 partisans resisted for a week, but gave up the region on 28 July after losing four hundred men. Vitsi was now cut off from the last remaining Democratic forces to the east, which were stationed in the Beles Mountains along the Bulgarian frontier. Operation Torch proper would have its hands free to concentrate on the last bastion.

Papagos's plan envisaged a diversionary attack on Grammos followed by a general offensive on Vitsi, after which his forces would fold back towards Grammos from the north and south to close the pocket. Six governmental divisions were to take part in the operation, while two more divisions supported by two independent brigades were sent to annihilate the Beles stronghold, now isolated from the bulk of the democratic forces.

Zachariadis had 8,000 partisans at Vitsi and 5,000 high up on Grammos. The first diversionary attack started on 5 August. The Government Army leaned steadily on the defenders of Grammos for a week, emptying the last villages in the region as they did so. On 10 August the three divisions of the 1st Government Army Corps turned to face Vitsi and, after an intensive bombardment, attacked simultaneously at eight points spread out from north to south.

The partisans offered their usual kamikaze resistance among the napalm-blackened crags. The fighting was so bitter that a few Albanian soldiers came to help the partisans of their own accord; this force, improvized for a brief forty-eight hours, was the only 'International Brigade' of the Greek revolution. On 14 August, through a deluge of bombs, the partisans tried to counterattack in the direction of Konitsa; they were driven back but returned to their previous positions, which they held all the next day. On the 16th they had to withdraw, leaving 997 dead strewn around Zachariadis's impregnable fortifications. Of the six brigades that pulled out, only one was almost intact; the others retreated in disorganized tatters. About 4,000 exhausted partisans reached Grammos to brace themselves for the second shock.

Elsewhere, the Third Government Army Corps hurled itself at the Beles mountains on 19 August. The whole air force supported this operation before turning its attention back to Grammos. The partisans' positions were untenable, but they held out for four days before the 1,000 survivors crossed the Bulgarian frontier: the beginning of the exodus.

Now Papagos could throw everything at Grammos. The Americans reinforced his air power by lending him fifty-one Curtiss Helldivers, the latest thing in ground support aircraft, with machine-guns, cannon and two tons of bombs which they could place with pinpoint accuracy. The final deluge began on 25 August in the presence of King Paul, who graciously consented to observe the bonfire. Outnumbering the partisans ten to one and commanding a firepower seldom if ever seen before, the regular forces took the peaks along the frontier one by one. The last symbol vanished when Grammos itself fell on the 27th. On the 28th governmental forces sealed off Starias and Baroukas, the two main passes through to Albania.

For three days longer the partisans defended their universe of chaos, making the enemy pay dear for every inch of rock, fighting artillery with booby traps, firing their Bren guns at aeroplanes and dying by the hundred after losing their last illusions. Kamenik, the last stronghold, fell at five in the morning on 30 August. 8,000 men managed to reach Albania before the governmental pincer clanged shut. It was over, finished. By ten in the morning Grammos was silent as the grave.

The last surviving partisan groups were being hunted from pillar to post, jinking and zigzagging like hares as they ran for the frontier. Albania, which was still officially at war with Greece, had taken an anti-Tito position and now found itself alone facing the whole Greek governmental army, which was massed along its frontier. On 26 August, at the beginning of the battle of Grammos, Enver Hoxha had made a statement undertaking to disarm any Greek partisans who crossed into Albania. On 5 September the Tirana papers announced that Albanian troops had disarmed 127 Greek rebels during that week. Bulgaria made similar pledges in its turn. Finally, on 1 October, the Soviet Union rejoined the Balkan Commission and issued various platonic appeals for reconciliation.

Radio Free Greece announced the end of the fighting on Sunday, 16 October:

The Greek Provisional Government is ceasing hostilities 'to prevent the total destruction of Greece'. The Democratic Army has not laid its weapons aside, but has suspended its operations for the time being. This should not be taken to mean that the Greeks are giving up the struggle for the rights of the people. The Anglo-American Imperialists and their monarcho-fascist agents would be mistaken if they assumed that the struggle was over and that the Democratic Army had ceased to exist.

Although the war was over and the Left defeated, the Athens government used the tone of this declaration as a pretext for further massacres. For obvious reasons connected with the flow of American aid, the Athens leaders refused to accept the reality of Zachariadis's ceasefire.

158,000 Greeks died in the civil war. If this figure is added to the total of victims of the German/Italian occupation, a tenth of the Greek population had perished since the beginning of the Second World War. 3,500 people had been condemned to death and 1,500 executed. Between 50,000 and 100,000 Greeks crossed the frontier and took refuge in the People's

Democracies. But even that was not the end; the way forward was blocked. The counter-revolution was under way. It is still going on.

Just for the record, the Athens government did, once, announce the end of the war: in July 1962, thirteen years after the last battle on Grammos. But even this did not bring the long night to an end. Caught between two giants, torn apart between the armoured West and an abstract revolution, the Greek people had its victory stolen before its eyes and lost all control of its own history which, suddenly, took on a quite different appearance. This is still happening. The true face of the Greek people has been stolen and is hidden from the world.

Epilogue

THE LOST GENERATION

'We have won. Communism fell at Vitsi and Grammos; now it's going to eat dirt at Makronisos.' The fingers of his right hand thrust into the opening in his tunic, Xirouchakis, licensed specialist in redemption, was softening up stubborn elements.

A long, bare rock lying a few kilometres offshore from the Temple of Poseidon in the cool air-current from the Aegean, Makronisos has been used since Antiquity for the purpose for which the laws of man, and the harsh forgetfulness of nature, make it especially suitable. It is one of the oldest military prisons in Greece, the accursed arch-jail, purified by the wind and patrolled by sharks. There were 13,000 men on the island, divided into three brigades. The Third Brigade was composed of political exiles who had been arriving since January 1948 from Limnos, Ikaria and Agios Eustratios.

In February 1949 the authorities started a big new 'persuasion' campaign. They dissolved the Third Brigade, which numbered about 10,000 men, and distributed its members between the other two brigades, which contained most of the 'penitents'. Theos, Nikiforos, Gozakis and 3,000 prisoners aged under thirty were sent to the First Brigade and immediately subjected to forty-eight hours of torture. After the 'treatment' there were 17 dead, 30 attempted suicides, 600 bone fractures and 250 mental cases.

Sarafis, Gavrilidis and a hundred ELAS officers were among those sent to the Second Brigade, where they were divided into small groups and taken to hear Xirouchakis's welcoming speech.

'You could be killed out of hand; we have the right to do it. If we let you live, it's because we have decided to make little nationalists of you. We stop at nothing. We are the winners, you are the losers: hard luck on the losers.

'You are probably wondering why we've put you in the Second Brigade. It's because the time has come to crush you, as you were squashed at

Vitsi. You submit or you die. The army runs things here. We, the army, represent everything, force, the State, power, the government; the lot. We have all the rights and all the power and we want you to know it. We have the right and the ability to exterminate you to the last man, and nobody would even ask us why we'd done it. Now go and have a little chat with your former comrades who have become nationalists. Either you return with your declaration in your hand, or you die. If you want to believe we're doing you a favour, then it's a favour. If you'd rather think of it as a provocation, it's a provocation. If you decide it's a moral rape, very well, it's a moral rape.'

Then the new arrivals were dragged away and tortured. Xirouchakis got a few signatures.

On the night of 8 December 1949 the prisoners were woken by the thundering of footsteps. The guards were charging the tents and clubbing them to death through the fabric. Beatings continued over the next few days; on the evening of 8 December, those who were still unconvinced were gathered together again.

'Bulgarians outside, hurry it up darlings.'

A man called Panagopoulos, who had recently had both feet amputated, was beaten and kicked until he managed to stand on the newly-healed stumps. Seven hundred prisoners were taken to an amphitheatre built by the soldiers. After sitting through another of Xirouchakis's elegant little pep-talks, they were dragged into trenches ten at a time. Screams came out of the trenches. An east wind was blowing and the howling of tortured men could be heard distinctly from Lavrion, ten kilometres away across the water, until dawn.

A hundred or so of the seven hundred victims allowed themselves to be redeemed. The others refused to sign and were placed behind barbed wire: Sarafis, Hajimichalis and the officers in one compound and Iliou, Koulambas, Gavrilidis and the political cadres in another. The men were divided into three categories according to their physical strength, and were set to breaking stones day and night for a road leading nowhere. Sofoulis had died at the age of eighty-eight on 24 June 1949. The old Liberal had died in harness after presiding faithfully over the civil war since September 1947.

The fighting over, the Americans felt that it was time for a new election: they were not eager to install Papagos, the victor of Grammos, as a sort of cut-price Franco. Greece started along a path which 'offers the original spectacle of a "democracy" dominated by the spirit of fascism, which maintains the institutions while abolishing, in practice, every constitutional guarantee of the rights of man and of the citizens'.[1]

The first elections after the civil war were held on 5 March 1950. The Liberals and Centrists won a majority, but their group was split by rivalries between Plastiras and the parties of Venizelos and Papandreou. The old general favoured a general amnesty, while his partners were fiercely opposed to anything of the kind. Venizelos, with British support, formed a government in alliance with the Right; it lasted a month. The Americans were determined that certain forms should be respected, and on 15 April they imposed a coalition led by Plastiras. In order to take office, however, the Prime Minister had to renounce the greater part of his initial programme, and many prosecutions and some executions took place in the following years, including the famous Beloyanis trial in 1952. It was also during this period that, despite Plastiras's honest but fumbling efforts, the emergency regulations were laid down which still control Red-hunting throughout the country to this day.

The Greek government had embarked on a costly crusade which had to be paid for in hard currency. The Americans were always there to sign the bill. In the fullness of time repression became an institution, its complex arsenal of legal and para-legal methods stretching from the police horse-play practised in the countryside (e.g. exorbitant fines because a suspect's house is not painted white, because his dog was off its lead in a village where all the dogs run free, absurd but very expensive trials, and so on), through the emergency laws to the establishment of a compulsory 'certificate of civic responsibility'.

Law 509 of 29 December 1947, which outlawed the KKE, was extended by Law 1975 of 1951 which conferred the powers of a military tribunal on the appeal courts. Most trials continued to be held before military tribunals, however, as spying charges were dealt with under Law 375, promulgated in 1936 under the Metaxas dictatorship. Former partisans who could not be simply prosecuted for common-law offences (interpreted with great latitude by the authorities) were held to be spies because they had been 'agents of Bulgarian Pan-Slavism', and these cases had to be tried by courts martial.

The 'certificates of civic responsibility' were obtained from the police, who were usually all too ready to label people 'crypto-communists'. Based on another emergency law, No. 516 of 8 January 1948, they went well

---

[1] Ilias Iliou at a meeting of West European lawyers for the restoration of freedom in Greece, 26 May 1962.

beyond its original scope, which was only intended to cover candidates for public service. These certificates were soon required of anyone enrolling in the schools or universities, applicants for grants, for driving and hunting licences, pedlars' licences and often, in private enterprise, of applicants for the most menial jobs.

Every right inscribed in the Constitution, for example the freedom of the press or tenure of a civil service post, was counterbalanced by an emergency law which trampled down the appropriate safeguards. Eventually, in defiance of every principle maintaining the liberty of the individual, administrative deportation became an entrenched institution, and was often applied without the most elementary guarantees either of the right to appeal or of the duration of the sentence. This is the framework in which post-war legality was set up in Greece. A ludicrous but sinewy charade perpetuating despotism.

EXILE

Tens of thousands of Greeks banned for ever from their native country were living through a different form of tyranny abroad. From now on the KKE Central Committee was functioning in exile. Zachariadis, Bartzotas and Vlantas hurriedly shed the responsibility for the disasters and shared it out among the dissidents. Led by Partsalidis, a substantial group of militants was demanding explanations and an honest critique of the line the Party had been following for the past few years. A dialogue began at the Seventh Plenum, which met in Bulgaria on 14 May 1950, but Zachariadis stopped it by turning on Partsalidis:

There can be no right to criticize, no democracy, no freedom of expression for enemies of the Party, anti-Party elements who seek to use criticism and democracy to damage, weaken and liquidate the Party.[1]

Partsalidis kept his head and weathered the inevitable flood of epithets. Bartzotas called him a liar, Vlantas a Trotskyist, splittist and opportunist, and an unnamed political cadre who had no fear of words condemned him as an 'egotist corrupted by excessive reading and the study of mathematics'.

When the flow of invective petered out a resolution was passed 'unanimously'. It called on Greek Communists still inside the country to collaborate with legal organizations without disclosing their Party connections,

[1] Karageorgis.

and to carry out the Central Committee's directives on their own account. With the passage of time, these directives were to become increasingly restrictive and intransigent as the remnants of the dismantled organization risked slipping further and further out of Zachariadis's orthodox control.

The history of the KKE in the years to come would be remarkable for this conflict between the needs of the political struggle within the country and the dogmatic rigidity of the hierarchy, which had always leaned heavily towards revolutionary abstraction and was henceforward cut off from all reality. The war was over, but thousands of exiled Greek partisans who had lost everything on Grammos and Vitsi were exposed to Zachariadis's new purges.

On 6 June 1950 Karageorgis sent a letter to the Central Committee in which, like Markos a year earlier, he strongly criticized the decisions and methods of the Party. He protested against the 'unanimous' condemnation of the views of Markos and Chrysa Hajivasiliou by an assembly of lackeys, he protested against the insults heaped on Partsalidis, and he condemned in general terms the submissive spirit 'which, far from being any sort of proof of a monolithic Bolshevik unity . . . bears witness, rather, to a manifest political and ideological stagnation'. He demanded an objective critique of the line followed since the beginning of the world war, and the publication of all documents which might shed some light on the issues involved.

I note that Zachariadis led us to our first defeat through the agency of the men he promoted (Ioannidis, Siantos) and that he led us to our second defeat in person, in both cases by way of a sequence of errors permeating every level and every period of the Party's existence. I note also – and this is the worst thing of all – that the word 'self-criticism' does not exist in Comrade Zachariadis's vocabulary.[1]

Like Markos, Karageorgis was building a case against himself, and in due course his letter became 'Comrade Karageorgis's opportunist platform'. After the time of sackings and furtive liquidations, new purges were on the way to enliven the bitterness of exile. The war was over but the purges went on, reminiscent of exorcism ceremonies in their sinister passion to distort history.

The first broadside was fired at the Third Congress in October 1950. Siantos, Partsalidis, Markos Vafiadis and Karageorgis were expelled from the Party. Siantos and Markos, who were not present, were shot to pieces: Siantos's posthumous condemnation as a British agent and class enemy

[1] Karageorgis.

was supposed to put a final end to the history of EAM-ELAS. Zachariadis was holding a seance and venting his rage on phantoms. Some of the blame rebounded on Karageorgis and Partsalidis, but Markos, who was not there to defend himself, was saddled with most of the responsibility for the carnage and became 'an incompetent arriviste who has never been a real Communist'.

In a frenzy of exorcism the Central Committee named the traitors, monarchists and Titoists who, according to their indictments, had caused the last defeats by 'stabbing the revolution in the back'. 1,500 partisans, 1,500 exiled Greeks huddling miserably in Bulgaria after losing everything in the struggle, were added to the list of sacrificial victims.

This senseless fraud, carried out in the face of a people which had been fighting for eight years, defaced the future for many years to come. Reality, like dead beheaded Aris, had lost its face. The history of Greece was and is treated with vitriol, scarred and dissolved by both sides. It wants to be reborn; it has not stopped looking for its own image in the shifting mosaic so thoroughly obscured by the complementary impostures of the revolutionary order and the order of reaction.

Aftermath

History marks time.

Unified Democratic Left (EDA), supported and led by former members of EAM, created. It obtained 10·7% of the vote in elections held on 9 September 1951 in which it put up deportees and prisoners as candidates, ten of whom were elected, including Sarafis and Glezos. Venizelos sought coalition with the Right. Marshal Papagos, supported by the Americans, stayed in reserve. Plastiras governed with the aid of a very weak centrist majority. His amnesty projects got nowhere. 30 March 1952: Beloyannis executed.

US ambassador Peurefoy brought pressure to bear in the hope of bringing down the government and called the Greeks to the polls yet again, this time using the majority count which would favour Papagos. Plastiras, exhausted and helpless, also came out in favour of the majority count. The elections on 16 November 1953 ensured the triumph of Papagos. With 49·22% of the votes, he won 82·30% of the seats in the National Assembly.

1953–1956

A military agreement between Greece and the US institutionalized the presence of American forces on Greek territory.

Cypriot national demands hardened. Armed struggle opened by EOKA under the leadership of General Grivas, the founder of the extreme right-wing X Organization under the occupation.

Marshal Papagos died in October 1955. The Americans and the Palace imposed Constantine Karamanlis in his place. Karamanlis dissolved Papagos's party (Hellenic Assembly) and formed ERE (National Radical Union) which won a majority of the seats in elections held on 19 February 1956.

After being disqualified from parliament after their election in 1951, EDA representatives gained admittance. Sarafis, parliamentary deputy for Larisa, elected Secretary-General of EDA. Liberal opposition front won 44% of the vote. Karamanlis and the Americans seized the opportunity to point to the 'red peril' and extend the emergency measures.

FEBRUARY 1956–1958

Twentieth Congress of the Communist Party of the Soviet Union.

KKE Sixth Plenum criticized the line followed in recent years. The Lebanon and Caserta agreements were denounced as 'unjustifiable capitulations' and the 1946 election boycott is called a 'monstrous error'. But the basic report was presented by the six Cominform parties; the KKE was de-Stalinized from the outside, liberalized despite itself.

October 1957: Zachariadis expelled from the KKE. Bartzotas and Vlantas followed a few weeks later. The Cominform parties named the KKE's new General Secretary: Kostas Koliyannis.

Karageorgis, soon to be rehabilitated, was found to have died in a cell built into the cellar of Zachariadis's private house.

Markos was rehabilitated for a time, but his 'excessively vehement' criticisms led to his renewed expulsion in 1961.

The liberalization showed in new overtures which lead to a wide rallying of social and political forces. The KKE's underground organizations were dissolved and their militants work within the EDA framework.

In the elections of February 1957, Sarafis was re-elected deputy with the second largest personal majority in the country. On 31 May 1957 he was killed by a US serviceman's car. It was said to be an accident.

MAY 1958–1963

EDA gained 25% of the votes in the new elections. Karamanlis returned to power with 41·17% of the votes, two-thirds of the seats in parliament. EDA's success resuscitated the anti-Communist campaign and unleashed new waves of repression.

The Americans, growing uneasy, persuaded Papandreou and Venizelos to form a third force by setting up a new party: EK, the Centre Union.

New elections were held on 29 October 1961, in a climate of terror. Direct military intervention took place in the countryside and the electoral lists were rigged (Papandreou claimed that they were swollen by 500,000 illegally-registered names).

Karamanlis gained 50·81% of the vote and 58·66% of the seats. The Centre Union won 33·66% of the votes, taking some support from EDA. The opposition protested about this 'electoral coup d'état' but Karamanlis was still the Americans' trusted man and ruled for another two years. He tried to wield the power of the State in his dealings with highly-placed army figures with Palace connections, and came into conflict with the Royal Family.

The Kennedy administration began to envisage a centrist solution for Greece.

MAY 1963–NOVEMBER 1963

The assassination in Salonika of the leftist deputy Lambrakis (Z) crystallized popular anger. The police complicity and semi-legal right-wing practices which emerged at the trial undermined the government's authority. In an atmosphere heavy with menace, half a million people followed Lambrakis's cortège through the streets of Athens.

18 May: Karamanlis submitted his government's resignation to the King. Pipinellis became Prime Minister with a majority of two votes. Papandreou demanded new elections.

NOVEMBER 1963–JULY 1965

The elections held on 3 November 1963 gave Papandreou a relative but not absolute majority (42·04% of the votes and 46% of the seats). Papandreou refused to govern in collaboration with EDA (12% of the votes) and resigned on 24 December.

New elections were held on 16 February 1964. This time the Centre Union won an absolute majority (57% of the seats). Greece emerged timidly from its long night. Police terrorism abated in the countryside. The emergency regulations were not lifted but certain practices (e.g. 'certificates of civic responsibility') fell into disuse. Files on exiles and political prisoners were examined on their own merits, and deportations ceased. Thousands of Greeks condemned to the dungeons or the underground recovered a fragile sense of liberty.

The Right unleashed its fury on Papandreou. The man who refused to ally himself with EDA, the stage-manager of the British landing in Athens in October 1944, was called a crypto-communist every time he managed to achieve a faltering step towards a restoration of legality.

King Paul died in 1964 and Constantine's accession to the throne, in the shadow of the Queen Mother Frederika, strengthened the opposition of a superpower determined to defend its 'private domains'.

The Greek government's policy towards Cyprus, attempting to equip itself with Soviet arms, is not to Johnson's taste. The days of freedom are numbered.

Papandreou found himself being torn between his party's conservative wing, led by the Minister of Defence Garoufalias, and the progressive wing led by his son Andreas Papandreou, which spearheaded democratic and social demands and was beginning to overtake him on the left.

Papandreou tried to impose State authority on the service Staffs, thus disturbing royal taboos. He exhumed the 'Pericles' plan which governed the army's role in rigging the 1961 elections. Garoufalias's opposition hardened and the Centre Union was threatened with disintegration.

The Right riposted immediately, accusing Papandreou of fomenting the 'Aspida' plot in the army in collusion with a subversive military organization.

15 July 1965: Papandreou visited the King to announce his intention of replacing Garoufalias. Constantine refused to sign the decree. The Premier threatened to resign if he could not reshuffle the government. Constantine replied, in violation of the very letter of the Constitution: 'Very well, if that's the way you feel, resign!'

After twenty months of convalescent democracy the paths of legality were barred once again. Thousands of Greeks who had hardly begun to know liberty were soon to know terror once more.

The 'Royal coup d'état' of 15 July hampered the normal functioning of the institutions for a considerable time.

JULY 1965–APRIL 1967

Large popular demonstrations were held in Athens and every other town in Greece to demand respect for constitutional legality and democratic order.

The Palace tried to exploit the split in the Centre Union by recruiting from the movement's right wing. The first government formed on this basis was installed in September 1965, led by Stefanopoulos.

The support given to this operation by the Centre Union's 'apostates' caused the tendency led by Andreas Papandreou to move to the left. The great majority of EDA leaders supported united action. But the guardians of orthodoxy were watching from Bucharest. The resolutions made in 1956 were still in force. Since the Eighth Congress of 1961 the Party leadership within the country had been excluded from all discussions and subjected to ukases from abroad.

It was the same old pattern: at one time it was Athens cut off from the mountains, now it was Bucharest cut off from the whole of Greece, which drew up blueprints and institutionalized mistrust. During the crisis summer of 1965 the Koliyannis Central Committee decided to reconstitute the Party's underground organizations in Greece and ordered them to function inside the EDA formations, to ensure the application of the 'pure' orthodox line elaborated on the other side of the iron curtain.

EDA lost all its autonomy. Urgent decisions were delayed by tortuous procedures which progressively undermine left-wing unity in Greece.

The emergency measures relaxed by the Papandreou government regained all their old vigour. Lambrakis's youth organization was threatened with dissolution; the trumped-up case against Aspida (an alleged plot by democratic officers) was aimed at Andreas Papandreou's movement, which was also denied KKE support as a result of policies imposed from Bucharest. The Palace embarked on a large-scale purge of the army and security services. Stefanopoulos was replaced as head of the government by Paraskevopoulos, who was supposed to forge a new Centre-right alliance before the end of the legislature. He failed to do so. Kanellopoulos succeeded him with the task of grouping a parliamentary majority around ERE (Karamanlis's old party) and organizing the next elections.

March 1967: KKE Central Committee met in Bucharest to hold the Tenth Plenum.

Elections were approaching, and the resolutions were particularly concerned with the dangerous influence of the Centre Union on left-supporting voters. Any prospect of unified action was utterly torpedoed, while the traditional Right and the Americans prepared a coup d'état for the day before or the day after the elections due to be held on 28 May. It was to be some time before these elections actually took place.

Disturbing rumours circulated. The fragmented Left was totally unprepared for the disaster about to be precipitated by an entirely new political factor.

On the morning of 21 April 1967, a month before the date planned by the Staffs and the Palace, tanks surrounded all public buildings in Athens and a monster wave of arrests decapitated the democratic opposition. It was not the traditional Right which seized power, but the officer caste excluded from the power clique centred on the Palace – the colonels, using a scheme elaborated by the CIA and ruining all the carefully-laid plans of their superiors.

21 APRIL 1967–1969

Papadopoulos and Pattakos set about turning Greece into something the latter called, in one of his Ubuesque discourses, an 'armoured democracy'.

Their basic programme consists of anti-Communism and 'morality' (a far-reaching concept which covers the banning of certain plays by Aristophanes, Sophocles and Aeschylus, of modern mathematical methods, of mini-skirts and long hair, of any mention of Sophocles's pederasty, etc.).

Confronted with the *fait accompli*, the king gave his provisional legal backing to the operation.

The prisons, the islands of Yaros and Leros, began filling up again within a few weeks. Thousands of Greeks who had hardly begun to emerge into the daylight were flung back into the colonels' dungeons to rot. Thousands of others made their way into exile.

The resistance began timidly organizing itself from about May 1967 onwards. The Communist Party and EDA announced the formation of a Patriotic Front which was to collaborate with two new organizations: Democratic Defence, formed by left-wing members of the Centre Union, and PAK (Panhellenic Liberation Movement) centred on Andreas Papandreou.

The activities of this resistance were limited but it achieved an embryonic unity at grass-roots level.

13 December 1967: King Constantine, supported by the Chiefs of Staffs and financial interests with Palace connections, tried to seize back the initiative which he lost at the winning-post eight months earlier. In a comic-opera manoeuvre, he appealed to his army and his good people to rise against the junta; but nobody felt involved in stories about kings and queens, nobody was interested in the internal squabbles of the Right. It was a laughable fiasco and Constantine fled to Rome. His men were winkled out of the government. His portrait remained on the walls of

barbers' shops, and a Regency was constituted to ensure the symbolic continuation of the monarchy, but the colonels had a free hand.

Nothing seemed likely to displace the junta. The great foreign powers, both Western and Communist, made their formal protests but soon resumed diplomatic relations with Greece.

February 1968: the KKE's Twelfth Plenum drew its conclusions from recent events, just as it had in the good old days. Koliyannis fired the Party leaders inside the country and, resorting to the Zachariadis method, blamed everything on Partsalidis's group. This time, however, the base revolted. The three main pariahs, Partsalidis, Zografos and Dimitriou, captured the Party radio station, denounced the leadership's methods and listed the errors committed over the last few years. Koliyannis found himself in a minority. He left Rumania, refused to hold a conference of all the Party organizations and persisted in representing himself as the trustee of orthodoxy. This was the basis for a split in the Party.

In Greece, the colonels submitted a draft constitution to the judgment of the citizens. The referendum began on 20 September 1968, in the shadow of martial law. The official results claimed that 92% of Greeks approved the regime's basic policies. Both public and individual liberties continued to be suspended by the whole arsenal of emergency regulations and the daily outrages of the security services.

3 November 1968: An enormous crowd gathered in Constitution Square to follow the funeral cortège of George Papandreou.

His 1964 administration and the persecutions of recent months bestowed a democratic aura on the man of 1944. Because the crowd owed him the few breaths of fresh air it had during the last two years, it identified to some extent with the ambiguous figure of the old Centrist leader. The square was crawling with plain-clothes policemen and informers. A few voices shouted the first slogans: 'Down with the Junta!' 'Down with the dictatorship!' Glances met for a moment. Suddenly half a million voices exploded skyward expressing the anger of Greece; it was the regime's true referendum.

At the end of 1968 the KKE's 'Bureau of the Interior' decided to assume leadership of all the Party organizations so as to prepare for a meeting of representatives of all the Greek Communists. The new Party face which emerges from this conference will perhaps, at last, be that of the Greek revolution.

Bibliography

Bassis, H., and Biniaris, A., *L'Armée démocratique grecque*, Paris, 1948.

Byford-Jones, W., *The Greek Trilogy*, London, 1945.

Capell, Richard, *Simiomata : A Greek note book, 1944-1945*, London, 1946.

Churchill, W. S., *The Second World War*, Vol. V (*Closing the Ring*), Vol. VI (*Triumph and Tragedy*), London, 1948–54.

Clark, Alan, *The Fall of Crete*, London, 1962.

Critis, 'Mort et Renaissance d'un Parti communiste', in *Politique d'aujourd'hui*, No. 4, April 1969.

Darivas, Basil, 'De la Résistance à la Guerre civile en Grèce', in *Recherches internationales*, Nos 44–45, Paris, 1964.

Djilas, Milovan, *Conversations with Stalin*, Harmondsworth, 1963.

Dzelepy, E. N., *Le Drame de la Résistance grecque*, Paris, 1946.

Glinos, Dimitris, 'Le double jeu de Churchill', in *Les Temps Modernes*, No. 109, January/February 1955.

Hampe, Roland, *Die Rettung Athens*, Wiesbaden, 1951.

Hamson, Denys, *We Fell Among Greeks*, London, 1946.

Hillgrüber, Andreas, *Kriegstagebuch des Oberkommandos der Wehrmacht*, Frankfurt, 1963.

Iannakakis, Ilias, 'The Greek Communist Party', in *New Left Review*, No. 54, London, 1969.

Kedros, André, *Peuple roi*, Paris, 1966.

Kedros, André, *La Résistance grecque, 1940–1944*, Paris, 1966.

Kofos, Evangelos, *Nationalism and Communism in Macedonia*, Thessaloniki, 1964.

Kousoulas, D. G., *The Price of Freedom*, Syracuse, 1953.

Kousoulas, D. G., *Revolution and Defeat*, London, 1965.

Leeper, Reginald, *When Greek Meets Greek*, London, 1950.

Livadis, J., 'Bref résumé d'un drame de vingt-cinq ans', in *Politique d'aujourd'hui*, No. 4, April n.d

Loverdo, Costa de, *Les Maquis rouges dans les Balkans*, Paris, 1967.

Loverdo, Costa de, *Le Bataillon sacré*, Paris, n.d.

McNeill, William Hardy, *The Greek Dilemma*, London, 1947.

Meynaud, Jean, *Les Forces politiques en Grèce*, Lausanne, 1965.

Meynaud, Jean, *Rapport sur l'abolition de la Démocratie en Grèce*, Montreal, 1965.

Michel, Henri, *The Shadow War*, London, 1972.

Milliex, Roger, *A l'école du peuple grec*, Paris, 1946.

Mulgan, John, *Report on Experience*, London, 1947.

Myers, Edmund, C., *Greek Entanglement*, London, 1955.

Neubacher, Hermann, *Sonderauftrag Südost*, Göttingen, 1956.

Noel-Baker, Francis, *Greece: The Whole Story*, London, 1946.

O'Ballance, Edgar, *The Greek Civil War, 1944–1949*, London, 1966.

Pyromaglou, Komninos, 'La Résistance grècque et les Alliés', published by the International Congress for the History of the Resistance, Milan, 1961.

Sarafis, Stefanos, *Greek Resistance Army*, London, 1951 (abridged from the original Greek edition).

Sheppard, A. W., *Britain in Greece*, London, 1947.

Sheppard, A. W., *Les enfants grecs ont retrouvé la paix et la liberté*.

Stavrianos, Nicolas, 'A Study in Resistance Organizations and Adminis-tration', in *Journal of Modern History*, March/December, 1952.

Stettinius, E. R., *Roosevelt and the Russians*, London, 1950.

Svoronos, Nicolas, *Histoire de la Grèce moderne*, Paris, 1953.

Tery, Simone, *Ils se battent aux Thermopylae*, Paris, 1948.

Tsoucalas, Constantine, *The Greek Tragedy*, Harmondsworth, 1969.

Trevor Roper, Hugh (ed.), *Hitler's Table Talk, 1941–1944*, London, 1953.

Voigt, F. A., *The Greek Sedition*, London, 1949.

Voix de la Grèce (an underground newspaper published in French by the Provisional Democratic Government of Greece, from May 1948).

Vukmanović-Tempo, S., *Über die Volksrevolution in Griechenland*, Belgrade, 1950.

Vukmanović-Tempo, S., *How and Why the People's Liberation Struggle of Greece met with Defeat*, London, 1950.

Wilson of Libya, Lord, *Eight Years Overseas*, London, 1948.

Woodhouse, C. M., *Apple of Discord*, London, 1948.

Woodhouse, C. M., 'Zur Geschichte der Resistance in Griechenland', in *Vierteljahreshefte für Zeitgeschichte*, April 1958.

Woodhouse, C. M., 'The Oath of Hippocrates' and 'The Code' in *One Omen* (short stories), London, 1950.

Democratic Organizations of Greece, *Third Blue Book*, September, 1950.

Gouvernement Démocratique Provisoire de Grèce, *Livre Bleu*, August 1948; *Deuxième Livre Bleu*, August, 1969.
National Liberation Front (EAM), *White Book, May 1944–March 1945*, New York, 1945.

Books and pamphlets in Greek consulted by the author

Bartzotas, Vasilis, *Politiki stelechon tou KKE sta televtaia deka chronia* ('Policy of KKE cadres during the last ten years'), Athens, 1950.
Dimitriou-Nikiforos, D. N., *Andartis sta vouna tis Roumelis* ('A Partisan in the Roumeli mountains'), Athens, 1965.
Glinos, Dimitris, *Ti inai kai ti theli to EAM* ('What is EAM and what are its aims?'), Athens, 1942.
Grigoriades, Fivos, *To Andartiko* ('The Partisan War'), Athens, 1964.
Ioannou, L., 'I Mesi Anatoli, 1941–1945' ('The Middle East'), in *Ethniki Antistasi*, Prague, 1963.
Karageorgis, Kostas, *Gyro apo to Dekemvri* ('On the December events'), Athens, 1945.
Karageorgis, Kostas, Letter to the Central Committee of KKE published as 'The Anti-Party Liquidationist Platform of Costas Gyftodimos', in *Neos Kosmos*, No. 8, August 1950.
Lagdas, Panos, *Aris Velouchiotis*, Athens, 1964.
Papandreou, Georgios, *I Apeleftherosis tis Ellados* ('The Liberation of Greece'), Athens, 1945.
Papandreou, Georgios, *O Tritos Polemos* ('The Third War'), Athens, 1948.
Pyromaglou, Komninos, *O Dourios Ippos* ('The Trojan Horse'), Athens, 1958.
Pyromaglou, Komninos, *I Ethniki Antistasis* ('The National Resistance'), Athens, 1947.
Pyromaglou, Komninos, *O Georgios Kartalis kai i epochi tou 1934–1957* ('George Kartalis and his Time'), Athens, 1965.
Sarafis, Stefanos, *O ELAS*, Athens, 1946.
Tsouderos, E. I., *Ellinikes Anomalies sti Mesi Anatoli* ('Greek Conflicts in the Middle East'), Athens, 1945.
Vafiadis-Markos, Letter to the Central Committee of KKE published as 'The Opportunist Platform of Markos Vafiades', in *Neos Kosmos*, 1950.
Vratsanos-Angeloulis, Antonis, *Vrontaï o Olymbos*, Athens, 1945.
Zachariadis, Nikos, *Deka Chronia Agonos, 1935–1945* ('Ten Years of Struggle'), Athens, 1945.

Zachariadis, Nikos, *Kainourgia Katastasi, Kainourgia Kathikonta* ('New Situation, New Duties'), Nicosia, 1950.

Zachariadis, Nikos, *Thesis gia tin Istoria tou KKE* ('Towards a History of KKE'), Athens, 1945.

Zevgos, Yannis, *I Laïki Antistasi tou Dekemvri kai to neoelliniko provlima* ('The Popular Resistance of December and the Problems of Modern Greece'), Athens, 1945.

Index

of the main participants, organizations and events

NOTTINGHAM UNIVERSITY LIBRARY

MONTHLY REVIEW

an independent socialist magazine

edited by Paul M. Sweezy and Harry Magdoff

Business Week: ". . . a brand of socialism that is thorough-going and tough-minded, drastic enough to provide the sharp break with the past that many left-wingers in the underdeveloped countries see as essential. At the same time they maintain a sturdy independence of both Moscow and Peking that appeals to neutralists. And their skill in manipulating the abstruse concepts of modern economics impresses would-be intellectuals. . . . Their analysis of the troubles of capitalism is just plausible enough to be disturbing."

Bertrand Russell: "Your journal has been of the greatest interest to me over a period of time. I am not a Marxist by any means as I have sought to show in critiques published in several books, but I recognize the power of much of your own analysis and where I disagree I find your journal valuable and of stimulating importance. I want to thank you for your work and to tell you of my appreciation of it."

The Wellesley Department of Economics: " . . . the leading Marxist intellectual (not Communist) economic journal published anywhere in the world, and is on our subscription list at the College library for good reasons."

Albert Einstein: "Clarity about the aims and problems of socialism is of greatest significance in our age of transition. . . . I consider the founding of this magazine to be an important public service." (In his article, "Why Socialism" in Vol. I, No. 1.)

DOMESTIC: $9 for one year, $16 for two years, $7 for one-year student subscription.

FOREIGN: $10 for one year, $18 for two years, $8 for one-year student subscription. (Subscription rates subject to change.)

116 West 14th Street, New York, New York 10011